Symmetry and Asymmetry Study in Graph Theory

Symmetry and Asymmetry Study in Graph Theory

Guest Editor

Mujiangshan Wang

MDPI

Basel • Beijing • Wuhan • Barcelona • Belgrade • Novi Sad • Cluj • Manchester

Guest Editor
Mujiangshan Wang
Institute of Advanced
Computing and Digital
Engineering
Chinese Academy of Sciences
Shenzhen
China

Editorial Office
MDPI AG
Grosspeteranlage 5
4052 Basel, Switzerland

This is a reprint of the Special Issue, published open access by the journal *Symmetry* (ISSN 2073-8994), freely accessible at: https://www.mdpi.com/journal/symmetry/special_issues/4K09C637XJ.

For citation purposes, cite each article independently as indicated on the article page online and as indicated below:

Lastname, A.A.; Lastname, B.B. Article Title. *Journal Name* **Year**, *Volume Number*, Page Range.

ISBN 978-3-7258-8179-6 (Hbk)
ISBN 978-3-7258-8180-2 (PDF)
https://doi.org/10.3390/books978-3-7258-8180-2

Contents

About the Editor

Mujiangshan Wang

Mujiangshan Wang is an Assistant Professor at the Shenzhen Institute of Advanced Technology, Chinese Academy of Sciences, and Vice President of Research and Development for AI-related work at Shenzhen Kaihong Digital Industry Development Co., Ltd. His research interests include graph theory, interconnection networks, network diagnosability, combinatorial optimization, graph neural networks, knowledge graphs, ontology-based AI, and intelligent operating systems. He received his Ph.D. in Computer Science from the University of Newcastle, Australia, and previously conducted postdoctoral research at the School of Software, Tsinghua University. He has published more than 40 academic papers in areas related to graph theory, network reliability, artificial intelligence, and intelligent systems, with a number of works appearing in journals and conferences in theoretical computer science, discrete mathematics, and applied AI. He also serves as a reviewer for more than 40 international journals and is involved in interdisciplinary projects connecting mathematical theory, graph-based learning, AI agents, and industrial intelligent systems. His recent work focuses on integrating graph structures, ontology modeling, and large language model-based agents to support explainable, controllable, and reusable enterprise level AI applications.

Preface

Symmetry and asymmetry are fundamental concepts in graph theory, complex networks, and intelligent information processing. They provide useful perspectives for understanding structural regularity, heterogeneous relations, optimization mechanisms, robustness, uncertainty, and decision-making in both theoretical and applied systems. This Reprint collects recent contributions that explore these ideas from multiple angles, ranging from graph neural networks, community detection, bipartite matching, knowledge graphs, and structured label dependencies to applications in cloud imaging, medical image classification, blockchain-based control, equipment maintenance, optical phase mask optimization, and mechanical drilling speed prediction.

The motivation for preparing this Reprint is to present a coherent collection of studies showing how graph-based models and symmetry-inspired methods can support modern computational science. The selected papers demonstrate that graph structures are not only mathematical objects, but also practical tools for representing real world interactions, constraints, dependencies, and dynamic processes. By combining graph theory with machine learning, optimization, and domain specific modeling, these works contribute to the development of more interpretable, adaptive, and robust computational methods.

This Reprint is intended for researchers, graduate students, engineers, and practitioners working in graph theory, artificial intelligence, network science, applied mathematics, computer science, and interdisciplinary intelligent systems. I hope that the collection will provide readers with useful insights into the evolving role of symmetry and asymmetry in graph-based modeling and will encourage further studies at the intersection of mathematical theory, learning algorithms, and practical applications.

Mujiangshan Wang

Guest Editor

symmetry

MDPI

Article

HybridGNN: A Self-Supervised Graph Neural Network for Efficient Maximum Matching in Bipartite Graphs

Chun-Hui Pan [1,†], Yi Qu [2], Yao Yao [3] and Mu-Jiang-Shan Wang [4,*,†]

[1] Shanghai World Foreign Language Academy, Shanghai 200233, China; chunhuipan_2026@stu.swfla.org
[2] Shanghai Aerospace Electronic Technology Institute, Shanghai 201109, China; quyi2026@163.com
[3] Shenzhen Nanshan Experimental Education Group OCT Senior High School, Shenzhen 518058, China; ya_yo_11@126.com
[4] Institute of Advanced Computing and Digital Engineering, Shenzhen Institute of Advanced Technology, Chinese Academy of Sciences, Shenzhen 518055, China
* Correspondence: mjs.wang@siat.ac.cn
† These authors contributed equally to this work.

Abstract: Solving maximum matching problems in bipartite graphs is critical in fields such as computational biology and social network analysis. This study introduces HybridGNN, a novel Graph Neural Network model designed to efficiently address complex matching problems at scale. HybridGNN leverages a combination of Graph Attention Networks (GATv2), Graph SAGE (SAGEConv), and Graph Isomorphism Networks (GIN) layers to enhance computational efficiency and model performance. Through extensive ablation experiments, we identify that while the SAGEConv layer demonstrates suboptimal performance in terms of accuracy and F_1-score, configurations incorporating GATv2 and GIN layers show significant improvements. Specifically, in six-layer GNN architectures, the combinations of GATv2 and GIN layers with ratios of 4:2 and 5:1 yield superior accuracy and F_1-score. Therefore, we name these GNN configurations $HybridGNN_1$ and $HybridGNN_2$. Additionally, techniques such as mixed precision training, gradient accumulation, and Jumping Knowledge networks are integrated to further optimize performance. Evaluations on an email communication dataset reveal that HybridGNNs outperform traditional algorithms such as the Hopcroft–Karp algorithm, the Hungarian algorithm, and the Blossom/Edmonds' algorithm, particularly for large and complex graphs. These findings highlight HybridGNN's robust capability to solve maximum matching problems in bipartite graphs, making it a powerful tool for analyzing large-scale and intricate graph data. Furthermore, our study aligns with the goals of the Symmetry and Asymmetry Study in Graph Theory special issue by exploring the role of symmetry in bipartite graph structures. By leveraging GNNs, we address the challenges related to symmetry and asymmetry in graph properties, thereby improving the reliability and fault tolerance of complex networks.

Keywords: HybridGNN; maximum matching; bipartite graphs; graph neural networks (GNNs); time complexity; graph attention networks (GATs); graph isomorphism networks (GINs); self-supervised learning; mixed precision training

MSC: 68T07; 05C85; 05C40

1. Introduction

Graphs are widely regarded as one of the most versatile data structures across numerous disciplines for modeling pairwise relationships. A prominent challenge in graph theory is solving the maximum matching problem, particularly in bipartite graphs, where the objective is to identify the largest set of non-overlapping edges. While classical algorithms such as the Hungarian algorithm, Edmonds' Blossom algorithm, and the Hopcroft–Karp algorithm [1–3] have proven effective, they often face limitations when dealing with larger or more complex graphs. As datasets continue to expand in size and intricacy, the demand for more scalable and generalizable solutions has become increasingly apparent.

Graph Neural Networks (GNNs) offer a promising approach by learning from graph-structured data and leveraging the inherent relationships within graphs [4,5]. This paper introduces HybridGNN, a model that integrates GATv2, Graph SAGE (SAGEConv), and GIN layers, further enhanced through self-supervised learning techniques. These candidate GNN layers are chosen for their diverse capabilities in capturing graph structure and node relationships. The integration of self-supervised learning techniques allows the model to be trained without the need for manually labeled datasets, making it a flexible solution for large-scale graph-based tasks.

This paper is structured as follows: Section 1 introduces the motivations and contributions of this study, emphasizing the challenges in solving maximum matching problems in bipartite graphs and the potential of Graph Neural Networks (GNNs). Section 2 provides a comprehensive literature review, discussing prior work on combinatorial optimization problems, GNN architectures, and their applications to graph-based tasks, as well as related foundational studies in graph theory and connectivity. Section 3 covers graph theory fundamentals, particularly bipartite graphs and their relevance in large-scale applications. Section 4 discusses classical and neural approaches to graph matching, with a focus on the limitations of traditional algorithms and the advantages of Graph Neural Networks (GNNs). In Section 5, we present the architecture of HybridGNN and the innovations it introduces for solving maximum matching problems. Section 6 explains the self-supervised learning strategies used to train HybridGNN using pseudo-labels. Section 7 outlines the regularization and early stopping mechanisms to prevent overfitting, followed by Section 8, which details the dynamic pseudo-label updating method. Section 9 provides the experimental setup, including the dataset and data augmentation techniques. Section 10 provides a comprehensive analysis of computational efficiency, which includes time complexity and memory efficiency. The latter covers mixed precision training, gradient accumulation, and scalability considerations. Section 11 presents a detailed discussion on the results and challenges encountered, and outlines future research directions, concluding with final remarks. Section 12 highlights the reproducibility of the study and includes the code availability details. Appendix A details the algorithms involved in this paper for further clarity.

The primary contributions of this work are as follows:

Firstly, we address the classic maximum matching problem in bipartite graphs using a novel Graph Neural Network (GNN)-based approach. While previous studies, such as those of Wu and Li [6] and others [7–10], have applied GNNs to related combinatorial optimization problems, our work stands out by introducing a methodology that integrates classical graph algorithms as prior knowledge into the GNN training process. This hybrid approach leverages the strengths of classical algorithms to generate pseudo-labels, guiding the self-supervised learning of GNNs. By doing so, we create a specialized GNN model capable of efficiently addressing the maximum matching problem, advancing both the theoretical and practical applications of GNNs.

Secondly, we present a thoughtfully designed architecture by combining existing GNN layers to optimize the model for this specific task. This approach leverages well-established GNN layer structures, configured to meet the unique requirements of the maximum matching problem. This layered design demonstrates superior performance compared to traditional algorithms, validating its effectiveness through extensive experiments.

Additionally, we introduce pseudo-label generation for self-supervised learning, which incorporates classical matching algorithms into the GNN training process. By generating pseudo-labels, our framework combines the interpretability and effectiveness of classical algorithms with the representational power of GNNs, creating a hybrid solution that adapts traditional algorithmic insights to a modern learning paradigm.

Furthermore, we implement Jumping Knowledge (JK) networks and self-supervised learning techniques, enhancing the model's capability to capture multi-layer information adaptively. This integration effectively addresses the structural challenges of bipartite matching tasks, allowing our model to exploit multi-hop dependencies more flexibly.

Finally, we incorporate mixed precision training and gradient accumulation, significantly improving the model's efficiency and resource utilization for large-scale graph data. These optimizations ensure that HybridGNN is not only theoretically robust but also practically scalable to complex graph structures.

These contributions advance the application of GNNs to classical graph theory challenges, providing a foundation for further research and development in this intersection of GNN and combinatorial optimization.

2. Literature Review

Angelini and Ricci-Tersenghi [7] compared modern Graph Neural Networks (GNNs) with classical greedy algorithms for solving combinatorial optimization problems, such as the maximum independent set (MIS). Their findings reveal that while GNNs demonstrate scalability to larger problem instances, they often fall short in performance compared to simpler algorithms like greedy approaches. This highlights the need for further optimization in GNN design, especially when addressing NP-hard problems like MIS. These insights emphasize the importance of exploring advanced GNN architectures, as demonstrated in our work, to bridge the gap between scalability and computational performance for complex graph problems such as bipartite matching.

Brusca et al. [8] proposed a GNN framework for solving the maximum independent set (MIS) problem, utilizing a dynamic programming-inspired recursive algorithm. Their work demonstrates how self-training processes, combined with dynamic programming principles, can improve the annotation accuracy of graph comparisons for combinatorial optimization problems. This approach highlights the potential of leveraging recursive strategies within GNNs to address complex graph-based tasks, aligning with our study's focus on enhancing GNN architectures to tackle maximum matching problems in bipartite graphs effectively.

Schuetz et al. [9] introduced a framework for solving combinatorial optimization problems using Graph Neural Networks inspired by statistical physics. Their approach applies relaxation strategies and unsupervised training processes to address canonical NP-hard problems such as maximum cut and maximum independent set. The study highlights the scalability and adaptability of GNNs for complex optimization tasks, providing insights that are closely aligned with our focus on leveraging GNNs to address maximum matching problems in bipartite graphs effectively.

Zaicevs [10] explored the application of Graph Neural Networks (GNNs) to the Maximum Weighted Matching (MWM) problem using supervised learning. While the study found that GNNs slightly underperformed compared to standard greedy algorithms in average cases, it demonstrated the potential of GNNs to handle more challenging graph datasets where greedy algorithms struggled. These findings highlight the complementary strengths of GNNs and classical algorithms, aligning with our approach of leveraging GNNs to tackle bipartite matching tasks and improving upon traditional methodologies.

Earlier research on graph diagnosability and connectivity, such as the work on bubble-sort star graphs and leaf-sort graphs [11,12], highlights the critical importance of robust graph structures in solving complex graph-based problems. These studies provide foundational insights into the fault tolerance and structural properties of various network configurations, which are closely aligned with the challenges HybridGNN seeks to address.

Advancements in labelings and graph structures, including the edge-magic total labelings of wheels and fans [13], the constructions of magic and antimagic graph labelings [14], and the face antimagic labelings of plane graphs [15], further highlight the role of specialized graph structures in ensuring efficient performance in GNNs. Moreover, studies in applying graph structures to broader machine learning tasks, such as fake news detection [16], emphasize the versatility of graph models in various domains. Techniques like iMER for entity extraction [17] also underscore the power of graph-based approaches in structured data extraction, directly relevant to the learning tasks addressed in HybridGNN.

Wang et al. [18] presented an innovative method for generalizing aggregation functions within GNNs by using nonlinear aggregation techniques. This approach effectively builds high-capacity and robust GNN models, which demonstrates the effectiveness of combining different aggregation techniques to address specific problems. This insight supports HybridGNN's strategy of integrating various GNN layers to enhance its adaptability and robustness in handling complex graph problems like bipartite matching.

Abadal et al. [19] provided a comprehensive survey discussing the evolution of GNN architectures, emphasizing the combination of different layers and modules to meet computational challenges. Their findings highlight that the strategic integration of GNN components is a standard practice in GNN research, reinforcing HybridGNN's design approach as a validated method for optimizing performance.

Zhang et al. [20] introduced GCV-Turbo, which combines CNN layers with GNN layers to accelerate computer vision tasks on FPGA. This research illustrates how combining different neural network layers effectively meets the specific demands of complex applications, demonstrating that integrating different GNN layers, as performed in HybridGNN, is a powerful and versatile approach for tackling diverse computational tasks.

Shohei Satake et al.'s work on explicit non-malleable codes from bipartite graphs [21] offered another critical perspective, particularly in the context of using bipartite expander graphs for building robust, tamper-resistant communication systems. This is especially relevant in designing algorithms that ensure high reliability, aligning with the bipartite matching challenges addressed by HybridGNN. Their exploration of constructing codes from graph structures further supports the importance of leveraging advanced graph theory techniques for broader computational and communication tasks.

Wang et al. [22] explored the structural characteristics of center k-ary n-cubes, particularly their diagnosability and connectivity properties, which are crucial for maintaining optimal graph performance. These insights inspired the design of HybridGNN by highlighting the importance of robust graph structures in solving bipartite matching problems.

Furthermore, Wang et al. [23] emphasized the importance of ensuring graph robustness under edge failures through edge-restricted connectivity conditions. This aligns closely with HybridGNN's objective of improving fault tolerance and reliability in bipartite matching tasks.

Finally, Wu and Li [6] proposed a Deep Reinforcement Learning (DRL)-based framework, L2M, to address the Maximum Weighted Matching (MWM) problem on large-scale graphs. Their work models MWM as a Markov Decision Process (MDP), leveraging message-passing networks and a pruning method to efficiently select edges and accelerate computation. While L2M and our work on Maximum Matching (MM) share overlapping goals in improving graph matching solutions using machine learning, the significance of our work lies in presenting a novel methodology: incorporating classical graph algorithms as prior knowledge into the GNN training framework. By generating pseudo-labels to guide self-supervised learning, our approach develops specialized GNN models with better performance for specific problems. This method not only complements classical algorithms in addressing graph matching tasks but also demonstrates adaptability to broader challenges in graph-based applications.

3. Graph Theory Fundamentals

3.1. *Definitions*

Graphs, typically denoted as $G = (V, E)$, are fundamental data structures composed of a vertex set V and an edge set E, with each edge encapsulating a relationship between two distinct entities [24]. A significant subset of graphs is the class of bipartite graphs, characterized by the partitioning of the vertex set V into two mutually exclusive subsets U and W, where no edges exist between vertices within the same subset [25]. This inherent structure has applications in numerous fields, including network theory and algorithm design. Subgraphs, a core concept in graph theory, are defined as any subset of vertices and edges that themselves form a graph, preserving the original relationships from the parent graph [26].

The degree of a vertex, defined as the count of edges incident to it, provides insight into the local connectivity of a graph, while the minimum degree across all vertices represents a key measure of the graph's overall sparsity or density [24]. Additionally, the notion of connectivity is vital to understanding graph structure; a graph is said to be connected if there exists a path between every pair of vertices [25]. In a more granular sense, edge connectivity is defined as the minimum number of edges that must be removed to render the graph disconnected, highlighting its robustness against link failures [26].

A pivotal challenge in graph theory is solving the maximum matching problem. This problem seeks to identify the largest possible set of non-overlapping edges, particularly in bipartite graphs where such matching maximizes relationships between the two distinct vertex sets [27]. The ability to efficiently compute maximum matchings in large-scale graphs is critical for applications ranging from resource allocation to network flow optimization.

3.2. Bipartite Graphs in Large-Scale Applications

Bipartite graphs are a cornerstone of many real-world applications, owing to their distinctive structure, which separates the vertex set into two disjoint groups. This partitioning allows for the effective modeling of problems where interactions occur between two distinct classes of entities, such as in task scheduling, network flow optimization, and resource allocation [27]. For example, in scheduling, tasks and resources can be represented as vertices in a bipartite graph, with edges indicating feasible assignments, enabling efficient optimization of the task assignment process [25].

One of the most well-known algorithms for finding maximum matchings in bipartite graphs is the Hopcroft–Karp algorithm [3]. This classical algorithm has been widely adopted due to its $O(n^{5/2})$ time complexity, making it suitable for many medium-sized graph instances. However, as the size and complexity of datasets continue to grow, the performance of classical methods like Hopcroft–Karp begins to degrade, particularly in large-scale graphs where the number of vertices and edges can reach millions [26]. The inherent computational complexity of these methods becomes a bottleneck, limiting their scalability in modern applications. To illustrate the contrast between classical approaches and modern solutions, Figure 1 provides a visual comparison of the processes involved in both classical algorithms and GNN-based models.

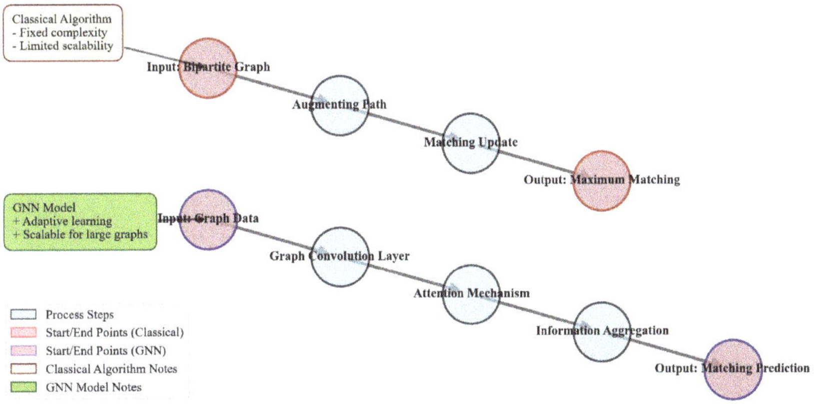

Figure 1. Comparison of classical algorithm and GNN model for bipartite matching.

To address these limitations, recent research has turned to Graph Neural Networks (GNNs) as a means to generalize and scale bipartite graph algorithms for larger, more complex structures. By leveraging the ability of GNNs to learn from graph-structured data, we can design models that not only retain the combinatorial properties of classical approaches but also adaptively handle large-scale and intricate graph instances [4]. As shown in Figure 1, the GNN-based model incorporates advanced learning mechanisms that enhance scalability and adaptability, making it a more robust approach to overcome the computational challenges posed by traditional algorithms and ensuring applicability to diverse real-world problems.

4. Classical and Neural Approaches to Graph Matching

Graph matching has been approached from both classical algorithmic perspectives and, more recently, through neural network-based techniques. Classical methods, such as the Hungarian algorithm, Edmonds' Blossom algorithm, and the Hopcroft–Karp algorithm, have long been considered efficient solutions for solving maximum matching problems in general and bipartite graphs, respectively. These algorithms rely on combinatorial optimization and have been extensively used in theoretical applications. However, their scalability is often limited when faced with large and dynamically changing graph structures.

In contrast, the advent of Graph Neural Networks (GNNs) has opened up new possibilities for tackling graph matching problems. By utilizing deep learning techniques to learn from graph-structured data, GNNs are capable of generalizing across diverse graph types and efficiently processing large-scale graphs. This shift towards neural approaches represents a promising avenue for overcoming the limitations of classical algorithms, particularly in real-world applications where graphs can be noisy, large, and complex [4,28].

4.1. Challenges of Classical Approaches in Graph Matching

Classical algorithms are cornerstone methods for solving the maximum matching problem in bipartite and general graphs, respectively. The Hopcroft–Karp algorithm, known for its efficient time complexity of $O(n^{5/2})$, operates by iteratively finding augmenting paths to increase the size of the current matching in bipartite graphs [3]. Similarly, Edmonds' Blossom algorithm solves the more complex case of general graphs by introducing the concept of blossoms to handle odd-length cycles, providing a polynomial-time solution [2].

Despite their theoretical efficiency, these algorithms face significant challenges when applied to real-world datasets. As graph sizes increase, both algorithms exhibit scaling limitations, particularly with respect to memory usage and processing time. The practical performance of these methods often deteriorates as the graph structure becomes more complex, with millions of vertices and edge. Furthermore, their reliance on handcrafted optimization procedures limits their ability to generalize across different types of graphs, particularly in dynamic or noisy environments, where graph structures may evolve over time.

These limitations have prompted a shift towards more scalable, learning-based methods, particularly Graph Neural Networks (GNNs). By leveraging the inherent structure of graphs, GNNs offer a more flexible framework for tackling large-scale graph matching problems, where traditional approaches fall short [29].

4.2. Graph Neural Networks (GNNs)

Graph Neural Networks (GNNs) have revolutionized the field of graph representation learning by extending deep learning techniques to graph-structured data. These models, such as Graph Convolutional Networks (GCNs) introduced by Kipf and Welling [28], and Graph Attention Networks (GATs) developed by Veličković et al. [4], have shown remarkable success in tasks like node classification, link prediction, and graph matching. GCNs apply convolutional operations to aggregate information from neighboring nodes, effectively capturing the local structure of graphs, while GATs introduce attention mechanisms that assign different importance weights to different neighbors, allowing the model to focus on the most relevant connections.

To illustrate this process, Figure 2 demonstrates how nodes aggregate 1-hop and 2-hop neighborhood information across different GNN layers. In a GNN, each node at the kth layer aggregates information from its k-hop neighbors (see Definition 1). For ease of understanding, we focus on specific nodes in the figure: nodes 2, 3, and 6 (highlighted in red) in the first layer, and nodes 1, 4, 5, 7, and 9 (highlighted in green) in the second layer. The red nodes—2, 3, and 6—are connected by red edges to their respective 1-hop neighbors: $\{1, 4\}$, $\{1, 4, 7\}$, and $\{5, 7\}$. Similarly, the green nodes—1, 4, 5, 7, and 9—aggregate information from their 2-hop neighbors connected by green edges: $\{4, 7\}$, $\{1, 7, 9\}$, $\{1, 4, 5, 9\}$, and $\{4, 6, 7\}$, respectively.

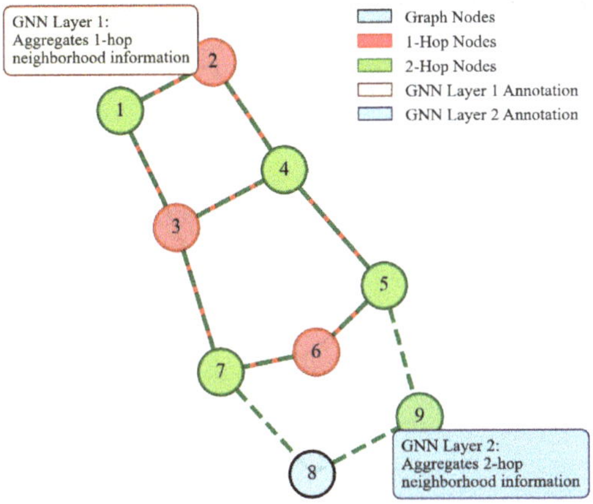

Figure 2. Visualization of GNN layer operations. The figure shows how nodes aggregate 1-hop and 2-hop neighborhood information across different GNN layers. The highlighted nodes and edges represent the flow of information, illustrating the step-by-step aggregation process in a GNN model.

Definition 1. *Given a graph $G = (V, E)$ and a node $v \in V$, the k-hop neighborhood of v is defined as the set of nodes that are reachable from v by traversing at most k edges. Formally, the k-hop neighborhood $N_k(v)$ is*

$$N_k(v) = \{u \in V \mid distance(v, u) \leq k\},$$

where $distance(v, u)$ represents the shortest path distance between nodes v and u.

The success of these models lies in their ability to learn directly from the graph data, without the need for handcrafted features or complex optimization procedures. GNNs can adapt to different graph structures and scales, making them highly generalizable and efficient even when applied to large-scale, real-world graphs. Moreover, their ability to incorporate both node features and edge relationships enables them to capture complex patterns within the data, making them particularly well suited for solving challenging graph matching problems [30].

As graph-based tasks continue to grow in complexity, the application of GNNs to these problems offers a promising path forward. By leveraging the expressive power of neural networks, GNN-based models are capable of solving problems that classical algorithms find intractable, particularly in scenarios involving noisy, dynamic, or large-scale graphs [29].

5. HybridGNN: Architectural Design and Innovation

The HybridGNN model is designed to integrate the complementary strengths of Graph Attention Network (GATv2), Graph SAGE (SAGEConv), and Graph Isomorphism Network (GIN) layers, enabling it to effectively capture both local node-level relationships and global graph-wide patterns. These three types of layers were selected as candidates for the architecture due to their unique capabilities in processing graph-structured data.

The GATv2, GraphSAGE, and GIN layers each bring unique strengths to the HybridGNN architecture. GATv2 layers use attention mechanisms to assign varying importance to neighboring nodes, which helps in identifying key connections within heterogeneous graphs [4]. GraphSAGE layers enable inductive learning, allowing the model to generate embeddings for unseen nodes and adapt to larger, evolving graphs without retraining [5]. GIN layers are designed to capture detailed structural information by mimicking the Weisfeiler–Lehman (WL) graph isomorphism test, making them highly effective for tasks that require distinguishing subtle differences in graph structure [29].

The construction of the final HybridGNN model is based on the results of ablation experiments that compare the performance of these candidate layers. By combining GATv2, SAGEConv, and GIN layers, HybridGNN can capture both fine-grained and coarse-grained patterns in the graph, making it an ideal solution for complex graph-based tasks such as bipartite matching.

A key innovation in the HybridGNN architecture is the incorporation of the Jumping Knowledge (JK) mechanism, which aggregates representations from multiple layers of the network. Unlike traditional GNNs that rely solely on the final layer's output, the JK mechanism ensures that both shallow and deep layer representations are utilized, allowing the model to effectively leverage information from various levels of granularity [31]. This feature is particularly important when addressing graphs with hierarchical structures, where both local and global information are critical for accurate prediction.

In addition, HybridGNN employs mixed precision training and gradient accumulation techniques to optimize memory usage and computational efficiency, especially when working with large-scale graphs. This makes it a scalable and efficient solution for real-world applications where resource limitations and data size present significant challenges.

To meet the structural and computational demands of the maximum matching problem in bipartite graphs, the HybridGNN model integrates GATv2, GraphSAGE, and GIN layers, each contributing unique strengths to the task. Specifically, GATv2 layers capture essential node-to-node dependencies through attention mechanisms, allowing the model to focus on critical interactions between nodes. GraphSAGE layers enhance this by aggregating neighborhood information efficiently, a feature crucial for scaling to larger graphs. Finally, GIN layers add expressive power to the model by capturing fine-grained structural similarities, particularly valuable in distinguishing subtle graph patterns. This layer combination thus enables HybridGNN to balance both local and global information flows, making it well suited for combinatorial problems like bipartite maximum matching.

Architectural Components of HybridGNN

The HybridGNN model is specifically designed to address the intricate relationships present in bipartite graphs. It incorporates several key components to effectively capture and process graph-structured data:

- **Graph Attention Networks v2 (GATv2)** The Graph Attention Network v2 (GATv2) is an enhanced version of the original GAT model, designed to overcome certain limitations, particularly those associated with the non-negative attention coefficients in GAT. GATv2 introduces a more flexible attention mechanism, allowing the attention coefficients to assume both positive and negative values. This enhancement enables GATv2 to more effectively capture complex relationships between nodes, even in noisy or highly intricate graphs, thereby improving overall task performance.
  The core operation of GATv2 is represented as follows:

$$\alpha_{ij} = \frac{\exp(\text{LeakyReLU}(\mathbf{a}^T[\mathbf{W}h_i \,||\, \mathbf{W}h_j]))}{\sum_{k \in \mathcal{N}(i)} \exp(\text{LeakyReLU}(\mathbf{a}^T[\mathbf{W}h_i \,||\, \mathbf{W}h_k]))}$$

  where h_i and h_j represent the feature vectors of nodes i and j, $\mathbf{W}$ is a learnable weight matrix, and $\mathbf{a}$ represents the attention mechanism. Unlike the original GAT, GATv2 allows for negative attention scores, significantly increasing its expressiveness and enabling the model to better handle complex and non-linear interactions in graph structures. This improvement is crucial for tasks that require a nuanced understanding of node relationships, especially in noisy or complex graph environments.

- **SAGEConv Layers:** By aggregating information from neighboring nodes, the SAGEConv layers generate more comprehensive node representations, facilitating a deeper understanding of both local and global graph structures [5]. This aggregation process enables the model to generalize effectively across diverse graph topologies.
- **Graph Isomorphism Networks (GINs)**: The Graph Isomorphism Network (GIN) is a highly expressive GNN architecture specifically designed to capture detailed structural information from graphs by mimicking the Weisfeiler–Lehman (WL) graph isomorphism test [29]. The GIN achieves this by aggregating node features from neighboring nodes using a learned weighted sum, making it particularly effective for tasks requiring a fine-grained understanding of graph structure. This high level of discriminative power makes GIN especially suitable for graph matching tasks and other applications where subtle structural differences in the graph are critical.
  The GIN aggregation rule is defined as

$$h_v^{(k)} = \mathrm{MLP}\left(\left(1+\epsilon^{(k)}\right)h_v^{(k-1)} + \sum_{u\in\mathcal{N}(v)} h_u^{(k-1)}\right)$$

  where $h_v^{(k)}$ represents the feature of node v at the k-th layer, $\epsilon^{(k)}$ is a learnable parameter, and $\mathcal{N}(v)$ denotes the set of neighboring nodes of v. The Multi-Layer Perceptron (MLP) in the GIN plays a crucial role in enhancing the model's expressiveness, enabling it to capture complex and intricate graph structures. This architecture's ability to differentiate between non-isomorphic graphs gives it a significant advantage in learning highly discriminative graph representations.
- **Focal Loss:** This is a focal version of the standard cross-entropy loss function, specifically designed to address the challenges posed by class imbalance in classification tasks. In scenarios where certain classes dominate the dataset, models often become biased toward these majority classes, resulting in poor performance on underrepresented minority classes. Focal Loss mitigates this issue by reducing the relative loss contribution from easily classified examples and placing more emphasis on hard-to-classify instances. The Focal Loss function is mathematically defined as:

$$FL(p_t) = -\alpha_t(1-p_t)^{\gamma}\log(p_t)$$

  where p_t represents the predicted probability for the target class, α_t is a weighting factor for class t, and γ is a focusing parameter that controls the down-weighting rate of easy examples. By increasing γ, the loss function places greater focus on difficult-to-classify examples, effectively forcing the model to pay more attention to minority or misclassified data points. This mechanism enhances the model's ability to perform well on imbalanced datasets, addressing a common limitation of traditional loss functions.
- **Jumping Knowledge (JK):** The JK mechanism integrates representations from multiple layers, allowing the model to retain and utilize information at various depths of the network [31]. This ensures that the model captures both shallow and deep patterns, enhancing its ability to handle graphs with multi-level complexities.

To provide a better understanding of the design and innovation behind the HybridGNN model, Figure 3 illustrates the complete process from input data to the final output of node matching probabilities. The diagram outlines how pseudo-labels are generated using classic algorithms as part of the input, which is then processed through a combination of GATv2, SAGEConv, and GIN layers. Note that these three types of layers serve as our candidate layers, and the selection and configuration of these layers within HybridGNN are determined based on the results of ablation experiments. Supported by the Jumping Knowledge mechanism, these layers enable multi-layer aggregation and flexibility. The Focal Loss is employed during training to address class imbalance, ensuring that the model places greater focus on difficult-to-classify examples. This comprehensive approach effectively captures graph structure information and facilitates solving complex graph matching tasks.

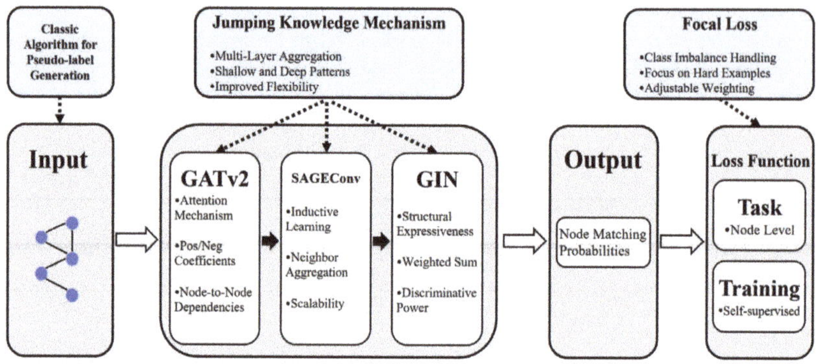

Figure 3. HybridGNN architectural overview.

6. Self-Supervised Learning for Graph-Based Tasks

In many real-world applications, acquiring labeled data for graph-based tasks is both time consuming and expensive. To address this challenge, we utilize a self-supervised learning approach, which allows the model to generate pseudo-labels directly from the data without the need for manual annotations. By leveraging the graph's inherent structure, the model can perform downstream supervised tasks, such as classification or link prediction, more effectively.

Self-supervised learning has gained significant attention for its ability to uncover hidden patterns within data, particularly in domains where labeled datasets are limited [32]. This technique aligns closely with the goals of Graph Neural Networks, as it enables the model to learn meaningful representations by predicting parts of the graph or relationships between nodes, thereby reducing the dependence on large labeled datasets. Recent research has demonstrated that self-supervised learning can substantially improve performance across a wide range of tasks, making it a scalable and robust solution for graph-related problems [33].

6.1. Pseudo-Labeling Strategies for Bipartite Graphs

To generate pseudo-labels that are specifically suited for bipartite graphs, we implement a method combining degree-based node classification, neighborhood similarity metrics, and participation in maximum matching. This hybrid approach ensures that the generated pseudo-labels align closely with the structural characteristics of bipartite graphs, providing more meaningful labels for subsequent tasks.

The pseudo-labeling process comprises three key steps:

- **Node Degree-Based Labeling:** Nodes within each vertex set of the bipartite graph are first classified based on their degree. Nodes exhibiting similar degree values are grouped under the same pseudo-label, thereby capturing the local connectivity patterns [34].
- **Neighborhood Disparity Adjustment:** For each node, the feature vector similarity with its neighboring nodes is calculated. Nodes that exhibit significant disparity between their feature vectors and those of their neighbors are reclassified and assigned new pseudo-labels, reflecting their distinct roles in the graph.
- **Maximum Matching Participation:** Nodes that participate in the maximum matching of the bipartite graph are assigned unique pseudo-labels to highlight their central importance in maintaining the overall structure of the graph [27]. This ensures that critical nodes are treated differently, aligning the pseudo-labeling process with the structural properties of maximum matchings.

6.2. Supervised Training of HybridGNN Using Pseudo-Labels

After generating the pseudo-labels, HybridGNN is trained in a supervised fashion, where these pseudo-labels serve as ground-truth annotations. By treating the pseudo-labels as proxies for manually annotated data, the model is able to perform classification tasks, thereby optimizing its internal parameters. This approach leverages the structural properties of bipartite graphs, ensuring that the pseudo-labels provide meaningful supervision for the model.

During the training process, HybridGNN utilizes the pseudo-labels to minimize a predefined loss function, such as cross-entropy, which measures the difference between the predicted labels and the pseudo-labels. Through backpropagation, the model iteratively adjusts its weights to improve prediction accuracy [35]. This method not only reduces the reliance on manually labeled datasets but also allows the model to scale more effectively to large, complex graphs [36]. Moreover, the self-supervised nature of the pseudo-label generation helps to mitigate the risk of overfitting, as the model learns from a broader and more diverse set of graph features.

7. L2 Regularization and Early Stopping Mechanisms

To prevent overfitting during the training of the HybridGNN model, we employ two widely recognized techniques: L2 regularization (commonly known as weight decay) and an early stopping mechanism. These approaches are essential for ensuring that the model generalizes effectively to unseen data, especially in the context of large and complex graph structures.

7.1. L2 Regularization for Overfitting Prevention

L2 regularization is a well-established technique in machine learning that penalizes large weight values, thereby discouraging overly complex models. By adding a regularization term, which is the sum of the squared magnitudes of the model's weights, to the loss function, L2 regularization constrains the model's ability to overfit to the training data. This, in turn, enhances the model's generalization to new, unseen data [37]. In our implementation, we apply a weight decay value of 1×10^{-4} to the optimizer, carefully selecting this parameter to maintain a balance between model flexibility and the regularization strength. This approach allows the model to learn effectively without becoming overly dependent on specific patterns in the training data.

The modified loss function that incorporates L2 regularization can be expressed as

$$L_{total} = L_{cross\_entropy} + \lambda \sum_i w_i^2$$

where $L_{cross\_entropy}$ represents the original cross-entropy loss, λ denotes the regularization parameter (set to 1×10^{-4} in our experiments), and w_i corresponds to the individual weights of the model.

7.2. F_1-Score-Driven Early Stopping Mechanism

In addition to employing L2 regularization, we incorporate an early stopping mechanism to further mitigate the risk of overfitting during extended training sessions. Early stopping works by monitoring a selected performance metric throughout the training process and halting the process if no improvement is observed for a predefined number of consecutive epochs, a parameter known as *patience* [38].

For this work, we select the F_1-score as the primary metric for early stopping. The F_1-score is particularly well suited for imbalanced classification tasks, as it balances precision and recall, offering a more comprehensive measure of model performance. Given the potential class imbalances in our data, the F_1-score provides a nuanced assessment of how well the model generalizes across both classes. The patience parameter is set to five epochs; if no improvement in the F_1-score is observed during this period, training is stopped. This approach optimizes training efficiency by preventing unnecessary iterations when model performance plateaus, while also reducing the risk of overfitting to the training data.

By combining L2 regularization with an F_1-score-driven early stopping mechanism, we significantly enhance the generalization ability of the HybridGNN model. This dual-strategy approach allows us to maintain high performance while ensuring that the model remains robust and does not overfit to the specificities of the training dataset.

8. Dynamic Pseudo-Label Updating

Dynamic pseudo-label updating is an approach used in self-supervised learning to iteratively improve pseudo-label accuracy as the model learns. In the initial stages of training, pseudo-labels are generated through clustering techniques such as K-means. As the model improves over training epochs, predictions with high confidence scores are used to update the pseudo-labels, thereby enhancing the training signal.

The dynamic updating process proceeds as follows:

1. **Initial Pseudo-Label Generation:** Use a clustering method (e.g., K-means) to assign pseudo-labels to the nodes based on their embeddings.
2. **Confidence Score Calculation:** At each epoch, compute the confidence of model predictions using softmax probabilities.
3. **Update Rule:** For nodes where the confidence exceeds a predefined threshold (e.g., 70%), update their pseudo-labels to the predicted class.
4. **Iterative Refinement:** This process is repeated over multiple epochs, ensuring that the pseudo-labels become more accurate as the model improves.

This dynamic updating mechanism allows the model to gradually refine the training labels, leading to better generalization performance, especially in cases with limited labeled data.

9. Experimental Setup

9.1. Dataset Overview: Email Communication Network

The evaluation of the HybridGNN model was conducted using an email communication network dataset obtained from the Stanford Network Analysis Project (SNAP) repository [39]. In this dataset, nodes correspond to individual users, and edges represent email communications between users, forming a bipartite graph structure. This dataset is well suited for evaluating graph-based models due to its complex, real-world interactions and sparse connectivity patterns.

For the experiments, 80% of the dataset is randomly selected as the training set, while the remaining 20% is reserved as the test set for subsequent evaluation. This partitioning strategy ensures that the model is trained effectively, and its performance is assessed on unseen data to validate its generalizability.

To facilitate the training process, pseudo-labels are generated using K-means clustering, which groups nodes based on structural similarities and communication patterns within the graph [40]. This pseudo-labeling approach enables the model to perform supervised learning tasks without requiring manually annotated labels, thus enhancing scalability and flexibility in handling large-scale, unlabeled datasets.

9.2. DropEdge Data Augmentation

DropEdge is a regularization technique, where edges are randomly dropped from the graph during training to prevent overfitting. The DropEdge mechanism improves the model's generalization by reducing the model's reliance on specific edges.

9.3. Optimization and Training Procedures for HybridGNN

The HybridGNN model is optimized using binary cross-entropy loss, a common objective function for classification tasks, which measures the divergence between predicted outputs and the ground truth [35]. The Adam optimizer is employed with an initial learning rate of 0.001, chosen for its ability to adaptively adjust the learning rate during training, thereby improving convergence speed and stability [41].

To mitigate the memory constraints typically encountered during training on large datasets, gradient accumulation is employed. This technique allows for the accumulation of gradients over multiple mini-batches before performing a weight update, reducing the memory footprint while maintaining training efficacy [42]. By incorporating these optimization strategies, the model is able to effectively handle large-scale graph data, improving both computational efficiency and performance.

10. Experimental Results and Analysis

10.1. Metrics for Assessing HybridGNN Performance

To comprehensively evaluate the performance of HybridGNN, we employ several key metrics. These metrics are commonly used in graph matching and classification tasks to provide insights into both the accuracy and generalization capability of the model.

- **Accuracy:** Accuracy is used to measure the proportion of edges correctly predicted as part of the maximum matching. This metric provides a straightforward indication of how well the model identifies true matches within the graph [35].
- **F_1-Score:** The F_1-score, a harmonic mean of precision and recall, is used to balance the trade-off between these two measures, especially in cases where the class distribution is imbalanced. It is particularly useful for evaluating the model's performance in binary classification tasks related to edge prediction [43].

10.2. Ablation Study

We conduct the following experiments (all incorporating the optimization techniques mentioned above) to assess the impact of different layer combinations on the performance of our GNN model:

1. **Three-layer GNN Experiments:** We evaluate the performance of a three-layer GNN composed of GATv2, SAGEConv, and GIN layers. We also compare it against two-layer GNNs where one layer is removed from the original three-layer configuration.
   Analysis of Experimental Results: The comparison is based on both *Accuracy* and *F_1-score* metrics. Based on the experimental results, as shown in Figures 4 and 5, we observe that the model without the SAGEConv layer performs the best in both metrics during training. Consequently, we decide to exclude the SAGEConv layer and proceed to analyze the relative performance between the GATv2 and GIN layers based on their *Accuracy* and *F_1-score*.
2. **Alternative Three-layer Configurations:** We explore two variations of the three-layer GNN, one in which the SAGEConv layer is replaced by an additional GATv2 layer, and another where the SAGEConv layer is replaced by a GIN layer. These configurations are evaluated and compared based on *Accuracy* and *F_1-score*.
   Analysis of Experimental Results: We observe that the model with the GIN layer shows a slight advantage during the initial training phase. However, as seen in Figures 6 and 7, the configuration using the additional GATv2 layer demonstrates superior performance in the later stages of training. This superiority is marked by a clear upward trend, indicating a more significant overall advantage in both *Accuracy* and *F_1-score*.
3. **Six-layer GNN Configurations:** We extend the GNN to six layers, using only GATv2 and GIN layers. We examine all six possible combinations, with the number of GATv2 layers ranging from 0 to 6 and the number of GIN layers ranging from 6 to 0. The *Accuracy* and *F_1-score* of these six configurations are compared to determine the optimal layer distribution.
   Analysis of Experimental Results: Referring to the results illustrated in Figures 8 and 9, we observe that the GNN models exhibit the most optimal performance in terms of both accuracy and F_1-score when configured with GATv2 and GIN in the ratios of 4:2 and 5:1. Consequently, we designate the former configuration as $HybridGNN_1$ and the latter as $HybridGNN_2$.

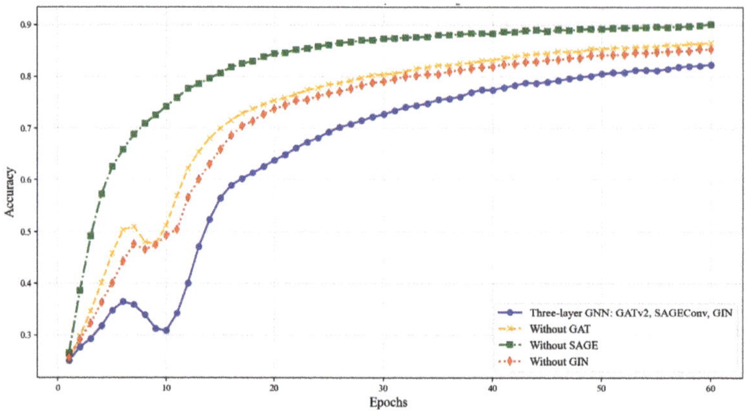

Figure 4. Comparison of training accuracy over 60 epochs for different GNN configurations.

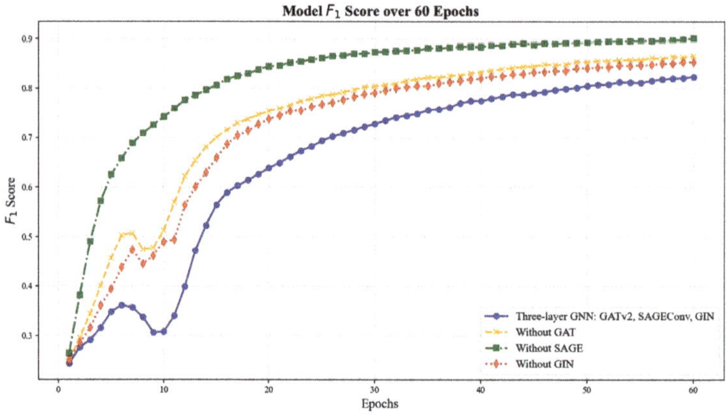

Figure 5. Comparison of training F_1-score over 60 epochs for different GNN configurations.

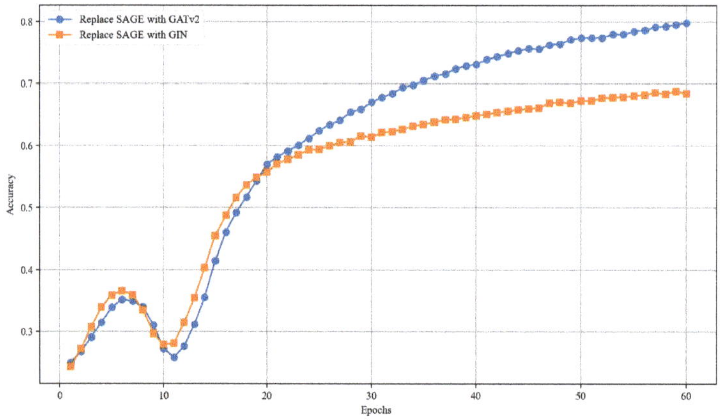

Figure 6. Comparison of training accuracy over 60 epochs for the experiments replacing SAGE with GATv2 and GIN.

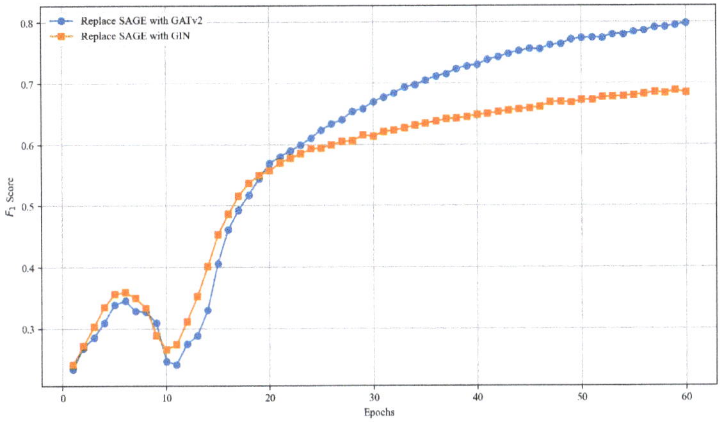

Figure 7. Comparison of F_1-score over 60 epochs for the experiments replacing SAGE with GATv2 and GIN.

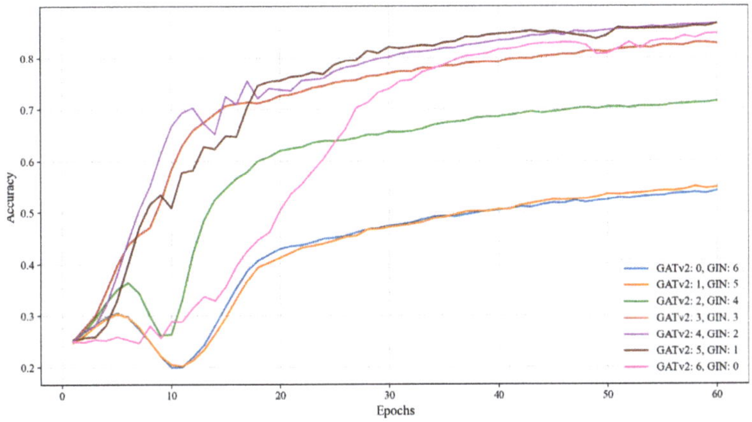

Figure 8. Training accuracy comparison over 60 epochs for different GNN configurations.

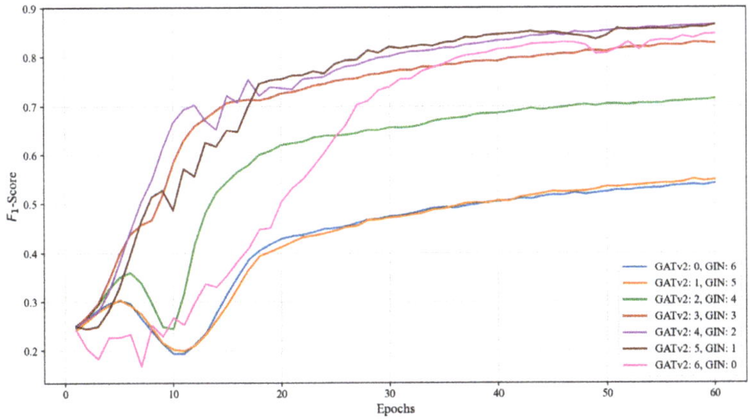

Figure 9. Training F_1-score comparison over 60 epochs for different GNN configurations.

Through a series of training experiments, we initially establish that SAGEConv demonstrated suboptimal performance for the specific problem addressed in this paper. The outcomes from our initial experiments consistently indicate that SAGEConv does not contribute significantly to the overall effectiveness of the GNN model. As a result, we decide to exclude SAGEConv from our GNN configuration, focusing on more promising architectures for subsequent tests.

In the second set of experiments, we conduct a comparative analysis between GATv2 and GIN layers to observe their respective advantages and disadvantages throughout the training process. These experiments are crucial in identifying which configuration would yield better accuracy and F_1-score during the learning phase. The findings reveal that, while both GATv2 and GIN provide certain benefits, the balance between these two types of layers has a notable impact on the overall model performance.

By testing all possible combinations of GATv2 and GIN layers within a six-layer GNN structure, we determine that the configurations with a 4:2 and 5:1 ratio of GATv2 to GIN layers show the most optimal results in terms of both accuracy and F_1-score. Therefore, we designate these configurations as HybridGNN_1 and HybridGNN_2, respectively, to represent the two most effective architectures based on our findings.

Moving forward, we plan to conduct further experiments using the email Eron training dataset and the email EU testing dataset. These additional tests will allow us to evaluate the performance of our proposed HybridGNNs against three classical algorithms, focusing on accuracy and F_1-score as the primary metrics for comparison. This will help solidify the effectiveness of HybridGNN_1 and HybridGNN_2 and provide deeper insights into their potential for practical applications.

10.3. Training Set Performance Comparison with Classical Algorithms

The performance of HybridGNN models, specifically HybridGNN_1 (GATv2: 4, GIN: 2) and HybridGNN_2 (GATv2: 5, GIN: 1), is evaluated against classical algorithms commonly used for maximum matching in bipartite graphs: the Hopcroft–Karp algorithm [3], the Hungarian algorithm [1], and the Blossom/Edmonds' algorithm [2]. The training accuracy and F_1-score results over 60 epochs (Figures 10 and 11) reveal distinct performance characteristics between these methods.

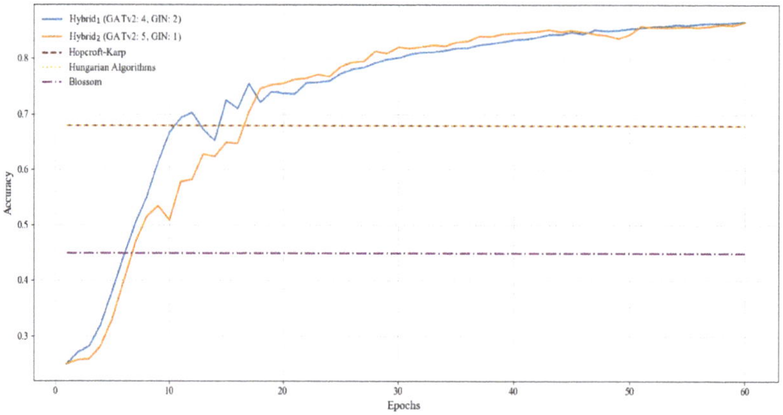

Figure 10. Training accuracy comparison over 60 epochs for HybridGNN_1, HybridGNN_2, and classical algorithms (Hopcroft–Karp, Hungarian, and Blossom).

In these experiments, HybridGNN models exhibit superior performance in terms of both accuracy and F_1-score when compared to the classical algorithms. While the Hopcroft–Karp and Hungarian algorithms show comparable accuracy levels, they both plateau below 0.7 and demonstrate less adaptability to varying graph structures. The Blossom algorithm, though robust for certain graph types, consistently displays lower scores and does not achieve competitive performance compared to the GNN-based approaches.

The classical algorithms are efficient for specific cases but show limitations when handling large and heterogeneous datasets. The Hopcroft–Karp algorithm, for instance, performs well for medium-scale bipartite graphs but faces increased computational demands on larger datasets. Similarly, the Hungarian algorithm is effective for structured assignment problems but scales poorly with graph size. The Blossom algorithm, although powerful for non-bipartite graphs, struggles with extensive datasets in terms of efficiency.

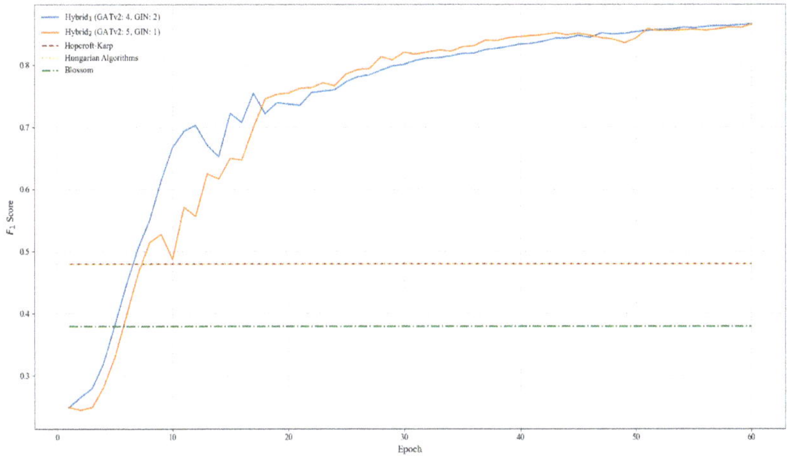

Figure 11. Training F_1-score comparison over 60 epochs for $HybridGNN_1$, $HybridGNN_2$, and classical algorithms (Hopcroft–Karp, Hungarian, and Blossom).

$HybridGNN_1$ and $HybridGNN_2$, on the other hand, demonstrate their neural network-based strengths by efficiently processing large-scale graphs, achieving consistent improvements across training epochs. Their ability to learn graph representations enables them to adapt to complex and evolving graph structures, showing marked robustness and flexibility over static classical methods. This reinforces the advantages of integrating GNNs in tackling the computational challenges associated with graph data, supporting the findings from recent studies in Graph Neural Networks [29].

These results highlight the potential of HybridGNN models to offer enhanced performance in applications that involve large and complex graphs, emphasizing their practical relevance in scenarios where traditional algorithms may not suffice.

10.4. Test Set Performance Comparison with Classical Algorithms

The comparison of test set performance between $HybridGNN_1$, $HybridGNN_2$, and classical graph algorithms highlights the effectiveness of our models in addressing the maximum matching problem in bipartite graphs. The results, as shown in Figure 12, demonstrate that both $HybridGNN_1$ and $HybridGNN_2$ achieve significantly higher accuracy and F_1-scores compared to classical methods like Hopcroft–Karp, Hungarian, and Blossom algorithms.

$HybridGNN_1$ achieves an accuracy of 0.84 and an F_1-score of 0.84, while $HybridGNN_2$ closely follows with an accuracy of 0.83 and an F_1-score of 0.83. In contrast, the classical algorithms show comparatively lower performance: the Hopcroft–Karp and Hungarian algorithms reach similar accuracy levels around 0.69 but have notably lower F_1-scores at 0.49. The Blossom algorithm, although effective for specific non-bipartite cases, records the lowest metrics, with an accuracy of 0.47 and an F_1-score of 0.38.

It is important to note that our test set evaluation is conducted over a single epoch after training the models for 60 epochs. The results on the test set are found to be consistent with the training set performance, showing minimal deviation. This observation indicates that overfitting does not occur, as the models maintain their accuracy and F_1-score levels when evaluated on unseen data.

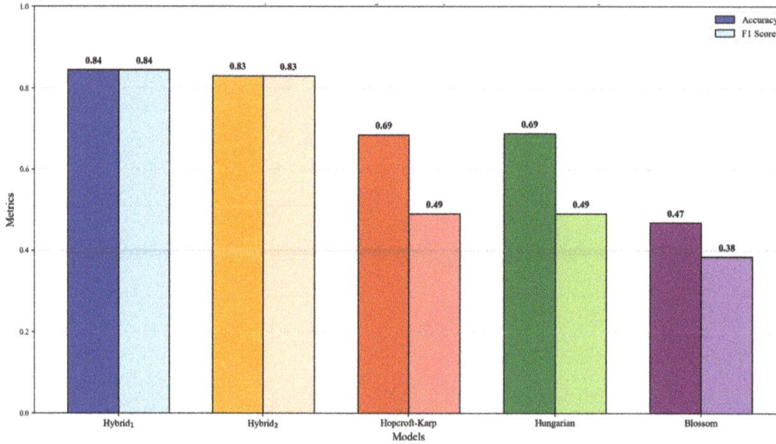

Figure 12. Test set accuracy and F_1-score comparison for $HybridGNN_1$, $HybridGNN_2$, and classical algorithms (Hopcroft–Karp, Hungarian, Blossom).

These findings underscore the robustness of the HybridGNN models, which leverage the combined power of GATv2 and GIN layers to effectively capture both local and global dependencies in the graph structure. The models' strong performance compared to traditional algorithms, especially in handling complex graph structures, highlights their suitability for large-scale real-world applications. The consistency between training and test results further supports the generalization capability of $HybridGNN_1$ and $HybridGNN_2$.

11. Computational Efficiency Analysis

In this section, we analyze the computational efficiency of the proposed HybridGNN models, $Hybrid_1$ (GATv2: 4, GIN: 2) and $Hybrid_2$ (GATv2: 5, GIN: 1), focusing on both time complexity and memory usage. By integrating GATv2 and GIN layers in varying proportions and employing optimization techniques, these models leverage the strengths of each component to handle specific aspects of the maximum matching problem efficiently.

11.1. Time Complexity

The time complexity analysis breaks down the computational demands of each layer within the HybridGNN models:

- **GATv2Conv Layers**: For a single layer with K attention heads, the time complexity is

$$T_{\text{GATv2}} = O(E \cdot H + N \cdot H)$$

- **GINConv Layers**: For a single GINConv layer, where d_{MLP} is the depth of the MLP, the time complexity is

$$T_{\text{GIN}} = O(E \cdot H + N \cdot H \cdot d_{\text{MLP}})$$

The overall time complexity T_{total} for a forward pass through the HybridGNN models, given their configurations, can be expressed as

$$T_{\text{total}} = 4 \cdot T_{\text{GATv2}} + 2 \cdot T_{\text{GIN}} + T_{\text{FC}} \quad (\text{Hybrid}_1)$$

$$T_{\text{total}} = 5 \cdot T_{\text{GATv2}} + T_{\text{GIN}} + T_{\text{FC}} \quad (\text{Hybrid}_2)$$

where $T_{FC} = O(N \cdot H \cdot C)$ represents the final fully connected layer. Substituting the individual complexities, and assuming $E \gg N$ for sparse graphs, the dominant term simplifies to

$$T_{\text{total}} = O(L \cdot E \cdot H)$$

This complexity is typical for GNNs operating on sparse graphs, dominated by edge-wise computations in the convolutional layers.

11.2. Memory Efficiency

To mitigate memory constraints and enhance scalability, we implement two pivotal optimization strategies: **mixed precision training** and **gradient accumulation**.

Figure 13 presents a comprehensive comparison of memory consumption between HybridGNN_1 (GATv2: 4, GIN: 2) and HybridGNN_2 (GATv2: 5, GIN: 1) against traditional algorithms such as the Hungarian, Blossom, and Hopcroft–Karp methods. The analysis reveals that HybridGNN_1 and HybridGNN_2 achieve notable memory efficiency, with recorded usage of 50 MB and 53 MB, respectively. In comparison, the Blossom algorithm exhibits the highest memory footprint at 70 MB, while the Hungarian and Hopcroft–Karp algorithms record intermediate memory usage levels of 47 MB and 60 MB, respectively.

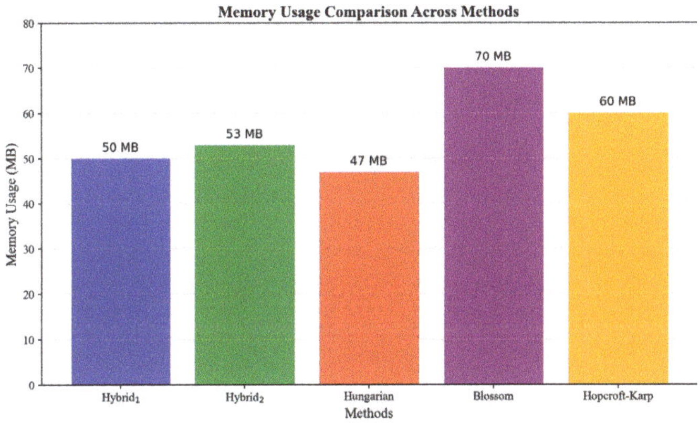

Figure 13. Comparison of memory usage across HybridGNN models and classical algorithms.

11.2.1. Mixed Precision Training

Mixed precision training leverages 16-bit floating point (FP16) precision for selected operations, while preserving 32-bit precision (FP32) for key model parameters to maintain numerical stability. This hybrid approach optimizes memory usage, effectively reducing it by approximately half, which enables the use of larger batch sizes and lowers the risk of memory allocation issues, particularly in large-scale graphs with high-dimensional node features.

Moreover, modern hardware, such as NVIDIA Tensor Cores, is designed to execute FP16 operations more efficiently than FP32. This dual advantage results in a decreased memory footprint and faster computation times, positioning mixed precision training as a robust solution for the resource-intensive demands of complex GNN architectures.

11.2.2. Gradient Accumulation

Gradient accumulation is an effective strategy for enabling larger effective batch sizes by accumulating gradients over multiple smaller mini-batches before updating the model parameters. In our implementation, gradients are accumulated over every four mini-batches (`accumulation_steps=4`), thereby decreasing the memory requirement per mini-batch. This method is particularly advantageous for GNNs, where the high degree of inter-node dependencies significantly amplifies memory usage during graph convolution operations.

By alleviating the per-mini-batch memory constraints, gradient accumulation facilitates training within the available hardware memory limits, thereby improving training stability and maintaining computational efficiency without compromising performance.

11.3. Scalability Considerations and Conclusion

Minor computational components, such as residual connections, batch normalization, and activation functions, add $O(N \cdot H)$ complexity per layer, but these have minimal impact relative to the edge-based computations of $O(E \cdot H)$. The HybridGNN model's complexity scales linearly with the number of layers L, the number of edges E, and the hidden dimension H. This linear scalability makes it suitable for large-scale graph applications. To efficiently handle larger datasets, we employ strategies such as the following:

- **Sampling Methods**: Techniques like GraphSAGE neighbor sampling reduce the number of edges processed per batch.
- **Sparse Matrix Operations**: Leveraging efficient sparse matrix computations improves computational efficiency.
- **Mini-Batch Training**: Processing graph subsets reduces memory requirements per iteration.

In conclusion, while the HybridGNN model combines multiple architectures to enhance performance, its overall time complexity per epoch remains $O(L \cdot E \cdot H)$. With the above optimizations, it achieves computational efficiency suitable for real-world scalability.

12. Discussion and Concluding Remarks

12.1. Analysis of Results and Challenges

The experiments demonstrated that HybridGNN_1 (GATv2: 4, GIN: 2) and HybridGNN_2 (GATv2: 5, GIN: 1) excel in solving the maximum matching problem in complex bipartite graphs. By combining GATv2 and GIN layers, these models effectively capture both local and global dependencies, achieving better accuracy and F_1-scores compared to traditional methods like the Hopcroft–Karp and Hungarian algorithms.

The powerful attention mechanism in GATv2 and the expressive capabilities of GIN layers contribute to the models' strong generalization across different graph structures. Data augmentation further strengthens the training, enabling robustness against noisy or incomplete data. The use of pseudo-labels from classical algorithms facilitates effective self-supervised training without large labeled datasets.

However, HybridGNN_1 and HybridGNN_2 face challenges, including high computational demands, especially for large graphs, which require significant resources. Performance can also plateau as graph size increases due to fixed model layer sizes and aggregation limitations, potentially leading to overfitting or diminished returns. Additionally, reliance on pseudo-labels, while useful, can affect performance if the data are highly irregular or disconnected.

12.2. Future Research Directions

To enhance HybridGNN_1 and HybridGNN_2, future research could explore several directions. First, advanced architectures and pooling methods such as DiffPool or SAGPool could be integrated to better handle large graphs. Second, model efficiency could be improved by reducing computational costs through model compression, quantization, and distributed training. Third, models could be tested on real-world data, including social, biological, and communication networks, while also incorporating temporal dynamics for evolving graphs. Fourth, self-supervised learning enhancements, such as exploring contrastive learning, graph augmentation, improved pseudo-labels, and leveraging graph autoencoders and GANs, could be pursued. Fifth, extending the models to handle multi-graph and heterogeneous graph scenarios would allow for more complex applications. Finally, improving the explainability of the models through graph saliency maps or attention-based visualizations could provide better interpretability.

12.3. Concluding Remarks

This paper introduced $HybridGNN_1$ and $HybridGNN_2$, which integrate GATv2 and GINConv layers with Jumping Knowledge mechanisms for maximum matching in bipartite graphs. The models demonstrated superior performance over classical algorithms and showed potential for scalable real-world applications due to self-supervised learning with pseudo-labels.

While these models performed well, challenges such as high computational costs and potential performance plateaus indicate areas for improvement. Future work should focus on optimizing efficiency and expanding real-world applicability, solidifying the role of GNNs in solving classical graph problems and bridging traditional and modern approaches to graph-based problem-solving.

13. Reproducibility and Code Availability

To ensure the reproducibility of our results and facilitate further research, we have made the code for training HybridGNN models, the implementation of various training optimizations, and the ablation study experiments publicly available. This repository also includes the code for conducting comparative experiments between HybridGNNs and classical algorithms in terms of accuracy and F_1-scores, as well as the code for memory usage comparison.

All code, datasets, and detailed instructions for reproducing the results presented in this paper can be accessed at our dedicated GitHub repository under the following account: https://github.com/Dandypan/GNN- (accessed on 30 November 2024).

Researchers and practitioners are encouraged to use this repository to replicate our experiments, analyze the training process, and build upon our findings to further enhance Graph Neural Network applications for maximum matching problems and beyond.

Author Contributions: Conceptualization, M.-J.-S.W.; Methodology, M.-J.-S.W. and C.-H.P.; Software, C.-H.P.; Validation, C.-H.P. and Y.Y.; Formal Analysis, Y.Y. and C.-H.P.; Investigation, C.-H.P. and Y.Q.; Resources, M.-J.-S.W.; Data Curation, C.-H.P.; Writing—Original Draft Preparation, C.-H.P. and M.-J.-S.W.; Writing—Review and Editing, M.-J.-S.W.; Visualization, C.-H.P.; Supervision, M.-J.-S.W.; Project Administration, M.-J.-S.W.; Funding Acquisition, M.-J.-S.W. All authors have read and agreed to the published version of the manuscript.

Funding: This research was funded by the National Science and Technology Major Project undertaken by the Shenzhen Technology and Innovation Council (Grant No. CJGJZD20220517141800002).

Data Availability Statement: The data supporting the reported results in this study are publicly available from the Stanford Large Network Dataset Collection (https://snap.stanford.edu/data/, accessed on 15 October 2024).

Acknowledgments: The corresponding author, Mu-Jiang-Shan Wang, conceived the idea of combining classical graph theory problems with GNNs, and developed the research concept for comparing traditional methods with GNN-based approaches for bipartite graph matching. The first author, Chun-Hui Pan, implemented the research idea, conducted the experiments, and performed detailed result analysis. Yi Qu provided invaluable and precise suggestions during the code debugging process, such as the use of predefined labels instead of randomly generated ones, effectively resolving key issues. Yao Yao systematically verified and reproduced the overall framework of the GNN model, demonstrating its compatibility, and contributed significantly by helping to analyze the time complexity. Her contributions were both valuable and substantial. Lastly, we would like to express our sincere gratitude to all the members of the editorial team and the reviewers for their invaluable suggestions and contributions to this paper.

Conflicts of Interest: The authors declare no conflicts of interest. The funders had no role in the design of the study; in the collection, analyses, or interpretation of data; in the writing of the manuscript; or in the decision to publish the results.

Appendix A. Algorithms Involved in This Paper

Algorithm A1: HybridGNN$_1$ and HybridGNN$_2$ Model Implementation.

Input: Input node features x, edge index *edge_index*
Output: Node classification output x

```
Model Initialization: Define HybridGNN_1 with GATv2 (4 heads) and GIN (2 layers), and
  HybridGNN_2 with GATv2 (5 heads) and GIN (1 layer).;
Input Parameters: input_dim, hidden_dim, output_dim, num_layers, gat_heads, dropout;
Layer Structure: - Add initial GATv2Conv layers with skip connections (4 layers for
  HybridGNN_1, 5 layers for HybridGNN_2).;
- Add GINConv layers (2 layers for HybridGNN_1, 1 layer for HybridGNN_2).;
- Initialize batch normalization for each layer.;
- Final linear classifier fc.;
Forward Pass: foreach layer i in convs do
    residual ← x;
    if i < num_gatv2_layers then
        x ← convs[i](x, edge_index);
        x ← batch_norms[i](x);
        x ← F.elu(x) + skip_proj[i](residual);
    else if i < num_gatv2_layers + num_gin_layers then
        x ← convs[i](x, edge_index);
        x ← batch_norms[i](x);
        x ← F.relu(x) + residual;
    x ← dropout(x);
x ← fc(x);
return x;
```

Algorithm A2: Generating Pseudo-Labels for Bipartite Graphs.

Input: Graph *data*, number of classes k
Output: Pseudo-labels *pseudo_labels*

```
Step 1: Classify nodes by degree ;
node_degrees ← compute degrees of nodes ;
degree_thresholds ← quantiles of node_degrees ;
pseudo_labels ← initialize to zeros ;
for i ← 0 to k − 1 do
    Assign labels based on degree ranges ;
Step 2: Adjust labels by neighborhood disparity ;
foreach node v do
    neighbors ← get neighbors of v ;
    if neighbors exist then
        cos_sim ← compute cosine similarity ;
        if cos_sim < 0.5 then
            Adjust pseudo_labels[v] ;
Step 3: Adjust by maximum matching participation ;
node_mask ← get matching nodes ;
Adjust pseudo_labels[node_mask] ;
return pseudo_labels
```

Algorithm A3: Training HybridGNN with Pseudo-Labels.

Input: Model *model*, data loader *data_loader*, pseudo-labels *pseudo_labels*, class weights *class_weights*, epochs *epochs*, learning rate *lr*, accumulation steps *accumulation_steps*, patience *patience*

Output: Training losses *losses*, accuracies *accuracies*

```
Initialize optimizer and scheduler ;
criterion ← FocalLoss(class_weights, γ = 2) ;
pseudo_labels_tensor ← tensor(pseudo_labels) ;
best_acc, patience_counter ← 0, 0 ;
for epoch ← 1 to epochs do
    optimizer.zero_grad() ;
    foreach batch in data_loader do
        out ← model(batch) ;
        target ← pseudo_labels_tensor[batch.n_id] ;
        loss ← criterion(out,target) / accumulation_steps ;
        loss.backward() ;
        if (i + 1)%accumulation_steps == 0 then
            optimizer.step(), optimizer.zero_grad() ;
    Evaluate model and calculate accuracy ;
    if accuracy > best_acc then
        best_acc ← accuracy, patience_counter ← 0 ;
    else
        patience_counter ← patience_counter + 1 ;
        if patience_counter ≥ patience then
            break (Early stopping) ;
    Update pseudo-labels dynamically ;
    scheduler.step() ;
return losses, accuracies ;
```

Algorithm A4: DropEdge Implementation.

Input: Data loader *data_loader*, drop rate *drop_rate*

Output: Original edge index *original_edge_index*

```
original_edge_index ← data_loader.dataset[0].edge_index.clone();
num_edges ← size(original_edge_index, 1);
perm ← randperm(num_edges);
retain_edges ← int(num_edges × (1 − drop_rate));
edge_index ← original_edge_index[:, perm[: retain_edges]];
data_loader.dataset[0].edge_index ← edge_index;
return original_edge_index;
```

Algorithm A5: Training the HybridGNN Model.

```
Input: Model model, Data loader data_loader, Pseudo-labels pseudo_labels, Class
       weights class_weights
Output: Training losses and accuracies
Initialize optimizer, scheduler, criterion (Focal Loss);
Set best_acc ← 0, patience_counter ← 0;
Convert pseudo_labels to tensor;
for each epoch do
    Apply DropEdge augmentation: Randomly drop edges from data_loader;
    Train model: ;
        for each batch in data_loader do
            Compute output out ← model(batch);
            Compute loss and backpropagate;
            if batch index % accumulation_steps == 0 then
                Update model parameters;
    Restore original edge index;
    Evaluate model: ;
        Compute predictions preds;
        Calculate accuracy accuracy;
    Update best accuracy and early stopping: ;
        if accuracy > best_acc then
            Update best_acc;
            Reset patience_counter;
        else
            Increment patience_counter;
            if patience_counter ≥ patience then
                Stop training early;
    Dynamic pseudo-label update;
    Update pseudo_labels using model predictions;
return losses, accuracies;
```

References

1. Kuhn, H.W. The Hungarian Method for the Assignment Problem. *Nav. Res. Logist. Q.* **1955**, *2*, 83–97. [CrossRef]
2. Edmonds, J. Paths, trees, and flowers. *Can. J. Math.* **1965**, *17*, 449–467. [CrossRef]
3. Hopcroft, J.E.; Karp, R.M. An $n^{5/2}$ algorithm for maximum matchings in bipartite graphs. *SIAM J. Comput.* **1973**, *2*, 225–231. [CrossRef]
4. Veličković, P.; Cucurull, G.; Casanova, A.; Romero, A.; Lio, P.; Bengio, Y. Graph attention networks. *arXiv* **2017**, arXiv:1710.10903. [CrossRef]
5. Hamilton, W.L.; Ying, R.; Leskovec, J. Inductive representation learning on large graphs. In Proceedings of the Advances in Neural Information Processing Systems, Long Beach, CA, USA, 4–9 December 2017; pp. 1024–1034.
6. Wu, B.; Li, L. Solving maximum weighted matching on large graphs with deep reinforcement learning. *Inf. Sci.* **2022**, *614*, 400–415. [CrossRef]
7. Angelini, M.C.; Ricci-Tersenghi, F. Modern graph neural networks do worse than classical greedy algorithms in solving combinatorial optimization problems like maximum independent set. *Nat. Mach. Intell.* **2023**, *5*, 29–31. [CrossRef]
8. Brusca, L.; Quaedvlieg, L.C.; Skoulakis, S.; Chrysos, G.; Cevher, V. Maximum independent set: Self-training through dynamic programming. In *Advances in Neural Information Processing Systems*; Curran Associates, Inc.: Newry, UK, 2023; Volume 36, pp. 40637–40658.
9. Schuetz, M.J.; Brubaker, J.K.; Katzgraber, H.G. Combinatorial optimization with physics-inspired graph neural networks. *Nat. Mach. Intell.* **2022**, *4*, 367–377. [CrossRef]
10. Zaicevs, N. Solving Maximum Weighted Matching Problem Using Graph Neural Networks. Master's Thesis, The University of Bergen, Bergen, Norway, 2024.
11. Wang, M.; Lin, Y.; Wang, S. The nature diagnosability of bubble-sort star graph networks under the PMC model and MM* model. *Int. J. Eng. Appl. Sci.* **2017**, *4*, 55–60.

12. Wang, S.; Wang, Y.; Wang, M. Connectivity and matching preclusion for leaf-sort graphs. *J. Interconnect. Netw.* **2019**, *19*, 1940007. [CrossRef]
13. Lin, Y.; Miller, M.; Simanjuntak, R. Edge-magic total labelings of wheels, fans and friendship graphs. *Bull. ICA* **2002**, *35*, 89–98.
14. Baca, M.; Lin, Y.; Miller, M.; Simanjuntak, R. New constructions of magic and antimagic graph labelings. *Util. Math.* **2001**, *60*, 229–239.
15. Lin, Y. Face antimagic labelings of plane graphs Pab. *Ars Comb.* **2006**, *80*, 259–273.
16. Alghamdi, J.; Luo, S.; Lin, Y. A comprehensive survey on machine learning approaches for fake news detection. *Multimed. Tools Appl.* **2024**, *83*, 51009–51067. [CrossRef]
17. Javed, M.; Lin, Y. iMER: Iterative process of entity relationship and business process model extraction from the requirements. *Inf. Softw. Technol.* **2021**, *135*, 106558. [CrossRef]
18. Wang, B.; Jiang, B.; Tang, J.; Luo, B. Generalizing aggregation functions in GNNs: Building high capacity and robust GNNs via nonlinear aggregation. *IEEE Trans. Pattern Anal. Mach. Intell.* **2023**, *45*, 13454–13466. [CrossRef]
19. Abadal, S.; Jain, A.; Guirado, R.; López-Alonso, J.; Alarcón, E. Computing graph neural networks: A survey from algorithms to accelerators. *ACM Comput. Surv. (CSUR)* **2021**, *54*, 1–38. [CrossRef]
20. Zhang, B.; Kannan, R.; Busart, C.; Prasanna, V. GCV-Turbo: End-to-end Acceleration of GNN-based Computer Vision Tasks on FPGA. *arXiv* **2024**, arXiv:2404.07188. [CrossRef]
21. Satake, S.; Gu, Y.; Sakurai, K. Explicit Non-malleable Codes from Bipartite Graphs. In *Arithmetic of Finite Fields 9th International Workshop, WAIFI 2022, Chengdu, China, 29 August–2 September 2022, Revised Selected Papers*; Springer: Berlin/Heidelberg, Germany, 2022; pp. 221–236.
22. Wang, M.; Wang, S. Connectivity and diagnosability of center k-ary n-cubes. *Discret. Appl. Math.* **2021**, *294*, 98–107. [CrossRef]
23. Wang, M.; Lin, Y.; Wang, S.; Wang, M. Sufficient conditions for graphs to be maximally 4-restricted edge connected. *Australas. J. Comb.* **2018**, *70*, 123–136.
24. Bondy, J.A.; Murty, U.S.R. *Graph Theory with Applications*; Macmillan: London, UK, 1976; Volume 290.
25. West, D.B. *Introduction to Graph Theory*; Prentice Hall Upper Saddle River: Upper Saddle River, NJ, USA, 2001.
26. Diestel, R. *Graph Theory*; Reinhard Diestel (eBooks); Springer: New York, NY, USA, 2024.
27. Lovász, L.; Plummer, M. *Matching Theory*; American Mathematical Society: Providence, RI, USA, 2009.
28. Kipf, T.N.; Welling, M. Semi-supervised classification with graph convolutional networks. *arXiv* **2016**, arXiv:1609.02907. [CrossRef]
29. Xu, K.; Hu, W.; Leskovec, J.; Jegelka, S. How powerful are graph neural networks? *arXiv* **2018**, arXiv:1810.00826. [CrossRef]
30. Battaglia, P.W.; Hamrick, J.B.; Bapst, V.; Sanchez-Gonzalez, A.; Zambaldi, V.; Malinowski, M.; Tacchetti, A.; Raposo, D.; Santoro, A.; Faulkner, R.; et al. Relational inductive biases, deep learning, and graph networks. *arXiv* **2018**, arXiv:1806.01261. [CrossRef]
31. Xu, K.; Li, C.; Tian, Y.; Sonobe, T.; Kawarabayashi, K.i.; Jegelka, S. Representation learning on graphs with jumping knowledge networks. In Proceedings of the 35th International Conference on Machine Learning, Stockholm, Sweden, 10–15 July 2018; pp. 5453–5462.
32. Jing, L.; Tian, Y. Self-supervised learning: A survey. *arXiv* **2020**, arXiv:2006.08218.
33. Hu, W.; Liu, B.; Gomes, J.; Zitnik, M.; Liang, P.; Pande, V.; Leskovec, J. Strategies for pre-training graph neural networks. In Proceedings of the International Conference on Learning Representations, Addis Ababa, Ethiopia, 30 April 2020.
34. Zhao, J.; Zhou, H.; Liu, W. Degree-based classification in bipartite networks. *Phys. Rev. E* **2006**, *74*, 056109.
35. Goodfellow, I.; Bengio, Y.; Courville, A. *Deep Learning*; MIT Press: Cambridge, MA, USA, 2016.
36. Liu, X.; Zhang, F.; Hou, Z.; Mian, L.; Wang, Z.; Zhang, J.; Tang, J. Self-supervised learning: Generative or contrastive. *IEEE Trans. Knowl. Data Eng.* **2021**, *35*, 857–876. [CrossRef]
37. Ng, A.Y. Feature selection, L_1 vs. L_2 regularization, and rotational invariance. In Proceedings of the Twenty-First International Conference on Machine Learning, Banff, AB, Canada, 4–8 July 2004; Association for Computing Machinery: New York, NY, USA, 2004; p. 78.
38. Prechelt, L. Early stopping-but when? *Neural Networks: Tricks of the Trade*; Springer: Berlin, Heidelberg/Germany, 1998; pp. 55–69.
39. Leskovec, J.; Sosic, R. SNAP: A general-purpose network analysis and graph mining library. In *ACM Transactions on Intelligent Systems and Technology (TIST)*; Association for Computing Machinery: New York, NY, USA, 2014; Volume 8, p. 1.
40. Lloyd, S. Least squares quantization in PCM. *IEEE Trans. Inf. Theory* **1982**, *28*, 129–137. [CrossRef]
41. Kingma, D.P.; Ba, J. Adam: A method for stochastic optimization. *arXiv* **2014**, arXiv:1412.6980.
42. Paszke, A.; Gross, S.; Chintala, S.; Yang, E.; DeVito, Z.; Lin, Z.; Desmaison, A.; Antiga, L.; Lerer, A. Automatic differentiation in PyTorch. In Proceedings of the Advances in Neural Information Processing Systems, Long Beach, CA, USA, 4–9 December 2017.
43. Sasaki, Y. The Truth of the F-Measure. 2017. Available online: https://www.researchgate.net/publication/268185911_The_truth_of_the_F-measure (accessed on 15 October 2024).

symmetry

MDPI

Article

The Heterogeneous Network Community Detection Model Based on Self-Attention

Gaofeng Zhou [1,*] and Rui-Feng Wang [2,3]

[1] College of Computer Science & Technology, Qingdao University, Qingdao 266071, China
[2] College of Engineering, China Agricultural University, 17 Qinghua East Road, Haidian, Beijing 100083, China; sweefongreggiewong@cau.edu.cn
[3] National Innovation Center for Digital Fishery, China Agricultural University, Beijing 100083, China
* Correspondence: zhougaofeng@qdu.edu.cn

Abstract: With the advancement of representation learning, graph representation learning has gained significant attention in the field of community detection for heterogeneous networks. A prominent approach in this domain involves the use of meta-paths to capture higher-order relationships between nodes, particularly when bidirectional or reciprocal relationships exist. However, defining effective meta-paths often requires substantial domain expertise. Moreover, these methods typically depend on additional clustering algorithms, which can limit their practical applicability. To address these challenges, context paths have been introduced as an alternative to meta-paths. When combined with a self-attention mechanism, models can dynamically assess the relative importance of different context paths. By leveraging the inherent symmetry within context paths, models enhance their ability to capture balanced relationships between nodes, thereby improving their representation of complex interactions. Building on this idea, we propose BP-GCN, a self-attention-based model for heterogeneous community detection. BP-GCN autonomously identifies node relationships within symmetric context paths, significantly improving community detection accuracy. Furthermore, the model integrates the Bernoulli–Poisson framework to establish an end-to-end detection system that eliminates the need for auxiliary clustering algorithms. Extensive experiments on multiple real-world datasets demonstrate that BP-GCN consistently outperforms existing benchmark methods.

Keywords: heterogeneous network; community detection; self-attention; Bernoulli–Poisson model; contextual path; graph neural network

1. Introduction

With the advent of the big data era and the increasing research interest in complex networks [1], heterogeneous networks have emerged as a key focus in this field. Heterogeneous networks are intricate structures composed of multiple types of nodes and edges. Unlike homogeneous networks, which consist of a single type of entity and relationship, heterogeneous networks encode a broader range of structural and semantic information. These networks are prevalent across various domains, including academic networks [2] (which involve nodes such as papers, authors, conferences and topics), movie networks [3] (comprising entities like actors, directors and films) and knowledge graphs, which represent entities and their relationships. While the diversity of node and edge types in heterogeneous networks enriches their semantic information, it also introduces significant challenges in terms of modeling and analysis.

Deng Cai et al. [4] proposed a query-based approach for mining heterogeneous social networks, which has significantly advanced the study of such networks. This method employs regression-based graph matrix analysis to uncover detailed and nuanced semantic relationships within social networks. Guo-Jun Qi et al. [5] introduced a clustering algorithm based on heterogeneous random fields, which models the structure and content of heterogeneous graphs through anomalous edges. By integrating content information from social media objects with the link structures, this approach enhances clustering performance. Chuan Shi et al. [6] proposed a ranking-based clustering method that projects heterogeneous graphs into subgraphs for analysis, facilitating effective community detection.

While traditional methods for heterogeneous community detection have made significant strides, they still struggle to capture higher-order complex relationships within heterogeneous networks. A common approach in these methods is the use of meta-paths for community detection. A meta-path connects different types of nodes and reveals higher-order relationships between them.

For instance, consider nodes a1 and a5 in Figure 1. These nodes should belong to the same community (Community 1), but traditional methods, which rely on direct relationships (such as "association"), would not group them together since no direct connection exists between them (r4). However, a1 and a5 are the authors of papers p1 and p4, and these papers share a common theme, t1. Additionally, a5 is directly connected to a4, who has collaborated with a1 on the same research theme, t1. These indirect connections provide strong evidence that a1 and a5 should be grouped together. Predefined meta-paths (such as "Author–Paper–Theme–Paper–Author") facilitate a more accurate community assignment for a1 and a5. Furthermore, the symmetry of meta-paths enriches and enhances the flexibility of the relationships between nodes. For instance, the relationship between a1 and a5 through papers p1 and p4 and theme t1 is not one-way. Due to symmetry, both a1 and a5 act as "authors", which strengthens their similarity. This symmetric connection aids in more accurately identifying their shared community.

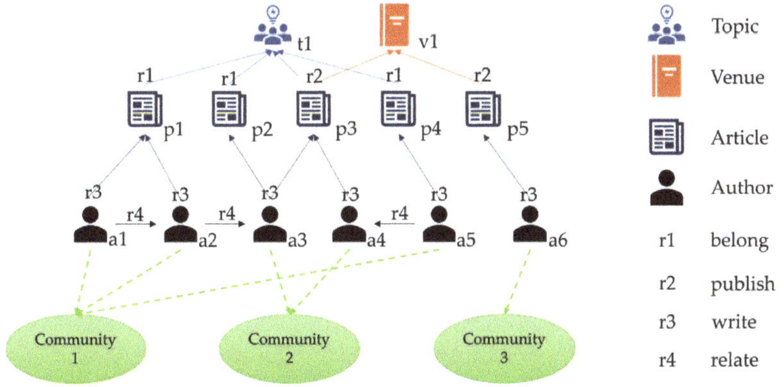

Figure 1. Heterogeneous bibliographic network.

Meta-paths, by capturing higher-order relationships that direct connections may overlook (such as indirect links through papers and themes), provide a more reliable and comprehensive representation of interactions between different node types in heterogeneous networks.

With the advancement of deep learning [7–10] and the increasing research interest in complex networks [11,12], the study of heterogeneous networks has become a significant focus in network science. However, most existing community detection methods primarily target homogeneous networks, which consist of a single node type. These methods often perform poorly when applied to heterogeneous networks, as they fail to effectively capture the intricate relationships between diverse node types. Consequently, the development of algorithms capable of accounting for multiple node types and their complex interrelationships in heterogeneous networks has become a critical area of current research.

In community detection methods [13–16] based on representation learning, many techniques leverage meta-paths to capture node relationships within heterogeneous networks. For example, the HIN2Vec [17] method employs a neural network to model relationships between nodes via meta-paths, embedding this relational information into a low-dimensional space. By learning relationship vectors, it differentiates between various types of relationships while preserving contextual information. The Metapath2Vec [18] method constructs heterogeneous neighborhoods of nodes using meta-path-based random walks and then performs node embeddings through a heterogeneous skip-gram model. This process automatically uncovers hidden connections between different node types.

The HAN model [2] is a semi-supervised heterogeneous graph neural network that employs an attention mechanism with hierarchical layers at both the node and semantic levels. Specifically, node-level attention identifies correlations between nodes and their meta-path neighbors, while semantic-level attention evaluates the significance of different meta-paths. The CDBMA model [16] consists of both a structural information encoder and a semantic information encoder. By incorporating a multi-attention mechanism and integrating self-supervised learning, this model achieves the joint optimization of structural and semantic information, effectively reducing dependency on community labels. The HGT model [19] adopts an attention-based architecture that accounts for both node and edge types. Unlike traditional methods, it eliminates the need for predefined meta-paths by learning 'soft' meta-paths through message passing. This approach is particularly effective for large-scale heterogeneous graphs, as it dynamically aggregates information from high-order neighbors of various types.

The effectiveness of these methods is closely tied to the quality of meta-paths, which are often designed based on domain knowledge. Constructing effective meta-paths requires a comprehensive understanding of both the network's structure and its semantics, making the process inherently difficult and complex. As meta-path length increases, the number of potential combinations grows exponentially, rendering it impractical to evaluate every possible meta-path in detail. While methods based on Heterogeneous Graph Transformers (HGTs) circumvent the challenge of manual meta-path definition, they are limited in that they only capture one-hop neighbor information. This constraint fails to account for higher-order relationships within the network, reducing the model's robustness and generalization ability and making it less effective at capturing complex, high-order connections.

Moreover, most existing community detection methods treat node representation learning and clustering tasks as separate processes. Although this approach is effective in certain cases, it does not fully integrate the network structure and node relationships, ultimately diminishing the overall effectiveness of community detection. The key challenge, therefore, is to merge node representation learning with community detection within a unified framework, thereby enhancing performance in heterogeneous networks.

In this study, we introduce BP-GCN, a self-attention-based model for community detection in heterogeneous networks, utilizing the Bernoulli–Poisson model [20,21] as an optimization function. BP-GCN employs context paths to capture semantic relationships between nodes, replacing traditional meta-paths. The self-attention mechanism enables the model to assess the importance of different paths, facilitating the effective aggregation of higher-order relationships. BP-GCN generates a community affiliation matrix and performs end-to-end community detection. A key advantage of context paths is their adaptability: they evolve based on specific tasks while maintaining node-type symmetry. This ensures that nodes of the same type learn similar semantic contexts, while different node types develop their representations within a balanced space. Such symmetry enhances model robustness by reducing noise, mitigating bias and improving overall efficiency. Additionally, this approach lowers computational complexity while preserving expressive power. By effectively aggregating high-order relationships, BP-GCN enhances both accuracy and scalability in community detection.

2. BP-GCN Model

2.1. Concept Definition

This section assumes a given heterogeneous graph $HG(V, E, A, \mathbb{R})$, where V denotes the set of nodes, including various types of nodes; E represents the set of edges, consisting of different edge types; A is the set of node types, indicating the type of each node; and $\mathbb{R}$ is the set of edge types, representing the different types of edges in the graph. Node types are associated with elements in A through the node mapping function $\phi(v)$, while edge types are linked to elements in $\mathbb{R}$ via the edge mapping function $\psi(e)$. To ensure that the heterogeneous graph can represent diverse structures, it is required that $|A|+|\mathbb{R}|> 2$, representing that both the number of node and edge types must exceed two. The Table A1 in the Appendix A provides a detailed explanation of the symbols used in this paper. Community detection in heterogeneous graphs must account for the various types of nodes and edges, as well as their diverse relationships. The results of this process are analogous to those in homogeneous graphs, where nodes of the same type with high association are clustered together.

Definition 1. Primary Node and Auxiliary Node [22]. *In community detection tasks, clustering is typically performed on a specific type of node, referred to as the primary node (P). Other nodes in the heterogeneous network are termed auxiliary nodes, and together they form the type set A'. Notably, any node in the network can be considered as a primary node type.*

Definition 2. Primary Graph and Auxiliary Graph. *Given a heterogeneous graph HG, the primary graph is a subgraph composed of primary nodes of type P, denoted as $HG_P = (V_P, E_P)$. Each node $v \in V_P$ belongs to the primary node type P, and each edge, $(v_i, v_j) \in E_P\ for\ (v_i, v_j) \in V_P$ and $v_i \neq v_j$,* is a homogeneous edge directly connecting primary nodes. The primary graph serves as the main target graph in community detection tasks. The auxiliary graph is a subgraph formed by the auxiliary nodes A′ and their associated edges, denoted as $HG_{A'} = (V_{A'}, E_{A'})$. Each node $v \in V_{A'}$ in the auxiliary graph has a corresponding node $\varphi(v) = A' \in A$ in the primary graph. The auxiliary graph provides contextual information and supplementary semantics by capturing relationships between auxiliary nodes as well as between auxiliary and primary nodes, thereby enhancing the effectiveness of community detection.

Definition 3. Context Path [23]. *Given a heterogeneous graph HG, a context path is a path connecting two nodes, v_i and v_j, in the primary graph HG_P, denoted as $\rho_K = (v_i, R_K, v_j)$, where R_K is any path connecting v_i and v_j consisting of K nodes; this path can be either a symmetric loop or an asymmetric path. When K = 0, R_K is empty, indicating that v_i and v_j are directly connected. Nodes connected through context paths are referred to as context neighbors.*

Due to the small-world phenomenon [24,25], most nodes in a network can be connected through relatively short paths. In the case of context paths, this is reflected in their ability to link primary nodes via a small number of auxiliary nodes. This characteristic enables context paths to effectively capture higher-order semantic relationships between nodes, providing theoretical support for the definition and utilization of context neighbors. In contrast, meta-paths require domain experts to manually configure combinations of auxiliary nodes along the context path. As the number of node types and path lengths increases, the number of possible combinations grows exponentially, leading to a rapid increase in computational complexity. Therefore, context paths help mitigate the impact of path length on computational complexity.

Furthermore, context paths encompass all possible K-step relationships for a given path length K, allowing them to capture a wider range of latent semantic connections. According to the six degrees of separation theory [26,27], the distance between any two nodes in a network typically does not exceed six steps. Building on this theory, empirical selection or the optimization of path length K via a context path length attention mechanism can effectively cover the primary relationships between nodes while avoiding redundancy and the computational overhead associated with excessively long paths. This approach significantly enhances computational efficiency while boosting the model's expressive capability.

As shown in Figure 2, in these paths, R* represents the auxiliary nodes, such as works or directors, that form the path. These auxiliary nodes may include films jointly acted in by both actors, directors they collaborated with, or other relevant entities. Such paths capture both direct relationships between actors and more complex indirect connections, thereby providing rich semantic information for context-based network analysis. For example, in Figure 2, paths R1 and R2 can be represented by a context path of length 3.

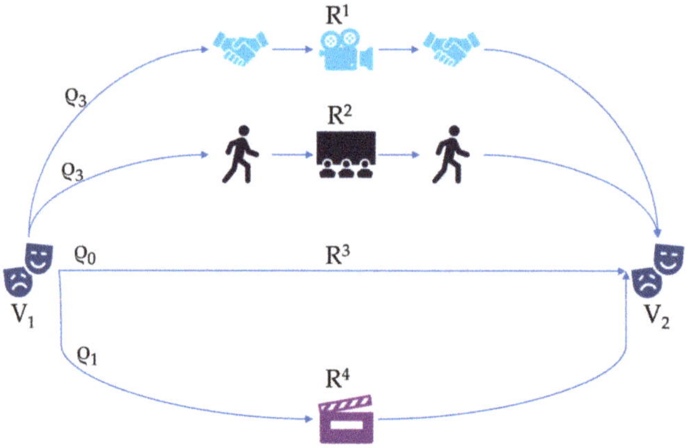

Figure 2. The context path gives four possible context paths ρ*, each of different lengths, to connect participants V1 and V2.

2.2. Loss Function

A target function L(BP), based on the Bernoulli–Poisson model, was designed to construct an end-to-end detection model and enhance the quality of clustering results. The following section provides an introduction to this loss function.

The Bernoulli–Poisson model (B-P model) is a bipartite membership network model capable of accurately detecting community structures in a network, including non-overlapping, overlapping and nested community structures. The core of the model lies in fitting the adjacency matrix A based on the community membership matrix ***F***. This approach enables the detection of complex community patterns, ensuring that the model effectively represents various types of relationships within the network.

$$A_{ij} = Bemoulli(1 - \exp(-F_i F_j^T)) \tag{1}$$

The community membership matrix is used to approximate the adjacency matrix of the primary graph with the improved formula, expressed as follows:

$$\mathrm{HG}_{\mathrm{P}_{ij}} = Bemoulli(1 - \exp(-F_i F_j^T)) \quad (2)$$

According to the theory of the B-P model, the edge connection probability between any two primary nodes, $\mathrm{v_i}$ and $\mathrm{v_j}$, is positively correlated with the number of shared communities. The element $\mathrm{F_{ij}}$ of the membership matrix F represents the probability that the primary node $\mathrm{v_i}$ belongs to community $\mathrm{C_j}$. If $\mathrm{F_{ij}}$ exceeds a predefined threshold probability p, the primary node $\mathrm{v_i}$ is assigned to community $\mathrm{C_j}$. Therefore, the row vector $\mathrm{F_i}$ of the matrix F characterizes the community affiliation of node $\mathrm{v_i}$. By optimizing the following function L(BP) using the B-P model, the following community membership matrix F for the primary graph is obtained:

$$L(BP) = \sum_{(u,v)\in E_P} \log(1 - \exp(-F_i F_j^T)) - \sum_{(u,v)\notin E_P} F_i F_j^T \quad (3)$$

Here, $1 - \exp(-F_i F_j^T)$ represents the probability of connection between two primary nodes $\mathrm{v_i}$ and $\mathrm{v_j}$. In a real network, if nodes $\mathrm{v_i}$ and $\mathrm{v_j}$ are connected, the inner product of $F_i F_j^T$ should equal 1, making the first part of the equation equal to 1. If the two nodes are not connected, $F_i F_j^T$ should be 0. Given that real-world networks are typically sparse, with the actual number of edges being much smaller than the total number of possible edges, the second part of the equation generally contributes significantly. To ensure the accuracy of the resulting structure, an appropriate balance between the two parts of the equation is required. The balanced formula is as follows:

$$L(BP) = -E_{(u,v)\sim P_E}\left[\log\left(1 - \exp\left(-F_i F_j^T\right)\right)\right] + E_{(u,v)\sim P_N}\left[F_i F_j^T\right] \quad (4)$$

In this context, $\mathrm{P_E}$ and $\mathrm{P_N}$ represent the uniform distribution of edges and non-edges in the primary graph, respectively.

2.3. BP-GCN Model Architecture

This section introduces BP-GCN, a self-attention-based graph neural network model designed to learn the community membership matrix of primary nodes within heterogeneous graphs, thereby enabling end-to-end community detection. The overall architecture of the model is illustrated in Figure 3.

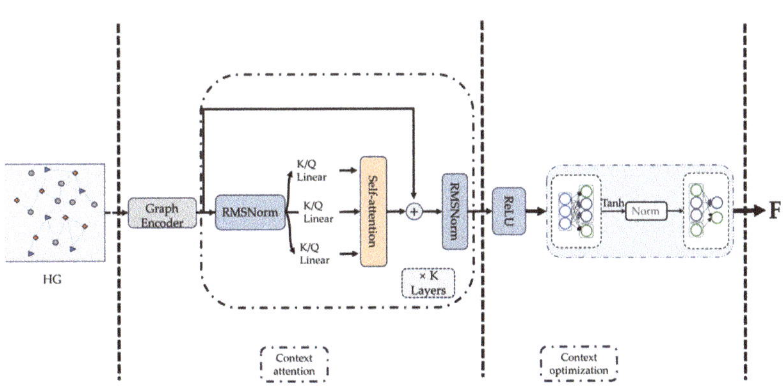

Figure 3. BP-GCN Model Architecture.

Initially, for a given heterogeneous graph (HG), all context paths of length K are extracted for each node in the primary graph (HG_P). A self-attention mechanism is then applied to further differentiate the semantic information of various contexts. Subsequently, a partial decoder architecture from the Transformer model is adopted. The BP-GCN model integrates Graph Convolutional Networks (GCNs) with the Bernoulli–Poisson loss function to learn the community membership matrix. The key implementation details of the model are discussed in the following sections.

The model reinterprets the processes of embedding transformation and context path aggregation in heterogeneous networks as a systematic generative decoding process [28,29]. By sequentially generating node context information through the decoder layer by layer, BP-GCN effectively incorporates higher-order relationships and contextual details within the graph. This iterative approach refines the embedding representation of each node, facilitating a more accurate capture of structural features and intricate relational patterns inherent in the graph.

In heterogeneous networks, node relationships may exhibit irregularities, where certain nodes experience unstable information propagation due to missing edges or erroneous connections. To address this, the Dropout mechanism [30–32] was introduced to enhance model robustness. By randomly dropping a fraction of the outputs, this mechanism prevents the model from over-relying on specific nodes or features, effectively reducing model overfitting and improving generalization capabilities.

$$HG' = Dropout(HG) \tag{5}$$

Subsequently, BP-GCN employs an averaging operation to obtain the global graph representation, thereby enhancing the model's expressive capacity and stability. This step involves averaging the embedding vectors of all nodes, seamlessly integrating local information from each node to form a unified global representation. The averaging operation is particularly advantageous due to its simplicity and robust expressiveness, as it consolidates information from all nodes without introducing significant computational complexity.

$$hg = Mean(C') \tag{6}$$

C' integrates the context information vectors of all nodes in the heterogeneous graph HG', providing richer node representations for subsequent community detection tasks.

The design of BP-GCN contrasts with traditional Graph Convolutional Networks (GCNs), which typically rely on explicit graph structure traversal and node adjacency information for message passing. In contrast, BP-GCN leverages the auto-regressive nature of its decoder architecture to progressively generate the contextual information of the nodes.

During this generation process, BP-GCN integrates a self-attention mechanism, which assigns varying levels of importance to different contextual paths, enabling selective aggregation across multiple relationships. The attention score for the h-th head is computed as follows:

$$Q^{hg}(hg_{\mathrm{T}}^{1}) = QLinear_{\mathrm{T}}^{1}(hg_{\mathrm{T}}^{1}) \tag{7}$$

$$K^{hg}(hg_{\mathrm{S}}^{1}) = KLinear_{\mathrm{S}}^{1}(hg_{\mathrm{S}}^{1}) \tag{8}$$

$$\alpha_{ST}^{hg,l} = Softmax\frac{Q^{hg}(hg_l^T)K^{hg}(hg_l^S)}{\sqrt{d}} \tag{9}$$

Let S and T denote the source and target node types in the node relation r_{ST}. For the one-layer heterogeneous subgraphs HG_S and HG_T, let hg_S^1 and hg_T^1 represent their graph-aggregated vectors. To compute the attention scores, two linear projection functions, QLinear and KLinear, are applied to map the graph-aggregated vectors into query and key vectors. This mapping enables the model to capture the relationships between different nodes and their importance to the final node embeddings.

To enhance the model's expressive capability, a multi-head attention mechanism [33] is incorporated. This involves the use of H distinct attention heads, each with independent parameters that are progressively learned and optimized during the training process. Each attention head is designed to focus on different aspects of the relationships within the graph, thereby enabling the model to capture more comprehensive relational information. The attention weight, denoted as $\alpha_{ST}^{hg,l}$, represents the attention weight of relation r_{ST} at layer l on head h, reflecting the contribution of the relation to the node embeddings. This setup allows each layer of the decoder to dynamically calculate the attention weights for various relations based on the output of the preceding layer and the contextual information relevant to the current node. By employing this mechanism, the model can automatically assess the importance of different relation types during the decoding process, avoiding the reliance on static graph structures characteristic of traditional methods. As a result, the aggregation of node information becomes more flexible and efficient. The aggregation of multiple attention heads enables the model to capture the diverse influences of different relations. In determining the contextual information vector for node v_i, the contextual information vectors of its neighbors from the $(l-1)$-th layer are used, along with the attention scores for each relation, to perform a weighted aggregation.

$$c_i^l = W_2^l\left(\sum_{h=1}^{H} \sigma\left(W_1^l \sum_{r_{ST}} \alpha_{ST}^{hg,l} \sum_{v_j \in N_S(i)} c_i^{l-1}\right) + B\right) \tag{10}$$

Let $N_S(i)$ denote the set of neighboring nodes of node v_i and H represent the number of attention heads. After K layers of computation, the final output is denoted as c_p^K. By employing multi-head attention aggregation at each layer, this approach effectively integrates information derived from multiple relations, thereby capturing richer contextual associations among nodes.

To optimize contextual information and effectively address the potential issue of over-smoothing that may occur during the deep propagation of node embeddings, the BP-GCN model specifically incorporates a Gated Recurrent Unit (GRU) mechanism [34–36]. The GRU mechanism helps to preserve the diversity of node embeddings and prevents the gradual loss of information throughout the multi-layer decoding process.

$$c_p^K = GRU(c_p^{K-1}, BP - GCNLayer(c_p^{K-1}, c_{A\prime}^{K-1})) \tag{11}$$

To further enhance the model's expressive capacity, BP-GCN applies the ReLU activation function to the generated contextual information, effectively filtering out redundant embedding features. This approach not only reduces information redundancy but also improves the precision of the embeddings. Additionally, the contextual information of the primary graph nodes, as generated by the model, serves as the input for a Graph Convolutional Network (GCN), which produces the final community affiliation matrix for the primary graph. By leveraging a message-passing mechanism, the GCN propagates node feature information to neighboring nodes, thereby capturing the intricate relationships within the network. In some respects, this message-passing process mimics real-world information dissemination, increasing the likelihood that the derived community structures accurately represent real-world scenarios. The single-layer convolutional formula of the GCN is expressed as follows:

$$H^{(l+1)} = \sigma(\tilde{D}^{-\frac{1}{2}}\tilde{A}\tilde{D}^{-\frac{1}{2}}H^{(l)}W^{(l)}) \tag{12}$$

Here, σ denotes the activation function, such as Sigmoid, Tanh or ReLU. $\tilde{A} = A + I_N$ represents the adjacency matrix combined with self-loops, and D is the degree matrix of the adjacency matrix A. The convolution process in the GCN involves an iterative procedure that continuously aggregates information from both the node itself and its neighbors, where each iteration corresponds to a feature transformation. For large-scale networks, the BP-GCN method employs a two-layer convolution to further process contextual information, c_p^K, with the following specific modifications:

$$F = \mathrm{ReLU}(\tilde{HG_P}(\mathrm{Tanh}(\tilde{HG_P}c_p^K W^{(1)})W^{(2)})) \tag{13}$$

In this context, $\tilde{HG_P} = D_P^{-\frac{1}{2}}(HG_P)D_P^{-\frac{1}{2}}$ denotes the degree matrix of the HG_P subgraph within the heterogeneous graph, and $\boldsymbol{F}$ corresponds to the community affiliation matrix of the primary graph. This matrix represents the final clustering results, enabling an end-to-end approach to community detection tasks.

3. Experiments

3.1. Dataset

This section comprises our evaluation of the performance of BP-GCN by comparing it with other benchmark models using the ACM [2], DBLP [37], IMDB [3] and AIFB [38] datasets. Detailed information regarding these datasets is provided in the Table 1 below:

Table 1. Dataset information (primary node types are marked with "*").

Dataset	Node Type	Nodes	Edge Type	Edges	Meta-Path
ACM	* Paper (P) Author (A) Subject (S) Facility (F)	12,499 17,431 73 1804	Paper–Paper Paper–Author Paper–Subject Author–Facility	30,789 37,055 12,499 30,424	PAP PSP
DBLP	* Paper (P) * Author (A) Conference (C) Term (T)	14,475 14,736 20 8920	Paper–Conference Author–Paper Paper–Term	14,736 41,794 114,624	APCPA APA APTPA
IMDB	* Movie Actor Director Keyword	4275 5432 2083 7313	Movie–Actor Movie–Director Movie–Keyword	12,831 4181 20,428	MAM MDM MKM
AIFB	A total of 7 types of nodes	7262	A total of 104 types of edges	48,810	-

ACM Dataset: This dataset consisted of a paper information network with four types of nodes. The primary node was the paper node, which formed the main graph. The other three node types served as auxiliary nodes, contributing to the construction of an auxiliary graph. Two predefined meta-paths were utilized: Paper–Author–Paper (PAP) and Paper–Subject–Paper (PSP). The PAP meta-path captured the relationship between papers and authors by linking papers co-authored by the same individuals, thereby revealing collaboration networks and paper patterns. The PSP meta-path, on the other hand, highlighted the relationship between papers and subjects, connecting papers through shared research topics to illustrate academic relationships between research themes.

DBLP Dataset: The DBLP dataset included four types of nodes and was modeled in two stages. Initially, the author and paper nodes were chosen as the primary nodes, allowing for clustering based on these two categories. Subsequently, the dataset was presented in two forms: DBLP-P (paper-centered) and DBLP-A (author-centered). Three meta-paths were defined: Author–Paper–Author (APA), Author–Paper–Conference–Paper–Author (APCPA) and Author–Paper–Term–Paper–Author (APTPA). The APA meta-path highlighted the connections between authors through shared publications, reflecting collaboration patterns such as overlaps in research domains. The APCPA meta-path captured relationships between authors, their co-authored papers and the conferences they were associated with, showcasing the authors' influence in specific conference domains. Lastly, the APTPA meta-path linked authors through shared terminology, facilitating the identification of similarities in their research topics.

IMDB Dataset: This dataset featured four node types: "Director", "Actor", "Movie" and "Keyword". The movie node served as the primary node and was categorized into three genres: Action, Comedy and Drama. The remaining three nodes were auxiliary types. Three meta-paths were defined for the network. The first, Movie–Actor–Movie (MAM), captured the relationships between films through actors who co–starred, highlighting collaborations between films and actors. The second, Movie–Director–Movie (MDM), connected films through shared directors. The third, Movie–Keyword–Movie (MKM), linked films through shared keywords, enabling an analysis of thematic or content-based similarities between them.

AIFB Dataset: The AIFB dataset was based on a knowledge graph, consisting of seven distinct node types and 104 unique edge types. The primary node type was the 'Personen' node, which was further categorized into four different groups. Due to the dataset's complexity, some specific details are omitted from the table, though relevant meta-paths are provided where necessary.

3.2. Benchmark Methods

To evaluate the performance of BP-GCN, the proposed method was benchmarked against several state-of-the-art techniques, including both un-supervised and supervised approaches. Among the un-supervised methods, Node2vec [39] and Metapath2vec [18] were included, while the supervised methods consisted of GCN [40], GAT [41], LGNN [42], HAN [2] and HGT [19]. Notably, HGT is regarded as the current state-of-the-art method. The following section provides a comprehensive overview of the benchmark methods:

Node2vec: Node2vec formulates network feature learning as an optimization problem based on a graph search. It is designed to capture diverse connectivity patterns within a network by mapping nodes into a low-dimensional feature space. The objective is to maximize the preservation of node neighborhood probabilities, thereby enabling the efficient learning of node representations.

Metpath2vec: Metpath2vec is specifically tailored for heterogeneous networks with multiple node and edge types. It generates heterogeneous neighborhood embeddings for nodes using meta-path-based random walks and incorporates heterogeneous negative sampling techniques to enhance optimization. This enables Metpath2vec to capture both the structural and semantic relationships between different network objects.

GCN: GCN is a semi-supervised learning method designed for graph-structured data. The key idea is to approximate the spectral graph convolution in the first order locally. GCN introduces an effective hierarchical propagation rule that approximates the graph's Laplacian operator, using the graph's structure to establish dependencies between nodes.

This process enables node representations to be updated through information flow within local neighborhoods, making GCN particularly effective for node classification tasks.

GAT: GAT employs a masked self-attention mechanism that allows each node to attend to its neighboring nodes. This attention mechanism is used to compute hidden representations of nodes, with multiple layers stacking to capture neighborhood features more effectively. It also enables nodes to assign varying weights to each neighbor, avoiding computationally expensive operations like matrix inversion, and eliminates the need for prior knowledge about the graph structure.

LGNN: LGNN is an enhancement to the traditional Graph Neural Network (GNN) architecture, which allows the model to utilize edge adjacency information and incorporate a non-recursive graph operator. These improvements enhance the model's expressiveness, enabling it to capture more complex relationships in graph data.

HAN: HAN is a heterogeneous graph neural network that utilizes a hierarchical attention mechanism. It integrates attention at both the node and semantic levels. The node-level attention learns the importance of the relationships between nodes and their neighbors, based on meta-paths. The semantic-level attention focuses on determining the relative significance of different meta-paths. This hierarchical aggregation of features from meta-path neighbors results in more effective node embeddings.

HGT: HGT incorporates parameters that depend on node and edge types, allowing it to capture heterogeneous attention across edges. This enables the model to retain specialized representations for various node and edge types. Additionally, HGT introduces a heterogeneous mini-batch graph sampling algorithm called HG-Sampling, which facilitates efficient and scalable training on web-scale datasets.

3.3. Comparative Experiments

Three widely used evaluation metrics—F1 score, Normalized Mutual Information (NMI) and Adjusted Rand Index (ARI)—were employed to assess the quality of the clustering results in community detection. A brief overview of these metrics is provided below:

F1 score: F1 score is a standard evaluation metric for community detection, measuring the similarity between the detected community partition and the ground truth. It combines precision and recall by calculating their harmonic mean. F1 scores range from 0 to 1, where a higher score indicates better community partition quality and a lower score suggests a greater disparity between the detected and true communities.

NMI: NMI [43] quantifies the shared statistical information between two clusters, thus providing an assessment of clustering performance. NMI values range from 0 to 1. A value closer to 1 indicates a strong alignment between the clustering results and the correct community classification, while a value near 0 implies weak correspondence. NMI standardizes the metric to mitigate the effects of varying category numbers and dataset scales, ensuring consistent evaluation across different datasets and clustering algorithms.

ARI: The Adjusted Rand Index (ARI) is a widely used metric for clustering evaluation, measuring the degree of agreement between the clustering outcomes and the ground truth labels. The ARI adjusts the Rand Index to account for random chance, leading to a more accurate reflection of clustering quality. The ARI ranges from -1 to 1, with a score of 1 indicating perfect agreement between the clustering results and the ground truth, suggesting accurate capture of the data structure. A score of 0 means the clustering results are no better than random chance, indicating poor clustering performance. Negative values suggest clustering results that are worse than random, likely due to significant misclassification errors.

In this experiment, GCN, GAT, LGNN and HAN were employed to learn primary node embeddings. The resulting embedding matrices were then input into the K-Means algorithm for clustering, with the value of k set to match the number of primary node categories, facilitating community detection. The performance of each algorithm is presented in the Table 2 below. Meta-path-based methods, such as Metapath2Vec and HAN, were unable to perform community detection on the AIFB dataset due to the absence of predefined meta-paths. This limitation highlights the constraints of meta-path-based approaches.

Table 2. Experimental results.

Dataset	Metric	Node2vec	Metapath2vec	GCN	GAT	LGNN	HAN	HGT	BP-GCN
ACM	F1	0.6954	0.7142	0.5366	0.6876	0.6987	**0.7922**	0.7599	0.7496
	NMI	0.2666	0.3596	0.0966	0.2577	0.2746	0.394	**0.4509**	0.4231
	ARI	0.2469	0.2956	0.1022	0.1422	0.2368	0.319	0.3813	**0.4039**
DBLP-A	F1	0.7572	0.7144	0.32	0.9023	0.321	0.9023	**0.9386**	0.9261
	NMI	0.0638	0.2554	0.0186	0.618	0.0069	0.624	**0.7032**	0.6934
	ARI	0.0409	0.2722	0.0166	0.5264	−0.0012	0.665	0.7322	**0.7626**
DBLP-P	F1	0.3	0.3125	0.31	0.3	0.225	0.3375	0.4	**0.4875**
	NMI	0.0655	0.0034	0.0171	0.0495	0.0431	0.0732	0.1086	**0.4392**
	ARI	−0.0016	0.0013	−0.0048	−0.0029	0.0016	−0.0103	**0.0724**	0.0564
IMDB	F1	0.5494	0.488	0.3628	0.3587	0.3646	0.4888	0.3634	**0.546**
	NMI	0.0745	0.027	0.0018	0.0012	0.0158	0.1172	0.0101	**0.2298**
	ARI	0.0471	0.0146	0.0013	−0.0009	−0.0079	0.131	0.0083	**0.1135**
AIFB	F1	0.7517	-	0.6524	0.7375	0.6809	-	0.7163	**0.7659**
	NMI	0.2401	-	0.1567	0.2117	0.2435	-	0.3812	**0.3854**
	ARI	0.1518	-	0.1248	0.1142	0.079	-	0.3011	0.2836

When comparing un-supervised methods, Metapath2Vec outperforms Node2Vec. On the DBLP dataset, Metapath2Vec significantly surpasses Node2Vec in terms of F1, NMI and ARI metrics. These results suggest that longer meta-paths are more effective in capturing higher-order semantic relationships between nodes, leading to richer node representations. Furthermore, the design of meta-paths allows Metapath2Vec to better leverage semantic information in heterogeneous graphs, thereby enhancing its performance on heterogeneous network data. This underscores the crucial role of meta-paths in improving node embedding quality in un-supervised learning.

Among the supervised methods, GCN and LGNN exhibit the weakest performance, particularly on the DBLP-P network. On this dataset, GCN even produces negative metric values, while LGNN encounters similar issues on the DBLP-A and IMDB datasets. This is because GCN and LGNN are optimized for homogeneous networks and struggle to process the complex heterogeneous information present in heterogeneous graphs, making them unsuitable for community detection in such networks. In contrast, GAT, HAN and HGT, which employ attention mechanisms to assess the importance of different node relationships in heterogeneous graphs, demonstrate superior performance. Among them, HAN outperforms GAT due to its use of meta-paths, which extract deeper structural and semantic information, leading to better performance. However, HAN's reliance on predefined meta-paths limits its ability to detect communities in the AIFB dataset. Unlike HAN, HGT does not rely on meta-paths, providing greater flexibility across datasets, which enhances its robustness and generalization capability. Its community detection performance is comparable to that of HAN. However, HGT still requires labeled data for model optimization, which constrains its ability to generalize to unseen data.

The experimental results demonstrated that BP-GCN outperforms other methods across multiple datasets and evaluation metrics. On the ACM dataset, BP-GCN achieved an ARI score of 0.4039, the highest among the tested methods, showing a 2.2% improvement over HGT. On the DBLP-P dataset, BP-GCN achieved F1 and NMI scores of 0.4875 and 0.4392, respectively, with the NMI score exceeding HGT by more than 30%, highlighting BP-GCN's ability to effectively capture complex relationships between nodes. On the IMDB dataset, BP-GCN achieved an NMI score of 0.2298, significantly surpassing other methods, demonstrating its broad applicability in heterogeneous graphs. On the AIFB dataset, BP-GCN achieved F1 and NMI scores of 0.7569 and 0.3854, respectively, outperforming HGT and other baseline methods. This result underscores BP-GCN's capability to uncover higher-order relationships between diverse node types. Unlike meta-path-dependent methods such as HAN, BP-GCN does not require predefined meta-paths, making it more flexible and adaptable across different datasets. As a result, its learned node embeddings are better suited for community detection in heterogeneous networks. Compared to models designed for homogeneous graphs such as GCN and LGNN, BP-GCN demonstrates superior performance in heterogeneous graph analysis.

In conclusion, the design and optimization strategies of BP-GCN enable exceptional performance in community detection. The model's adaptability and robustness make it highly effective for analyzing heterogeneous graphs, positioning it as a state-of-the-art solution for heterogeneous network analysis.

3.4. *Parameter Sensitivity Analysis*

This section presents our systematic examination of the sensitivity of the model's performance though key hyperparameters, including the number of attention heads, embedding dimensions and context path length, through a series of experiments. Specifically, we analyzed how different parameter configurations influenced the model's performance across various datasets. By adjusting these hyperparameters, we assessed their impact on the model's final performance and present experimental results under multiple parameter settings for each dataset. These findings provide empirical evidence demonstrating the critical roles of attention heads, embedding dimensions and context path length in shaping the model's effectiveness.

3.4.1. Number of Attention Heads

Figures 4 and 5 illustrate the model's performance across varying numbers of attention heads on the ACM and DBLP datasets. The experiments evaluated the impact of different attention head configurations on model performance, comparing both smaller and larger numbers of attention heads. Due to hardware limitations, the maximum number of attention heads tested was 16. Nevertheless, the results offer valuable insights into how the number of attention heads affects model performance.

As depicted in Figures 4 and 5, the F1, NMI and ARI values reach their peak at 8 attention heads but begin to decline when the number increases to 16. This suggests that simply increasing the number of attention heads does not necessarily enhance model performance. When the number of attention heads is too low, the model struggles to capture complex features, leading to suboptimal results.

Although increasing the number of attention heads beyond 8 can enhance the model's capacity, it may also introduce redundant information, increasing both the number of parameters and computational complexity. This can lead to attention dispersion or the incorporation of noise, which negatively affects performance. Therefore, selecting the optimal number of attention heads is crucial for maximizing performance across different tasks and datasets. Based on the experimental results, setting the number of attention heads to 8 is recommended for community detection tasks on both the ACM and DBLP-A datasets, as it yielded the best overall performance.

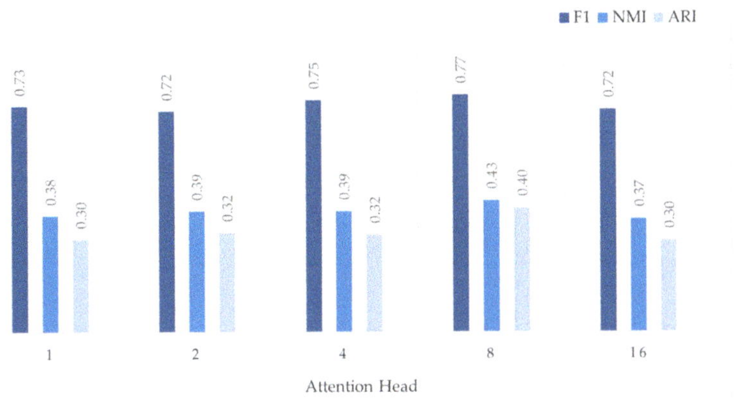

Figure 4. Performance of different attention head numbers on ACM dataset.

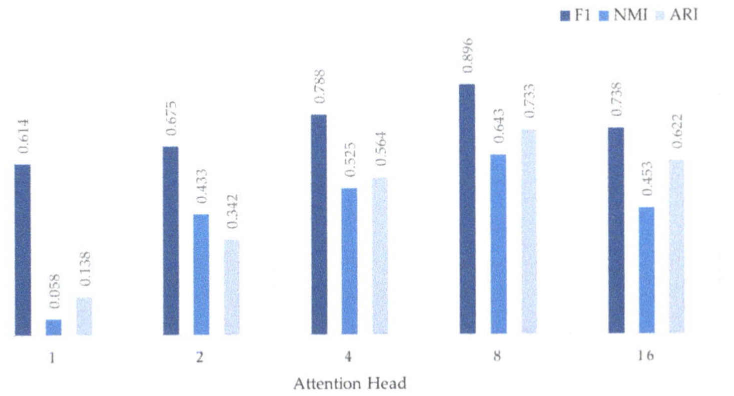

Figure 5. Performance of different attention head numbers on DBLP-A dataset.

3.4.2. Embedding Dimensions

Figures 6 and 7 evaluate the model's performance across different embedding dimensions for the ACM and DBLP datasets, providing insights into how embedding size influenced model effectiveness. The experimental results indicate a positive correlation between embedding dimensions and model performance across all datasets. However, the relationship between embedding size and performance is nonlinear.

When the embedding dimension was too small, the model struggled to effectively represent features, limiting its ability to capture complex relationships within the data. As the embedding dimension increased, the model's capacity to represent features improved, allowing it to capture richer semantic information. However, this also introduced potential redundancy, which can lead to overfitting and reduced generalization.

Moreover, increasing the embedding dimension expanded the number of model parameters, making training more computationally intensive and requiring additional computational resources. Due to experimental constraints, the embedding dimension for the ACM dataset was capped at 128, while for the DBLP-A and DBLP-P tasks, the maximum embedding dimension was set to 256. Although hardware limitations restricted the scope of the experiments, the results still provide valuable guidance for selecting appropriate embedding dimensions to optimize model performance.

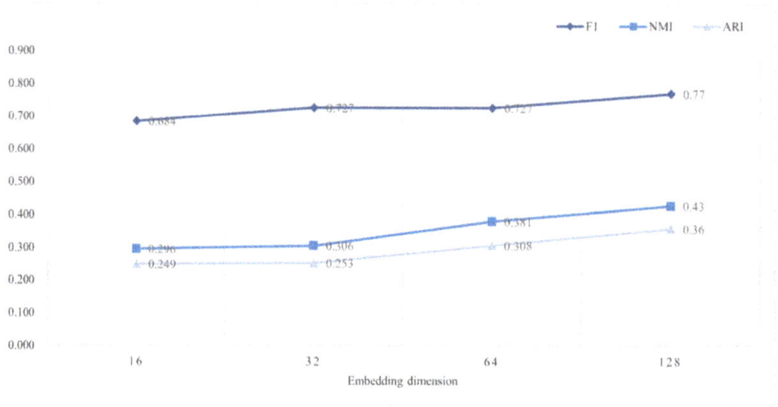

Figure 6. Performance of different embedding dimensions in ACM datasets.

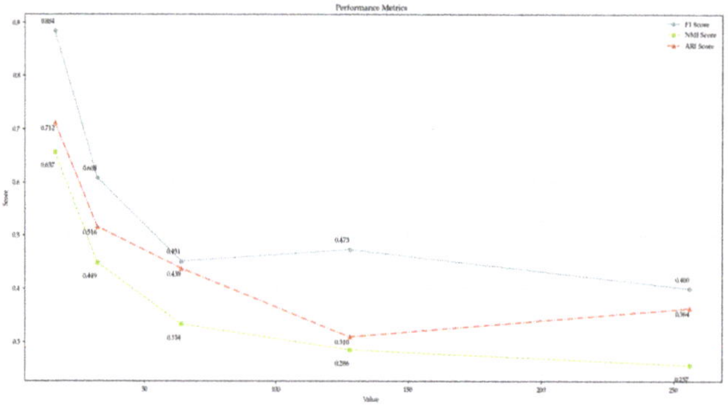

Figure 7. Performance of different embedding dimensions in DBLP-A datasets.

Based on the experimental results for attention head parameters, the model's performance on the ACM dataset was evaluated by maintaining a constant number of eight attention heads while varying the embedding dimensions. The results, presented in Figure 6, demonstrate a significant improvement in F1, NMI and ARI scores as the embedding dimension increased. These findings suggest that larger embedding dimensions enhanced the model's ability to represent features, allowing it to capture more complex relationships within the data, thereby improving performance.

However, increasing the embedding dimension also escalates computational demands and memory usage. This trade-off underscores the importance of balancing performance improvements with resource efficiency. The experiments revealed that an embedding dimension of 128, combined with eight attention heads, achieved the best performance on the ACM dataset. Therefore, this configuration is recommended to achieve an optimal balance between performance and efficiency for community detection tasks on this dataset.

Figure 7 illustrates the performance of community detection tasks on the DBLP dataset, with the Author node as the primary node. As previously mentioned, the model achieved optimal performance when the number of attention heads was set to 8 for the DBLP-A task. In this section, the experiments fixed the number of attention heads at 8 and focused on examining how embedding dimensions influenced model performance.

The results indicate that for the DBLP-A task, the model performed best when the embedding dimension was set to 16. Beyond this point, performance gradually declined as the embedding dimension increased. This decline can be attributed to the additional complexity introduced by higher embedding dimensions. While a larger feature space could enhance the model's expressiveness, it also increased the number of parameters, raising model complexity and making training more challenging. Furthermore, excessively high embedding dimensions may lead to overfitting, reducing the model's ability to generalize effectively on the test set.

Based on this analysis, setting the embedding dimension to 16 while maintaining 8 attention heads is recommended for achieving optimal performance in community detection tasks on the DBLP dataset.

3.4.3. Context Path Length

This study, through controlled variable experiments, revealed the nonlinear impact of context path length on the performance of the BP-GCN model. As illustrated in Figure 8a,b, on the ACM and DBLP-A datasets, the model achieved its peak performance in metrics such as F1 score, NMI and ARI when the path lengths were increased to K = 3 and K = 4, respectively. Notably, the performance of CP-GNN on the DBLP-A dataset further validated the core hypothesis: when K = 3, the model optimally captures higher-order relational information between nodes, thereby achieving superior performance in community detection tasks. This phenomenon underscores the critical role of high-order topological features in node semantic representation within complex network analysis.

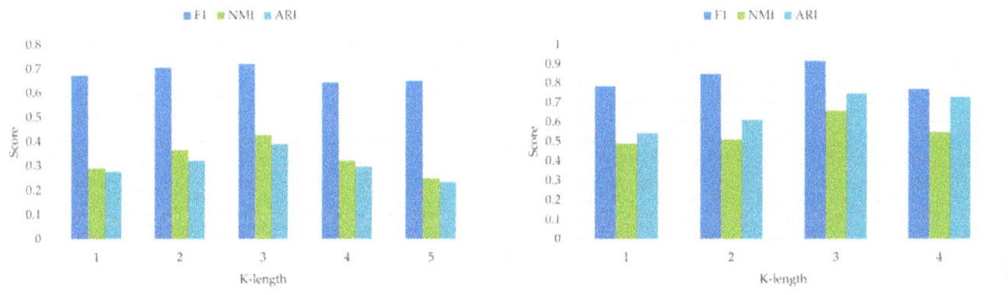

(**a**) ACM Dataset (**b**) DBLP-A Dataset

Figure 8. The influence of different context path lengths on model performance.

The inverted U-shaped variation pattern revealed by the experimental data can be attributed to a triple mechanism: (1) short path constraints ($K \leq 2$) lead the model into a local neighborhood trap, only perceiving shallow features of directly connected nodes; (2) within the optimal path range (K = 3–4), the expanded context window enables the model to achieve structural–semantic joint modeling of multi-hop neighborhoods, dynamically aggregating feature combinations with community discriminability through a self-attention mechanism; and (3) the network degradation effect induced by excessively long paths ($K > 4$) manifests as follows: when K exceeds a critical threshold, the effective neighborhood range of nodes expands sharply, eventually forming a fully connected topology. This over-connected state leads to two negative effects: firstly, node features undergo excessive smoothing (over-smoothing) during multi-layer propagation, blurring the discriminative boundaries between different communities; secondly, the exponential growth of path combinations causes the accumulation of semantic noise, resulting in a dilution effect of community-related features. Therefore, the selection of context path length requires a balance between information richness and noise control to achieve optimal model performance. This conclusion provides significant insights for subsequent research: a dynamic path length adjustment mechanism should be established in model design, rather than simply adopting fixed-length context paths.

Figure 9 illustrates the variation in runtime of the BP-GCN model under different context path lengths. It is important to note that, due to the limitations of the experimental machine's performance, the maximum context path length in the DBLP-A and DBLP-P datasets was set to 4, making it impossible to execute community detection tasks with a path length of 5.

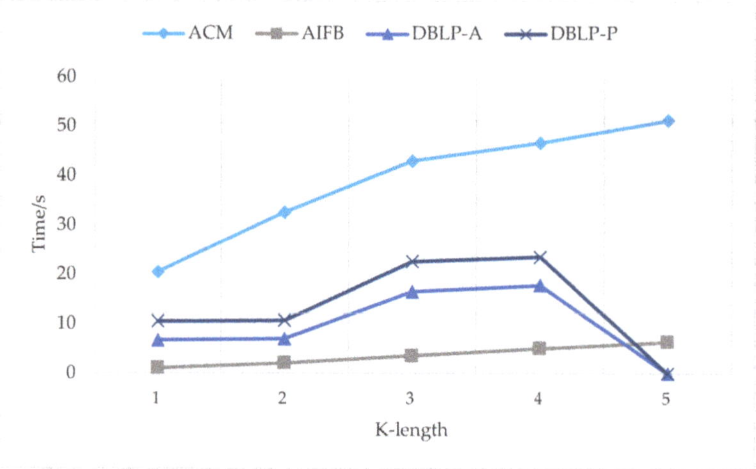

Figure 9. The running time of different context path lengths.

As shown in Figure 9, the runtime of the model significantly increased as the context path length grew. Specifically, when the path length increased from 1 to 2, the runtime grew relatively smoothly; however, when the path length increased from 2 to 3, the runtime rose sharply, and the model's performance also improved significantly (as shown in Figure 9). When the path length further increased from 3 to 5, the runtime surged dramatically, but the model's performance did not reach its optimum; instead, the best performance was achieved at a path length of 3. Therefore, the appropriate selection of context path length has a significant impact on both the performance and efficiency of the model. The reason for the increase in runtime with the context path length was that as the context path length increased, the range of information the model needed to process expanded significantly, and the computational complexity also rose. Specifically, longer context paths meant that the model needed to aggregate information over a larger neighborhood. Additionally, longer path lengths introduced more redundant information, increasing the overhead of self-attention semantic parsing and adding to the computational burden. Consequently, the runtime grew significantly with the increase in context path length. However, excessively long path lengths may lead to information overload or noise accumulation, which can degrade the model's performance. Thus, selecting an appropriate context path length is crucial for balancing model performance and computational efficiency.

4. Conclusions

This paper presents BP-GCN, a heterogeneous network community detection model based on a self-attention mechanism. BP-GCN leverages the Bernoulli–Poisson framework to address the challenges of community detection in heterogeneous graphs. The model excels in learning structural features within these graphs without relying on predefined meta-paths. By using a self-attention mechanism, BP-GCN captures higher-order relationships between nodes and highlights the significance of different context paths, overcoming the limitations of traditional meta-path-based methods. Moreover, BP-GCN eliminates the need for additional clustering algorithms in heterogeneous community detection, facilitating an end-to-end detection process. This approach enhances both efficiency and flexibility. Extensive experiments conducted on various real-world datasets show that BP-GCN outperforms existing benchmark methods, demonstrating its robust generalization ability and resilience.

Author Contributions: Conceptualization, G.Z.; Methodology, G.Z. and R.-F.W.; Software, G.Z.; Validation, G.Z. and R.-F.W.; Formal Analysis, G.Z. and R.-F.W.; Investigation, G.Z. and R.-F.W.; Resources, G.Z.; Data Curation, G.Z.; Writing—Original Draft Preparation, G.Z.; Writing—Review and Editing, G.Z. and R.-F.W.; Visualization, G.Z.; Project Administration, G.Z.; Funding Acquisition, G.Z. All authors have read and agreed to the published version of the manuscript.

Funding: This research was funded by Humanities and Social Sciences Planning Foundation of the Ministry of Education, grant number 21YJA860001 and Shandong Natural Science Foundation of China, grant number ZR2021MG006.

Data Availability Statement: Experimental datasets required in this study can be found online (https://github.com/xiaotaozi121096/BP-GCN/) last accessed on 12 March 2025.

Conflicts of Interest: The authors declare no conflict of interest.

Appendix A

This appendix provides a comprehensive list of symbols, notations and their corresponding meanings used throughout this thesis for clarity and ease of reference.

Table A1. Symbol Explanation.

Symbol	Explanation	Relation
HG	Heterogeneous graph	
HG_P	Primary graph of the heterogeneous graph	$HG_P \subseteq HG$
$HG_{A'}$	Auxiliary graph of the heterogeneous graph	$HG_{A'} \subseteq HG$
A	Node set of the heterogeneous graph	
P	Primary node type	$P \subseteq A$
A′	Auxiliary node type	$A' \subseteq A$
$\mathbb{R}$	Edge set of the heterogeneous graph	
ρ_K	Context path of length k	
F	Community membership matrix	

References

1. Wang, M.; Xiang, D.; Qu, Y.; Li, G. The diagnosability of interconnection networks. *Discret. Appl. Math.* **2024**, *357*, 413–428. [CrossRef]
2. Wang, X.; Ji, H.; Shi, C.; Wang, B.; Ye, Y.; Cui, P.; Yu, P.S. Heterogeneous graph attention network. In Proceedings of the World Wide Web Conference, San Francisco, CA, USA, 13–17 May 2019; pp. 2022–2032.
3. Wu, C.-Y.; Beutel, A.; Ahmed, A.; Smola, A.J. Explaining reviews and ratings with paco: Poisson additive co-clustering. In Proceedings of the 25th International Conference Companion on World Wide Web, Montréal, QC, Canada, 11–15 April 2016; pp. 127–128.
4. Cai, D.; Shao, Z.; He, X.; Yan, X.; Han, J. Mining hidden community in heterogeneous social networks. In Proceedings of the 3rd International Workshop on Link Discovery, Chicago, IL, USA, 21–25 August 2005; pp. 58–65.
5. Qi, G.-J.; Aggarwal, C.C.; Huang, T.S. On clustering heterogeneous social media objects with outlier links. In Proceedings of the Fifth ACM International Conference on Web Search and Data Mining, Seattle, WA, USA, 8–12 February 2012; pp. 553–562.
6. Shi, C.; Wang, R.; Li, Y.; Yu, P.S.; Wu, B. Ranking-based clustering on general heterogeneous information networks by network projection. In Proceedings of the 23rd ACM International Conference on Conference on Information and Knowledge Management, Shanghai, China, 3–7 November 2014; pp. 699–708.

7. Fan, S.; Zhu, J.; Han, X.; Shi, C.; Hu, L.; Ma, B.; Li, Y. Metapath-guided heterogeneous graph neural network for intent recommendation. In Proceedings of the 25th ACM SIGKDD International Conference on Knowledge Discovery & Data Mining, Anchorage, AK, USA, 4–8 August 2019; pp. 2478–2486.
8. Pan, C.-H.; Qu, Y.; Yao, Y.; Wang, M.-J.-S. HybridGNN: A Self-Supervised Graph Neural Network for Efficient Maximum Matching in Bipartite Graphs. *Symmetry* **2024**, *16*, 1631. [CrossRef]
9. Wang, R.-F.; Su, W.-H. The application of deep learning in the whole potato production Chain: A Comprehensive review. *Agriculture* **2024**, *14*, 1225. [CrossRef]
10. Cui, K.; Tang, W.; Zhu, R.; Wang, M.; Larsen, G.D.; Pauca, V.P.; Alqahtani, S.; Yang, F.; Segurado, D.; Fine, P.; et al. Real-time localization and bimodal point pattern analysis of palms using uav imagery. *arXiv* **2024**, arXiv:2410.11124.
11. Wang, M.; Lin, Y.; Wang, S. The nature diagnosability of bubble-sort star graphs under the PMC model and MM∗ model. *Int. J. Eng. Appl. Sci.* **2017**, *4*, 2394–3661.
12. Cui, K.; Li, R.; Polk, S.L.; Murphy, J.M.; Plemmons, R.J.; Chan, R.H. Unsupervised spatial-spectral hyperspectral image reconstruction and clustering with diffusion geometry. In Proceedings of the 2022 12th Workshop on Hyperspectral Imaging and Signal Processing: Evolution in Remote Sensing (WHISPERS), Rome, Italy, 13–16 September 2022; pp. 1–5.
13. Tu, Y.-H.; Wang, R.-F.; Su, W.-H. Active Disturbance Rejection Control—New Trends in Agricultural Cybernetics in the Future: A Comprehensive Review. *Machines* **2025**, *13*, 111. [CrossRef]
14. Xiang, D.; Hsieh, S.-Y. G-good-neighbor diagnosability under the modified comparison model for multiprocessor systems. *Theor. Comput. Sci.* **2025**, *1028*, 115027.
15. Cui, K.; Li, R.; Polk, S.L.; Lin, Y.; Zhang, H.; Murphy, J.M.; Plemmons, R.J.; Chan, R.H. Superpixel-based and Spatially-regularized Diffusion Learning for Unsupervised Hyperspectral Image Clustering. *IEEE Trans. Geosci. Remote. Sens.* **2024**, *62*, 1–18. [CrossRef]
16. Li, Y.; Wu, Z.; Wang, Z.; Li, P. CDBMA: Community Detection in Heterogeneous Networks Based on Multi-attention Mechanism. In Proceedings of the Chinese National Conference on Social Media Processing, Hefei, China, 23–26 November 2023; pp. 174–187.
17. Fu, T.-Y.; Lee, W.-C.; Lei, Z. Hin2vec: Explore meta-paths in heterogeneous information networks for representation learning. In Proceedings of the 2017 ACM on Conference on Information and Knowledge Management, Singapore, 6–10 November 2017; pp. 1797–1806.
18. Dong, Y.; Chawla, N.V.; Swami, A. metapath2vec: Scalable representation learning for heterogeneous networks. In Proceedings of the 23rd ACM SIGKDD International Conference on Knowledge Discovery and Data Mining, Halifax, NS, Canada, 13–17 August 2017; pp. 135–144.
19. Hu, Z.; Dong, Y.; Wang, K.; Sun, Y. Heterogeneous graph transformer. In Proceedings of the Web Conference 2020, Taipei, Taiwan, 20–24 April 2020; pp. 2704–2710.
20. Yang, J.; Leskovec, J. Community-affiliation graph model for overlapping network community detection. In Proceedings of the 2012 IEEE 12th International Conference on Data Mining, Brussels, Belgium, 10–13 December 2012; pp. 1170–1175.
21. Shchur, O.; Günnemann, S. Overlapping community detection with graph neural networks. *arXiv* **2019**, arXiv:1909.12201.
22. Luo, L.; Fang, Y.; Cao, X.; Zhang, X.; Zhang, W. Detecting communities from heterogeneous graphs: A context path-based graph neural network model. In Proceedings of the 30th ACM International Conference on Information & Knowledge Management, Queensland, Australia, 1–5 November 2021; pp. 1170–1180.
23. Barman, D.; Bhattacharya, S.; Sarkar, R.; Chowdhury, N. *k*-Context Technique: A Method for Identifying Dense Subgraphs in a Heterogeneous Information Network. *IEEE Trans. Comput. Soc. Syst.* **2019**, *6*, 1190–1205. [CrossRef]
24. Watts, D.J.; Strogatz, S.H. Collective dynamics of 'small-world'networks. *Nature* **1998**, *393*, 440–442. [CrossRef] [PubMed]
25. Du, H.; Li, S.; Yue, Z.; Yang, X. Research on Community Structure of Small-World Networks and Scale-Free Networks. *Chin. Phys. Soc.* **2007**, *56*, 6886–6893.
26. Guare, J. Six degrees of separation. In *The Contemporary Monologue: Men*; Routledge: London, UK, 2016; pp. 89–93.
27. Zhang, L.; Tu, W. Six Degrees of Separation in Online Society. 2009. Available online: https://citeseerx.ist.psu.edu/document?repid=rep1&type=pdf&doi=1febc4cc5199d36e50ec7d3533a8ac8a32889d7c (accessed on 10 March 2025).
28. Zhao, C.-T.; Wang, R.-F.; Tu, Y.-H.; Pang, X.-X.; Su, W.-H. Automatic Lettuce Weed Detection and Classification Based on Optimized Convolutional Neural Networks for Robotic Weed Control. *Agronomy* **2024**, *14*, 2838. [CrossRef]
29. Wang, Z.; Wang, R.; Wang, M.; Lai, T.; Zhang, M. Self-supervised transformer-based pre-training method with General Plant Infection dataset. In Proceedings of the Chinese Conference on Pattern Recognition and Computer Vision (PRCV), Urumqi, China, 18–20 October 2024; pp. 189–202.
30. Tinto, V. Dropout from higher education: A theoretical synthesis of recent research. *Rev. Educ. Res.* **1975**, *45*, 89–125. [CrossRef]
31. Srivastava, N.; Hinton, G.; Krizhevsky, A.; Sutskever, I.; Salakhutdinov, R. Dropout: A simple way to prevent neural networks from overfitting. *J. Mach. Learn. Res.* **2014**, *15*, 1929–1958.
32. Li, L.; Wang, H.; Wu, Y.; Chen, S.; Wang, H.; Sigrimis, N.A. Investigation of Strawberry Irrigation Strategy Based on K-Means Clustering Algorithm. *Trans. Chin. Soc. Agric. Mach.* **2020**, *51*, 295–302.

33. Voita, E.; Talbot, D.; Moiseev, F.; Sennrich, R.; Titov, I. Analyzing multi-head self-attention: Specialized heads do the heavy lifting, the rest can be pruned. *arXiv* **2019**, arXiv:1905.09418.
34. Dey, R.; Salem, F.M. Gate-variants of gated recurrent unit (GRU) neural networks. In Proceedings of the 2017 IEEE 60th International Midwest Symposium on Circuits and Systems (MWSCAS), Boston, MA, USA, 6–9 August 2017; pp. 1597–1600.
35. Sun, S.; Liu, J.; Sun, S. Hyperspectral subpixel target detection based on interaction subspace model. *Pattern Recognit.* **2023**, *139*, 109464. [CrossRef]
36. Wang, H.; Zhang, X.; Mei, S. Shannon-Cosine Wavelet Precise Integration Method for Locust Slice Image Mixed Denoising. *Math. Probl. Eng.* **2020**, *2020*, 4989735. [CrossRef]
37. Gao, J.; Liang, F.; Fan, W.; Sun, Y.; Han, J. Graph-based consensus maximization among multiple supervised and unsupervised models. In Proceedings of the 23rd International Conference on Neural Information Processing Systems, Vancouver, BC, Canada, 7–10 December 2009; Volume 22.
38. Ristoski, P.; De Vries, G.K.D.; Paulheim, H. A collection of benchmark datasets for systematic evaluations of machine learning on the semantic web. In Proceedings of the Semantic Web–ISWC 2016: 15th International Semantic Web Conference, Kobe, Japan, 17–21 October 2016; Proceedings, Part II 15. pp. 186–194.
39. Grover, A.; Leskovec, J. node2vec: Scalable feature learning for networks. In Proceedings of the 22nd ACM SIGKDD International Conference on Knowledge Discovery and Data Mining, San Francisco, CA, USA, 13–17 August 2016; pp. 855–864.
40. Kipf, T.N.; Welling, M. Semi-supervised classification with graph convolutional networks. *arXiv* **2016**, arXiv:1609.02907.
41. Veličković, P.; Cucurull, G.; Casanova, A.; Romero, A.; Lio, P.; Bengio, Y. Graph attention networks. *stat* **2017**, *1050*, 4.
42. Chen, Z.; Li, X.; Bruna, J. Supervised community detection with line graph neural networks. *arXiv* **2017**, arXiv:1705.08415.
43. Danon, L.; Diaz-Guilera, A.; Duch, J.; Arenas, A. Comparing community structure identification. *J. Stat. Mech. Theory Exp.* **2005**, *2005*, P09008. [CrossRef]

symmetry

MDPI

Article

Hybrid Optimization of Phase Masks: Integrating Non-Iterative Methods with Simulated Annealing and Validation via Tomographic Measurements

Zhiwen Li [1], Chao Sun [2], Haihua Wang [3,4,*] and Rui-Feng Wang [4,5,*]

[1] National Laboratory of Solid State Microstructures, College of Engineering and Applied Sciences, Nanjing University, Nanjing 210023, China; zhiwen_li@smail.nju.edu.cn
[2] School of Chemistry and Chemical Engineering, Nanjing University, Nanjing 210023, China; mg20240089@smail.nju.edu.cn
[3] College of Information and Electrical Engineering, China Agricultural University, 17 Qinghua East Road, Haidian, Beijing 100083, China
[4] National Innovation Center for Digital Fishery, China Agricultural University, Beijing 100083, China
[5] College of Engineering, China Agricultural University, 17 Qinghua East Road, Haidian, Beijing 100083, China
* Correspondence: whaihua@cau.edu.cn (H.W.); sweefongreggiewong@cau.edu.cn (R.-F.W.)

Abstract: The development of holography has facilitated significant advancements across a wide range of disciplines. A phase-only spatial light modulator (SLM) plays a crucial role in realizing digital holography, typically requiring a phase mask as its input. Non-iterative (NI) algorithms are widely used for phase mask generation, yet they often fall short in delivering precise solutions and lack adaptability in complex scenarios. In contrast, the Simulated Annealing (SA) algorithm provides a global optimization approach capable of addressing these limitations. This study investigates the integration of NI algorithms with the SA algorithm to enhance the optimization of phase mask generation in digital holography. Furthermore, we examine how adjusting annealing parameters, especially the cooling strategy, can significantly improve system optimization performance and symmetry. Notably, we observe a considerable improvement in the efficiency of the SA algorithm when non-iterative methods are employed to generate the initial phase mask. Our method achieves a perfect representation of the symmetry in desired light fields. The efficacy of the optimized phase masks is evaluated through optical tomographic measurements using two-dimensional mutually unbiased bases (MUBs), with the resulting average similarity reaching 0.99. These findings validate the effectiveness of our methodin optimizing phase mask generation and underscore its potential for high-precision optical mode recognition and analysis.

Keywords: phase mask; non-iterative algorithms; simulated annealing algorithm; orbital angular momentum; tomographic measurement; symmetry of optical field

1. Introduction

Over the past three decades, digital holography has garnered extensive attention, particularly in areas such as hyper-realistic imaging [1], ultra-high-speed data transmission [2], data storage [3], and real-time display [4]. Generally, the complete information of an optical wave, encompassing both amplitude and phase, can be reconstructed from the hologram [5,6]. Computer Generated Holograms (CGHs) offer the advantage of eliminating the need to record the hologram of a real physical scene, thereby enabling the use of virtual objects instead [7,8]. This has led to widespread applications in three-dimensional displays [9], virtual reality [10], and augmented reality [11].

Recently, researchers have also made new breakthroughs in the study of holograms and image reconstruction. Current deep learning approaches for holographic imaging largely rely on the statistical correlations within the training data [12,13]. This reliance can undermine their robustness in real-world imaging scenarios where various physical perturbations—such as mechanical motion and optical fluctuations—are present [14]. In 2023, Chanseok Lee et al. [15] introduced a novel deep learning framework that integrates a parameterized physical forward model, enabling the simultaneous reconstruction of both the complex amplitude and the object-to-sensor distance, even when the latter extends beyond the range covered by the training dataset. In 2024, SIWOO LEE et al. [16] introduced HoloSR, an innovative deep learning-driven super-resolution method that converts low-resolution RGBD inputs into high-resolution computer-generated holograms, thereby enabling real-time rendering of photorealistic three-dimensional scenes. By integrating an advanced deep super-resolution network with resizing and convolutional layers, HoloSR directly generates high-resolution holograms without the need for additional interpolation. Conventional holography often results in 3D scenes with unnatural defocus and prominent speckle noise, primarily due to the spatial light modulator's limited space-bandwidth product. In 2015, Zhenxing Dong et al. [17] proposed a Motion Hologram technique that achieves precise, photorealistic, and speckle-free 3D imaging. This method utilizes a single hologram alongside an adaptable, learnable motion trajectory, both of which are concurrently optimized within a deep reinforcement learning framework.

In holographic displays utilizing SLMs, the complex amplitude information is typically encoded into phase-only holograms (POHs) or amplitude-only holograms (AOHs), depending on the modulation modes of the SLM [18]. POHs, in contrast to AOHs, exhibit superior diffraction efficiency and eliminate the formation of conjugate images, attributes that have garnered considerable interest in the research community [19]. As a result, POHs have emerged as the dominant encoding technique in contemporary CGHs [20].

Several non-iterative methods exist for generating CGHs [21,22], including random phase mask methods [23], patterned phase-only holography[24], double-phase methods [25], and random phase-free methods [26]. However, due to the inherent nature of POHs, the holography generation problem lacks a simple direct solution, often requiring approximation methods to reach the optimal result. The Gerchberg–Saxton (GS) algorithm, an iterative technique for phase retrieval [27,28], recovers phase information from intensity data and was first introduced by Roy Gerchberg and Warren Saxton in 1972 [29]. Despite its broad application, the GS algorithm has inherent limitations [30], including the potential to become trapped in local optima during the iterative process. Additionally, the optimized light field distribution often exhibits significant Gibbs oscillations, leading to poor uniformity in the reconstructed image, especially at the edges.

The performance of the optical system also affects the quality of the generated light fields in CGHs. Optical aberrations, introduced by components such as lenses, including spherical aberration, coma, and air turbulence, can deteriorate the desired light field [31,32]. Addressing these challenges requires calibration based on actual measurements to ensure that the symmetry of the optical field is preserved and optimized [33].

To achieve the desired light field, we employ the SA algorithm to optimize the phase masks. In the early 1980s, Kirkpatrick, Gelatt, and Vecchi [34] introduced the novel application of annealing concepts to combinatorial optimization problems. Inspired by the physical annealing process in materials science, the SA algorithm is particularly suited for solving optimization problems, overcoming the limitation of Monte Carlo methods that often become trapped in local minima by using an efficient Metropolis acceptance criterion [35]. In addition, SA is recognized as a versatile metaheuristic approach [36–38] for tackling complex black-box [39] global optimization problems, especially in cases where the objective function is not directly available and its evaluation relies on computational simulations. Given the complexity of evaluating the objective function, involving a high-dimensional state space and substantial memory requirements, SA proves to be the appropriate method for addressing these challenges [40–42]. Among the various optimization techniques, the SA algorithm has emerged as a robust and versatile global optimization method in optical field [43,44]. Unfortunately, the efficiency of simulated annealing markedly decreases when applied to large-scale optimization problems. This reduction in performance is often attributed to premature convergence or the algorithm becoming stuck in a stagnation phase. In 2017, Mohamed Lalaoui et al. proposed a self-tuned SA algorithm. Their study sought to address this challenge by employing a self-adjusting strategy that utilized a machine learning technique known as the Hidden Markov Model. The fundamental concept involved enabling the SA to modify its cooling schedule autonomously at each iteration based on past search experiences [45]. In 2018, they focused on mitigating the challenges encountered in simulated annealing by integrating a fuzzy logic controller. The approach aimed to dynamically adapt the neighborhood structure during the simulated annealing process, thereby enhancing its performance and addressing inherent limitations [46].

Furthermore, we propose a diagnostic approach that utilizes vector mode decompositions tailored to individual modes, complemented by a tomographic method designed to quantitatively evaluate the orbital angular momentum (OAM) degree of freedom [47]. The initial measurement of quantum correlations in the OAM basis was reported by Mair and colleagues in 2001 [48,49]. Unlike polarization, which is confined to a two-dimensional Hilbert space, OAM spans an infinite-dimensional Hilbert space, theoretically enabling the encoding of an infinite amount of information onto a single photon [50]. Using CGHs recorded on holographic film, Mair et al. demonstrated that, like polarization and spin angular momentum, OAM is an intrinsic property of individual photons.

High-dimensional entangled photons provide substantial advantages in areas like quantum communication and cryptography. By encoding more information per photon than is possible with polarization alone, these states not only enhance the data capacity of each photon but also bolster security in communication protocols [51]. For instance, in 2013, Mhlambululi Mafu et al. investigated high-dimensional quantum key distribution protocols that utilize mutually unbiased bases, implemented via photons encoded with OAM [52]. In 2014, Mario Krenn et al. examined the generation of a (100×100)-dimensional entangled quantum system by exploiting the spatial modes of photons [53]. In 2017, Alicia Sit et al. demonstrated a single-photon quantum key distribution system that operated over a 0.3 km turbulent free-space link in the city of Ottawa by exploiting both the spin and OAM degrees of freedom of photons. Their findings revealed that even under moderate turbulence and without active wavefront correction, high-dimensional photon states significantly enhanced the secure transmission of information [54].

Quantum state tomography, initially proposed in 1957 [55], has become a well-established technique within quantum optics [56,57]. Jack et al. advanced this methodology by employing digital holograms encoded on SLMs to reconstruct the density matrix of a two-dimensional entangled state in the OAM basis [58]. Furthermore, quantum state tomography has been successfully implemented using MUBs. In this work, one set of MUBs is represented by the the pure OAM states ($|\psi\rangle = \pm|\ell\rangle$) and the other consists of superposition states of these pure OAM states ($|\psi\rangle = |\ell\rangle + \exp(i\phi)|-\ell\rangle$) [59]. In this study, we select Hermite–Gaussian(HG) modes and Laguerre–Gaussian(LG) modes to validate the superiority of the SA algorithm, as both serve as eigenfunctions of the Fourier transform and solutions to the paraxial wave equation and are eigenmodes of parabolic refractive index waveguides and quantum harmonic oscillators [60–62].

Based on the SA algorithm, we compare two methods for optimizing phase masks: a numerical optimization approach (NOSAA) executed solely on a computer, and an optical experimental approach (OESAA) in which the simulated annealing algorithm is integrated into a feedback system during optical experiments to adaptively optimize the phase masks. We propose a hybrid optimization approach that integrates NI algorithms with SA. In our method, the NI algorithms are first employed to rapidly generate an initial phase mask, which is subsequently refined using the SA algorithm. This combined strategy leverages the fast convergence of NI methods and the robust global search capabilities of SA, ultimately yielding phase masks that deliver excellent reconstruction accuracy and enhanced symmetry in the resulting light fields. Our method not only highlights the potential of SA algorithm in advancing the design of optical systems but also underscores its potential for broader adoption in cutting edge photonics research [63–65], particularly in applications that require the precise symmetry of light fields and optimization of complex optical modes [66–68].

2. Theory

2.1. LG Modes and HG Modes in Optical System

In recent years, laser beams carrying OAM have garnered significant attention [69–71]. These beams can be described using LG modes [72–74]. LG modes propagate with a rotating Poynting vector around the beam axis. They are defined by two numbers: the azimuthal integer (denoted ℓ) and the radial integer (denoted p) [75,76]. The standard formula for the amplitude of any normalized LG mode is expressed as [77]

$$u_{\ell p} = \sqrt{\frac{2p!}{\pi(p+|\ell|)!}}\frac{1}{w(z)}\left[r\sqrt{2}\frac{|\ell|}{w(z)}\right]\exp\left(-\frac{r^2}{w^2(z)}\right)L_p^{|\ell|}\left(\frac{2r^2}{w^2(z)}\right) \tag{1}$$

$$\times \exp[-i\ell\varphi]\exp\left[ik_0 r^2 z\left(\frac{1}{2(z^2+z_R^2)}\right)\right]\exp[-i\psi(z)]$$

where $z_R - \pi w_0^2/\lambda$ is the Rayleigh range with wavelength λ and wavevector $k_0 = 2\pi/\lambda$, $w(z) = w_0\left[(z^2+z_R^2)/z_R^2\right]^{1/2}$ is the radius of the beam with beam waist w_0 and $\psi(z) = [(2p+|\ell|)\arctan(z/z_R)]$ is the Gouy phase. In the context of LG modes, the radial index p and the azimuthal index ℓ delineate a spectrum of distinct modal configurations. Specifically, the parameter p assumes values as a non-negative integer, whereas ℓ spans the set of all integers. These indices facilitate the characterization of the modes through the application of generalized Laguerre polynomials L_p^ℓ, whose explicit formulation is described by the following equation:

$$L_p^\ell(x) = \sum_{n=0}^{p}(-1)^n\frac{(p+\ell)!}{(p-n)!(\ell+n)!n!}x^n \tag{2}$$

The HG modes constitute a set of solutions to the paraxial wave equation in free space when expressed within the Cartesian coordinate framework [78–82]. Along one dimension, an HG mode's electric field is [83]

$$u_n(x,z) = \left(\frac{2}{\pi}\right)^{\frac{1}{4}}\left(\frac{e^{-i(2n+1)\psi(z)}}{2^n n! w(z)}\right)^{\frac{1}{2}} \times H_n\left(\frac{\sqrt{2}x}{w(z)}\right)e^{-i\frac{kx^2}{2R(z)}}e^{-\frac{x^2}{w^2(z)}} \tag{3}$$

where n denotes the mode index for higher-order beams, k represents the wavevector, and H_n corresponds to the Hermite polynomial of degree n. The beam's radius $w(z)$, measured at a specific point z along its direction of propagation, is given by

$$w(z) = w_0 \left[1 + \left(\frac{z}{z_R}\right)^2\right]^{\frac{1}{2}} \tag{4}$$

where w_0 is the radius of the beam at the beam waist and the Rayleigh length is defined as $z_R = \pi w_0^2/\lambda$, with the wavelength of the beam denoted by λ. The Gouy phase is given by $\psi(z) = \tan^{-1}(z/z_R)$. The radius of curvature is $R(z) = z\left[1 + (z_R/z)^2\right]$.

The HG mode's 2D electric field is given by

$$u_{nm}(x, y, z) = u_n(x, z)u_m(y, z), \tag{5}$$

where $u_m(y, z)$ has a similar form to Equation (3).

2.2. SA Algorithm

The SA algorithm is an iterative optimization technique that uses acceptance probabilities to explore the solution space and find near-optimal solutions [84]. Compared to traditional optimization methods, the SA algorithm is less prone to becoming trapped in local optima, making it highly suitable for global optimization problems. This process involves cooling a solid to a low-energy state after raising its temperature. The flowchart of the SA algorithm is shown in Figure 1.

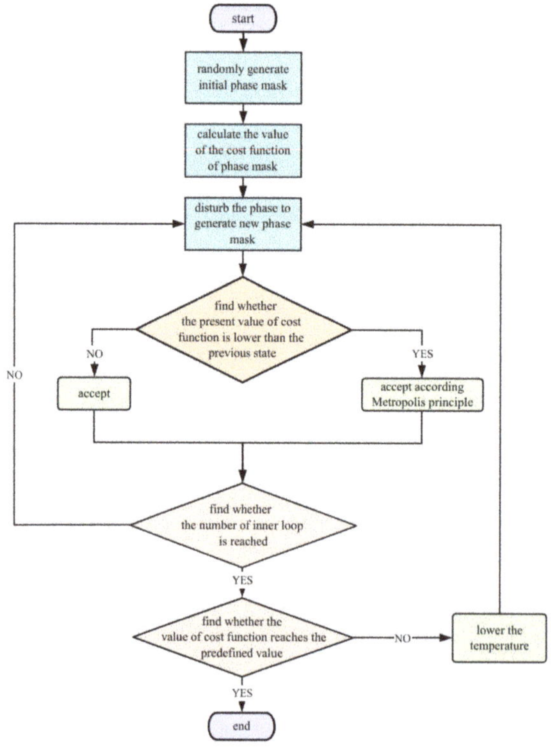

Figure 1. Flowchart of the SA algorithm used to optimize phase mask.

2.2.1. Initial Temperature

The core principle of the SA algorithm involves gradually decreasing a control parameter known as temperature, which governs the acceptance of solutions during the optimization process [85]. The temperature is updated iteratively as follows:

$$T_k = \alpha^k T_0 \quad (T_0 > 0,\ 0 < \alpha < 1,\ k = 1, 2, 3, \ldots) \tag{6}$$

where T_0 is the initial temperature and T_k is the temperature of the kth iteration. α is the decay factor which is a positive constant smaller than but close to one. Typical values for α range from approximately 0.8 to 0.99 [86]. The choice of the initial temperature plays an important role in the efficiency of subsequent optimization iterations.

The concept of the mushy state [87] provides guidance for selecting the initial temperature. It occurs at an initial temperature, characterized by an acceptance rate of 80–85%, where the algorithm accepts both better and worse solutions with significantly high probability. This allows extensive exploration of the solution space and avoids premature convergence to local minima.

There is another, more precise method for selecting the initial temperature. The initial temperature c_0 is computed following a well-defined and systematic procedure [86]. First, we let m_1 denote the total number of proposed transitions that strictly decrease the value of cost function, and m_2 represents the number of other proposed transitions. Additionally, $\Delta_f^{(+)}$ is defined as the average cost difference across all increasing transitions. The acceptance rate $\chi(c)$ is approximated by the expression

$$\chi(c) \approx \frac{m_1 + m_2 e^{-\frac{\Delta_f^{(+)}}{c}}}{m_1 + m_2}, \tag{7}$$

where c is the temperature control parameter.

The initial temperature c_0 is calculated from the acceptance rate:

$$c_0 \approx \frac{\Delta_f^{(+)}}{\ln\left(\frac{m_2}{m_2\chi(c) - m_1(1-\chi(c))}\right)}. \tag{8}$$

In practice, c_0 is first set to zero, and a sequence of transitions is generated to compute m_1 and m_2. The value of c_0 is then computed using Equation (8), where $\chi(c)$ is defined by us. This initial value of c_0 is used as the starting temperature in the cooling process. The procedure ensures that in the early stages of the SA algorithm, a larger number of state transitions are accepted, allowing for extensive exploration of the solution space. As the temperature decreases, the algorithm gradually becomes more selective, accepting only transitions that lead to improvements or minor deteriorations, which results in the algorithm eventually converging to a global optimum.

2.2.2. Decay of the Control Parameter

The temperature decay (Cooling Schedule) in the SA algorithm is determined by the relationship between successive control parameters c_k and c_{k+1}. The core idea is that as the temperature gradually decreases, the probability distribution of the SA algorithm should transition smoothly, avoiding drastic fluctuations. In order to ensure that the stationary distributions remain sufficiently close when the control parameter changes from c_k to c_{k+1}, this closeness can be quantified by the following formula [88,89]:

$$\forall i \in S, \quad \frac{1}{1+\delta} < \frac{q_i(c_k)}{q_i(c_{k+1})} < 1 + \delta, \tag{9}$$

where δ denotes a small positive constant specified in advance and S is the state space. $q_i(c_k)$ is stationary distribution which is typically represented by the Boltzmann distribution:

$$\forall i \in S, \quad q_i(c_k) = \frac{e^{-\frac{f(i)}{c_k}}}{\sum_{j \in S} e^{-\frac{f(j)}{c_k}}}, \tag{10}$$

where $f(i)$ denotes the objective function value (the energy associated with state i) and c_k represents the current temperature.

We consider the stationary distribution $q(c_k)$ of the Markov chain resulting from the simulated annealing process at iteration k. We let c_k and c_{k+1} be two consecutive values of the control parameter, with $c_{k+1} < c_k$. Then, Equation (9) is satisfied if

$$\forall i \in S, \quad e^{\Delta_i \left(\frac{1}{c_{k+1}} - \frac{1}{c_k} \right)} < 1 + \delta, \tag{11}$$

where $\Delta_i = f(i) - f_{\text{opt}}$, and f_{opt} denotes the optimal value of f.

An equivalent form of the necessary condition Equation (11) is given by

$$\forall i \in S, \quad c_{k+1} > \frac{c_k}{1 + \frac{c_k \ln(1+\delta)}{f(i) - f_{\text{opt}}}}. \tag{12}$$

It can be rigorously established that Condition (12) admits the following approximation:

$$\forall i \in S, \quad c_{k+1} > \frac{c_k}{1 + \frac{c_k \ln(1+\delta)}{3\sigma_{c_k}}}, \tag{13}$$

where σ_{c_k} denotes the standard deviation computed at temperature c_k.

The specified parameter δ governs the extent to which the temperature c is reduced. Larger values of δ lead to more substantial decreases in c, whereas smaller values cause more moderate reductions.

2.2.3. Cost Function

To evaluate the quality of the phase masks, the correlation coefficient β between the target image and the image reconstructed is used as the cost function [90]

$$\beta = \frac{\left| \iint R(x,y) T^*(x,y)\, dA \right|^2}{\iint |R(x,y)|^2\, dA \iint |T(x,y)|^2\, dA}. \tag{14}$$

It is the overlap integral between the replay field (R) in an area of interest (A) and some target distribution (T). In discrete domain, this corresponds to a normalized dot product:

$$\beta = \frac{\left| \sum_{i=0}^{n} R_i T_i^* \right|^2}{\sum_{i=0}^{n} |R_i|^2}. \tag{15}$$

As the temperature gradually decreases during the SA algorithm, this technique is more suitable for optimizing the minimum value of a problem rather than the maximum value. Hence, in the SA algorithm, we define the cost function as

$$E = 1 - \beta. \tag{16}$$

2.2.4. Metropolis Principle

The optimization begins with an initial phase mask, generated from a uniform distribution in the range $[0, 2\pi]$. The corresponding cost function is calculated, and a new phase mask is generated by introducing random perturbations. Then, the cost function of the new phase mask is calculated. The acceptance probability P for transitioning to the new solution is given by

$$P = \begin{cases} \exp\left(-\frac{E_{\text{new}} - E_{\text{old}}}{T_k}\right), & \text{if } E_{\text{new}} > E_{\text{old}}, \\ 1, & \text{otherwise.} \end{cases} \tag{17}$$

where E_{new} is the value of cost function of the new solution and E_{old} is the value of cost function of the old solution.

This probabilistic acceptance mechanism allows the algorithm to escape local minima by temporarily accepting solutions with worse performance. As the temperature decreases, the likelihood of accepting worse solutions diminishes, refining the search around promising regions in the solution space [91–93].

2.3. Analytical Optimization Approaches for Hologram Generation

In order to use phase-only SLM to reconstruct a desired optical field $E_{\text{desired}}(x, y) = A_{\text{desired}}(x, y)e^{i\Phi_{\text{desired}}(x,y)}$, a hologram $H(x, y)$ is adopted to transform an input field $E_{\text{in}}(x, y) = A_{\text{in}}(x, y)e^{i\Phi_{\text{in}}(x,y)}$ into the target field and to spatially separate the desired beam from the zero-order reflection.

This relationship can be expressed analytically as

$$E_{in}(x, y)e^{i\mathbf{k}'_{in}\cdot\hat{r}} \cdot e^{iH(x,y)} = E_{\text{desired}}(x, y)e^{i\mathbf{k}_{\text{desired}}\cdot\hat{r}}, \tag{18}$$

where $\mathbf{k}'_{in}$ in a transmissive SLM is the input wavevector and it refers to the reflected wavevector in a reflective SLM. Meanwhile, $\mathbf{k}_{desire}$ is the output wavevector. The hologram $H(x, y)$ is defined as

$$H(x, y) = f(A_{rel}(x, y))\Phi(x, y), \tag{19}$$

where $\Phi(x, y)$ is defined as:

$$\Phi(x, y) = \Phi_{desired}(x, y) - \Phi_{in}(x, y) + \Phi_{\text{grating}}(x, y), \tag{20}$$

where A_{rel} is the relative amplitude of input and output beams. f is a user-defined function to optimize the diffraction efficiency. $\Phi_{grating}(x, y)$ is grating phase to split the light into different diffraction orders in practice.

$H(x, y)$ can take various forms. In this work, we use three methods to calculate $H(x, y)$.

Method A, proposed by Davis et al. [94], is given by

$$H(x, y) = \left(1 - \frac{1}{\pi}\,\text{sinc}^{-1}(A(x, y))\right)\Phi(x, y), \tag{21}$$

$$f(A(x, y)) = 1 - \frac{1}{\pi}\,\text{sinc}^{-1}(A), \tag{22}$$

where $\text{sinc}(a) = \sin a/a$.

This technique encodes amplitude information onto a phase-only filter using a single liquid-crystal SLM. It offers several advantages: it preserves 100% of the incident light, ensuring no loss in transmission; it is straightforward to implement with a single liquid-crystal SLM, eliminating the need for complex setups or multiple modulators; and it combines amplitude and phase modulation, enabling versatile optical applications such as low-pass and high-pass filtering, as well as inverse filters.

Method B, proposed by Bolduc et al. [95], introduces an enhanced technique that applies a correction:

$$H(x,y) = M(\Phi(x,y) - \pi M), \quad (23)$$

$$M = 1 + \frac{1}{\pi}\text{sinc}^{-1}(A). \quad (24)$$

This approach enables the simultaneous encoding of both the amplitude and phase of an optical field into a phase-only hologram. The main benefits of this approach include precise control over spatial transverse modes, which is crucial for various applications in optics. It eliminates unwanted phase alterations caused by intensity masking, ensuring the accurate reproduction of the desired optical field.

Method C, proposed by Arrizón et al. [96], introduces an alternative method for generating holograms:

$$H(x,y) = \Phi(x,y) + f(A(x,y))\sin(\Phi(x,y)), \quad (25)$$

$$J_0[f(A(x,y))] = A(x,y), \quad (26)$$

whereJ_0 is the zero-order Bessel function.

The method offers several advantages for encoding scalar complex fields using phase CGHs. First, one of the proposed holograms can be implemented with a phase modulator that has a reduced phase range, making it adaptable to conventional liquid crystal SLMs. Second, this reduced phase range, close to ±1.2 rad, makes the holograms suitable for applications such as optical trapping in biological systems.

2.4. Tomographic Measurement

Modal decomposition is a technique that expresses an unknown optical field as a linear combination of basis functions. These basis functions are typically chosen from an orthogonal set of spatial modes. The optical field $u(\mathbf{r})$ can be written as

$$u(\mathbf{r}) = \sum_{l=1}^{\infty} c_l \psi_l(\mathbf{r}), \quad (27)$$

where $\mathbf{r} = (x, y)$ represents the spatial coordinates and $c_l = q_l e^{i\Delta\phi_l}$ is the complex expansion coefficient, with q_l being the amplitude and $\Delta\phi_l = \phi_l - \phi_0$ representing the intermodal phase. The function $\psi_l(\mathbf{r})$ denotes the basis function.

The process of modal decomposition involves measuring the coefficients that describe the unknown field. This field can be expressed as a combination of modes, each with specific weightings and phase relationships. The decomposition is performed by measuring the inner product between the field and each mode, yielding coefficients defined by $\rho_l^2 = |\langle u|\psi_l\rangle|^2$. This measurement provides an intensity in the Fourier plane (on-axis), which is proportional to the power content of each mode, normalized such that $\sum \rho_l^2 = 1$.

To evaluate the capability of encoding and detecting transverse spatial modes, we apply this method to generate and detect states in MUBs [97–100]. The eigenstates of the sets $\{|u_i\rangle\}$ and $\{|v_j\rangle\}$ are referred to as MUBs in a d-dimensional Hilbert space, with the condition that $|\langle u_i|v_j\rangle|^2 = 1/d$ for all i and j [101]. For each mode, a complete set of projections is conducted to identify the generated mode. The process of reconstructing a state from all measurement outcomes is known as quantum state tomography, which is highly reliable but requires extensive measurements, as it involves generating and detecting all independent eigenstates and superpositions.

Without loss of generality, we simplify the analysis by neglecting the radial component of the optical field and focusing only on the azimuthal part related to optical OAM [102]. An optical beam with an azimuthal phase term $\exp(i\ell\phi)$ carries a well-defined OAM value ℓ per photon, where ϕ is the azimuthal angle. Such beams correspond to the eigenstates associated with the z-axis component of the OAM operator, providing a comprehensive set of basis functions within the azimuthal coordinate system [103].

MUBs form a comprehensive set of bases. In a Hilbert space of dimension d, if d is a prime number or can be expressed as a power of a prime, the known maximum number of such bases is $d+1$ [59,104]. In the context of a two-dimensional OAM Hilbert space, three MUBs are specifically the eigenstates associated with the Pauli matrices [105]. In a two-dimensional Hilbert space, the complete set of MUBs is given by

$$\begin{aligned} \mathcal{I} &= \{|0\rangle, |1\rangle\} \\ \mathcal{II} &= \left\{\frac{|0\rangle + |1\rangle}{\sqrt{2}}, \frac{|0\rangle - |1\rangle}{\sqrt{2}}\right\}, \\ \mathcal{III} &= \left\{\frac{|0\rangle + i|1\rangle}{\sqrt{2}}, \frac{|0\rangle - i|1\rangle}{\sqrt{2}}\right\}. \end{aligned} \tag{28}$$

Tomographic measurements play a crucial role in quantum optics [106] and information processing [107], particularly in quantum entanglement [108], quantum communication [109], and quantum computation [106]. By combining digital holography and SLMs, these measurements allow for efficient reconstruction and analysis of quantum states [110]. This technique enables the extraction of key physical quantities, such as intensity, phase, wavefront, Poynting vector, polarization, and OAM density [111,112]. Digital holography, in conjunction with SLMs, enhances the precision of quantum state tomography, enabling the accurate reconstruction of the quantum state's density matrix [103,113]. This method has proven especially useful for high-dimensional quantum systems, where traditional two-level quantum states (like polarization) are extended to OAM states, offering greater potential in quantum communication and quantum key distribution [114]. The ability to perform high-dimensional quantum tomography significantly increases the information capacity per photon, making it a vital tool for improving the efficiency and security of quantum communication systems [115].

3. Experiment and Result

3.1. NI Algorithms for Hologram Generation

We conducted optical experiments to evaluate non-iterative methods for hologram generation techniques based on the quality of the obtained modes. The schematic diagram of the experimental setup is depicted in Figure 2. The light source is a He-Ne laser (Thorlabs S1FC660, Newton, NJ, USA) with a wavelength of 660 nm. The beam expander is used to expand and collimate the laser, projecting it onto the SLM (MeadowlarkOptics P1920-400 800-HDMI, Meadowlark Optics Inc., Frederick, CO, USA). A phase mask optimized by non-iterative methods is loaded onto the SLM. An 8-bit reflective phase-only SLM is employed, with a sampling interval of 9.2 μm × 9.2 μm and a resolution of 1920 × 1152. A $4-f$ system, consisting of Lens 3 (focal length: 200 mm) and Lens 4 (focal length: 200 mm) along with a spatial filter (SF), is utilized to remove the zero-order light effect from the SLM. To enhance the filtering of zero-order light, a blazed grating is added and superimposed onto the phase masks. The outgoing modes form an image on the camera. We used a charge-coupled device (Andor, iStar CCD 05577H, Oxford Instruments Technology (Shanghai) Co. Limited, Shanghai, China) to capture the reconstructed image.

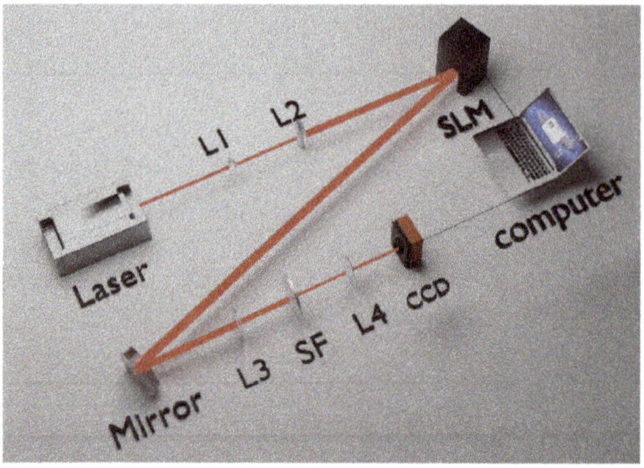

Figure 2. Experimental setup scheme of the optical system using SLM. The input laser beam is expanded and collimated by the beam expander, consisting of Lens 1 (L1) and Lens (L2), to produce a plane wave before the SLM. The SLM is used to modulate the input beam with a phase mask. A mirror is employed to fold the optical path and guide the modulated beam through a 4f imaging system L3 and L4. The SF is used to select the desired diffraction order. Finally, the CCD camera captures the modulated beam for data acquisition and analysis.

First, we performed numerical simulations to predict the experimental results. The results are shown in Figure 3. Figure 3a shows the numerical simulation results of the phase masks without optimization. Figure 3b–d, respectively, show the numerical simulation results of the phase masks optimized using Methods A, B, and C. We simulated this process by applying a Fourier transform to $E_{\text{desired}}(x,y)$ and then multiplying the transformed field with a circular mask, ensuring that all values outside the designated circular region are set to zero. An inverse Fourier transform was subsequently applied to the filtered data to reconstruct the amplitude and phase of the modified light field at the imaging plane of the SLM.

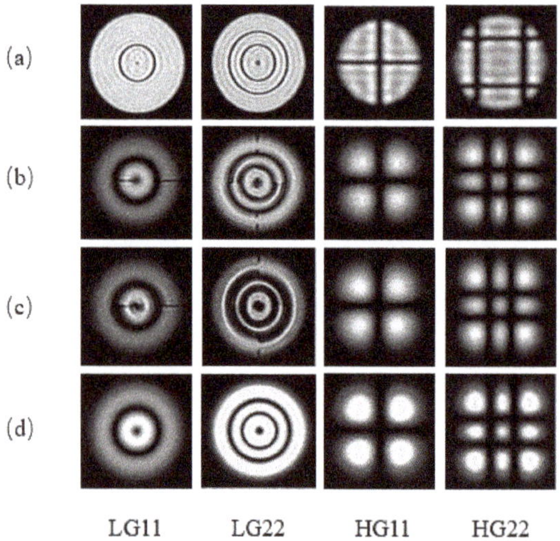

Figure 3. Numerical results of 4 different modes (LG11, LG22, HG11, HG22). (**a**) Reconstruction results using non-optimized phase masks. (**b**) Corresponding outcomes from Method A. (**c**) Outcomes from Method B. (**d**) Analysis results by Method C.

Then, we conducted the experiment according to the experimental setup diagram. The experimental results of non-iterative methods are shown in Figure 4. Figure 4a shows the desired modes (LG11, LG22, HG11, HG22). Figure 4b shows the phase distribution of the desired modes. To compare different optimization methods, Figure 4c presents the experimental results of the non-optimized phase masks. Figure 4d displays the modes obtained using the phase by Method A. Figure 4e presents the modes generated by Method B, while Figure 4f shows the modes obtained through Method C.

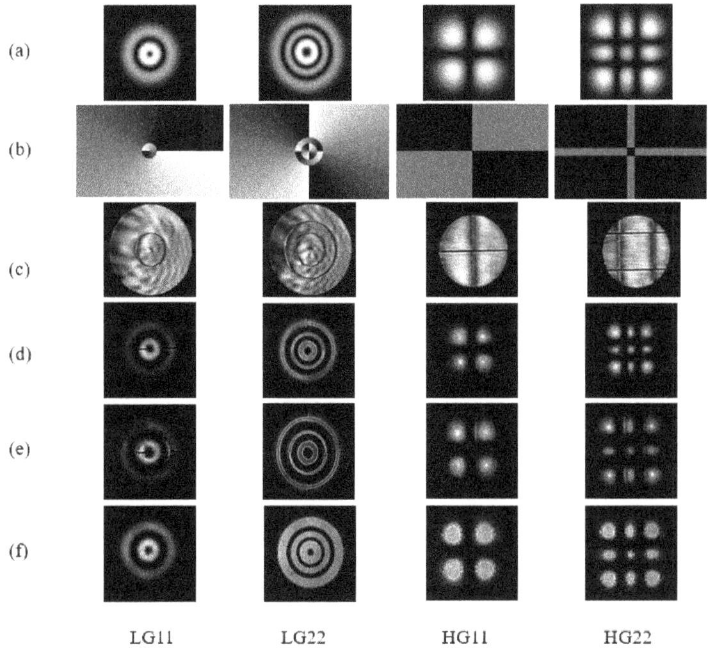

Figure 4. (**a**) Desired modes. (**b**) The phase distribution of desired modes. (**c**) Obtained modes without optimized mask. (**d**) Modes acquired by implementing Method A. (**e**) Modes captured utilizing Method B. (**f**) Modes obtained through the application of Method C.

We quantitatively compared the modes obtained using non-optimized and optimized masks by calculating their correlation coefficients. The line chart in Figure 5 illustrates the correlation coefficients obtained from the non-optimized mask and the mask optimized using non-iterative methods. As expected, we obtained lower correlation values with the non-optimized mask, whereas significantly higher correlation values were observed with the optimized mask. The correlation coefficients of desired modes from the non-optimized method were 53%, 57%, 62%, and 59%, respectively. In our analysis, Method A produced correlation coefficients of 91%, 82%, 94%, and 94%, respectively. In comparison, Method B produced slightly lower coefficients, measuring 87%, 78%, 91%, and 89%, while Method C yielded correlation coefficients of 95%, 82%, 85%, and 81%. These findings highlight the varying effectiveness of different methods in enhancing correlation. Our results indicate that Method A outperforms the others. Through experimental investigation, we found that the optimization effectiveness of the same method varies for different light fields. Overall, the NI optimization algorithm yields an imperfect representation of the symmetry in the desired light fields.

To address these issues, we propose using combination of NI algorithms and SA algorithm to optimize the phase masks, ensuring that ideal results can be obtained for any desired modes and images.

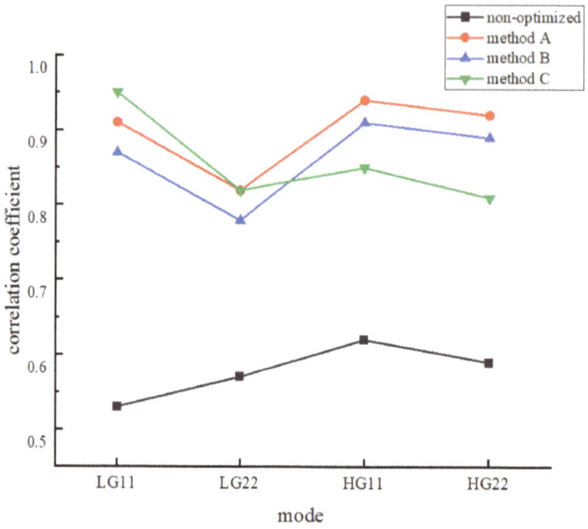

Figure 5. Comparison of correlation coefficients between non-optimized and various non-iterative optimization methods.

3.2. *Combination of NI Algorithms and SA Algorithm for Hologram Generation*

The GS algorithm is well known among iterative algorithms; however, it is prone to becoming trapped in local optima. To demonstrate the performance of the GS and SA algorithms in light field reconstruction, we selected the 'pine' image as the test image. Furthermore, we compared the result obtained using the SA algorithm with those obtained using the GS algorithm. Figure 6 shows the result from the GS algorithm, where it is evident that the algorithm becomes trapped in a local optimum during the iterative process.

Figure 6. Reconstruction result of the 'pine' image utilizing the GS algorithm.

To evaluate the symmetry of the reconstructed image, we employ the following computational method:

$$Symmetry = 1.0 - \frac{1}{255 \cdot h \cdot \left(\frac{w}{2}\right)} \sum_{y=0}^{h-1} \sum_{x=0}^{\frac{w}{2}-1} |I(y,x) - I(y,w-x-1)| \quad (29)$$

where h is the height (number of rows) of the image, w is the width (number of columns) of the image, $I(y, x)$ is the grayscale value at the yth row and xth column of the image, and $I(y, w - x - 1)$ is the grayscale value at the symmetric position on the right side of the image.

According to Equation (29), the symmetry of Figure 6 is calculated to be 86%. Subsequently, we generated CGHs using the SA algorithm, known as NOSAA, to reconstruct the 'pine' image. Figure 7 illustrates the entire process of NOSAA. Figure 7a shows the evolution of the phase masks from iteration 1 to 900, while Figure 7b presents the corresponding reconstructed images. It can be observed that, with an increasing number of iterations, more intricate image details are reconstructed, and the brightness of the resulting images becomes closer to that of the target image. All other parameters were kept constant as described in the simulation setup. The phase mask from the final iteration was loaded onto the SLM. For comparison, Figure 8a illustrates the target image. The reconstructed image is presented in Figure 8b.

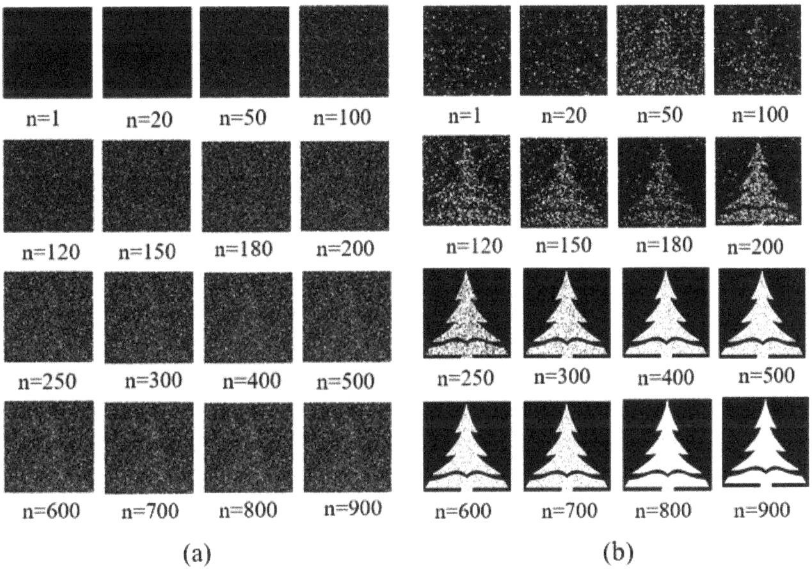

Figure 7. The entire process of NOSAA. (**a**) Variation of the phase mask with iteration number n ranging from 1 to 900. (**b**) Transformation of the reconstructed image as a function of iteration number n spanning from 1 to 900.

In Figure 8b, the reconstructed 'pine' image exhibits very poor quality. To mitigate the influence of objective factors such as laser instability and random fluctuations, we repeated the experiment hourly, for a total of five runs. The correlation coefficients were found to be 52%, 52%, 53%, 51%, and 52%, while the symmetry values were 76%, 75%, 75%, 77%, and 76% respectively. Experimental results demonstrated that when phase masks, generated by the NOSAA method, were loaded onto the SLM, the outcomes were less than perfect, leading to significant disruption of image symmetry. The result shows a discrepancy between the theoretical and experimental outcomes, which may arise from sensitivity to parameter configuration and sampling conditions. Specifically, this is because NOSAA requires extremely precise alignment of the actual optical path. In our theoretical calculations, we preseted the displacement of the first-order optical diffraction and the diameter of the circular aperture filter; however, our optical system cannot perfectly match these preset values. Moreover, objective factors such as lens aberrations and air turbulence within the optical path can affect the optimization results. Then, we used Method A for image reconstruction, with the results shown in Figure 8c. Through the calculations, the correlation coefficient is 92%, and the symmetry is 90%. The experiment demonstrates that the results obtained from the non-iterative optimization method are superior to those obtained from NOSAA within a limited time.

Experimental results confirm that for the reconstruction of ideal images, optimizing phase masks using the SA algorithm within an optical feedback system experiment, known as OESAA, is essential. Considering the disadvantages of NOSAA, such as long computation times and high requirements for experimental accuracy, we utilized the phase masks generated by non-iterative optimization methods as initial phase masks for OESAA. By adopting this combined optimization strategy, our method not only overcame the inefficiency of starting from scratch under the curse of dimensionality and the sensitivity of the experimental setup associated with NOSAA, but also provided a more robust initial value.

In this experiment, the SA algorithm is employed with two loops: an inner loop and an outer loop. In each inner loop, the phase mask randomly perturbed from the previous one is loaded to the SLM to modulate the light. A CCD capture the modulated light and send the captured image back to a computer to calculate the value of cost function. If the value of cost function is lower than the previous value, it can be accepted. If it is higher, it might still be accepted with a certain probability based on the Metropolis principle.

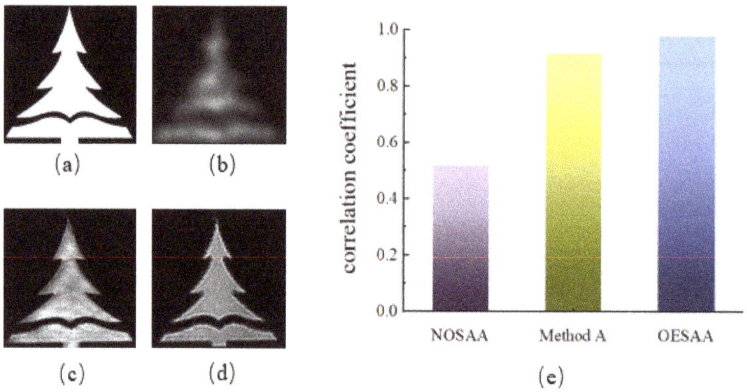

Figure 8. Optical results: (**a**) Target image. (**b**) The image captured by CCD after NOSAA. (**c**) Reconstructed result by Method A. (**d**) Reconstructed result by OESAA. (**e**) The results of the correlation coefficient.

The inner loop is limited to a preset maximum number of iterations. Once the maximum is reached, the system decreases the temperature and starts a new inner loop. This process continues until the value of cost function falls below a preset threshold.

The parameters of the OESAA used in our experiment are as follows. The temperature decay factor, α, is set to 0.97, with an initial high temperature of 10 and a final temperature of 0.001. In each inner loop iteration, the pixel value is randomly perturbed by 1. The Markov chain has a length of 100, indicating 100 iterations at each temperature level. A Markov chain is a stochastic process that models a sequence of potential events, where the probability of each event depends solely on the state achieved in the preceding event. Figure 8d shows the result obtained by combining the non-iterative method with the SA algorithm. According to the calculation, the correlation coefficient is 98%, and the symmetry is 97%. In Figure 8e, the bar chart illustrates the results of the correlation coefficient.

By reconstructing the 'pine' using different methods, the proposed approach shows significant improvement in both the correlation coefficient and symmetry compared to the GS algorithm and the NI optimization algorithm. The primary reason is that when using OESAA, we accounted for objective factors in the optical path, such as lens aberrations. Our proposed method can adaptively optimize the quality degradation resulting from these factors.

Due to the fact that LG modes and HG modes play an important role in many disparate areas of physics, we used the combination of NI algorithms and SA algorithm to optimize their phase masks.

Figure 9 shows the optimized phase masks through OESAA and their corresponding resulting modes. Figure 9a shows the desired modes (LG11, LG22, HG11, HG22) and Figure 9b shows the optimized phase masks by OESAA. Figure 9c,d show the numerical results and the modes obtained using the optimized phase masks from Figure 9b. By evaluating the cost function, the correlation coefficients of the modes are presented in Figure 10a. The results demonstrate that, through OESAA, the correlation coefficients of the modes reached 99%, 98%, 99%, and 98%, respectively, indicating significant improvements over NI algorithms. The results of symmetry reached 99%, 97%, 98%, and 97% in Figure 10b. The experimental results demonstrate that optimizing the light fields using a combination of NI algorithms and the SA algorithm yields a more perfect symmetry in the results.

Our experimental investigations substantiate that the integration of NI algorithms with the SA algorithm markedly improves optimization efficiency. To further confirm the reliability and efficacy of this combined approach, we performed tomographic measurements on the optimized light fields.

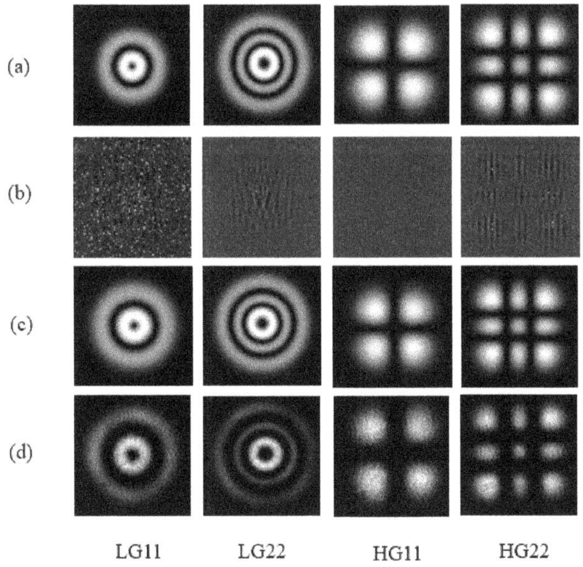

Figure 9. The results of OESAA. (**a**) Desired modes. (**b**) The optimized phase masks by OESAA. (**c**) Numerical results of 4 modes using optimized phases. (**d**) Obtained modes with optimized masks.

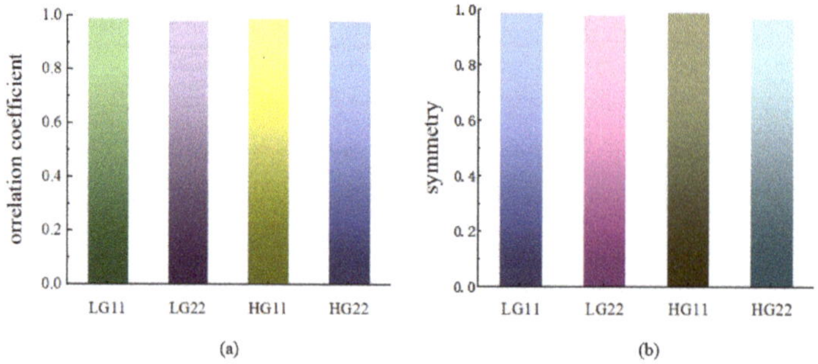

Figure 10. (**a**) Correlation coefficients of optimized masks by OESAA. (**b**) Symmetry of optimized masks by OESAA.

3.3. Experiment of Tomographic Measurement

The experimental setup for the MUBs test is illustrated in Figure 11. Projective measures are performed on the OAM degree of freedom using holograms encoded onto $SLM2$ (Hamatsu LCOS-SLM, X15213, HAMAMATSU PHOTONICS K.K., Iwata City, Japan). We created six different holograms on $SLM2$ to represent the two pure OAM modes as well as four orientations of the superposition states:

$$|\ell_1\rangle + \exp(i\theta)|\ell_2\rangle, \quad \theta = 0, \pi/2, \pi, 3\pi/2 \tag{30}$$

A modal decomposition is performed by performing an inner product of the incident field with a match hologram and measuring the on-axis intensity on a camera situated after lens L5. Results of tomographic measurements are shown in Figure 12. Figure 13 shows a specific quantitative description. The quality of the system is assessed using a measure called similarity S, which is analogous to fidelity in pair states. The calculated similarities of desired modes (LG11, LG22, HG11, HG22) are $S_{LG_{11}} = 0.995$, $S_{LG_{22}} = 0.987$, $S_{HG_{11}} = 0.992$, and $S_{HG_{22}} = 0.981$, respectively.

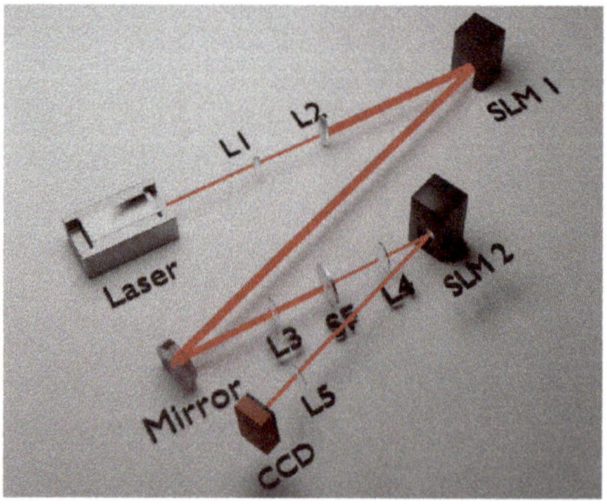

Figure 11. Experimental setup scheme of tomographic measurement.

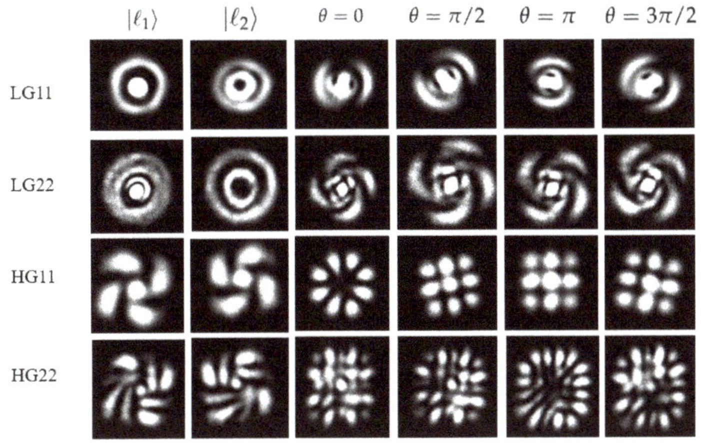

Figure 12. Tomography measurement obtained by projection of modes into six OAM states.

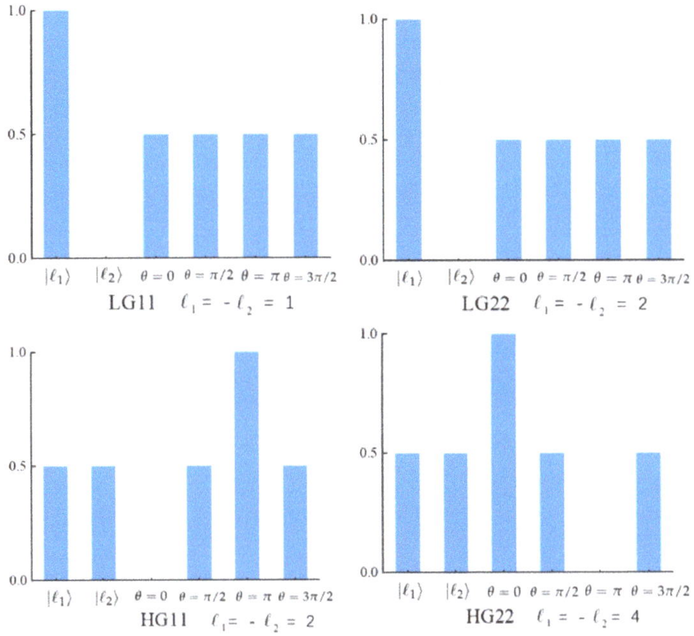

Figure 13. Characterization of projection measurements into the six states.

4. Conclusions

This study employed a hybrid approach combining NI algorithms with the SA algorithm to optimize phase masks for the generation of high-fidelity desired modes. Our experimental findings demonstrate that the optimized phase masks significantly enhance the correlation coefficient of the target mode. By comparing our method with traditional NI algorithms and other optimization techniques, we show that our approach yields superior results in terms of mode reconstruction accuracy and light field purity. The integration of the SA algorithm with non-iterative methods provides a notable improvement in computational efficiency, overcoming the individual limitations of each approach.

A quantitative comparison between the expected modes and the modulated modes through correlation measurements reveals that achieving optimal efficiency requires the careful optimization of the phase masks. The SA algorithm proves to be well suited for this task, effectively addressing the challenges of phase mask generation. These results confirm the practical applicability and superior performance of our method in optical field reconstruction. Furthermore, we introduce novel diagnostic techniques, vector mode decomposition and tomographic measurements, for evaluating the quality of the generated modes. These methods offer valuable insights into the underlying processes and the symmetry of the optical modes, providing a more comprehensive understanding of the phase mask optimization.

Our proposed method exhibits significant potential for enhancing the overall performance of optical systems. This technology not only enables precise control of the light field—improving directional transmission accuracy and stability in applications such as laser processing and optical trapping—but also effectively reduces noise and distortion through real-time adjustment of light field parameters in adaptive imaging, thereby significantly enhancing image resolution and quality for precise imaging solutions in biomedical and industrial inspections. Furthermore, our method facilitates high-precision encoding and decoding of optical signals in multimodal communication systems, improving transmission rates and signal-to-noise ratios, and providing robust support for high-speed, low-energy optical and quantum communications. Integrating this approach with emerging fields such as machine learning can further equip systems with self-adaptive learning and intelligent optimization capabilities, meeting the demands of real-time control in complex environments. Overall, this method demonstrates substantial research value and broad application prospects in both expanding new application areas and enhancing the performance of optical systems.

Author Contributions: Conceptualization: Z.L., H.W. and R.-F.W. Data curation: Z.L. and C.S. Fogrmal analysis: Z.L. and C.S. Investigation: Z.L. and C.S. Methodology: Z.L., H.W. and R.-F.W. Software: C.S. Validation: Z.L. and C.S. Visualization: Z.L. and C.S. Writing—original draft: Z.L. Writing—review and editing: Z.L., H.W., R.-F.W. and C.S. All authors have read and agreed to the published version of the manuscript.

Funding: This research was funded by Natural Science Foundation of Jiangsu Province grant number BK20243060.

Data Availability Statement: The original contributions presented in the study are included in the article; further inquiries can be directed to the corresponding authors.

Acknowledgments: The author Zhiwen Li acknowledges Lijian Zhang for helpful discussions; we thank the anonymous reviewers for their valuable comments and suggestions.

Conflicts of Interest: The authors declare no conflicts of interest.

Abbreviations

The following abbreviations are used in this manuscript:

SA	Simulated Annealing
SLM	Spatial Light Modulators
NI	Non-Iterative
MUB	Mutually Unbiased Bases
CGH	Computer-Generated Holography
POH	Phase-Only Holograms
AOH	Amplitude-Only Holograms
GS	Gerchberg-Saxton

OAM	Orbital Angular Momentum
HG	Hermite–Gaussian
LG	Laguerre–Gaussian
NOSAA	Numerical Optimization Strategy Based on Simulated Annealing Algorithm
OESAA	Optical Experiments Using the Simulated Annealing Algorithm

References

1. Schröter, J. Technologies beyond the Still and the Moving Image: The Case of the Multiplex Hologram. *Hist. Photogr.* **2011**, *35*, 23–32.
2. Gentet, P.; Joung, J.; Gentet, Y.; Lee, S.H. A Zerotrope™ with an ultra-realistic full-color digital hologram. In Proceedings of the Digital Holography and Three-Dimensional Imaging 2019, Bordeaux, France, 19–23 May 2019; p. M3A.7.
3. Yoneda, N.; Saita, Y.; Nomura, T. Computer-generated-hologram-based holographic data storage using common-path off-axis digital holography. *Opt. Lett.* **2020**, *45*, 2796–2799. [PubMed]
4. Zeng, T.; Zhu, Y.; Lam, E.Y. Deep learning for digital holography: A review. *Opt. Express* **2021**, *29*, 40572–40593. [PubMed]
5. Sahin, E.; Stoykova, E.; Mäkinen, J.; Gotchev, A. Computer-generated holograms for 3D imaging: A survey. *ACM Comput. Surv. (CSUR)* **2020**, *53*, 1–35.
6. Shi, L.; Li, B.; Kim, C.; Kellnhofer, P.; Matusik, W. Towards real-time photorealistic 3D holography with deep neural networks. *Nature* **2021**, *591*, 234–239. [CrossRef]
7. Shoydin, S.A.; Pazoev, A.L. Transmission of 3D holographic information via conventional communication channels and the possibility of multiplexing in the implementation of 3D hyperspectral images. *Photonics* **2021**, *8*, 448. [CrossRef]
8. Kim, M.K. Principles and techniques of digital holographic microscopy. *SPIE Rev.* **2010**, *1*, 018005.
9. Blinder, D.; Birnbaum, T.; Ito, T.; Shimobaba, T. The state-of-the-art in computer generated holography for 3D display. *Light Adv. Manuf.* **2022**, *3*, 572–600.
10. Qin, H.; Han, C.; Shi, X.; Gu, T.; Sun, K. Complex-valued generative adversarial network for real-time and high-quality computer-generated holography. *Opt. Express* **2024**, *32*, 44437–44451. [CrossRef]
11. Kara, K.; Lloret, J.; Romero, O.; Sendra, S. Performance Test of Holographic Video Communication System. In Proceedings of the 2024 International Conference on Multimedia Computing, Networking and Applications (MCNA), Valencia, Spain, 17–20 September 2024; pp. 15–20.
12. Nazir, A.; Hussain, A.; Singh, M.; Assad, A. A novel approach in cancer diagnosis: Integrating holography microscopic medical imaging and deep learning techniques—Challenges and future trends. *Biomed. Phys. Eng. Express* **2025**, *11*, 022002.
13. Ni, Y.; Feng, J.; Liu, J.; Yu, H.; Wei, H.; Du, Y.; Liu, L.; Sun, L.; Zhou, J.; Xu, W. An artificial nerve capable of UV-perception, NIR–vis switchable plasticity modulation, and motion state monitoring. *Adv. Sci.* **2022**, *9*, 2102036.
14. Wang, J.Z.; Zhao, S.; Wu, C.; Adams, R.B.; Newman, M.G.; Shafir, T.; Tsachor, R. Unlocking the emotional world of visual media: An overview of the science, research, and impact of understanding emotion. *Proc. IEEE* **2023**, *111*, 1236–1286.
15. Lee, C.; Song, G.; Kim, H.; Ye, J.C.; Jang, M. Deep learning based on parameterized physical forward model for adaptive holographic imaging with unpaired data. *Nat. Mach. Intell.* **2023**, *5*, 35–45.
16. Lee, S.; Nam, S.W.; Lee, J.; Jeong, Y.; Lee, B. HoloSR: Deep learning-based super-resolution for real-time high-resolution computer-generated holograms. *Opt. Express* **2024**, *32*, 11107–11122. [CrossRef]
17. Zhou, G.; Wang, R.F. The Heterogeneous Network Community Detection Model Based on Self-Attention. *Symmetry* **2025**, *17*, 432. [CrossRef]
18. Park, J.; Kang, H. Holo-VQVAE: VQ-VAE for phase-only holograms. *arXiv* **2024**, arXiv:2404.01330.
19. Fan, M.; Wang, J.; Du, C.; Yang, J.; Wang, H.; Xu, X. Generation of Non-Iterative POHs based on Optimized Hybrid Phase for Fresnel Lensless Holographic Projection. *Teh. Vjesn.* **2024**, *31*, 262–271.
20. Liu, Q.; Chen, J.; Qiu, B.; Wang, Y.; Liu, J. DCPNet: A dual-channel parallel deep neural network for high quality computer-generated holography. *Opt. Express* **2023**, *31*, 35908–35921.
21. Zhang, C.; Han, P.; Shi, J.; Zhou, H.; Zhang, Q.; Cheng, H.; Shen, C.; Zhang, F.; Han, C.; Wei, S. Non-Iterative 3D Computer-Generated Hologram Based on Single Full-Support Optimized Random Phase and Phase Compensation. *New J. Phys.* **2024**, *26*, 063032. [CrossRef]
22. Zhang, C.; Wu, F.; Zhou, J.; Wei, S. Non-iterative phase hologram generation for color holographic display. *Opt. Express* **2021**, *30*, 195–209. [CrossRef]
23. Wang, W.; Wang, X.; Xu, B.; Chen, J. Optical image encryption and authentication using phase-only computer-generated hologram. *Opt. Lasers Eng.* **2021**, *146*, 106722.
24. Tsang, P.; Chow, Y.T.; Poon, T.C. Generation of patterned-phase-only holograms (PPOHs). *Opt. Express* **2017**, *25*, 9088–9093. [CrossRef] [PubMed]

25. Kishk, S.; Javidi, B. Information hiding technique with double phase encoding. *Appl. Opt.* **2002**, *41*, 5462–5470. [CrossRef] [PubMed]
26. Chen, L.; Zhang, H.; He, Z.; Wang, X.; Cao, L.; Jin, G. Weighted constraint iterative algorithm for phase hologram generation. *Appl. Sci.* **2020**, *10*, 3652. [CrossRef]
27. Yang, G.Z.; Dong, B.Z.; Gu, B.Y.; Zhuang, J.Y.; Ersoy, O.K. Gerchberg–Saxton and Yang–Gu algorithms for phase retrieval in a nonunitary transform system: A comparison. *Appl. Opt.* **1994**, *33*, 209–218. [CrossRef]
28. Guo, C.; Liu, S.; Sheridan, J.T. Iterative phase retrieval algorithms. I: Optimization. *Appl. Opt.* **2015**, *54*, 4698–4708. [CrossRef]
29. Gaunt, A.; Hadzibabic, Z. Robust Digital Holography For Ultracold Atom Trapping. *Sci. Rep.* **2012**, *2*, 721.
30. Zhao, T.; Chi, Y. Modified Gerchberg–Saxton (G-S) Algorithm and Its Application. *Entropy* **2020**, *22*, 1354. [CrossRef]
31. Reddy, A.N.K.; Dev, V.; Pal, V.; Ganeev, R.A. The Effect of a Parabolic Apodizer on Improving the Imaging of Optical Systems with Coma and Astigmatism Aberrations. *Photonics* **2023**, *11*, 14. [CrossRef]
32. Wang, H.; Liu, J.; Liu, L.; Zhao, M.; Mei, S. Coupling technology of OpenSURF and Shannon-Cosine wavelet interpolation for locust slice images inpainting. *Comput. Electron. Agric.* **2022**, *198*, 107110.
33. Kelley, E.F. Calibration Requirements for Demanding Measurement Challenges. *Inf. Disp.* **2018**, *34*, 28–54. [CrossRef]
34. Bertsimas, D.; Tsitsiklis, J. Simulated annealing. *Stat. Sci.* **1993**, *8*, 10–15. [CrossRef]
35. Junior, H.A.; Ingber, L.; Petraglia, A.; Petraglia, M.R.; Machado, M.A.S. *Stochastic Global Optimization and Its Applications with Fuzzy Adaptive Simulated Annealing*; Springer Science & Business Media: Berlin/Heidelberg, Germany, 2012; Volume 35.
36. Osaba, E.; Villar-Rodriguez, E.; Del Ser, J.; Nebro, A.J.; Molina, D.; LaTorre, A.; Suganthan, P.N.; Coello, C.A.C.; Herrera, F. A tutorial on the design, experimentation and application of metaheuristic algorithms to real-world optimization problems. *Swarm Evol. Comput.* **2021**, *64*, 100888. [CrossRef]
37. Wang, S.; Wang, Y.; Wang, M. Connectivity and matching preclusion for leaf-sort graphs. *J. Interconnect. Netw.* **2019**, *19*, 1940007. [CrossRef]
38. Zhao, C.T.; Wang, R.F.; Tu, Y.H.; Pang, X.X.; Su, W.H. Automatic Lettuce Weed Detection and Classification Based on Optimized Convolutional Neural Networks for Robotic Weed Control. *Agronomy* **2024**, *14*, 2838. [CrossRef]
39. Dong, H.; Dong, Z. Surrogate-assisted grey wolf optimization for high-dimensional, computationally expensive black-box problems. *Swarm Evol. Comput.* **2020**, *57*, 100713. [CrossRef]
40. Lavin, A.; Krakauer, D.; Zenil, H.; Gottschlich, J.; Mattson, T.; Brehmer, J.; Anandkumar, A.; Choudry, S.; Rocki, K.; Baydin, A.G.; et al. Simulation intelligence: Towards a new generation of scientific methods. *arXiv* **2021**, arXiv:2112.03235.
41. Abdulazeez, D.H.; Askar, S.K. Offloading mechanisms based on reinforcement learning and deep learning algorithms in the fog computing environment. *IEEE Access* **2023**, *11*, 12555–12586. [CrossRef]
42. Tu, Y.H.; Wang, R.F.; Su, W.H. Active Disturbance Rejection Control—New Trends in Agricultural Cybernetics in the Future: A Comprehensive Review. *Machines* **2025**, *13*, 111. [CrossRef]
43. Yarmohamadi, H.; Mirhosseini, S. A new dynamic simulated annealing algorithm for global optimization. *J. Math. Comput. Sci* **2015**, *14*, 16–23. [CrossRef]
44. Wang, S.; Wang, M. The strong connectivity of bubble-sort star graphs. *Comput. J.* **2019**, *62*, 715–729.
45. Lalaoui, M.; El Afia, A.; Chiheb, R. A self-tuned simulated annealing algorithm using hidden markov model. *Int. J. Electr. Comput. Eng.* **2018**, *8*, 291–298. [CrossRef]
46. Lalaoui, M.; El Afia, A.; Chiheb, R. Simulated Annealing with Adaptive Neighborhood using Fuzzy Logic Controller. In Proceedings of the International Conference on Learning and Optimization Algorithms: Theory and Applications, New York, NY, USA, 2–5 May 2018; LOPAL '18.
47. Weng, Y.; Pan, Z. Orbital angular momentum based sensing and their applications: A review. *J. Light. Technol.* **2022**, *41*, 2007–2016.
48. Mair, A.; Vaziri, A.; Weihs, G.; Zeilinger, A. Entanglement of the orbital angular momentum states of photons. *Nature* **2001**, *412*, 313–316. [CrossRef] [PubMed]
49. Wang, H.; Mei, S.L. Shannon wavelet precision integration method for pathologic onion image segmentation based on homotopy perturbation technology. *Math. Probl. Eng.* **2014**, *2014*, 601841.
50. Forbes, A.; Dudley, A.; McLaren, M. Creation and detection of optical modes with spatial light modulators. *Adv. Opt. Photonics* **2016**, *8*, 200–227.
51. Ndagano, B.; Perez-Garcia, B.; Roux, F.S.; McLaren, M.; Rosales-Guzman, C.; Zhang, Y.; Mouane, O.; Hernandez-Aranda, R.I.; Konrad, T.; Forbes, A. Characterizing quantum channels with non-separable states of classical light. *Nat. Phys.* **2017**, *13*, 397–402.
52. Mafu, M.; Dudley, A.; Goyal, S.; Giovannini, D.; McLaren, M.; Padgett, M.J.; Konrad, T.; Petruccione, F.; Lütkenhaus, N.; Forbes, A. Higher-dimensional orbital-angular-momentum-based quantum key distribution with mutually unbiased bases. *Phys. Rev. A* **2013**, *88*, 032305.
53. Krenn, M.; Huber, M.; Fickler, R.; Lapkiewicz, R.; Ramelow, S.; Zeilinger, A. Generation and confirmation of a (100×100)-dimensional entangled quantum system. *Proc. Natl. Acad. Sci. USA* **2014**, *111*, 6243–6247.

54. Sit, A.; Bouchard, F.; Fickler, R.; Gagnon-Bischoff, J.; Larocque, H.; Heshami, K.; Elser, D.; Peuntinger, C.; Günthner, K.; Heim, B.; et al. High-dimensional intracity quantum cryptography with structured photons. *Optica* **2017**, *4*, 1006–1010.
55. Fano, U. Description of States in Quantum Mechanics by Density Matrix and Operator Techniques. *Rev. Mod. Phys.* **1957**, *29*, 74–93.
56. James, D.F.V.; Kwiat, P.G.; Munro, W.J.; White, A.G. Measurement of qubits. *Phys. Rev. A* **2001**, *64*, 052312.
57. de Burgh, M.D.; Langford, N.K.; Doherty, A.C.; Gilchrist, A. Choice of measurement sets in qubit tomography. *Phys. Rev. A* **2008**, *78*, 052122.
58. Jack, B.; Leach, J.; Ritsch, H.; Barnett, S.M.; Padgett, M.J.; Franke-Arnold, S. Precise quantum tomography of photon pairs with entangled orbital angular momentum. *New J. Phys.* **2009**, *11*, 103024.
59. Spengler, C.; Huber, M.; Brierley, S.; Adaktylos, T.; Hiesmayr, B.C. Entanglement detection via mutually unbiased bases. *Phys. Rev. A* **2012**, *86*, 022311.
60. Zhou, Y. *Optical Communication with Structured Photons Propagating Through Dynamic, Aberrating Media*; University of Rochester: Rochester, NY, USA, 2021.
61. Bastiaans, M.J. Applications of the Wigner distribution to partially coherent light beams. *Adv. Inf. Opt. Photonics* **2008**, *6*, 27.
62. Kovsh, D.I. *Laser Beam Propagation Through Bulk Nonlinear Media: Numerical Simulation and Experiment*; University of Central Florida: Orlando, FL, USA, 1999.
63. Wang, M.; Lin, Y.; Wang, S. The nature diagnosability of bubble-sort star graphs under the PMC model and MM model. *Int. J. Eng. Appl. Sci.* **2017**, *4*, 2394–3661.
64. Wang, M.; Ren, Y.; Lin, Y.; Wang, S. The tightly super 3-extra connectivity and diagnosability of locally twisted cubes. *Am. J. Comput. Math.* **2017**, *7*, 127–144.
65. Sun, S.; Liu, J.; Sun, S. Hyperspectral subpixel target detection based on interaction subspace model. *Pattern Recognit.* **2023**, *139*, 109464.
66. Wang, R.F.; Su, W.H. The application of deep learning in the whole potato production Chain: A Comprehensive review. *Agriculture* **2024**, *14*, 1225. [CrossRef]
67. Wang, Z.; Wang, R.; Wang, M.; Lai, T.; Zhang, M. Self-supervised transformer-based pre-training method with General Plant Infection dataset. In Proceedings of the Chinese Conference on Pattern Recognition and Computer Vision (PRCV), Urumqi, China, 18–20 October 2024; Springer: Berlin/Heidelberg, Germany, 2024; pp. 189–202.
68. Ni, Y.; Wang, Y.; Xu, W. Recent process of flexible transistor-structured memory. *Small* **2021**, *17*, 1905332.
69. Chen, J.; Wan, C.; Zhan, Q. Engineering photonic angular momentum with structured light: A review. *Adv. Photonics* **2021**, *3*, 064001.
70. Noor, S.K.; Yasin, M.N.M.; Ismail, A.M.; Osman, M.N.; Soh, P.J.; Ramli, N.; Rambe, A.H. A review of orbital angular momentum vortex waves for the next generation wireless communications. *IEEE Access* **2022**, *10*, 89465–89484.
71. Khare, K.; Lochab, P.; Senthilkumaran, P. *Orbital Angular Momentum States of Light: Propagation Through Atmospheric Turbulence*; IOP Publishing: Bristol, UK, 2024.
72. Padgett, M.; Arlt, J.; Simpson, N.; Allen, L. An experiment to observe the intensity and phase structure of Laguerre-Gaussian laser modes. *Am. J. Phys.* **1996**, *64*, 77–81.
73. Mardan Dezfouli, A. Generation and Detection of Optical Vortex Beam. Ph.D. Thesis, Department of Physics, Faculty of Science, University of Zagreb, Zagreb, Croatia, 2024.
74. Bae, J.Y.; Jeon, C.; Pae, K.H.; Kim, C.M.; Kim, H.S.; Han, I.; Yeo, W.J.; Jeong, B.; Jeon, M.; Lee, D.H.; et al. Generation of low-order Laguerre-Gaussian beams using hybrid-machined reflective spiral phase plates for intense laser-plasma interactions. *Results Phys.* **2020**, *19*, 103499.
75. Kovalev, A.; Kotlyar, V.; Porfirev, A. Asymmetric laguerre-gaussian beams. *Phys. Rev. A* **2016**, *93*, 063858.
76. Ghaderi Goran Abad, M.; Mahmoudi, M. Laguerre-Gaussian modes generated vector beam via nonlinear magneto-optical rotation. *Sci. Rep.* **2021**, *11*, 5972.
77. Longman, A.; Fedosejevs, R. Mode conversion efficiency to Laguerre-Gaussian OAM modes using spiral phase optics. *Opt. Express* **2017**, *25*, 17382–17392.
78. Pampaloni, F.; Enderlein, J. Gaussian, hermite-gaussian, and laguerre-gaussian beams: A primer. *arXiv* **2004**, arXiv:physics/0410021.
79. Kim, H.C.; Lee, Y.H. Hermite–Gaussian and Laguerre–Gaussian beams beyond the paraxial approximation. *Opt. Commun.* **1999**, *169*, 9–16.
80. Saghafi, S.; Sheppard, C.; Piper, J. Characterising elegant and standard Hermite–Gaussian beam modes. *Opt. Commun.* **2001**, *191*, 173–179. [CrossRef]
81. Casperson, L.W.; Tovar, A.A. Hermite–sinusoidal-Gaussian beams in complex optical systems. *J. Opt. Soc. Am. A* **1998**, *15*, 954–961. [CrossRef]
82. Laabs, H. Propagation of Hermite-Gaussian-beams beyond the paraxial approximation. *Opt. Commun.* **1998**, *147*, 1–4. [CrossRef]

83. Hofer, L.; Jones, L.; Goedert, J.; Dragone, R. Hermite–Gaussian mode detection via convolution neural networks. *J. Opt. Soc. Am. A* **2019**, *36*, 936–943. [CrossRef]
84. Luo, Y.Z.; Tang, G.J.; Zhou, L.N. Simulated annealing for solving near-optimal low-thrust orbit transfer. *Eng. Optim.* **2005**, *37*, 201–216. [CrossRef]
85. Delahaye, D.; Chaimatanan, S.; Mongeau, M. Simulated annealing: From basics to applications. In *Handbook of Metaheuristics*; Springer: Cham, Switzerland, 2019; pp. 1–35.
86. Burke, E.K.; Burke, E.K.; Kendall, G.; Kendall, G. *Search Methodologies: Introductory Tutorials in Optimization and Decision Support Techniques*; Springer: Berlin/Heidelberg, Germany, 2014.
87. Shakouri G., H.; Shojaee, K.; T. Behnam, M. Investigation on the choice of the initial temperature in the simulated annealing: A mushy state SA for TSP. In Proceedings of the 2009 17th Mediterranean Conference on Control and Automation, Thessaloniki, Greece, 24–26 June 2009; pp. 1050–1055.
88. Glover, F.W.; Kochenberger, G.A. *Handbook of metaheuristics*; Springer Science & Business Media: Berlin/Heidelberg, Germany, 2003; Volume 57.
89. Wang, H.; Zhang, X.; Mei, S. Shannon-Cosine Wavelet Precise Integration Method for Locust Slice Image Mixed Denoising. *Math. Probl. Eng.* **2020**, *2020*, 4989735. [CrossRef]
90. Carpenter, J.; Wilkinson, T.D. Graphics processing unit–accelerated holography by simulated annealing. *Opt. Eng.* **2010**, *49*, 095801. [CrossRef]
91. Gallego-Ruiz, R.; Álvarez-Castaño, M.; Herrera-Ramírez, J.; Correa, N. Optimization of phase masks using simulated annealing algorithm for mode conversion. *J. Phys. Conf. Ser.* **2020**, *1547*, 012007. [CrossRef]
92. Berdagué, S.; Facq, P. Mode division multiplexing in optical fibers. *Appl. Opt.* **1982**, *21*, 1950–1955. [CrossRef]
93. Fang, L.; Zuo, H.; Pang, L.; Yang, Z.; Zhang, X.; Zhu, J. Image reconstruction through thin scattering media by simulated annealing algorithm. *Opt. Lasers Eng.* **2018**, *106*, 105–110. [CrossRef]
94. Davis, J.A.; Cottrell, D.M.; Campos, J.; Yzuel, M.J.; Moreno, I. Encoding amplitude information onto phase-only filters. *Appl. Opt.* **1999**, *38*, 5004–5013. [PubMed]
95. Bolduc, E.; Bent, N.; Santamato, E.; Karimi, E.; Boyd, R.W. Exact solution to simultaneous intensity and phase encryption with a single phase-only hologram. *Opt. Lett.* **2013**, *38*, 3546–3549.
96. Arrizón, V.; Ruiz, U.; Carrada, R.; González, L.A. Pixelated phase computer holograms for the accurate encoding of scalar complex fields. *J. Opt. Soc. Am. A* **2007**, *24*, 3500–3507.
97. Lima, G.; Neves, L.; Guzmán, R.; Gómez, E.S.; Nogueira, W.; Delgado, A.; Vargas, A.; Saavedra, C. Experimental quantum tomography of photonic qudits via mutually unbiased basis. *Opt. Express* **2011**, *19*, 3542–3552. [PubMed]
98. Adamson, R.; Steinberg, A.M. Improving quantum state estimation with mutually unbiased bases. *Phys. Rev. Lett.* **2010**, *105*, 030406. [CrossRef]
99. Fernández-Pérez, A.; Klimov, A.; Saavedra, C. Quantum process reconstruction based on mutually unbiased basis. *Phys. Rev. A* **2011**, *83*, 052332.
100. Giovannini, D.; Romero, J.; Leach, J.; Dudley, A.; Forbes, A.; Padgett, M.J. Characterization of high-dimensional entangled systems via mutually unbiased measurements. *Phys. Rev. Lett.* **2013**, *110*, 143601.
101. Coles, P.J.; Berta, M.; Tomamichel, M.; Wehner, S. Entropic uncertainty relations and their applications. *Rev. Mod. Phys.* **2017**, *89*, 015002.
102. Padgett, M.J.; Courtial, J. Poincaré-sphere equivalent for light beams containing orbital angular momentum. *Opt. Lett.* **1999**, *24*, 430–432. [CrossRef]
103. Toninelli, E.; Ndagano, B.; Vallés, A.; Sephton, B.; Nape, I.; Ambrosio, A.; Capasso, F.; Padgett, M.J.; Forbes, A. Concepts in quantum state tomography and classical implementation with intense light: A tutorial. *Adv. Opt. Photonics* **2019**, *11*, 67–134. [CrossRef]
104. Wu, K.D.; Streltsov, A.; Regula, B.; Xiang, G.Y.; Li, C.F.; Guo, G.C. Experimental progress on quantum coherence: Detection, quantification, and manipulation. *Adv. Quantum Technol.* **2021**, *4*, 2100040.
105. Krenn, M.; Malik, M.; Erhard, M.; Zeilinger, A. Orbital angular momentum of photons and the entanglement of Laguerre–Gaussian modes. *Philos. Trans. R. Soc. A Math. Phys. Eng. Sci.* **2017**, *375*, 20150442.
106. Jullien, T.; Roulleau, P.; Roche, B.; Cavanna, A.; Jin, Y.; Glattli, D. Quantum tomography of an electron. *Nature* **2014**, *514*, 603–607. [PubMed]
107. Maire, E.; Withers, P.J. Quantitative X-ray tomography. *Int. Mater. Rev.* **2014**, *59*, 1–43.
108. Kokail, C.; van Bijnen, R.; Elben, A.; Vermersch, B.; Zoller, P. Entanglement Hamiltonian tomography in quantum simulation. *Nat. Phys.* **2021**, *17*, 936–942.
109. Cozzolino, D.; Da Lio, B.; Bacco, D.; Oxenløwe, L.K. High-dimensional quantum communication: benefits, progress, and future challenges. *Adv. Quantum Technol.* **2019**, *2*, 1900038.

110. Thekkadath, G.; England, D.; Bouchard, F.; Zhang, Y.; Kim, M.; Sussman, B. Intensity interferometry for holography with quantum and classical light. *Sci. Adv.* **2023**, *9*, eadh1439.
111. Pachava, S.; Dharmavarapu, R.; Vijayakumar, A.; Jayakumar, S.; Manthalkar, A.; Dixit, A.; Viswanathan, N.K.; Srinivasan, B.; Bhattacharya, S. Generation and decomposition of scalar and vector modes carrying orbital angular momentum: A review. *Opt. Eng.* **2020**, *59*, 041205.
112. Angelsky, O.; Bekshaev, A.Y.; Vasnetsov, M.; Zenkova, C.Y.; Maksimyak, P.; Zheng, J. Optical phase singularities: Physical nature, manifestations and applications. *Front. Phys.* **2022**, *10*, 1060787.
113. Defienne, H.; Ndagano, B.; Lyons, A.; Faccio, D. Polarization entanglement-enabled quantum holography. *Nat. Phys.* **2021**, *17*, 591–597.
114. Erhard, M.; Fickler, R.; Krenn, M.; Zeilinger, A. Twisted photons: New quantum perspectives in high dimensions. *Light Sci. Appl.* **2018**, *7*, 17146.
115. Ni, Y.; Yang, L.; Feng, J.; Liu, J.; Sun, L.; Xu, W. Flexible optoelectronic neural transistors with broadband spectrum sensing and instant electrical processing for multimodal neuromorphic computing. *SmartMat* **2023**, *4*, e1154.

symmetry

MDPI

Article

Dynamic State Equations and Distributed Blockchain Control: A Differential Game Model for Optimal Emission Trajectories in Shipping Networks

Zhongmiao Sun [1,*], Yike Xi [1], Baoli Shi [2,*] and Jinrong Liu [3]

1 School of Economics and Management, Shanghai Maritime University, Shanghai 201306, China; 202430710091@stu.shmtu.edu.cn
2 School of Management, Hangzhou Dianzi University, Hangzhou 310018, China
3 School of Business and Management, Shanghai Urban Construction Vocational College, Shanghai 201415, China; liujinrong@succ.edu.cn
* Correspondence: zmsun@shmtu.edu.cn (Z.S.); baolishi@hdu.edu.cn (B.S.)

Abstract: The shipping industry, a cornerstone of global trade, faces emissions reduction challenges amid tightening environmental policies. Blockchain technology, leveraging distributed symmetric architectures, enhances supply chain transparency by reducing information asymmetry, yet its dynamic interplay with emissions strategies remains underexplored. This study employs symmetry-driven differential game theory to model four blockchain scenarios in port-shipping networks: no blockchain (*N*), port-led (*PB*), shipping company-led (*CB*), and a joint platform (*FB*). By solving Hamilton–Jacobi–Bellman equations, we derive optimal emissions reduction efforts, green investments, and blockchain strategies under symmetric and asymmetric decision-making frameworks. Results show blockchain adoption improves emissions reduction and service quality under cost thresholds, with port-led systems maximizing low-cost profits and shipping firms gaining asymmetrically in high-freight contexts. Joint platforms achieve symmetry in profit distribution through fee-trust synergy, enabling win–win outcomes. Integrating graph-theoretic principles, we have designed dynamic state equations for emissions and service levels, segmenting shippers by low-carbon preferences. This work bridges dynamic emissions strategies with blockchain's network symmetry, fostering economic–environmental synergies to advance sustainable maritime supply chains.

Keywords: distributed blockchain; shipping networks; differential game; symmetric architectures; emissions reduction; dynamic state equations

1. Introduction

1.1. Background and Motivation

As the backbone of global commerce, shipping dominates over 80% of worldwide freight, driving trade, economic expansion, and societal advancement [1,2]. The symmetrically interconnected network of ports (nodes) and shipping routes (edges) underpins global trade, yet its structural symmetry in connectivity contrasts sharply with operational asymmetries in environmental impact. Ship operations emit pollutants and greenhouse gases disproportionately, creating ecological imbalances [3]. The International Maritime Organization (IMO) reports annual CO_2 emissions exceeding one billion metric tons (3% of global CO_2 output), which are projected to rise to 5% by 2050 [4]. The EU's 2024 Emissions Trading System mandates CO_2 monitoring for vessels over 5000 tons, challenging the industry to reconcile network symmetry (efficient connectivity) with operational asymmetry (uneven emissions). However, the multi-actor nature of the shipping network leads to significant information asymmetry and a dilemma for emissions reduction strategies. Ports have difficulty in tracking real-time ship emissions data, shipping companies lack trust in port green infrastructure, and cargo owners are unable to verify carbon footprint declarations in the transportation chain. This information barrier not only creates the risk of "greenwashing" but also makes it difficult to implement a coordinated emissions reduction mechanism. In this context, there is an urgent need for a technical tool that can realize real-time data sharing, tamper-proof process, and accurate traceability of responsibility, in order to solve the trust and collaboration problems in the emissions reduction network.

Blockchain technology, with its distributed ledger and smart contract characteristics, provides a new path for building a cross-organizational and highly credible carbon emissions monitoring network. For example, the Hong Kong GSBN-COSCO initiative (launched in 2024) employs blockchain to issue traceable green certificates, enhancing transparency in a graph-like supply chain where nodes (ports) and edges (routes) must align for sustainability. This technology enables combinatorial optimization of emissions strategies, akin to fault diagnosis in interconnected networks [5], identifying critical nodes (e.g., high-emission ports) and optimizing edge-level coordination [6]. However, decarbonization costs [7] and interdependencies between ports and shipping firms introduce asymmetric incentives, necessitating symmetric collaboration to balance economic and environmental objectives [8].

In the context of the increasingly stringent environmental policies of the IMO, green investments by port and shipping enterprises have become critical to enhancing competitiveness [9]. Some scholars have analyzed shipping companies' "on-chain" decisions by constructing a Stackelberg static equilibrium [10]; others have discussed introducing a carbon tax or a carbon trading mechanism [11] and considering consumers' preferences for logistics services and information [12]. These studies further provide references for promoting blockchain technology investment in emissions reduction strategies. Existing research on blockchain applications primarily focuses on technological roles and implementation challenges [13], neglecting the topic of integration into dynamic symmetry–asymmetry trade-offs within port-shipping networks. Therefore, by exploring blockchain's application in this context, we address a critical research gap. Our work not only leverages graph-theoretic symmetry to model emissions reduction trajectories but also introduces algorithmic complexity principles to optimize node-level (port) and edge-level (shipping route) decisions. This approach aligns with the restricted connectivity challenges of multiprocessor-like logistics systems, advancing the diagnosability of emission-critical nodes while harmonizing economic–environmental symmetry in maritime supply chains.

1.2. Research Questions and Innovations

Given the dual challenges of emissions reduction and digital transformation in the global shipping industry, we address the symmetry–asymmetry interplay in blockchain-driven supply chains through the following research questions:

Q1: How can symmetry-driven dynamic strategies enhance emissions reductions and blockchain investments, accounting for shippers' asymmetric preferences (low-carbon vs. non-low-carbon) and their impact on node-edge interactions (ports as nodes, shipping routes as edges) in maritime networks?

Q2: How does blockchain's distributed symmetric architecture reshape optimal emissions decisions, and what are the dynamic trajectories of emissions levels, service quality, demand, and profits under graph-theoretic equilibria (e.g., Stackelberg models with asymmetric leader–follower roles)?

Q3: What threshold conditions (e.g., cost symmetry, profit asymmetry) enable blockchain investments to achieve win–win outcomes for ports and shipping firms, and how do factors like restricted connectivity (e.g., port-shipping dependencies) and node-level diagnosability (e.g., emission-critical ports) influence these thresholds?

Q4: Which member (port or shipping firm) should lead blockchain investments to maximize network-wide symmetry in emissions reduction and service levels, considering their asymmetric roles as nodes (decision hubs) vs. edges (operational links) in the supply chain graph?

To address these questions, we developed a Stackelberg model within a shipping supply chain involving a port operator (leader) and a shipping firm (follower), framing their interactions as asymmetric node–edge dynamics in a graph-theoretic network (ports as nodes, shipping routes as edges). The port entity establishes green investment criteria, while shipping entities optimize emissions reduction initiatives under restricted connectivity constraints. We analyze four blockchain scenarios (*N*, *PB*, *CB*, *FB*) through sensitivity, comparative, and numerical analyses, incorporating blockchain green certification levels to assess how consumer trust symmetry influences emissions reductions.

The main innovations of this paper are threefold, as follows:

(1) Research Content: We pioneer the integration of blockchain investment levels with emissions strategies, segmenting cargo owners into asymmetric preference types (low/non-low-carbon) to model node-level heterogeneity in a graph-like supply chain. By unveiling the impact of shipping costs, cargo owner nature, and low-carbon coefficients, we demonstrate that port-led blockchain achieves profit symmetry under low operational costs, while shipping firms leverage asymmetric service sensitivity in high-freight environments. Joint platforms balance symmetry–asymmetry trade-offs through fee-trust synergy, akin to optimizing restricted connectivity in multiprocessor systems.

(2) Research Perspective: Transitioning from static to dynamic analysis, we design two symmetry-driven state equations for emissions reduction (node dynamics) and service quality (edge dynamics), revealing time-proportional convergence to symmetric steady states—mirroring graph neural networks (GNNs) in resolving algorithmic complexity for interconnected systems. This approach diagnoses critical nodes (e.g., high-emission ports) and optimizes edge-level coordination, advancing fault diagnosability in maritime networks.

(3) Research Methodology: We introduce optimal control theory to shipping supply chains, solving Hamilton–Jacobi–Bellman equations to derive emissions trajectories. This framework integrates combinatorial algorithms for node–edge optimization, addressing uncertainty in graph properties (e.g., fluctuating demand) and enhancing network reliability through dynamic symmetry–asymmetry equilibria.

1.3. Paper Organization and Structure

This paper is structured as follows. The literature is examined in Section 2. In Sections 3 and 4, hypotheses are formulated and models are developed. Section 5 presents parametric sensitivity analysis and comparative analysis of model results. Section 6 introduces the shipper green trust coefficient, designs new shipper utility and demand functions, and reanalyzes blockchain scenarios' impacts on shipping supply chain optimization under revised settings, expanding research boundaries to better align with real-world conditions. Section 7 employs MATLAB R2023a for numerical experiments, validating theoretical conclusions through empirical results to enhance research credibility. Section 8 summarizes this paper' s contributions and discusses their implications. Note: All proofs are in Supplementary S1, and the critical points are in Supplementary S2.

2. Literature Review

The available research delves into the impact of blockchain tech on cutting emissions in the port and shipping supply chain. As such, we distill the pertinent literature by examining three main avenues: the use of blockchain, emissions mitigation tactics within the shipping sector, and type of shippers.

2.1. The Application of Blockchain Technology

Academic research has expanded blockchain's use in the shipping industry (Liu et al., [14]; Xu et al., [15]; Li et al., [16]). Alahmadi et al. [17] examined the integration of blockchain into the port and shipping industry to facilitate digital transformation, finding that blockchain can streamline financial and documentation workflows. Chen and Yang [18] analyzed collaborative decision-making among supply chain stakeholders before and after blockchain adoption, examining data-sharing patterns and consumer concerns about information accuracy. Lorenz-Meyer et al. [19] highlighted blockchain's role in data sharing as a solution to challenges faced by maritime SMEs and the broader industry. Zhao et al. [20] revealed the role of blockchain services during port hours of operation, providing new ways to solve port congestion based on economic and environmental benefits, helping consumers to improve the service experience. Wang et al. [21] investigated shipping firms' blockchain investment tactics within competitive frameworks and their influence on consumer gains and societal welfare in various contexts. In addition, recent advances in graph-theoretic connectivity and diagnosability (Wang et al., [22,23]) provide theoretical foundations for analyzing blockchain's role in enhancing network reliability in shipping supply chains. For instance, studies on tightly super 3-extra connectivity in locally twisted cubes [22] and nature diagnosability in bubble-sort star graphs [23] align with blockchain's capacity to address node-level inefficiencies (e.g., port congestion) and edge-level coordination challenges (e.g., route optimization).

Moreover, researchers have investigated blockchain' s integration into various supply chain sectors. Babaei et al. [24] employed data-informed optimization techniques to evaluate the practicality of integrating blockchain technology into sustainable energy supply networks. Henrichs et al. [25] suggested an integrated model for utilizing blockchain in food and drug supply chain management, enhancing the prevention of low-quality product infiltration. Heydari [26] investigated the potential of blockchain to mitigate inefficiencies within construction supply chain coordination and teamwork. Meanwhile, Wang et al. [27] design a blockchain-based low-carbon incentive mechanism, enabling decentralized low-carbon management in building projects. Vu Nguyen Huynh Anh [28] employs organizational modeling techniques to develop blockchain smart contracts, demonstrating supply chain finance system processes and management principles. Furthermore, research on expanded k-ary n-cubes (Wang et al., [29]) highlights the importance of restricted connectivity in multiprocessor-like logistics systems, offering insights into blockchain's potential to streamline port-shipping interdependencies through decentralized data symmetry. Established studies have systematically explored the application of blockchain in different industries, but its potential for dynamic collaborative emissions reduction has not been fully explored. This provides space for this study to analyze the symmetric collaboration and asymmetric decision-making of port and shipping companies in blockchain scenarios through differential games.

2.2. Operational Strategies for Emissions Reduction in the Shipping Supply Chain

Our study directly relates to emissions reduction, with shipping emissions playing a significant role in global air pollutants [30]. Since the signing of the United Nations Framework Convention on Climate Change in 1992, the shipping industry' s emissions reduction strategies have garnered worldwide attention [31]. The goal of the Convention is to cut greenhouse gas emissions and drive carbon reduction efforts across all sectors, including shipping [32].

In the shipping supply chain, Pasha et al. [33] analyzed carbon emissions generated during ship operations, addressed major challenges to liner transportation strategies, and provided management insights. From a sustainable development perspective, emissions should be reduced through improved ship design and enhanced ocean governance policies [34,35]. Ji et al. [36] highlighted the dependency of emissions reduction strategies in fluctuating carbon quota markets on the performance of energy firms in cutting emissions. Wang and Mao [37] proposed a navigation optimization method to adjust marine engine power, reducing fuel consumption and air emissions while addressing three-dimensional route planning challenges. The connectivity and matching preclusion principles in leaf-sort graphs (Wang et al., [38]) resonate with optimizing emission-critical nodes (e.g., high-pollution ports) and edges (shipping routes), ensuring algorithmic reliability in dynamic emissions reduction models. These principles complement studies on navigation optimization [37] by addressing structural vulnerabilities in maritime networks. Zhu et al. [39] investigated optimal manufacturing approaches for both new and remanufactured goods within mixed-carbon regulatory frameworks, examining how production flexibility and certified emissions reduction (CER) mechanisms interact. Koohathongsumrit et al. [40] focused on the issue of routing in the intermodal supply chain and developed interactive freight planning and transportation policies. Their study analyzed key variables influencing operational decisions and overall carbon footprints under these hybrid environmental policies. Concurrently, Chen et al. [8] studied transport capacity deployment optimization, offering actionable insights for shipping companies to improve energy efficiency and emissions reduction. Additionally, Hoang et al. [4] pursued smart strategies leveraging renewable energy, clean fuels, smart grids, and energy-efficient measures to achieve emissions reduction targets.

In addition, scholars have explored dynamic and static decision-making in supply chains. In dynamic decision-making contexts, Zhang et al. [41] studied a two-tier supply chain involving a carbon-reducing manufacturer and a retailer, where emissions reduction factors exhibited dynamic changes. Ma and He [42] derived optimal green technology investments under three scenarios by constructing a Stackelberg game. Wu and Yang [43] incorporated consumer low-carbon preferences into a dynamic optimization model to analyze emissions reduction under decentralized and centralized decisions. Kang et al. [44] used differential game theory to analyze blockchain adoption and eco-friendly production in sustainable supply chains over time. Ma et al. [45] integrated cold chain logistics characteristics into a differential game model, studying preservation technology investments and emissions reduction behaviors dynamically. Regarding static decision-making, Yang et al. [46] developed Stackelberg and Nash game models to evaluate sustainable technology options within a port logistics network governed by cap-and-trade regulations. Yu et al. [47] investigated vertical and horizontal emissions reduction efforts alongside pricing strategies. Rashid et al. [48] employed a hybrid multi-decision approach and, through sensitivity analysis, pointed out the potential for future integration with fuzzy theory or extension to other decision-making scenarios. Concurrently, differential game models were utilized to assess government incentives' impact on enhancing emissions reduction levels (Chen et al., [49]; Meng et al., [50]).

The existing literature proposes diversified emissions reduction schemes from both static decision-making and dynamic optimization perspectives, but it has generally ignored two key issues. First, the long-term effects of emissions reduction strategies are limited by the coordination efficiency of nodes (ports) and edges (shipping companies), while established dynamic models do not analyze the symmetry constraints of the network structure in conjunction with graph theory; and second, the threshold effect of blockchain technology on the cost of emissions reduction has not been quantified. This study incorporates the above gaps into the dynamic optimization framework by designing state equations containing blockchain green trust coefficients. Additionally, the collaborative role among sectors such as ships, ports, and shipping firms in the emissions reduction process remains underexplored.

2.3. Type of Shippers

The low-carbon preferences of consumers have emerged as a crucial factor shaping emissions reduction. Chen et al. [8] derived critical insights into blockchain applications in shipping supply chains based on consumer information preferences. Yang and Chen [51] conducted a study analyzing the impact of retailers' profit-sharing and cost-splitting approaches on manufacturers' green technology investments and bottom-line performance. Zhou and Li [52] analyzed carbon reduction factors for ports and ships under carbon tax policies and consumer green preferences. Their research factored in two key market forces: growing consumer eco-consciousness and government-imposed carbon pricing mechanisms. Zhou et al. [53] employed a dynamic differential game model to assess long-term supply chain emissions in relation to low-carbon consumer preferences. Cheng et al. [54] applied an improved projection algorithm to solve game models and conducted static analyses of consumer preferences through numerical simulations. Ghosh et al. [55] demonstrated that consumer low-carbon preferences strongly influence supply chain order volumes and profit distributions. Regarding other aspects, Cai et al. [56] explored blockchain's dual effects on market demand and consumer privacy concerns through game-theoretic models. Yu et al. [57] discussed the coordination of pro-poor supply chains involving altruistic retailers, rural cooperatives, and blockchain adoption. Research has examined the impact of consumer eco-consciousness on pricing and manufacturing decisions in the electric vehicle supply chain [58,59].

Although scholars are aware of the role of low-carbon preference shippers in driving emissions reductions, existing categorizations are oversimplified: most studies default to shippers' homogeneity and fail to consider the feedback effect of their green trust differences on blockchain adoption. This omission makes it difficult for the model to explain why the same blockchain investment produces vastly different abatement effects under different shipper structures. This study fills this theoretical gap by disaggregating low-carbon preference/non-low-carbon preference and introducing a trust coefficient.

2.4. Research Gap

In summary, research in the aforementioned areas has achieved significant progress. Nonetheless, an extensive survey of the available research highlights numerous areas requiring further investigation. Table 1 highlights the distinctions between our study and prior works. Specifically, our study diverges from prior research in four main ways. First, our paper is primarily oriented towards the shipping industry. Although some literature has considered other factors, it has not focused on the shipping industry. Second, regarding modeling dynamic emissions reduction operations, we construct two state equations (emissions reduction level and shipping service level), while existing works often consider only emissions reduction dynamics. Third, we incorporate blockchain investment as a decision variable and investigate how it affects shipping supply chain management. Finally, we classify consumers into low-carbon-preference and non-low-carbon-preference groups, explicitly quantifying blockchain's direct impact on emissions reduction through a shipper green trust coefficient.

Table 1. Summary of some existing related literature.

Authors	Shipping Supply Chain	Dynamic Operations	Blockchain Adoption	Type of Shippers		Decision-Making	
				Non Low-Carbon Preference	Emission Reduction	Blockchain Investment	Low-Carbon Preference
Wang et al. [21]	√		√	√		√	
Liu et al. [14]	√		√	√			
Ji et al. [36]		√			√		
Zhu et al. [39]		√			√		
Wu and Yang [43]		√			√		√
Kang et al. [44]		√	√	√	√		
Yang et al. [46]	√					√	
Chen et al. [49]	√		√	√			√
Yang ang chen [51]					√		√
Zhou and Li [52]	√				√		√
Zhou et al. [53]		√			√		√
Cai et al. [56]			√				√
This paper	√	√	√	√	√	√	√

3. Description of the Problem and Assumptions

3.1. Description of the Problem

Green shipping is an unavoidable direction in the development of the international shipping industry, and governments, international organizations, ports, shipping companies, and relevant stakeholders are actively promoting this transformation. Currently, port companies mainly build green ports by investing in energy-saving and emission-reduction technologies such as 'oil-to-electricity' shore power and liquefied natural gas (LNG) terminals. To cut down on energy consumption and reduce their carbon footprint, shipping lines opt to harness shore power when docking, switch to low-sulfur fuels, or power their vessels with eco-friendly alternatives like methanol, or hydrogen.

As shown in Figure 1, this paper considers a green shipping supply chain system consisting of one green port (denoted by subscript P) and one shipping company (denoted by subscript S). There are two types of shippers in the shipping market; one type is low-carbon preference shippers with environmental awareness, and the other is non-low-carbon preference shippers without environmental awareness. To foster eco-friendly and sustainable growth within the shipping sector and boost the appeal of shippers who prioritize low-carbon choices, ports and shipping firms are incentivized to invest in green initiatives and undertake emission-cutting measures.

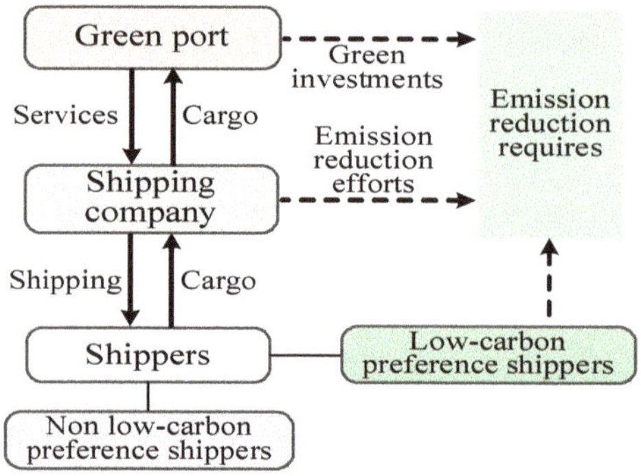

Figure 1. Structure of the green shipping supply chain.

In addition, driven by digital transformation, blockchain technology is fundamentally changing the operational mode of the shipping industry through its decentralization, tamper-proof data, and transparent transactions, such as improving port clearance efficiency, enhancing shipping logistics transparency, and improving shipping service levels. To explore investment strategies involving blockchain technology in the context of green shipping, we consider four blockchain scenarios, as shown in Figure 2, including: (1) Scenario *N*, the traditional shipping supply chain without blockchain; (2) Scenario *PB*, where the port is responsible for investing and establishing blockchain technology, with the shipping company participating; (3) Scenario *CB*, where the shipping company is responsible for investing in and establishing blockchain technology, with the port participating; (4) Scenario *FB*, where the port and shipping companies jointly participate in a shipping logistics blockchain platform.

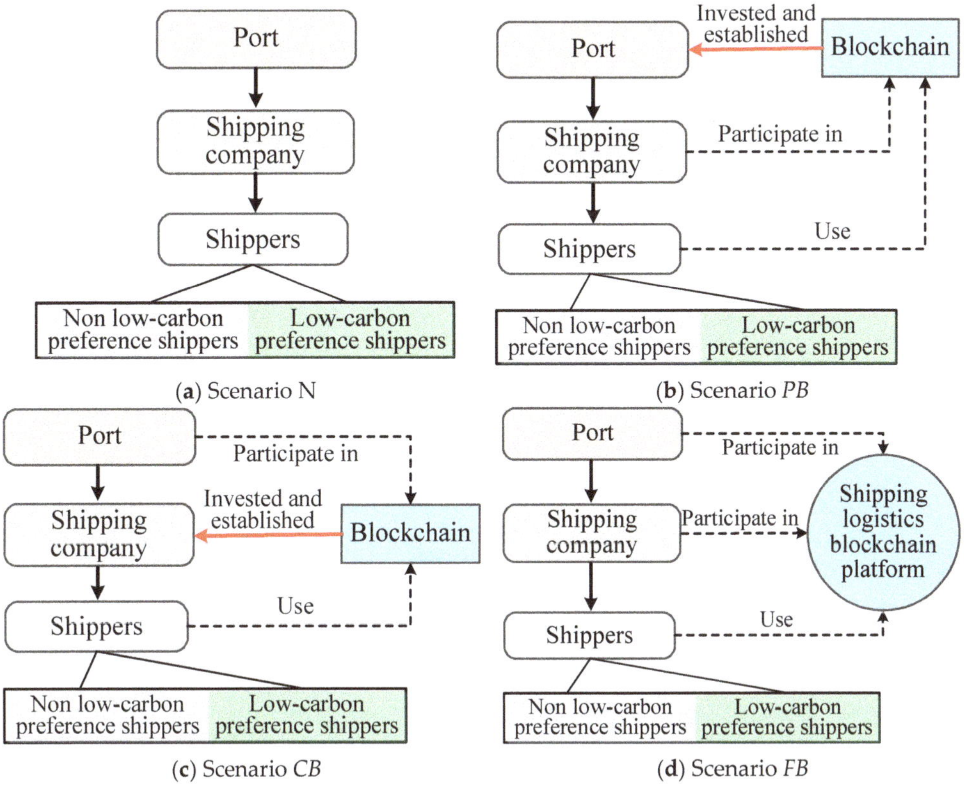

Figure 2. Four typical blockchain scenarios.

This paper characterizes the structural symmetry and decision-making asymmetry of the shipping network from the perspective of graph theory. As shown in Figure 2, the topology of the traditional shipping network (Structure A) contains two types of node-edge relationships. In the physical network, the nodes are ports and the edges are the routes operated by shipping companies. The structural symmetry is reflected in the connection efficiency between ports, but the decision-making asymmetry stems from the differences in emissions reduction targets and investment rights and responsibilities between ports and shipping companies. In the information network, the nodes are ports and shipping companies, and the edges are supply chain collaboration relationships. Their symmetry is limited by information transparency, while the introduction of blockchain technology will reconstruct the network topology. In Structure B, the shipping logistics blockchain platform, as a newly added super node, is embedded in the original network (Figure 2d). Through the consortium chain protocol, it establishes a two-way trust edge with all ports and shipping companies, forming a multi-center symmetric architecture. This topological transformation enables the traditional hierarchical channel strategy to evolve into a distributed collaborative decision-making model.

Under the framework of differential games, the graph theory characteristics of the network structure affect the equilibrium strategy in the following ways. Regarding node diagnosticality, the addition of blockchain platform nodes enhances the network's ability to identify high-emission ports (key nodes), and optimizes the nodal emissions reduction input through the dynamic state equation. In terms of edge coordination, the information symmetry driven by blockchain reduces the coordination cost between ports (nodes) and shipping companies (edges), transforming the game equilibrium from a non-cooperative Nash equilibrium to a Pareto-effective symmetrical cooperative equilibrium. Connectivity constraints in the traditional structure (Figure 2a–c) include restricted edge connections leading to local optima, while structure B (Figure 2d) extends global connectivity through cross-organizational smart contracts, supporting the graph neural network optimization of multi-party collaborative emissions reduction paths. The dynamic evolution of this network topology reveals differences in channel strategies under different blockchain scenarios; port dominance enhances node centrality, shipping dominance optimizes edge-level responses, while the joint platform achieves network-level symmetrical coordination through supernodes.

3.2. Model Assumptions

This study examines decision-making on emissions mitigation and blockchain investment in ports and shipping firms across varied contexts. Table 2 presents the model symbols and corresponding descriptions for simplified reference and analysis.

Based on the above description, the main assumptions of this paper are as follows:

Assumption 1. *We consider that emissions reduction in the shipping supply chain is a variable process, and the emissions reduction per unit of output mainly depends on the green investment of the port and the emissions reduction effort of the shipping company. In practice, the Port of Rotterdam has verified such dynamic synergy effects through green infrastructure such as shore power facilities and LNG refueling stations, in coordination with Maersk's fleet's adoption of low-carbon fuels and speed optimization. Based on the classical Nerlove–Arrow model (Nerlove et al., [60]) and referencing the existing literature (Meng et al., [50]; Zhu et al., [61]), it is assumed that the emissions reduction level (ERL) E(t) of the shipping supply chain at time t satisfies the following equation of state:*

$$dE(t) = u \cdot a(t)dt + \theta \cdot g(t)dt - \sigma \cdot E(t)dt,\ E(0) = E_0 \tag{1}$$

where a(t) and g(t) respectively represent the emissions reduction efforts (ERE) of the shipping company and the green investment level (GIL) of the port; u and θ, respectively reflect the impact of port GRL and shipping company ERE on the ERL of the shipping supply chain; $\sigma > 0$ indicates the attenuation rate of ERL, which may be attributed to the lack of emissions reduction awareness among managers, natural wear, and tear of emissions reduction equipment, etc. Furthermore, we assume that the initial emissions reduction level at time 0 is E(0) = E_0.

Table 2. Model symbols and descriptions.

Symbol	Description
t	Time, $t \in [0, +\infty)$
$b(t)$	Blockchain investment level (BIL) at time t
$a(t)$	The shipping company's emissions reduction efforts (ERE) at time t
$g(t)$	The port's green investment level (GIL) at time t
$E(t)$	Emissions reduction level (ERL) in the shipping supply chain at time t
σ	Attenuation rate of ERL
E_0	Initial emissions reductions level in the shipping supply chain, $E(0) = E_0$
λ	Channel preference coefficient of shippers utilizing shipping logistics blockchain platform
u	Influence factor of the shipping company ERE on ERL
θ	Influence factor of the port GIL on ERL
$S(t)$	The shipping service level (SSL) under blockchain technology at time t
S_0	Initial (without blockchain) shipping service level, $S(0) = S_0$
τ	Attenuation rate of SSL
φ	Influence factor of the BIL on ERL
α	Proportion of low-carbon-preference shippers
v	Valuation of shipping services by shippers, $v \sim U(0, 1)$
p	Shipping service price
r	Port service fee
β	The sensitivity of shippers to shipping services
γ	Low-carbon preference of shippers
m	Green trust coefficient of shippers on ERL
ρ	Discount rate
$D(t)$	Shipping demand at time t
k, h, η	Cost coefficients of GIL, ERE and BIL in the shipping supply chian
ω	Unit operating cost of blockchain
c_0	The unit operating cost of the port company
c_1	The unit operating cost of the shipping company
c_2	The unit operating cost of the shipping logistics blockchain platform
c_b	Blockchain usage fee charged by shipping logistics blockchain platform
π_P	Total expected profit of port company
π_C	Total expected profit of shipping company
π_F	Total expected profit of shipping logistics blockchain platform
V_P	Expected discounted profit of port company
V_C	Expected discounted profit of shipping company
V_F	Expected discounted profit of shipping logistics blockchain platform

Assumption 2. *Previous studies have shown that blockchain technology can create blockchain electronic bills of lading with permanent data records between ports, shipping companies, and shippers. For example, the GSBN platform in Hong Kong has reduced customs clearance time through blockchain bills of lading. This electronic bill of lading not only improves the clearance efficiency of shippers at ports, but also enhances the transparency of shipping logistics information, overall enhancing the shipper's shipping service experience (e.g., Xin et al., [15]; Wang et al., [21]; Li et al., [62]). Therefore, this paper assumes that the dynamic evolution of shipping service level (SSL) driven by blockchain technology is as follows:*

$$dS(t) = \varphi \cdot b(t)dt - \tau \cdot S(t)dt,\ S(0) = S_0 \tag{2}$$

In Equation (2), b(t) represents the blockchain investment level (BIL) in the shipping supply chain at time t, which has a positive impact on SSL due to the value of blockchain. The higher b(t), the higher the customs clearance efficiency of the port, the higher the transparency (service quality) of shipping logistics, and customers can have a better shipping service experience. τ represents the attenuation rate of SSL, which may be caused by the aging of blockchain technology equipment, data *processing redundancy, and competition with peer services. In addition, we assume that the initial shipping service level at time 0 is S(0) =* S_0. *It is worth noting that* S_0 *also indicates the shipping service level before blockchain adoption (i.e.,: when there is no blockchain).*

Assumption 3. *We assume that there are two types of shippers in the shipping market, including* α *proportion of low-carbon preference shippers (denoted by l) and* $1\text{-}\alpha$ *proportion of non-low-carbon preference shippers due to poor environmental awareness (denoted by n). In reality, Hapag-Lloyd's "Ship Green" service has been questioned as "greenwashing" due to the lack of verifiable emissions data, while Maersk's blockchain carbon tracking system enhances shippers' trust through on-chain deposits. Based on the scenario of blockchain and the type of shipper, we provide the utility function of the shipper in Table 3.*

Table 3. Shippers' utility function with and without blockchain.

Shipper Types	Without Blockchain	With Blockchain
Low-carbon-preference shippers	$v - p + \beta{\cdot}S_0 + \gamma{\cdot}E(t)$	$v - p + \beta{\cdot}S(t) + \gamma{\cdot}E(t)$
Non low-carbon-preference shippers	$v - p + \beta{\cdot}S_0$	$v - p + \beta{\cdot}S(t)$

In Table 3, let p represent shipping service price and v represent the shipper' s valuation of shipping services. Referring to the existing literature (e.g., Choi, [63]; Sui et al., [64]; Liu et al., [65]), we assume that the shippers have heterogeneous valuation v for the shipping service, in which v follows a uniform distribution from 0 to 1, with a probability density function (pdf) $f(v)$ and a cumulative distribution function (CDF) $F(v)$. In addition, β represents the sensitivity of shippers to shipping services, and γ represents the sensitivity of low-carbon-preference shippers to *ERL* in the shipping supply chain.

Furthermore, based on the utility function of shippers in Table 3, we can obtain the shipping demand without and under blockchain as follows:

$$\begin{aligned} D^N(t) &= \alpha \cdot \int_{p-\beta S_0-\gamma E(t)}^{1} f(v)dv + (1-\alpha)\cdot \int_{p-\beta S_0}^{1} f(v)dv \\ &= \alpha \cdot [1 - p + \beta S_0 + \gamma E(t)] + (1-\alpha)\cdot[1 - p + \beta S_0] \end{aligned} \tag{3}$$

$$\begin{aligned} D^B(t) &= \alpha \cdot \int_{p-\beta S(t)-\gamma E(t)}^{1} f(v)dv + (1-\alpha)\cdot \int_{p-\beta S(t)}^{1} f(v)dv \\ &= \alpha \cdot [1 - p + \beta S(t) + \gamma E(t)] + (1-\alpha)\cdot[1 - p + \beta S(t)] \end{aligned} \tag{4}$$

where $D^N(t)$ and $D^B(t)$ denote the shipping demand under the blockchain and without blockchain, respectively.

Assumption 4. *Following the existing literature (e.g., Meng et al., [50]; Xia et al., [66]; Cai et al., [67]), we assume that the green investment cost of the port at time t is* $k{\cdot}g^2(t)/2$, *the cost of emissions reduction efforts by the shipping company is* $h{\cdot}a^2(t)/2$, *and the blockchain investment cost is* $\eta{\cdot}b^2(t)/2$, *where k, h, and* η *are the corresponding cost coefficients. The context for this type of quadratic function aligns with the common convexity principle in economic theory and its underlying economic meaning is that the effects of emissions reduction and blockchain investment in the shipping supply chain are marginally diminishing. We referred to the research of Xin et al. [15], Jiang and Liu [68], and Wang et al. [21] regarding the assumption of investment costs in blockchain. These scholars believe that the investment cost of blockchain is related to its investment level and the marginal cost is increasing, which provides strong support for the research in this paper.*

Additionally, we assume that the port service fee is r, and the unit operating costs for the port, shipping company, and shipping logistics blockchain platform are c_0, c_1, and c_2, respectively. We also consider that the unit operating cost that blockchain investors need to bear is ω, and in the *FB* scenario, the unit blockchain usage fee charged by the shipping logistics blockchain platform to port and shipping companies is c_b.

4. Models

In this section, for the four scenarios, dynamic emissions reduction and blockchain investment decision models for shipping supply chains in different scenarios are constructed using continuous dynamic optimal control theory based on the state changes of shipping emissions reduction level (*ERL*) and shipping service level (*SSL*), respectively. This study uses differential game theory to analyze the dynamic emissions reduction decisions of ports and shipping companies. Its core is to give the optimal emissions reduction decision and the level of blockchain investment of port and shipping enterprises by solving the Hamilton–Jacobi–Bellman (HJB) equation. The HJB equation describes how a participant's value function varies with state and control variables. Its general form is as follows:

$$\rho V = \max_{u} [\pi(u) + V\prime \cdot f(u)] \tag{5}$$

where V is the value function, ρ is the discount rate, $\pi(u)$ is the instantaneous profit, and $f(u)$ is the equation of state. Solving the HJB equation determines the optimal control strategy to maximize the long-term profit of the participants via backward induction.

4.1. Without Blockchain (Scenario N)

As a benchmark, scenario N refers to ports and shipping companies in the traditional shipping supply chain that are not considering investing in blockchain technology. This assumption reflects independent decision-making between ports and shipping companies with no information sharing. For example, the Shenzhen port and companies such as COSCO Shipping and Maersk, which are anchored to the port, have historically agreed on service fees through long-term contracts, and there is a lack of real-time synergy between the port and the shipping companies in decision-making on emissions reduction, leading to asymmetrical node–edge decision-making. Based on the outlined issues and premises in Section 3, the blockchain investment level $b(t)$ at time t is 0, and the shipping service level $S(t)$ is S_0. Therefore, based on the state change of *ERL*, the differential game model of traditional shipping supply chain under scenario N is constructed as follows:

$$\max_{g^N(t)} \left\{ \begin{aligned} \pi_P{}^N &= \int_0^{+\infty} e^{-\rho \cdot t}[(r - c_0) \cdot D^N(t) - \frac{1}{2}k \cdot g^{N^2}(t)]dt \\ &= \int_0^{+\infty} e^{-\rho \cdot t}[(r - c_0) \cdot (\alpha \cdot (1 - p + \beta S_0 + \gamma E^N(t)) + (1 - \alpha) \cdot (1 - p + \beta S_0)) \\ &\quad - \frac{1}{2}k \cdot g^{N^2}(t)]dt \end{aligned} \right\} \tag{6}$$

$$\max_{a^N(t)} \left\{ \begin{aligned} \pi_C{}^N &= \int_0^{+\infty} e^{-\rho \cdot t}[(p - r - c_1) \cdot D^N(t) - \frac{1}{2}h \cdot a^{N^2}(t)]dt \\ &= \int_0^{+\infty} e^{-\rho \cdot t}[(p - r - c_1) \cdot (\alpha \cdot (1 - p + \beta S_0 + \gamma E^N(t)) + \\ &\quad (1 - \alpha) \cdot (1 - p + \beta S_0)) - \frac{1}{2}h \cdot a^{N^2}(t)]dt \end{aligned} \right\} \tag{7}$$

$$s.t. \left\{ \begin{array}{l} dE^N(t) = u \cdot a^N(t)dt + \theta \cdot g^N(t)dt - \sigma \cdot E^N(t)dt \\ E^N(0) = E_0 \end{array} \right. \tag{8}$$

where ρ represents the discount rate, and $\pi_P{}^N$ and $\pi_C{}^N$ denote the total expected profit of the port and the shipping company in the period $[0, +\infty)$ in scenario N, respectively.

Let $V_P{}^N(E^N)$ and $V_C{}^N(E^N)$ represent the optimal value functions of the port company and shipping company, respectively, which represent the total expected profits of the port company and shipping company during the operation period from time t to $+\infty$. $V_P{}^{N'}(E^N)$ is the first derivative of the optimal value function with respect to $V_P{}^N$, and $V_C{}^{N'}(E^N)$ is the first derivative of the optimal value function with respect to $V_C{}^N$. They represent the marginal contribution of emissions reductions in the shipping supply chain to the expected total profits of the port company and shipping company. In accordance with optimal control theory, the respective optimal value functions for the port and shipping companies fulfill the HJB equations depicted below:

$$\rho \cdot V_P{}^N(E^N) = \max_{g^N(t)} \left\{ \begin{array}{l} [(r - c_0) \cdot D^N(t) - \frac{1}{2}k \cdot g^{N^2}(t)] + V_P{}^N\prime(E^N)[ua^N(t)dt + \\ \theta g^N(t)dt - \sigma E^N(t)] \end{array} \right\} \tag{9}$$

$$\rho \cdot V_C{}^N(E^N) = \max_{a^N(t)} \left\{ \begin{array}{l} [(p - r - c_1) \cdot D^N(t) - \frac{1}{2}h \cdot a^{N^2}(t)] + V_C{}^{N\prime}(E^N)[ua^N(t)dt \\ +\theta g^N(t)dt - \sigma E^N(t)] \end{array} \right\} \tag{10}$$

By using optimal control theory to solve HJB Equations (8) and (9), we obtain Theorem 1.

Theorem 1. *In the Scenario N without blockchain, the optimal green investment level g^{N^*} of the port company and the optimal emissions reduction effort a^{N^*} of the shipping company in the shipping supply chain are as follows:*

$$g^{N*} = \frac{\alpha\gamma\theta(r - c_0)}{k(\rho + \sigma)} \tag{11}$$

$$a^{N*} = \frac{\alpha\gamma u(p - c_1 - r)}{h(\rho + \sigma)} \tag{12}$$

According to Theorem 1, Corollary 1 can further be obtained.

Corollary 1. *In the N Scenario without blockchain, the optimal dynamic trajectories of emissions reduction operational strategies for the shipping supply chain are as follows:*

$$\begin{aligned} E^{N*}(t) &= (E_0 - \tfrac{\alpha\gamma(h\theta^2(r-c_0)+ku^2(p-c_1-r))}{hk\sigma(\rho+\sigma)})e^{-\sigma \cdot t} \\ &+ \tfrac{\alpha\gamma(h\theta^2(r-c_0)+ku^2(p-c_1-r))}{hk\sigma(\rho+\sigma)} \end{aligned} \tag{13}$$

$$\begin{aligned} D^{N*}(t) &= \alpha(\gamma((E_0 - \tfrac{\alpha\gamma(h\theta^2(r-c_0)+ku^2(p-c_1-r))}{hk\sigma(\rho+\sigma)})e^{-\sigma \cdot t} \\ &+ \tfrac{1}{hk\sigma(\rho+\sigma)}(\alpha\gamma(h\theta^2(r - c_0) + ku^2(p - c_1 - r)))) \\ &-p + \beta S_0 + 1) + (1 - \alpha)(1 - p + \beta S_0) \end{aligned} \tag{14}$$

$$\begin{aligned} V_C{}^{N*}(t) &= \tfrac{\alpha\gamma(p-c_1-r)}{\rho+\sigma} \cdot ((E_0 - \tfrac{\alpha\gamma(h\theta^2(r-c_0)+ku^2(p-c_1-r))}{hk\sigma(\rho+\sigma)})e^{-\sigma \cdot t} + \\ &\tfrac{\alpha\gamma(h\theta^2(r-c_0)+ku^2(p-c_1-r))}{hk\sigma(\rho+\sigma)}) + \tfrac{(p-c_1-r)}{2\rho} \cdot (2(1 - p + \beta S_0) \\ &+ \tfrac{\alpha^2\gamma^2(2h\theta^2(r-c_0)+ku^2(p-c_1-r))}{hk(\rho+\sigma)^2}) \end{aligned} \tag{15}$$

$$\begin{aligned} V_P{}^{N*}(t) &= \tfrac{\alpha\gamma(r-c_0)}{\rho+\sigma} \cdot ((E_0 - \tfrac{\alpha\gamma(h\theta^2(r-c_0)+ku^2(p-c_1-r))}{hk\sigma(\rho+\sigma)})e^{-\sigma \cdot t} + \\ &\tfrac{\alpha\gamma(h\theta^2(r-c_0)+ku^2(p-c_1-r))}{hk\sigma(\rho+\sigma)}) + \tfrac{(r-c_0)}{2\rho} \cdot (2(1 - p + \beta S_0) \\ &+ \tfrac{\alpha^2\gamma^2(h\theta^2(r-c_0)+2ku^2(p-c_1-r))}{hk(\rho+\sigma)^2}) \end{aligned} \tag{16}$$

4.2. Blockchain Established by the Port (Scenario PB)

Unlike the N scenario without blockchain, in the PB scenario, the investment level of blockchain technology is decided by the port company, continuously improving the shipping service experience of shippers by enhancing the transparency and clearance efficiency of the shipping supply chain, reflecting the practice where ports dominate the technical standards (e.g., GSBN platform is driven by the Hong Kong Port Authority) and shipping companies are passively adaptive. Therefore, based on the state changes in ERL and SSL, a differential game model for blockchain-supported shipping supply chain in the PB scenario is established as follows:

$$\max_{g^{PB}(t),\, b^{PB}(t)} \left\{ \begin{aligned} \pi_P{}^{PB} &= \int_0^{+\infty} e^{-\rho\cdot t}[(r-\omega-c_0)\cdot D^{PB}(t) - \frac{1}{2}k\cdot g^{PB^2}(t) - \frac{1}{2}\eta\cdot b^{PB^2}(t)]dt \\ &= \int_0^{+\infty} e^{-\rho\cdot t}[(r-\omega-c_0)\cdot(\alpha\cdot(1-p+\beta S(t)+\gamma E(t)) \\ &\quad +(1-\alpha)\cdot(1-p+\beta S(t))) - \frac{1}{2}k\cdot g^{PB^2}(t) - \frac{1}{2}\eta\cdot b^{PB^2}(t)]dt \end{aligned} \right\} \tag{17}$$

$$\max_{a^{PB}(t)} \left\{ \begin{aligned} \pi_{C^{PB}} &= \int_0^{+\infty} e^{-\rho\cdot t}[(p-r-c_1)\cdot D^{PB}(t) - \frac{1}{2}h\cdot a^{PB^2}(t)]dt \\ &= \int_0^{+\infty} e^{-\rho\cdot t}[(p-r-c_1)\cdot(\alpha\cdot(1-p+\beta S(t)+\gamma E(t)) \\ &\quad +(1-\alpha)\cdot(1-p+\beta S(t))) - \frac{1}{2}h\cdot a^{PB^2}(t)]dt \end{aligned} \right\} \tag{18}$$

$$s.t. \begin{cases} dE^{PB}(t) = ua^{PB}(t)dt + \theta g^{PB}(t)dt - \sigma E^{PB}(t)dt \\ dS^{PB}(t) = \varphi b^{PB}(t)dt - \tau S^{PB}(t)dt \\ E^{PB}(0) = E_0 \\ S^{PB}(0) = S_0 \end{cases} \tag{19}$$

Theorem 2. *In the PB Scenario where the blockchain technology established by the port company, we obtain the optimal blockchain technology investment level of port company in the shipping supply chain as follows:*

$$b^{PB*} = \frac{\beta\varphi(r-c_0-\omega)}{\eta(\rho+\tau)} \tag{20}$$

The optimal green investment level g^{PB^*} *of port company and the optimal emissions reduction effort* a^{PB^*} *of shipping company under PB blockchain technology are as follows:*

$$g^{PB*} = \frac{\alpha\gamma\theta(r-c_0-\omega)}{k(\rho+\sigma)} \tag{21}$$

$$a^{PB*} = \frac{\alpha\gamma u(p-c_1-r)}{h(\rho+\sigma)} \tag{22}$$

Corollary 2. *In the PB Scenario where the blockchain technology established by the port company, the optimal dynamic trajectories of emissions reduction operational strategies for the shipping supply chain are as follows:*

$$E^{PB*}(t) = E_0\cdot e^{-\sigma\cdot t} + \frac{\alpha\gamma(h\theta^2(r-c_0-\omega)+ku^2(p-c_1-r))}{hk\sigma(\rho+\sigma)}\cdot(1-e^{-\sigma\cdot t}) \tag{23}$$

$$S^{PB*}(t) = S_0\cdot e^{-\tau\cdot t} + \frac{\beta\varphi^2(r-c_0-\omega)}{\eta\tau(\rho+\tau)}\cdot(1-e^{-\tau\cdot t}) \tag{24}$$

$$\begin{aligned} D^{PB*}(t) &= 1 - p + \alpha\gamma(E_0 \cdot e^{-\sigma \cdot t} + \tfrac{\alpha\gamma(h\theta^2(r-c_0-\omega)+ku^2(p-c_1-r))}{hk\sigma(\rho+\sigma)} \\ &\cdot(1 - e^{-\sigma \cdot t})) + \beta(S_0 \cdot e^{-\tau \cdot t} + \tfrac{\beta\varphi^2(r-c_0-\omega)}{\eta\tau(\rho+\tau)} \cdot (1 - e^{-\tau \cdot t})) \end{aligned} \tag{25}$$

$$\begin{aligned} V_C{}^{PB*}(t) &= \tfrac{\alpha\gamma(p-c_1-r)}{\rho+\sigma} \cdot E^{PB*}(t) + \tfrac{\beta(p-c_1-r)}{\rho+\tau} \cdot S^{PB*}(t) + \\ &\tfrac{1}{2\rho}(\tfrac{2\alpha\gamma(p-c_1-r)}{\rho+\sigma}(ua^{PB*} + \theta g^{PB*}) - ha^{PB*2} \\ &+ \tfrac{2\varphi\beta(p-c_1-r)b^{PB*}}{\rho+\tau} + 2(1-p)(p-r-c_1)) \end{aligned} \tag{26}$$

$$\begin{aligned} V_P{}^{PB*}(t) &= \tfrac{\alpha\gamma(r-c_0-\omega)}{\rho+\sigma} \cdot E^{PB*}(t) + \tfrac{\beta(r-c_0-\omega)}{\rho+\tau} \cdot S^{PB*}(t) + \\ &\tfrac{1}{2\rho}(\tfrac{2\alpha\gamma(r-c_0-\omega)}{\rho+\sigma}(ua^{PB*} + \theta g^{PB*}) \\ &\tfrac{2\alpha\gamma(r-c_0-\omega)(ua^{PB*}+\theta g^{PB*})}{\rho+\sigma} - \eta a^{PB*2} \\ &+ \tfrac{2\varphi\beta(r-c_0-\omega)b^{PB*}}{\rho+\tau} - g^{PB*2}k + \\ &2(1-p)(r-c_0-\omega)) \end{aligned} \tag{27}$$

4.3. Blockchain Established by the Shipping Company (Scenario CB)

In the *CB* scenario, shipping companies decide on the level of investment in blockchain technology. For example, Maersk TradeLens and COSCO Shipping's blockchain platforms are led by shipping companies and aim to improve the operational efficiency of global routes. Therefore, based on the state changes in *ERL* and *SSL*, a differential game model for blockchain-supported shipping supply chain in *CB* scenario is established as follows:

$$\max_{a^{CB}(t),b^{CB}(t)} \left\{ \begin{aligned} \pi_C{}^{CB} &= \int_0^{+\infty} e^{-\rho \cdot t}[(p - \omega - r - c_1) \cdot D^{CB}(t) \\ &-\frac{1}{2}h \cdot a^{CB^2}(t) - \frac{1}{2}\eta \cdot b^{CB^2}(t)]dt \end{aligned} \right\} \tag{28}$$

$$\max_{g^{CB}(t)} \left\{ \pi_P{}^{CB} = \int_0^{+\infty} e^{-\rho \cdot t}[(r - c_0) \cdot D^{CB}(t) - \frac{1}{2}k \cdot g^{CB^2}(t)]dt \right\} \tag{29}$$

$$s.t. \begin{cases} dE^{CB}(t) = ua^{CB}(t)dt + \theta g^{CB}(t)dt - \sigma E^{CB}(t)dt \\ dS^{CB}(t) = \varphi b^{CB}(t)dt - \tau S^{CB}(t)dt \\ E^{CB}(0) = E_0 \\ S^{CB}(0) = S_0 \end{cases} \tag{30}$$

Theorem 3. *In the CB Scenario where the blockchain technology established by the shipping company, we obtain the optimal blockchain technology investment level of shipping company in the shipping supply chain as follows:*

$$b^{CB*} = \frac{\beta\varphi(p - r - \omega - c_1)}{\eta(\rho + \tau)} \tag{31}$$

The optimal green investment level g^{CB^*} of port company and the optimal emissions reduction effort a^{CB^*} of the shipping company under CB blockchain technology are as follows:

$$g^{CB*} = \frac{\alpha\gamma\theta(r - c_0)}{k(\rho + \sigma)} \tag{32}$$

$$a^{CB*} = \frac{\alpha\gamma u(p - r - \omega - c_1)}{h(\rho + \sigma)} \tag{33}$$

Corollary 3. *In the CB Scenario where the blockchain technology is established by the shipping company, the optimal dynamic trajectories of emissions reduction operational strategies for the shipping supply chain are as follows:*

$$E^{CB*}(t) = E_0 \cdot e^{-\sigma \cdot t} + \frac{\alpha\gamma\left(h\theta^2(r-c_0) + ku^2(p-r-\omega-c_1)\right)}{hk\sigma(\rho+\sigma)} \cdot (1-e^{-\sigma \cdot t}) \tag{34}$$

$$S^{CB*}(t) = S_0 \cdot e^{-\tau \cdot t} + \frac{\beta\varphi^2(p-c_1-r-\omega)}{\eta\tau(\rho+\tau)} \cdot (1-e^{-\tau \cdot t}) \tag{35}$$

$$D^{CB*}(t) = 1 - p + \alpha\gamma E^{CB*}(t) + \beta S^{CB*}(t) \tag{36}$$

$$\begin{aligned} V_C{}^{CB*}(t) &= \tfrac{\alpha\gamma(p-c_1-r-\omega)}{\rho+\sigma} \cdot E^{CB*}(t) + \tfrac{\beta(p-c_1-r-\omega)}{\rho+\tau} \cdot S^{CB*}(t) \\ &+ \tfrac{1}{2\rho}(-ha^{CB*^2} + \tfrac{2\alpha\gamma(p-c_1-r-\omega)(ua^{CB*}+\theta g^{CB*})}{\rho+\sigma} - \\ &b^{CB*^2}\eta + \tfrac{2\varphi\beta(p-c_1-r-\omega)b^{CB*}}{\rho+\tau} + 2c_1(p-1) + \\ &2p(1-p+r+\omega) - 2r - 2\omega) \end{aligned} \tag{37}$$

$$\begin{aligned} V_P{}^{CB*}(t) &= \tfrac{\alpha\gamma(r-c_0)}{\rho+\sigma} \cdot E^{CB*}(t) + \tfrac{\beta(r-c_0)}{\rho+\tau} \cdot S^{CB*}(t) \\ &+ \tfrac{1}{2\rho}(\tfrac{2\alpha\gamma(r-c_0)(ua^{CB*}+\theta g^{CB*})}{\rho+\sigma} + \tfrac{2\varphi\beta(r-c_0)b^{CB*}}{\rho+\tau} \\ &+ 2(1-p)(r-c_0) - kg^{CB*^2}) \end{aligned} \tag{38}$$

4.4. *Join a Shipping Logistics Blockchain Platform (Scenario FB)*

In Scenario *FB*, ports and shipping companies pay blockchain fees to the shipping logistics blockchain platform for technical support. In this case, we must consider the cost and profitability of the shipping logistics blockchain platform. Therefore, we assume that blockchain usage fee charged by shipping logistics blockchain platform c_b and the unit operating cost of the shipping logistics blockchain platform c_2. Therefore, based on the state changes in *ERL* and *SSL*, a differential game model for blockchain-supported shipping supply chain in *FB* scenario is established as follows:

$$\max_{b^{FB}(t)} \left\{ \pi_F{}^{FB} = \int_0^{+\infty} e^{-\rho \cdot t}[(2c_b - c_2 - \omega) \cdot D^{FB}(t) - \frac{1}{2}\eta \cdot b^{FB^2}(t)]dt \right\} \tag{39}$$

$$\max_{a^{FB}(t)} \left\{ \pi_C{}^{FB} = \int_0^{+\infty} e^{-\rho \cdot t}[(p - r - c_1 - c_b) \cdot D^{FB}(t) - \frac{1}{2}h \cdot a^{FB^2}(t)]dt \right\} \tag{40}$$

$$\max_{g^{FB}(t)} \left\{ \pi_P{}^{FB} = \int_0^{+\infty} e^{-\rho \cdot t}[(r - c_b - c_0) \cdot D^{FB}(t) - \frac{1}{2}k \cdot g^{FB^2}(t)]dt \right\} \tag{41}$$

$$s.t. \begin{cases} dE^{FB}(t) = ua^{FB}(t)dt + \theta g^{FB}(t)dt - \sigma E^{FB}(t)dt \\ dS^{FB}(t) = \varphi b^{FB}(t)dt - \tau S^{FB}(t)dt \\ E^{FB}(0) = E_0 \\ S^{FB}(0) = S_0 \end{cases} \tag{42}$$

Theorem 4. *In the FB Scenario where the port and shipping companies jointly participate in a shipping logistics blockchain platform, the optimal blockchain technology investment level of the platform in the shipping supply chain is as follows:*

$$b^{FB*} = \frac{\beta\varphi(1+\lambda)(2c_b - c_2 - \omega)}{\eta(\rho+\tau)} \tag{43}$$

The optimal green investment level g^{FB^*} of port company and the optimal emissions reduction effort a^{FB^*} of the shipping company under FB blockchain technology are as follows:

$$g^{FB*} = \frac{\alpha\gamma\theta(1+\lambda)(r-c_0-c_b)}{k(\rho+\sigma)} \tag{44}$$

$$a^{FB*} = \frac{\alpha\gamma u(1+\lambda)(p-c_1-c_b-r)}{h(\rho+\sigma)} \tag{45}$$

Corollary 4. *In the FB Scenario where the port and shipping companies jointly participate in a shipping logistics blockchain platform, the optimal dynamic trajectories of emissions reduction operational strategies for the shipping supply chain are as follows:*

$$\begin{aligned} E^{FB*}(t) &= E_0 \cdot e^{-\sigma \cdot t} + \tfrac{\alpha\gamma(1+\lambda)(h\theta^2(r-c_0-c_b)-ku^2(p-r-c_1-c_b))}{hk\sigma(\rho+\sigma)} \\ &\cdot(1-e^{-\sigma \cdot t}) \end{aligned} \tag{46}$$

$$S^{FB*}(t) = S_0 \cdot e^{-\tau \cdot t} + \frac{\beta\varphi^2(1+\lambda)(2c_b-c_2-\omega)}{\eta\tau(\rho+\tau)} \cdot (1-e^{-\tau \cdot t}) \tag{47}$$

$$D^{FB*}(t) = (1+\lambda)(1-p+\alpha\gamma E^{FB*}(t)+\beta S^{FB*}(t)) \tag{48}$$

$$\begin{aligned} V_C{}^{FB*}(t) &= \tfrac{\alpha\gamma(1+\lambda)(p-r-c_1-c_b)}{\rho+\sigma} \cdot E^{FB*}(t) \\ &+ \tfrac{\beta(1+\lambda)(p-r-c_1-c_b)}{\rho+\tau} \cdot S^{FB*}(t) + \tfrac{(1+\lambda)}{\rho}(p-r-c_b-c_1) \\ &(1-p+\tfrac{\alpha\gamma(a^{FB*}u+\theta g^{FB*})}{\rho+\sigma} + \tfrac{\varphi\beta b^{FB*}}{\rho+\tau}) - \tfrac{h a^{FB*2}}{2\rho} \end{aligned} \tag{49}$$

$$\begin{aligned} V_P{}^{FB*}(t) &= \tfrac{(r-c_0-c_b)(1+\lambda)\alpha\gamma}{\rho+\sigma} \cdot E^{FB*}(t) + \tfrac{(r-c_0-c_b)(1+\lambda)\beta}{\rho+\tau} \cdot S^{FB*}(t) \\ &+ \tfrac{1}{2\rho}(-g^{FB*2}k + 2(r-c_0-c_b)(1+\lambda)(\tfrac{\alpha\gamma(g^{FB*}\theta+a^{FB*}u)}{\rho+\sigma} \\ &+(1-p) + \tfrac{\varphi\beta b^{FB*}}{\rho+\tau})) \end{aligned} \tag{50}$$

$$\begin{aligned} V_F{}^{FB*}(t) &= \tfrac{\alpha\gamma(1+\lambda)(2c_b-c_2-\omega)}{\rho+\sigma} \cdot E^{FB*}(t) + \tfrac{\beta(1+\lambda)(2c_b-c_2-\omega)}{\rho+\tau} \cdot S^{FB*}(t) \\ &+ \tfrac{1}{2\rho}(-\eta b^{FB*2} + 2(1+\lambda)(2c_b-c_2-\omega) \\ &(1-p+\tfrac{\alpha\gamma(ua^{FB*}+\theta g^{FB*})}{\rho+\sigma} + \tfrac{\varphi\beta b^{FB*}}{\rho+\tau})) \end{aligned} \tag{51}$$

5. Model Analysis

5.1. Dynamic Emissions Reduction Operational Strategy

This section investigates strategic recommendations for port and shipping businesses by analyzing the optimal dynamic changes in demand, emissions reduction level, and other relevant factors, thereby supporting the development of sustainable and technologically adaptive growth strategies for the shipping industry.

Proposition 1. *N Scenario:*

(i) *When $t < t_{th}{}^N$, we find that if* $\begin{cases} E_0 \le E_\infty{}^N \text{ or } p \ge p_{th}{}^N \text{ or } \alpha \ge \alpha_{th}{}^N \\ \text{or } \gamma \ge \gamma_{th}{}^N \text{ or } u \ge u_{th}{}^N \text{or } \theta \ge \theta_{th}{}^N \text{or } k \le k_{th}{}^N \\ \text{or } h \le h_{th}{}^N \text{or } c_0 \le c_{0th}{}^N \text{ or } c_1 \le c_{1th}{}^N \text{or } [(\frac{h}{k} \ge \frac{u^2}{\theta^2}) \wedge (r \ge r_{th}{}^N)] \\ \text{or } [(\frac{h}{k} < \frac{u^2}{\theta^2}) \wedge (r < r_{th}{}^N)] \end{cases}$ *, then* $\frac{\partial E^N}{\partial t} > 0, \frac{\partial D^N}{\partial t} > 0, \frac{\partial V_C{}^N}{\partial t} > 0, \frac{V_P{}^N}{\partial t} > 0$*; otherwise* $\frac{\partial E^N}{\partial t} < 0, \frac{\partial D^N}{\partial t} < 0, \frac{\partial V_C{}^N}{\partial t} < 0, \frac{\partial V_P{}^N}{\partial t} < 0$*; where $t_{th}{}^N$ is the time node in (0, +∞);*

(ii) *When* $t \geq t_{th}{}^{N}$, *we have* $\frac{\partial E^N}{\partial t} = 0, \frac{\partial D^N}{\partial t} = 0, \frac{\partial V_C{}^N}{\partial t} = 0, \frac{\partial V_P{}^N}{\partial t} = 0$;

(iii) *We confirm that the relevantimportant critical points in Scenario N can be found in Supplementary S2.*

Proposition 1 shows the relationships between the emissions reduction level E^N, shipping demand D^N, expected discounted profit of shipping company $V_C{}^N$, expected discounted profit of port company $V_P{}^N$, and time t. We find that when time t is sufficiently small, E^N, D^N, $V_C{}^N$, $V_P{}^N$ increase with t if the initial emissions reduction level E_0, cost coefficient k, h, c of the shipping supply chain are small. This indicates a trend where companies aim to elevate emission cuts and boost demand, concurrently lowering costs, thereby enhancing profitability. It is also worth noting that the evolution of E^N, D^N, $V_C{}^N$, $V_P{}^N$ with time t will eventually converge to a steady state, regardless of the changes in other parameters. This is because in the long run, companies will strive to increase their level of emissions reduction and increase their profits by reducing costs while increasing demand. In this process, companies constantly adjust their own decisions, such as emissions reduction efforts and green investment levels, to achieve a balance between costs and benefits. When a relatively stable state is reached, levels of emissions reductions, demand, and profits also tend to be stable.

Proposition 2. *PB Scenario:*

(i) *When* $t < t_{th0}{}^{PB}$, *we find that if* $\begin{cases} E_0 \leq E_\infty{}^{PB} \text{ or } p \geq p_{th0}{}^{PB} \text{ or } \alpha \geq \alpha_{th0}{}^{PB} \text{or } \gamma \geq \gamma_{th0}{}^{PB} \text{ or} \\ u \geq u_{th0}{}^{PB} \text{ or } \theta \geq \theta_{th0}{}^{PB} \text{or } k \leq k_{th0}{}^{PB} \text{ or } h \leq h_{th0}{}^{PB} \text{ or} \\ \omega \leq \omega_{th0}{}^{PB} \text{ or } c_0 \leq c_{0th0}{}^{PB} \text{ or } c_1 \leq c_{1th0}{}^{PB} \text{or} \\ [(\frac{h}{k} \geq \frac{u^2}{\theta^2}) \wedge (r \geq r_{th0}{}^{PB})] \text{ or } [(\frac{h}{k} < \frac{u^2}{\theta^2}) \wedge (r < r_{th0}{}^{PB})] \end{cases}$,
then $\frac{\partial E^{PB}}{\partial t} > 0$; *otherwise,* $\frac{\partial E^{PB}}{\partial t} < 0$; *When* $t \geq t_{th0}{}^{PB}$, *we have* $\frac{\partial E^{PB}}{\partial t} = 0$; *where* $t_{th0}{}^{PB}$ *is the time node in* $(0, +\infty)$;

(ii) *When* $t < t_{th1}{}^{PB}$, *we find that if* $\begin{cases} S_0 \leq S_\infty{}^{PB} \text{ or } r \geq r_{th1}{}^{PB} \text{ or } \beta \geq \beta_{th1}{}^{PB} \text{or } \varphi \geq \varphi_{th1}{}^{PB} \text{ or} \\ \eta \leq \eta_{th1}{}^{PB} \text{ or } \omega \leq \omega_{th1}{}^{PB} \text{ or } c_0 \leq c_{0th1}{}^{PB} \end{cases}$,
then $\frac{\partial S^{PB}}{\partial t} > 0$; *otherwise,* $\frac{\partial S^{PB}}{\partial t} < 0$; *When* $t \geq t_{th1}{}^{PB}$, *we have* $\frac{\partial S^{PB}}{\partial t} = 0$; *where* $t_{th1}{}^{PB}$ *is the time node in* $(0, +\infty)$;

(iii) *When* $t < \max\{t_{th0}{}^{PB}, t_{th1}{}^{PB}\}$, *we find that if* $[(E_0 \leq E_\infty{}^{PB}) \wedge (S_0 \leq S_\infty{}^{PB})]$, *then* $D^{PB}(t)$, $V_C{}^{PB}(t)$, *and* $V_P{}^{PB}(t)$ *will inevitably increase with time t; When* $t \geq \max\{t_{th0}{}^{PB}, t_{th1}{}^{PB}\}$, *we have* $\partial D^{PB}/\partial t = 0$, $\partial V_C{}^{PB}/\partial t = 0$, *and* $\partial V_P{}^{PB}/\partial t = 0$; *Otherwise,* $D^{PB}(t)$, $V_C{}^{PB}(t)$, *and* $V_P{}^{PB}(t)$ *may increase or decrease with time t, depending on the rate of increase or decrease in the state equations* $E^{PB}(t)$ *and* $S^{PB}(t)$;

(iv) *We confirm that the relevant important critical points in Scenario PB can be found in Supplementary S2.*

Proposition 2 states that in the *PB* scenario, the dynamic evolution process of emissions reduction level E^{PB}, shipping service level S^{PB}, demand D^{PB}, and related profit function with time has obvious regularity. When time t is small enough, we find that the shipping service level S^{PB} is proportional to t if the initial shipping service level S_0, η, ω, c_0 decrease, or if r, β, φ increase. This is because in this case, the benefits of ports investing in blockchain technology, such as improved efficiency in customs clearance and enhanced transparency in logistics, can notably improve shipping service quality due to alterations in initial conditions and variables, which in turn lead to a positive correlation between service levels and time. When t is less than the maximum value between two critical values, $D^{PB}(t)$, $V_C{}^{PB}(t)$, and $V_P{}^{PB}(t)$ increase with time t if the condition that both E_0 and S_0 decrease is satisfied. Moreover, when t is infinite, its dynamic evolution will eventually converge to the steady state. The port company achieves a greater degree of emissions reduction by introducing blockchain technology. At the same time, the application of these technologies also improves service levels, thereby increasing profits.

Proposition 3. *CB Scenario:*

(i) When $t < t_{th0}{}^{CB}$, we find that if $\begin{cases} E_0 \leq E_{\infty}{}^{CB} \text{ or } p \geq p_{th0}{}^{CB} \text{ or } \alpha \geq \alpha_{th0}{}^{CB} \text{ or } \gamma \geq \gamma_{th0}{}^{CB} \text{ or} \\ u \geq u_{th0}{}^{CB} \text{ or } \theta \geq \theta_{th0}{}^{CB} \text{ or } k \leq k_{th0}{}^{CB} \text{ or } h \leq h_{th0}{}^{CB} \text{ or} \\ \omega \leq \omega_{th0}{}^{CB} \text{ or } c_0 \leq c_{0th0}{}^{CB} \text{ or } c_1 \leq c_{1th0}{}^{CB} \text{ or} \\ [(\frac{h}{k} \geq \frac{u^2}{\theta^2}) \wedge (r \geq r_{th0}{}^{CB})] \text{ or } [(\frac{h}{k} < \frac{u^2}{\theta^2}) \wedge (r < r_{th0}{}^{CB})] \end{cases}$, then $\frac{\partial E^{CB}}{\partial t} > 0$; otherwise, $\frac{\partial E^{CB}}{\partial t} < 0$; When $t \geq t_{th0}{}^{CB}$, we have $\frac{\partial E^{CB}}{\partial t} = 0$; where $t_{th0}{}^{PB}$ is the time node in $(0, +\infty)$;

(ii) When $t < t_{th1}{}^{CB}$, we find that if $\begin{cases} S_0 \leq S_{\infty}{}^{CB} \text{ or } r \leq r_{th1}{}^{CB} \text{ or } \beta \geq \beta_{th1}{}^{CB} \text{ or } \varphi \geq \varphi_{th1}{}^{CB} \text{ or} \\ \eta \leq \eta_{th1}{}^{CB} \text{ or } \omega \leq \omega_{th1}{}^{CB} \text{ or } c_1 \leq c_{1th1}{}^{CB} \end{cases}$, then $\frac{\partial S^{CB}}{\partial t} > 0$; otherwise, $\frac{\partial S^{CB}}{\partial t} < 0$; When $t \geq t_{th1}{}^{CB}$, we have $\frac{\partial S^{CB}}{\partial t} = 0$; where $t_{th1}{}^{CB}$ is the time node in $(0, +\infty)$;

(iii) When $t < max\{t_{th0}{}^{CB}, t_{th1}{}^{CB}\}$, we find that if $[(E_0 \leq E_{\infty}{}^{CB}) \wedge (S_0 \leq S_{\infty}{}^{CB})]$, then $D^{CB}(t)$, $V_C{}^{CB}(t)$, and $V_P{}^{CB}(t)$ will inevitably increase with time t; When $t \geq max\{t_{th0}{}^{CB}, t_{th1}{}^{CB}\}$, we have $\partial D^{CB}/\partial t = 0$, $\partial V_C{}^{CB}/\partial t = 0$, and $\partial V_P{}^{CB}/\partial t = 0$; Otherwise, $D^{PB}(t)$, $V_C{}^{CB}(t)$, and $V_P{}^{CB}(t)$ may increase or decrease with time t, depending on the rate of increase or decrease in the state equations $E^{CB}(t)$ and $S^{CB}(t)$;

(iv) *We confirm that the relevant important critical points in Scenario CB can be found in Supplementary S2.*

Proposition 3 is similar to Proposition 2. When t is sufficiently small and certain conditions are satisfied, E^{CB}, S^{CB}, $D^{CB}(t)$, $V_C{}^{CB}(t)$, and $V_P{}^{CB}(t)$ increase with t, with a vice versa decrease. All of these eventually converge to the steady state as time t evolves. Proposition 3 (*iii*) states that when $t < max\{t_{th0}{}^{CB}, t_{th1}{}^{CB}\}$, if the initial emissions reduction level and service level meet certain conditions, $D^{CB}(t)$, $V_C{}^{CB}(t)$ and $V_P{}^{CB}(t)$ are proportional to time t.

Although blockchain adoption by shipping companies increases investment costs, it enhances supply chain management efficacy. Through blockchain technology, companies gain real-time cargo tracking, optimize routes, and improve handling efficiency, thereby reducing operational costs. Simultaneously, blockchain improves transparency and operational efficiency, enabling shippers to monitor cargo status more accurately, which strengthens trust and supports emissions reduction initiatives. Furthermore, elevated service levels and customer satisfaction attract more clients, expand market share, and boost profits. These dynamics demonstrate the *CB* scenario's positive impacts: blockchain investments create synergistic relationships across supply chain factors, offering critical insights for corporate decision-making.

Proposition 4. *FB Scenario:*

(i) When $t < t_{th0}{}^{FB}$, we find that if $\begin{cases} E_0 \leq E_{\infty}{}^{FB} \text{ or } p \geq p_{th0}{}^{FB} \text{ or } \alpha \geq \alpha_{th0}{}^{FB} \text{ or } \gamma \geq \gamma_{th0}{}^{FB} \text{ or} \\ u \geq u_{th0}{}^{FB} \text{ or } \theta \geq \theta_{th0}{}^{FB} \text{ or } k \leq k_{th0}{}^{FB} \text{ or } h \leq h_{th0}{}^{FB} \text{ or} \\ c_b \leq c_{bth0}{}^{FB} \text{ or } c_0 \leq c_{0th0}{}^{FB} \text{ or } c_1 \leq c_{1th0}{}^{FB} \text{ or} \\ [(\frac{h}{k} \geq \frac{u^2}{\theta^2}) \wedge (r \geq r_{th0}{}^{FB})] \text{ or } [(\frac{h}{k} < \frac{u^2}{\theta^2}) \wedge (r < r_{th0}{}^{FB})] \end{cases}$, then $\frac{\partial E^{FB}}{\partial t} > 0$; otherwise, $\frac{\partial E^{FB}}{\partial t} < 0$; When $t \geq t_{th0}{}^{FB}$, we have $\frac{\partial E^{FB}}{\partial t} = 0$; where $t_{th0}{}^{FB}$ is the time node in $(0, +\infty)$;

(ii) *When* $t < t_{th1}{}^{FB}$, *we find that if* $\left\{ \begin{array}{l} S_0 \leq S_\infty{}^{FB} \text{ or } \beta \geq \beta_{th1}{}^{FB} \text{ or } \varphi \geq \varphi_{th1}{}^{FB} \text{ or } c_b \leq c_{bth1}{}^{FB} \\ \text{or } \eta \leq \eta_{th1}{}^{FB} \text{ or } \omega \leq \omega_{th1}{}^{FB} \text{ or } c_2 \leq c_{2th1}{}^{FB} \end{array} \right.$, *then* $\frac{\partial S^{FB}}{\partial t} > 0$; *otherwise,* $\frac{\partial S^{FB}}{\partial t} < 0$; *When* $t \geq t_{th1}{}^{FB}$, *we have* $\frac{\partial S^{FB}}{\partial t} = 0$; *where* $t_{th1}{}^{FB}$ *is the time node in* $(0, +\infty)$;

(iii) *When* $t < max\{t_{th0}{}^{FB}, t_{th1}{}^{FB}\}$, *we find that if* $[(E_0 \leq E_\infty{}^{FB}) \wedge (S_0 \leq S_\infty{}^{FB})]$, *then* $D^{FB}(t)$, $V_C{}^{FB}(t)$, $V_P{}^{FB}(t)$, *and* $V_F{}^{FB}(t)$ *will inevitably increase with time t; When* $t \geq max\{t_{th0}{}^{CB}, t_{th1}{}^{CB}\}$, *we have* $\partial D^{FB}/\partial t = 0$, $\partial V_C{}^{FB}/\partial t = 0$, $\partial V_P{}^{FB}/\partial t = 0$, *and* $\partial V_F{}^{FB}/\partial t = 0$; *Otherwise,* $D^{FB}(t)$, $V_C{}^{FB}(t)$, $V_P{}^{FB}(t)$, *and* $V_F{}^{FB}(t)$ *may increase or decrease with time t, depending on the rate of increase or decrease in the state equations* $E^{FB}(t)$ *and* $S^{FB}(t)$;

(iv) *We confirm that the relevant important critical points in Scenario FB can be found in Supplementary S2.*

Proposition 4 indicates that E^{FB} is proportional to t if E_0, k, h, c_b, c_0, c_1 are satisfied when $t < t_{th0}{}^{FB}$ is sufficiently small. Unlike Proposition 3, Proposition 4 considers the blockchain usage fee charged by shipping logistics blockchain platform c_b, and E^{FB} is also proportional to t when $c_b < c_{bth0}{}^{FB}$. The reverse is inversely proportional. When $t < t_{th1}{}^{FB}$, the shipping service level S^{FB} is proportional to t if S_0, c_b, η, ω, c_2 is smaller or β, φ is larger; otherwise, it is inversely proportional. In addition, when t is less than the maximum value between two critical values, $D^{FB}(t)$, $V_C{}^{FB}(t)$, and $V_P{}^{FB}(t)$ increase with time t if the condition that both E_0 and S_0 decrease is satisfied. When t is infinitely large, its dynamic evolution will eventually converge to the steady state.

This proposition demonstrates that blockchain technology provides a secure, transparent, efficient, and convenient shared-service network platform for port and shipping enterprises. Through blockchain platforms, diversified services and multi-tier functional frameworks can be implemented across controlled processes, enabling online-offline collaboration for cargo operations, dynamic logistics chain tracking, operational efficiency improvements, and overall cost reduction. For instance, the Shanghai Blockchain Paperless Order Exchange Platform has established a high-reliability alliance chain infrastructure, integrating all port and shipping logistics stakeholders as nodes. This system facilitates blockchain-based recording of user profiles, logistics data, and business interactions.

5.2. Parameter Analysis

As detailed in Section 5.1, the port's vessel emission rates (*VERs*) stabilize across various scenarios, reaching equilibrium without further temporal fluctuations. Consequently, this section conducts a steady-state parametric analysis of port *VERs*, offering valuable insights into the enduring effects of government policies aimed at encouraging emissions reductions by port operators.

Proposition 5. *In different Scenarios, the impacts of shipping price p and port service fee r on the optimal decisions are analyzed as follows:*

(i) $\frac{\partial a^{i*}}{\partial p} > 0$, $\frac{\partial a^{i*}}{\partial r} < 0$;

(ii) $\frac{\partial g^{i*}}{\partial p} = 0$, $\frac{\partial g^{i*}}{\partial r} > 0$;

(iii) $\frac{\partial b^{j*}}{\partial p} \left\{ \begin{array}{l} = 0, \text{ when } j = PB, FB \\ > 0, \text{ when } j = CB \end{array} \right.$, $\frac{\partial b^{j*}}{\partial r} \left\{ \begin{array}{l} > 0, \text{ when } j = PB \\ < 0, \text{ when } j = CB \\ = 0, \text{ when } j = FB \end{array} \right.$;

(iv) $\frac{\partial E^{i*}}{\partial p} > 0$, $\left\{ \begin{array}{l} if\ \theta \geq \sqrt{\frac{ku^2}{h}}, \text{ then } \frac{\partial E_\infty{}^{i*}}{\partial r} \geq 0 \\ if\ \theta < \sqrt{\frac{ku^2}{h}}, \text{ then } \frac{\partial E_\infty{}^{i*}}{\partial r} < 0 \end{array} \right.$;

(v) $\frac{\partial S^{j*}}{\partial p}\begin{cases} = 0, \ when \ j = PB, FB \\ > 0, \ when \ j = CB \end{cases}, \frac{\partial S^{j*}}{\partial r}\begin{cases} > 0, \ when \ j = PB \\ < 0, \ when \ j = CB \\ = 0, \ when \ j = FB \end{cases};$

(vi) $\begin{cases} if \ \alpha \geq {\alpha_{th1}}^{i}, \ then \ \frac{\partial D^{i*}}{\partial p} \geq 0 \\ if \ \alpha < {\alpha_{th1}}^{i}, \ then \ \frac{\partial D^{i*}}{\partial p} < 0 \end{cases}, \begin{cases} if \ \theta \geq \sqrt{\frac{ku^2}{h}}, \begin{cases} then \ \frac{\partial D^{N,\ PB,\ FB*}}{\partial r} \geq 0 \\ and \begin{cases} \varphi \leq {\varphi_{th2}}^{CB}, \ then \ \frac{\partial D^{CB*}}{\partial r} \geq 0 \\ \varphi > {\varphi_{th2}}^{CB}, \ then \ \frac{\partial D^{CB*}}{\partial r} < 0 \end{cases} \end{cases} \\ if \ \theta < \sqrt{\frac{ku^2}{h}}, \begin{cases} then \ \frac{\partial D^{N,\ CB,\ FB*}}{\partial r} < 0 \\ and \begin{cases} \varphi \leq {\varphi_{th2}}^{PB}, \ then \ \frac{\partial D^{PB*}}{\partial r} \leq 0 \\ \varphi > {\varphi_{th2}}^{PB}, \ then \ \frac{\partial D^{PB*}}{\partial r} > 0 \end{cases} \end{cases} \end{cases}$

;

i = N, PB, CB, FB; j = PB, CB, FB.
See Supplementary S2 for relevant important critical points regarding Proposition 5.

Proposition 5 shows that the shipping company's emissions reduction efforts a^{i^*} are positively correlated with p and negatively correlated with r. This means that shipping companies will see their costs increase as they undertake emissions reduction efforts. In order to cover these additional costs, shipping companies may increase their shipping fees. Improving operational efficiency through emissions reduction measures reduces the cost of services provided by shipping companies at ports. The port's green investment level g^{i^*} is not correlated with p but is positively correlated with r, which suggests that the port will increase the service fee to increase the level of green investment. In the *PB* and *FB* cases, blockchain investment level b^{j^*} is not correlated to p. In *CB*, b^{j^*} is positively correlated with p. So b^{j^*} has a different relationship with r in the three scenarios. Emissions reduction level E^{i^*} is positively correlated with p. If θ is large enough, E^{i^*} is positively related to r. The shipping service level S^{j^*} is positively or negatively correlated or is uncorrelated with p and r under certain conditions. In addition, when α is large enough, shipping demand D^{i^*} is positively related to p. When θ is large enough, $D^{N,PB,FB}$ are positively correlated with r, and D^{CB} is positively correlated with r when φ is small enough. This suggests that the relationship between shipping demand and p and r is also affected by relevant influencing factors, so shipping companies and ports need to better cope with the uncertainty of shipping demand, improve competitiveness, and maintain sustainable development in the changing market environment.

Proposition 6. *In different Scenarios, the impacts of parameters related to low-carbon-preference shippers (i.e., α, β, γ) on the optimal decisions are analyzed as follows:*

(i) $\frac{\partial a^{i*}}{\partial \alpha} > 0, \frac{\partial a^{i*}}{\partial \beta} = 0, \frac{\partial a^{i*}}{\partial \gamma} > 0;$

(ii) $\frac{\partial g^{i*}}{\partial \alpha} > 0, \frac{\partial g^{i*}}{\partial \beta} = 0, \frac{\partial g^{i*}}{\partial \gamma} > 0;$

(iii) $\frac{\partial b^{j*}}{\partial \alpha} = 0, \frac{\partial b^{j*}}{\partial \beta} > 0, \frac{\partial b^{j*}}{\partial \gamma} = 0;$

(iv) $\frac{\partial E^{i*}}{\partial \alpha} > 0, \frac{\partial E^{i*}}{\partial \beta} = 0, \frac{\partial E^{i*}}{\partial \gamma} > 0;$

(v) $\frac{\partial S^{j*}}{\partial \alpha} = 0, \frac{\partial S^{j*}}{\partial \beta} > 0, \frac{\partial S^{j*}}{\partial \gamma} = 0;$

(vi) $\frac{\partial D^{i*}}{\partial \alpha} > 0, \frac{\partial D^{i*}}{\partial \beta} = 0, \frac{\partial D^{i*}}{\partial \gamma} > 0;$

where i = N, PB, CB, FB; j = PB, CB, FB.

Proposition 6 reveals that a^{i^*}, g^{i^*}, E^{i^*}, D^{i^*} are positively correlated with α, γ and uncorrelated with β. There is a positive correlation between shipping companies' emissions reduction efforts and ports' green investments, indicating that ports' green infrastructure and technology investments enhance shipping companies' low-carbon transportation outcomes. If the proportion of low-carbon-priority shippers rises, this reflects growing demand for low-carbon transportation, steering the industry toward a greener trajectory. However, b^{j*}, S^{j*} are uncorrelated with α, γ and positively correlated with β. This suggests that the proportion of low-carbon-preference shippers and their low-carbon preferences do not significantly affect blockchain investment levels or shipping service levels under blockchain systems. The positive correlation indicates that as the application level of blockchain technology in shipping services increases, shippers' satisfaction with transportation services also rises. In other words, higher blockchain adoption levels lead to greater shipper sensitivity to service quality as expectations for high-quality service are met.

Proposition 7. *In different Scenarios, the impacts of parameters related to port and shipping emissions reduction and shipping service (i.e., u, θ, φ) on the optimal decisions are analyzed as follows:*

(i) $\frac{\partial a^{i*}}{\partial u} > 0, \frac{\partial a^{i*}}{\partial \theta} = 0, \frac{\partial a^{i*}}{\partial \varphi} = 0;$

(ii) $\frac{\partial g^{i*}}{\partial u} = 0, \frac{\partial g^{i*}}{\partial \theta} > 0, \frac{\partial g^{i*}}{\partial \varphi} = 0;$

(iii) $\frac{\partial b^{j*}}{\partial u} = 0, \frac{\partial b^{j*}}{\partial \theta} = 0, \frac{\partial b^{j*}}{\partial \varphi} > 0;$

(iv) $\frac{\partial E^{i*}}{\partial u} > 0, \frac{\partial E^{i*}}{\partial \theta} > 0, \frac{\partial E^{i*}}{\partial \varphi} = 0;$

(v) $\frac{\partial S^{j*}}{\partial u} = 0, \frac{\partial S^{j*}}{\partial \theta} = 0, \frac{\partial S^{j*}}{\partial \varphi} > 0;$

(vi) $\frac{\partial D^{i*}}{\partial u} > 0, \frac{\partial D^{i*}}{\partial \theta} > 0, \frac{\partial D^{i*}}{\partial \varphi}\begin{cases} = 0, \text{ when } i = N \\ > 0, \text{ when } i = PB, CB, FB \end{cases};$

where i = N, PB, CB, FB; j = PB, CB, FB.

Proposition 7 shows that a^{i*}, E^{i*}, D^{i*} is positively correlated with u. Similarly, g^{i*}, E^{i*}, D^{i*} is positively correlated with θ. Furthermore, b^{j*}, S^{j*} is positively correlated with φ. Where D^{i*} is uncorrelated with φ in scenario N and positively correlated in the other scenarios. Proposition 7 (*i*)–(*iii*) illustrate that when ports, shipping companies, and blockchain technology have greater factors affecting the level of emissions reduction in the shipping supply chain, their respective investment levels are higher. The uncorrelation of E^{i*} and φ in Proposition 7 *(iv)* suggests that current blockchain investments are not being effectively used in emissions reduction efforts in the shipping supply chain, or that the application of blockchain technology is not yet mature enough to have a significant impact on emissions reductions. Proposition 7 (*v*) shows that the shipping service level S^{j*} is only related to the influence of the *BIL* on *ERL* φ. From the conclusions of Proposition 7 (*iv*) and Proposition 7 (*v*), (*vi*) can be introduced.

Proposition 8. *In different Scenarios, the impacts of cost-related parameters on the shipping supply chain (i.e., k, h, η, ω, c_0, c_1, c_2, c_b) on the optimal decisions are analyzed as follows:*

(i) $\frac{\partial a^{i*}}{\partial k} = 0, \frac{\partial a^{i*}}{\partial h} < 0, \frac{\partial a^{i*}}{\partial \eta} = 0, \frac{\partial a^{i*}}{\partial \omega}\begin{cases} = 0, \text{ when } i = N, PB, FB \\ < 0, \text{ when } i = CB \end{cases}, \frac{\partial a^{i*}}{\partial c_0} = 0, \frac{\partial a^{i*}}{\partial c_1} < 0,$

$\frac{\partial a^{FB*}}{\partial c_2} = 0, \frac{\partial a^{FB*}}{\partial c_b} < 0;$

(ii) $\frac{\partial g^{i*}}{\partial k} < 0, \frac{\partial g^{i*}}{\partial h} = 0, \frac{\partial g^{i*}}{\partial \eta} = 0, \frac{\partial g^{i*}}{\partial \omega}\begin{cases} = 0, \text{ when } i = N, CB, FB \\ < 0, \text{ when } i = PB \end{cases}, \frac{\partial g^{i*}}{\partial c_0} < 0, \frac{\partial g^{i*}}{\partial c_1} = 0,$

$\frac{\partial g^{FB*}}{\partial c_2} = 0, \frac{\partial g^{FB*}}{\partial c_b} < 0;$

(iii) $\frac{\partial b^{j*}}{\partial k} = 0, \frac{\partial b^{j*}}{\partial h} = 0, \frac{\partial b^{j*}}{\partial \eta} < 0, \frac{\partial b^{j*}}{\partial \omega} < 0, \frac{\partial b^{j*}}{\partial c_0}\begin{cases} < 0, \text{ when } j = PB \\ = 0, \text{ when } j = CB, FB \end{cases},$

$\frac{\partial b^{j*}}{\partial c_1}\begin{cases} = 0, \text{ when } j = PB, FB \\ < 0, \text{ when } j = CB \end{cases}, \frac{\partial b^{FB*}}{\partial c_2} < 0, \frac{\partial b^{FB*}}{\partial c_b} > 0;$

(*iv*) $\frac{\partial E^{i*}}{\partial k} < 0$, $\frac{\partial E^{i*}}{\partial h} < 0$, $\frac{\partial E^{i*}}{\partial \eta} = 0$, $\frac{\partial E^{i*}}{\partial \omega}\begin{cases} = 0, \ when \ i = N, FB \\ < 0, \ when \ i = PB, CB \end{cases}$, $\frac{\partial E^{i*}}{\partial c_0} < 0$, $\frac{\partial E^{i*}}{\partial c_1} = 0$,
$\frac{\partial E^{FB*}}{\partial c_2} = 0$, $\frac{\partial E^{FB*}}{\partial c_b} < 0$;

(*v*) $\frac{\partial S^{j*}}{\partial k} = 0$, $\frac{\partial S^{j*}}{\partial h} = 0$, $\frac{\partial S^{j*}}{\partial \eta} < 0$, $\frac{\partial S^{j*}}{\partial \omega} < 0$, $\frac{\partial S^{j*}}{\partial c_0}\begin{cases} < 0, \ when \ j = PB \\ = 0, \ when \ j = CB, FB \end{cases}$,
$\frac{\partial S^{j*}}{\partial c_1}\begin{cases} = 0, \ when \ j = PB, FB \\ < 0, \ when \ j = CB \end{cases}$, $\frac{\partial S^{FB*}}{\partial c_2} < 0$, $\frac{\partial S^{FB*}}{\partial c_b} > 0$;

(*vi*) $\frac{\partial D^{i*}}{\partial k} < 0$, $\frac{\partial D^{i*}}{\partial h} < 0$, $\frac{\partial D^{i*}}{\partial \eta}\begin{cases} = 0, \ when \ i = N \\ < 0, \ when \ i = PB, CB, FB \end{cases}$, $\frac{\partial D^{i*}}{\partial \omega}\begin{cases} = 0, \ when \ i = N \\ < 0, \ when \ i = PB, CB, FB \end{cases}$,
$\frac{\partial D^{i*}}{\partial c_0} < 0$, $\frac{\partial D^{i*}}{\partial c_1} = 0$, $\frac{\partial D^{FB*}}{\partial c_2} < 0$,
$\begin{cases} if \ \varphi \geq {\varphi_{th2}}^{FB}, \ then \ \frac{\partial D^{FB*}}{\partial p} \geq 0 \\ if \ \varphi < {\varphi_{th2}}^{FB}, \ then \ \frac{\partial D^{FB*}}{\partial p} < 0 \end{cases}$;

i = *N*, *PB*, *CB*, *FB*; *j* = *PB*, *CB*, *FB*.
See Supplementary S2 for relevant important critical points regarding Proposition 8.

Proposition 8 shows how cost factors influence optimal choices across scenarios. For example, in Proposition 8 (*i*), a^{i^*} is not correlated with k, η, c_0, c_2 and is uncorrelated with ω in each scenario. In Proposition 8 (*ii*), the port's green investment level g^{i^*} is uncorrelated with h, η, c_1, c_2 and uncorrelated with ω in a given scenario. An increase in k results in a decrease in the port's green investment level g^{i^*}, suggesting that an increase in the green cost factor will squeeze the budget for blockchain investments. Meanwhile, the tightening of regulatory policies can be indirectly manifested in the increase of port green investment cost coefficient k in the model, which explains why in reality, some ports prioritize meeting compliance requirements over adopting blockchain technologies. In Proposition 8 (*iii*), the blockchain investment level b^{j^*} is uncorrelated with k and correlated with h. E^{i^*} in Proposition 8 (*iv*) is uncorrelated with k, h, c_1, c_b. S^{j^*} in Proposition 8 (*v*) is uncorrelated with k, h uncorrelated with c_0, c_1 in each scenario, and positively correlated with c_b. In addition, the shipping demand D^{i^*} in Proposition 8 (*vi*) is uncorrelated with η, ω, c_1 in the given scenario. Normally, an increase in the cost coefficient leads to a decrease in the optimal decision because the larger the input cost parameter is, the greater the input cost becomes. However, through the above analysis, we find that cost coefficients may be uncorrelated or even positively correlated with the optimal decision under certain circumstances, which may be attributed to the dynamics of the cost-revenue trade-off. When the rate of revenue increase matches the rate of cost coefficient growth, the firm's optimal decision may remain unchanged. Although the cost coefficient increases, it can attract more shippers who prioritize information technology and service quality. This is beneficial to the port's sustainable development in the long run, resulting in a positive correlation between the cost coefficient and the optimal decision.

5.3. Effects of Blockchain Technology

Our analysis of port *VER* parameters in Section 5.2's steady-state examination revealed multiple advantages for both ports and shipping firms engaging in emissions reduction initiatives. Building on these findings, this section contrasts various blockchain scenarios against non-blockchain approaches, demonstrating how such technological integration can significantly enhance emissions reduction efforts.

Proposition 9. *Effects of blockchain technology established by the port company on the optimal decisions of the shipping supply chain are as follows:*

(*i*) $a^{PB*} = a^{N*}$; (*ii*) $g^{PB*} < g^{N*}$; (*iii*) $E^{PB*} < E^{N*}$; (*iv*) $\begin{cases} if\ \omega \leq \omega_{th2},\ then\ S^{PB*} \geq S_0 \\ if\ \omega > \omega_{th2},\ then\ S^{PB*} < S_0 \end{cases}$;

(*v*) $\begin{cases} if\ \frac{\varphi^2}{\eta} \geq X_{th1},\ then\ D^{PB*} \geq D^{N*} \\ if\ \frac{\varphi^2}{\eta} < X_{th1},\ then\ D^{PB*} < D^{N*} \end{cases}$;

See Supplementary S2 for relevant important critical points regarding Proposition 9.

Proposition 9 analyzes changes in emissions reduction levels and service levels when ports invest in blockchain platforms compared with non-blockchain scenarios. Proposition 9 (*i*) demonstrates that neither blockchain investment nor non-investment affects shipping companies' emissions reduction efforts. From Proposition 9 (*ii*) and (*iii*), it can be observed that ports' investment in blockchain technology reduces both the green investment level and emissions reduction level in the shipping supply chain compared to non-blockchain scenarios. This finding is unexpected due to the fact that in the *PB* scenario, ports are responsible for blockchain investments while shipping companies adjust their strategies as followers. The port's investment in the blockchain may have taken away resources that would have been used for green investment. The Cost Assumptions section mentions that both the cost of green investment and the cost of blockchain investment are quadratic functions, which implies increasing marginal costs. The port allocates its budget between the two. An increase in blockchain investment may lead to a decrease in green investment. Proposition 9 (*iv*) indicates that shipping service levels under blockchain technology become higher when ω is sufficiently small, i.e., when blockchain unit operating costs remain low. When the blockchain unit operating cost ω exceeds a critical value ω_{th2}, the level of blockchain investment b^{j*} by ports and shipping companies drops significantly, even if the technology has perfect functionality. This maps to the reality of IBM-Maersk TradeLens' dilemma, where small and medium-sized shipping companies have low adoption rates due to excessive technology licensing fees. In other words, elevated ω in the model directly affects the quality of service $S(t)$ and the demand $D(t)$ through the decline in b^{j*}. According to Proposition 9 (*v*), transportation demand under blockchain technology exceeds that of non-blockchain scenarios beyond a specific threshold. This is because technological advancements following blockchain implementation reduce operational costs, aligning increased market demand with market dynamics and consequently expanding market share.

Proposition 10. *Effects of blockchain technology established by the shipping company on the optimal decisions of the shipping supply chain are as follows:*

(*i*) $a^{CB*} < a^{N*}$; (*ii*) $g^{CB*} = g^{N*}$; (*iii*) $E^{CB*} < E^{N*}$; (*iv*) $\begin{cases} if\ \omega \leq \omega_{th3},\ then\ S^{CB*} \geq S_0 \\ if\ \omega > \omega_{th3},\ then\ S^{CB*} < S_0 \end{cases}$;

(*v*) $\begin{cases} if\ \frac{\varphi^2}{\eta} \geq X_{th2},\ then\ D^{CB*} \geq D^{N*} \\ if\ \frac{\varphi^2}{\eta} < X_{th2},\ then\ D^{CB*} < D^{N*} \end{cases}$;

See Supplementary S2 for relevant important critical points regarding Proposition 10.

Proposition 10 analyzes shipping companies' investment in blockchain technology. Proposition 10 (*ii*) demonstrates that blockchain investment decisions (whether to invest or not) do not affect the port' s green investment level. From Proposition 10 (*i*) and (*iii*), it can be observed that a shipping company' s blockchain investment reduces both the port' s emissions reduction efforts and emissions reduction levels compared to non-blockchain scenarios. At first glance, this outcome appears to run counter to blockchain technology's fundamental purpose. However, when shipping firms invest in blockchain systems, they incur substantial expenses—from acquiring specialized equipment to training personnel and covering various ancillary costs. These additional financial pressures have forced enterprises to reduce their budgets for research and development of emissions reduction technologies and equipment upgrading in the short term, thus objectively weakening their investment in environmental protection, and leading to a stage-by-stage decline in the effectiveness of emissions reduction. From Proposition 10 (*iv*), the shipping service level under blockchain technology is higher if ω is smaller, i.e., the blockchain unit operating cost is lower. This is because the lower blockchain unit operating costs allow shipping companies to leverage the benefits of blockchain technology more fully. According to Proposition 10 (*v*), the demand under blockchain technology is greater than the no blockchain scenario for a certain threshold. This is because as technological advances following blockchain investments bring down costs, the increase in market demand is in line with the changing patterns of the market, thus increasing market share.

Proposition 11. *Effects of the shipping logistics blockchain platform on the optimal decisions of the shipping supply chain are as follows:*

(*i*) $\begin{cases} if\ c_b \geq \frac{\lambda(p-c_1-r)}{1+\lambda},\ then\ a^{FB*} \leq a^{N*} \\ if\ c_b < \frac{\lambda(p-c_1-r)}{1+\lambda},\ then\ a^{FB*} > a^{N*} \end{cases};$

(*ii*) $\begin{cases} if\ c_b > \frac{\lambda(r-c_0)}{1+\lambda},\ then\ g^{FB*} \leq g^{N*} \\ if\ c_b < \frac{\lambda(r-c_0)}{1+\lambda},\ then\ g^{FB*} > g^{N*} \end{cases};$

(*iii*) $\begin{cases} if\ c_b \geq \frac{\lambda(ku^2(p-c_1-r)+h\theta^2(r-c_0))}{(1+\lambda)(ku^2+h\theta^2)},\ then\ E^{FB*} \leq E^{N*} \\ if\ c_b < \frac{\lambda(ku^2(p-c_1-r)+h\theta^2(r-c_0))}{(1+\lambda)(ku^2+h\theta^2)},\ then\ E^{FB*} > E^{N*} \end{cases};$

(*iv*) $\begin{cases} if\ \omega \leq \omega_{th4},\ then\ S^{FB*} \geq S_0 \\ if\ \omega > \omega_{th4},\ then\ S^{FB*} < S_0 \end{cases};$

(*v*) $\begin{cases} if\ \frac{\varphi^2}{\eta} \geq X_{th\ 3},\ then\ D^{FB*} \geq D^{N*} \\ if\ \frac{\varphi^2}{\eta} < X_{th\ 3},\ then\ D^{FB*} < D^{N*} \end{cases};$

See Supplementary S2 for relevant important critical points in Proposition 11.

Proposition 11 focuses on the impact of a shipping logistics blockchain platform on optimal decision-making in the shipping supply chain, comparing scenarios with and without blockchain technology. Proposition 11 (*i*)–(*iii*) illustrate that when the blockchain usage fee charged by the shipping logistics blockchain platform is low, the shipping company's emissions reduction efforts, the port's green investment level, and emissions reduction levels in the shipping supply chain are generally higher than in non-blockchain scenarios. This is because the lower blockchain usage fee lowers the threshold for port and shipping enterprises to use the technology, making them more willing to increase the application of blockchain technology at a manageable cost. When port and shipping companies join the shipping logistics blockchain platform, they can exchange data in real time and work together to formulate emissions reduction plans to further promote emissions reductions. From Proposition 11 (*iv*), it can be observed that blockchain platform operating costs decrease when ω is sufficiently small, i.e., when blockchain unit operating costs remain low. This enables improved shipping service levels following substantial blockchain technology investments. Blockchain' s cost-efficient operations allow the platform to run with minimal expenses, paving the way for widespread adoption by port and shipping companies. This economic advantage makes the technology a viable solution for large-scale implementation across the industry. According to Proposition 11 (*v*), the demand under blockchain technology is greater than the no-blockchain case for a certain threshold. The application of blockchain technology can optimize supply chain management, improve transportation efficiency, and reduce operating costs. These cost reductions can translate into price advantages, attracting more customers to choose the shipping company's services.

5.4. Blockchain Investment Strategy

Section 5.3 reveals that blockchain technology investments can boost demand under specific circumstances. Building on these findings, this section examines how operational approaches evolve when various stakeholders adopt blockchain solutions.

Proposition 12. *The comparative analysis of the two blockchain scenarios PB and CB is as follows:*

$$(i)\ a^{PB*} > a^{CB*};\ (ii)\ g^{PB*} < g^{CB*};\ (iii) \begin{cases} if\ p \le 2r - c_0 + c_1,\ then\ b^{PB*} \ge b^{CB*} \\ if\ p > 2r - c_0 + c_1,\ then\ b^{PB*} < b^{CB*} \end{cases};$$

$$(iv) \begin{cases} if\ \frac{k}{\theta^2} \ge \frac{h}{u^2},\ then\ E^{PB*} \ge E^{CB*} \\ if\ \frac{k}{\theta^2} < \frac{h}{u^2},\ then\ E^{PB*} < E^{CB*} \end{cases};$$

$$(v) \begin{cases} if\ r \ge \frac{1}{2}(p + c_0 - c_1),\ then\ S^{PB*} \ge S^{CB*} \\ if\ r < \frac{1}{2}(p + c_0 - c_1),\ then\ S^{PB*} < S^{CB*} \end{cases};$$

$$(vi) \begin{cases} if\ \left\{r > \frac{1}{2}(p + c_0 - c_1),\ \frac{k}{\theta^2} > \frac{h}{u^2}\right\},\ then\ D^{PB*} > D^{CB*} \\ if\ \left\{r \le \frac{1}{2}(p + c_0 - c_1),\ \frac{k}{\theta^2} \le \frac{h}{u^2}\right\},\ then\ D^{PB*} \le D^{CB*} \\ if \begin{cases} \frac{\varphi^2}{\eta} \le X_{th\ 4},\ then\ D^{PB*} \ge D^{CB*} \\ \frac{\varphi^2}{\eta} > X_{th\ 4},\ then\ D^{PB*} < D^{CB*} \end{cases} \end{cases};$$

See Supplementary S2 for relevant important critical points regarding Proposition 12.

Proposition 12 compares the differences in operational strategies between *PB* and *CB* blockchain scenarios. Proposition 12 (*i*) and (*ii*) state that if a port invests in blockchain technology, shipping companies will take more aggressive emissions reduction measures than under the *CB* model, while the port' s green investment will be correspondingly lower. In the *CB* scenario, shipping companies as "edges" grasp core data such as ship emission trajectories and route efficiency, and ports as "nodes" rely on their shared information to adjust service strategies. This information symmetry structure of "strong edges and weak nodes" leads to a lower synergy efficiency of shipping emissions reduction efforts than in the *PB* scenario. In the *PB* scenario, the port, as the leading party of blockchain investment, has a guiding effect on the entire supply chain. Ports have improved supply chain transparency and collaboration through blockchain technology, prompting shipping companies to increase their efforts to reduce emissions to adapt to the new environment and remain competitive. As ports have focused on investing in blockchain technology, this has resulted in relatively fewer resources for green investment, which in turn has reduced the level of green investment. When the port service fee is higher, ports have higher levels of blockchain investment, emissions reductions, demand, and shipping service levels than shipping companies. When the port service fee is higher, the port's level of blockchain investment, level of emissions reductions, level of de-demanding and level of shipping services are higher than those of the shipping company. This inconsistency with the common intuition that port-led investments better integrate resources and reduce costs is due to the fact that ports need to incur more blockchain infrastructure construction costs in *PB* scenarios, which in turn raises the cost of service. The more the port invests, the lower price makes consumer demand increase, which in turn leads to an increase in the level of emissions reduction and the level of service.

Proposition 13. *The comparative analysis of the two blockchain scenarios PB and FB is as follows:*

$$(i) \begin{cases} if\ c_b \ge \frac{\lambda(p-c_1-r)}{1+\lambda},\ then\ a^{PB*} \ge a^{FB*} \\ if\ c_b < \frac{\lambda(p-c_1-r)}{1+\lambda},\ then\ a^{PB*} < a^{FB*} \end{cases};\ (ii) \begin{cases} if\ c_b \ge \frac{\lambda(r-c_0)+\omega}{1+\lambda},\ then\ g^{PB*} \ge g^{FB*} \\ if\ c_b < \frac{\lambda(r-c_0)+\omega}{1+\lambda},\ then\ g^{PB*} < g^{FB*} \end{cases};$$

$$(iii)\begin{cases} if\ c_b \leq \frac{1}{2}(\frac{r-c_0-\omega}{1+\lambda}+c_2+\omega),\ then\ b^{PB*} \geq b^{FB*} \\ if\ c_b > \frac{1}{2}(\frac{r-c_0-\omega}{1+\lambda}+c_2+\omega),\ then\ b^{PB*} < b^{FB*} \end{cases};$$

$$(iv)\begin{cases} if\ c_b \leq \frac{h\theta^2\omega+\lambda(ku^2(p-c_1-r)+h\theta^2(r-c_0))}{(1+\lambda)(ku^2+h\theta^2)},\ then\ E^{PB*} \leq E^{FB*} \\ if\ c_b > \frac{h\theta^2\omega+\lambda(ku^2(p-c_1-r)+h\theta^2(r-c_0))}{(1+\lambda)(ku^2+h\theta^2)},\ then\ E^{PB*} > E^{FB*} \end{cases};$$

$$(v)\begin{cases} if\ c_b \leq \frac{(r-c_0+c_2(1+\lambda)+\lambda\omega)}{2(1+\lambda)},\ then\ S^{PB*} \geq S^{FB*} \\ if\ c_b > \frac{(r-c_0+c_2(1+\lambda)+\lambda\omega)}{2(1+\lambda)},\ then\ S^{PB*} < S^{FB*} \end{cases};$$

$$(vi)\begin{cases} if\ \frac{\varphi^2}{\eta} > X_{th\ 5},\ and \begin{cases} c_b \leq c_{bth\ 2},\ then\ D^{PB*} \geq D^{FB*} \\ c_b > c_{b\ th\ 2},\ then\ D^{PB*} < D^{FB*} \end{cases} \\ if\ \frac{\varphi^2}{\eta} < X_{th\ 5},\ and \begin{cases} c_b \geq c_{b\ th\ 2},\ then\ D^{PB*} \geq D^{FB*} \\ c_b < c_{b\ th\ 2},\ then\ D^{PB*} < D^{FB*} \end{cases} \\ if\ \frac{\varphi^2}{\eta} = X_{th\ 5},\ and \begin{cases} c_2 \geq c_{2\ th\ 2},\ then\ D^{PB*} \geq D^{FB*} \\ c_2 < c_{2\ th\ 2},\ then\ D^{PB*} < D^{FB*} \end{cases} \end{cases};$$

See Supplementary S2 for relevant important critical points regarding Proposition 13.

Proposition 13 analyzes the blockchain usage fee charged by shipping logistics blockchain platforms. When royalty fees are set at higher levels, emissions reduction efforts by shipping companies and green investment levels by ports under the *PB* scenario exceed those under the *FB* scenario. This occurs because shipping companies and ports proactively intensify emissions reduction initiatives to achieve cost savings. In the *PB* scenario, where the port leads blockchain investments, elevated user fees incentivize ports to prioritize operational efficiency improvements and energy consumption reduction as compensatory measures. These strategic adjustments further motivate shipping companies to enhance their emissions reduction efforts in alignment with the port' s overarching sustainability goals. Conversely, in the *FB* scenario, despite joint participation by ports and shipping enterprises in the blockchain platform, high operational costs create significant pressure on cost-sharing mechanisms among stakeholders. This financial burden may partially inhibit enthusiasm for green investments and emissions reduction initiatives. When the fee is low, the port still bears the main investment cost. This may limit the port's ability to invest in other emissions reduction related areas, resulting in a relatively low level of emissions reduction. However, ports have absolute control over the application of technology and service enhancement resulting in higher service levels. The multi-party consensus mechanism in the FB scenario ensures that the green investment effect of the port is synchronized with the emissions reduction efforts of the shipping companies in real time, forming a positive feedback mechanism of "node emission reduction–edge response". In the PB scenario, the port, as the single dominant party, may ignore the actual operational constraints of the shipping company, resulting in a decrease in symmetric collaboration efficiency.

Proposition 14. *The comparative analysis of the two blockchain scenarios CB and FB is as follows:*

$$(i)\begin{cases} if\ c_b \geq \frac{\lambda(p-r-c_1)+\omega}{1+\lambda},\ then\ a^{CB*} \geq a^{FB*} \\ if\ c_b < \frac{\lambda(p-r-c_1)+\omega}{1+\lambda},\ then\ a^{CB*} < a^{FB*} \end{cases};$$

$$(ii)\begin{cases} if\ c_b \geq \frac{\lambda(r-c_0)}{1+\lambda},\ then\ g^{CB*} \geq g^{FB*} \\ if\ c_b < \frac{\lambda(r-c_0)}{1+\lambda},\ then\ g^{CB*} < g^{FB*} \end{cases};$$

$$(iii)\begin{cases} if\ c_b \leq \frac{1}{2}(\frac{p-r-c_1-\omega}{1+\lambda}+c_2+\omega),\ then\ b^{CB*} \geq b^{FB*} \\ if\ c_b > \frac{1}{2}(\frac{p-r-c_1-\omega}{1+\lambda}+c_2+\omega),\ then\ b^{CB*} < b^{FB*} \end{cases}$$

$$(iv)\begin{cases} if\ c_b \leq \frac{hu^2\omega+\lambda(ku^2(p-c_1-r)+h\theta^2(r-c_0))}{(1+\lambda)(ku^2+h\theta^2)},\ then\ E^{CB*} \leq E^{FB*} \\ if\ c_b > \frac{hu^2\omega+\lambda(ku^2(p-c_1-r)+h\theta^2(r-c_0))}{(1+\lambda)(ku^2+h\theta^2)},\ then\ E^{CB*} > E^{FB*} \end{cases};$$

$$(v) \begin{cases} if\ c_b \le \frac{(p-r-c_1+c_2(1+\lambda)+\lambda\omega)}{2(1+\lambda)},\ then\ S^{CB*} \ge S^{FB*} \\ if\ c_b > \frac{(p-r-c_1+c_2(1+\lambda)+\lambda\omega)}{2(1+\lambda)},\ then\ S^{CB*} < S^{FB*} \end{cases};$$

$$(vi) \begin{cases} if\ \frac{\varphi^2}{\eta} > X_{th\ 5},\ and \begin{cases} c_b \le c_{b\ th\ 3},\ then\ D^{CB*} \ge D^{FB*} \\ c_b > c_{b\ th\ 3},\ then\ D^{CB*} < D^{FB*} \end{cases} \\ if\ \frac{\varphi^2}{\eta} < X_{th\ 5},\ and \begin{cases} c_b \ge c_{b\ th\ 3},\ then\ D^{CB*} \ge D^{FB*} \\ c_b < c_{b\ th\ 3},\ then\ D^{CB*} < D^{FB*} \end{cases} \\ if\ \frac{\varphi^2}{\eta} = X_{th\ 5},\ and \begin{cases} c_2 \ge c_{2\ th\ 3},\ then\ D^{CB*} \ge D^{FB*} \\ c_2 < c_{2\ th\ 3},\ then\ D^{CB*} < D^{FB*} \end{cases} \end{cases};$$

See Supplementary S2 for relevant important critical points regarding Proposition 14.

Proposition 14 aligns with the conclusions derived from Proposition 13. The level of blockchain investment in the case of shipping companies investing in blockchain technology is higher than that in the case of port and shipping companies jointly participating in a shipping logistics blockchain platform when the fees charged are higher. Distinguished from the single-subject dominance of the *PB* or *CB* scenario, the *FB* scenario ensures complete symmetry of key parameters such as emissions reduction level $E(t)$, service level $S(t)$, and cost of blockchain usage c_b through a multi-node consensus algorithm, eliminating "node–edge" or "edge–node" information privileges. In the *CB* scenario, as primary investors in blockchain infrastructure, shipping companies actively intensify their blockchain investments to offset high operational costs. Given the substantial capital commitment, these firms exhibit heightened expectations regarding investment returns. By increasing blockchain technology investments, they aim to achieve enhanced supply chain efficiency, thereby strengthening market competitiveness and securing greater profit margins. Conversely, in the *FB* scenario, despite collaborative participation by ports and shipping companies in the blockchain platform, the overall blockchain investment level remains comparatively subdued when confronted with high usage costs.

6. Extended Analysis

Earlier analyses overlooked how investing in blockchain technology directly affects carbon emissions in shipping transport. However, if we were to factor in the environmental credibility provided by blockchain-based green certification, how would this alter the outcome? In this section, the green trust coefficient of shippers $m = 1 - \overline{m}$ is introduced into the N case, indicating low-carbon preference shippers' trust in the emissions reduction process in the shipping industry. Consequently, leveraging the inquiries, the differential game model of traditional shipping supply chain under scenario *N1* is constructed as follows:

$$\max_{a^{N1}(t)} \left\{ \pi_C{}^{N1} = \int_0^{+\infty} e^{-\rho \cdot t}[(p-r-c_1) \cdot D^{N1}(t) - \frac{1}{2}h \cdot a^{N1^2}(t)]dt \right\} \tag{52}$$

$$\max_{g^{N1}(t)} \left\{ \pi_P{}^{N1} = \int_0^{+\infty} e^{-\rho \cdot t}[(r-c_0) \cdot D^{N1}(t) - \frac{1}{2}k \cdot g^{N1^2}(t)]dt \right\} \tag{53}$$

$$s.t. \begin{cases} dE^{N1}(t) = ua^{N1}(t)dt + \theta g^{N1}(t)dt - \sigma E^{N1}(t)dt \\ E^{N1}(0) = E_0 \end{cases} \tag{54}$$

The demand of shippers without blockchain is expressed as follows:

$$\begin{aligned} D^{N1}(t) &= \alpha \cdot \int_{p-\beta S_0-\gamma(1-\overline{m})E(t)}^{1} f(v)dv + (1-\alpha) \cdot \int_{p-\beta S_0}^{1} f(v)dv \\ &= \alpha \cdot [1-p+\beta S_0+\gamma(1-\overline{m})E(t)] + (1-\alpha) \cdot [1-p+\beta S_0] \end{aligned} \tag{55}$$

The demand of shippers with blockchain is expressed as follows:

$$\begin{aligned} D^B(t) &= \alpha \cdot \int_{p-\beta S(t)-\gamma E(t)}^{1} f(v)dv + (1-\alpha) \cdot \int_{p-\beta S(t)}^{1} f(v)dv \\ &= \alpha \cdot [1 - p + \beta S(t) + \gamma E(t)] + (1-\alpha) \cdot [1 - p + \beta S(t)] \end{aligned} \tag{56}$$

Theorem 5. *In scenario N1 where there is no blockchain and considering low-carbon-preference shippers are distrustful of shipping industry emissions reductions, the optimal green investment level g^{N1^*} of port company and the optimal emissions reduction effort a^{N1} shipping company in the shipping supply chain are as follows:*

$$g^{N1*} = \frac{\alpha\gamma(1-\overline{m})\theta(r-c_0)}{k(\rho+\sigma)} \tag{57}$$

$$a^{N1*} = \frac{\alpha\gamma u(1-\overline{m})(p-c_1-r)}{h(\rho+\sigma)} \tag{58}$$

Corollary 5. *In scenario N1 where there is no blockchain and considering low-carbon-preference shippers are distrustful of shipping industry emissions reductions, the optimal dynamic trajectories of emissions reduction operation strategies for the shipping supply chain are as follows:*

$$\begin{aligned} E^{N1*}(t) &= (E_0 - \tfrac{\alpha\gamma(1-\overline{m})(h\theta^2(r-c_0)+ku^2(p-c_1-r))}{hk\sigma(\rho+\sigma)})e^{-\sigma\cdot t} + \\ &\tfrac{\alpha\gamma(1-\overline{m})(h\theta^2(r-c_0)+ku^2(p-c_1-r))}{hk\sigma(\rho+\sigma)} \end{aligned} \tag{59}$$

$$\begin{aligned} D^{N1*}(t) &= \alpha(\gamma((E_0 - \tfrac{\alpha\gamma(1-\overline{m})(h\theta^2(r-c_0)+ku^2(p-c_1-r))}{hk\sigma(\rho+\sigma)})e^{-\sigma\cdot t} \\ &+ \tfrac{1}{hk\sigma(\rho+\sigma)}(\alpha\gamma(1-\overline{m})(h\theta^2(r-c_0)+ku^2(p-c_1-r)))) \\ &-p+\beta S_0+1) + (1-\alpha)(1-p+\beta S_0) \end{aligned} \tag{60}$$

$$\begin{aligned} {V_C}^{N1*}(t) &= \tfrac{\alpha\gamma(1-\overline{m})(p-c_1-r)}{\rho+\sigma} \cdot ((E_0- \\ &\tfrac{\alpha\gamma(1-\overline{m})(h\theta^2(r-c_0)+ku^2(p-c_1-r))}{hk\sigma(\rho+\sigma)})e^{-\sigma\cdot t} \\ &+\tfrac{\alpha\gamma(1-\overline{m})(h\theta^2(r-c_0)+ku^2(p-c_1-r))}{hk\sigma(\rho+\sigma)}) \\ &+\tfrac{(p-c_1-r)}{2\rho} \cdot (2(1-p+\beta S_0) \\ &+\tfrac{\alpha^2\gamma^2(1-\overline{m})^2(2h\theta^2(r-c_0)+ku^2(p-c_1-r))}{hk(\rho+\sigma)^2}) \end{aligned} \tag{61}$$

$$\begin{aligned} {V_P}^{N1*}(t) &= \tfrac{\alpha\gamma(1-\overline{m})(r-c_0)}{\rho+\sigma} \\ &\cdot((E_0 - \tfrac{\alpha\gamma(1-\overline{m})(h\theta^2(r-c_0)+ku^2(p-c_1-r))}{hk\sigma(\rho+\sigma)})e^{-\sigma\cdot t} \\ &+\tfrac{\alpha\gamma(1-\overline{m})(h\theta^2(r-c_0)+ku^2(p-c_1-r))}{hk\sigma(\rho+\sigma)}) \\ &+\tfrac{(r-c_0)}{2\rho} \cdot (2(1-p+\beta S_0) \\ &+\tfrac{\alpha^2\gamma^2(1-\overline{m})^2(h\theta^2(r-c_0)+2ku^2(p-c_1-r))}{hk(\rho+\sigma)^2}) \end{aligned} \tag{62}$$

Under blockchain technology $(1-\overline{m}) = 1$, by comparing *PB*, *CB*, and *FB* with *N1*, it can be inferred that when blockchain technology is utilized for green certification during the emissions reduction process of the shipping supply chain to boost shippers' green trust, the impact of the blockchain technology established by port companies on the optimization decision of the shipping supply chain is as follows:

Proposition 15. *When blockchain technology can be used for green certification in emissions reduction processes to enhance shippers' green trust, the effects of blockchain technology established by the port company on the optimal decisions of the shipping supply chain are as follows:*

$$(i)\ a^{PB*} > a^{N1*};\ (ii) \begin{cases} if\ \frac{\overline{m}}{\omega} \geq \frac{1}{r-c_0},\ then\ g^{PB*} \geq g^{N1*} \\ if\ \frac{\overline{m}}{\omega} < \frac{1}{r-c_0},\ then\ g^{PB*} < g^{N1*} \end{cases};$$

$$(iii) \begin{cases} if\ \frac{\overline{m}}{\omega} \geq \frac{h\theta^2}{k(p-r-c_1)u^2+h(r-c_0)\theta^2},\ then\ E^{PB*} \geq E^{N1*} \\ if\ \frac{\overline{m}}{\omega} < \frac{h\theta^2}{k(p-r-c_1)u^2+h(r-c_0)\theta^2},\ then\ E^{PB*} < E^{N1*} \end{cases};$$

$$(iv) \begin{cases} if\ \frac{\varphi^2}{\eta} \geq X_{th\ 1}{}',\ then\ D^{PB*} \geq D^{N1*} \\ if\ \frac{\varphi^2}{\eta} < X_{th\ 1}{}',\ then\ D^{PB*} < D^{N1*} \end{cases};$$

See Supplementary S2 for relevant important critical points regarding Proposition 15.

Proposition 15 (*i*) indicates that the emissions reduction efforts in the *PB* scenario are higher than those in the *N1* scenario. In the *PB* scenario, after the port company invests in blockchain technology, the characteristics of blockchain make all aspects of the supply chain more transparent and traceable. Contrastingly, in the *N1* scenario, the port' s ability to oversee and handle the shipping firm is hamstrung by the absence of blockchain support. This shortfall diminishes the company' s motivation to slash emissions, leaving efforts to reduce pollutants somewhat lackluster. Proposition 15 (*ii*), (*iii*) shows that when low-carbon-preference shippers have a higher level of distrust in the shipping industry' s emissions reduction efforts, investing in blockchain can improve transparency and trust, thereby enhancing the level of emissions reduction. This suggests that even if initial trust is low, the transparency of the blockchain can significantly increase the effectiveness of mitigation, challenging the conventional wisdom that low trust is difficult to reverse. The shipping sector' s faith in the efficacy of carbon-reduction measures among eco-conscious shippers significantly influences their selection of shipping options. In the *N1* scenario, shippers' lack of trust in the shipping industry' s ability to reduce emissions could lead them to reduce their demand for shipping services or to opt for greener but more costly alternative modes of transport. Proposition 15 (*iv*) shows that when there are other factors influencing the scenario, investing in blockchain technology increases demand due to enhanced shipper trust.

Proposition 16. *When blockchain technology can be used for green certification in emissions reduction processes to enhance shippers' green trust, the effects of blockchain technology established by the shipping company on the optimal decisions of the shipping supply chain are as follows:*

$$(i) \begin{cases} if\ \frac{\overline{m}}{\omega} \geq \frac{1}{p-r-c_1},\ then\ a^{CB*} \geq a^{N1*} \\ if\ \frac{\overline{m}}{\omega} < \frac{1}{p-r-c_1},\ then\ a^{CB*} < a^{N1*} \end{cases};\ (ii)\ g^{CB*} > g^{N1*};$$

$$(iii) \begin{cases} if\ \frac{\overline{m}}{\omega} \geq \frac{ku^2}{k(p-r-c_1)u^2+h(r-c_0)\theta^2},\ then\ E^{CB*} \geq E^{N1*} \\ if\ \frac{\overline{m}}{\omega} < \frac{ku^2}{k(p-r-c_1)u^2+h(r-c_0)\theta^2},\ then\ E^{CB*} < E^{N1*} \end{cases};$$

$$(iv) \begin{cases} if\ \frac{\varphi^2}{\eta} \geq X_{th\ 2}{}',\ then\ D^{CB*} \geq D^{N1*} \\ if\ \frac{\varphi^2}{\eta} < X_{th\ 2}{}',\ then\ D^{CB*} < D^{N1*} \end{cases};$$

See Supplementary S2 for relevant important critical points regarding Proposition 16.

Proposition 16 (*i*), (*iii*) show that the emissions reduction efforts in the *CB* scenario are higher than those in the *N1* scenario. In the *CB* scenario, shipping companies' investment in blockchain technology enables them to monitor and manage carbon emissions from ship operations more accurately. Blockchain technology can record a ship's fuel consumption, sailing routes, and other operational data in real time, providing shipping companies with precise carbon emission analytics. Leveraging this data, shipping companies can systematically enhance the level of emissions reduction. In contrast, in the *N1* scenario, shippers' distrust of emissions reduction claims makes them more cautious about their choice of shipping services, which negatively impacts the business volume of shipping companies. Proposition 16 (*iv*) demonstrates that when other factors are considered, the *CB* scenario increases demand by strengthening shippers' trust. In this scenario, blockchain technology not only contributes to emissions reduction but also offers significant advantages in improving service quality and customer experience.

Taken together, Propositions 15 and 16 point to the same fundamental insight: when environmentally conscious shippers grow increasingly skeptical about the shipping sector's commitment to cutting emissions, blockchain investments yield substantially greater returns. The findings reveal a direct correlation—the deeper this distrust runs among eco-minded shipping clients, the more value blockchain technology delivers.

Proposition 17. *When blockchain technology can be used for green certification in emissions reduction processes to enhance shippers' green trust, the effects of the shipping logistics blockchain platform on the optimal decisions of the shipping supply chain are as follows:*

$$(i)\begin{cases} if\ \overline{m} \geq \frac{c_b(1+\lambda)}{p-r-c_1} - \lambda,\ then\ a^{FB*} \geq a^{N1*} \\ if\ \overline{m} < \frac{c_b(1+\lambda)}{p-r-c_1} - \lambda,\ then\ a^{FB*} < a^{N1*} \end{cases};(ii)\begin{cases} if\ \overline{m} \geq \frac{c_b(1+\lambda)}{r-c_0} - \lambda,\ then\ g^{FB*} \geq g^{N1*} \\ if\ \overline{m} < \frac{c_b(1+\lambda)}{r-c_0} - \lambda,\ then\ g^{FB*} < g^{N1*} \end{cases};$$

$$(iii)\begin{cases} if\ \overline{m} < -\frac{c_b(ku^2+h\theta^2)(1+\lambda)}{c_1ku^2-k(p-r-c_1)u^2-h(r-c_0)\theta^2} - \lambda,\ then\ E^{FB*} \geq E^{N1*} \\ if\ \overline{m} \geq -\frac{c_b(ku^2+h\theta^2)(1+\lambda)}{c_1ku^2-k(p-r-c_1)u^2-h(r-c_0)\theta^2} - \lambda,\ then\ E^{FB*} < E^{N1*} \end{cases};$$

$$(iv)\begin{cases} if\ \frac{\varphi^2}{\eta} \geq X_{th\ 3'},\ then\ D^{FB*} \geq D^{N1*} \\ if\ \frac{\varphi^2}{\eta} < X_{th\ 3'},\ then\ D^{FB*} < D^{N1*} \end{cases}$$

See Supplementary S2 for relevant important critical points in Proposition 17.

Proposition 17 (*i*) and (*ii*) compare the emissions reduction efforts of shipping companies and the green investment levels of ports in the *FB* scenario versus the *N1* scenario. When shippers' distrust is higher, both the emissions reduction efforts of shipping companies and the green investment levels of ports in the *FB* scenario exceed those in the *N1* scenario. In the *FB* scenario, ports and shipping companies jointly participate in the blockchain platform, and the abatement data jointly provided by multiple parties can strengthen customer selection and create a scale effect on the demand side. In the face of stringent emissions regulation, the *FB* scenario can meet compliance requirements more efficiently and avoid the cost of repeatedly interfacing with different regulatory systems due to the unified data format and multi-party consensus mechanism. However, in Proposition 17 (*iii*), the lower the degree of distrust that shippers have toward the shipping industry' s emissions reduction efforts, the higher will be the levels of emissions reductions achieved through joint participation of ports and shipping enterprises in the shipping logistics blockchain platform. This is because shippers are more willing to provide incentives for low-carbon transportation services, such as reduced insurance rates and prioritized freight payments, thereby creating an effective mechanism to encourage ports and shipping companies to actively reduce emissions under the blockchain-enabled collaboration. In contrast, if the shippers do not trust these emissions reductions, ports and shipping companies may face market pressures, economic losses, and insufficient incentives to increase investments in emissions reduction. Additionally, in the *FB* scenario, blockchain technology' s ability to enhance cargo owners' trust can also lead to increased demand under specific conditions.

7. Experiment and Results

This section delves into the influence of investing in blockchain technology on the emissions reductions of port and shipping firms, considering the dynamic path of the optimal decision and the alteration of key parameters across diverse scenarios. This part discusses in depth the impact of investing in blockchain technology on emissions reductions in harbor and shipping enterprises and considers the dynamic path of optimal decision-making and changes in key parameters in different scenarios. In this context, this paper refers to the related literature (Meng et al., [50]) and constructs a parameter system that aligns with realistic scenarios through field research and public data collection. Specifically, the cost parameters are set with reference to the technology deployment cost of Shanghai Port's "Blockchain Paperless Order Exchange Platform"; the green investment level is based on the measured data from Shenzhen Yantian Port's "Oil-to-Electricity" project; and the proportion of low-carbon preference is derived from Maersk Group's research on low-carbon customers, reflecting the current global shipping market. The low-carbon preference ratio, based on Maersk Group's customer survey data, indicates that approximately 70% of cargo owners in the global shipping market currently have a clear demand for green certification services. These parameters were obtained through quantitative analysis of typical cases. Numerical simulations were performed using MATLA—MATLAB R2023a software, and the system parameters are set as follows: $\sigma = 0.3$; $E_0 = 5$; $\mu = 0.58$; $\theta = 0.55$; $S_0 = 2$; $\tau = 0.25$; $\varphi = 0.6$; $\alpha = 0.7$; $p = 10$; $r = 5$; $\beta = 1.5$; $\gamma = 2.5$; $m = 0.85$; $\rho = 0.8$; $k = 1.8$; $h = 2$; $\eta = 1$; $\omega = 0.2$; $c_0 = 0.17$; $c_1 = 0.2$; $c_2 = 0.01$; $c_b = 0.5$; $\lambda = 0.6$.

7.1. Dynamic Trajectory of Shipping Supply Chain Operation Strategy

Figures 3–5 show the trajectory plots of the emissions reductions levels in the shipping supply chain E, the shipping service level S, and the shipping demand D over time t under five scenarios. When E_0 is less than E_∞, the emissions reductions level increases with time; when E_0 is greater than E_∞, it decreases with time t. This phenomenon indicates that if the initial emissions reductions level is relatively low during the early stages of the shipping supply chain's operation, the emissions reduction measures implemented by ports and shipping companies will gradually become effective as time progresses.

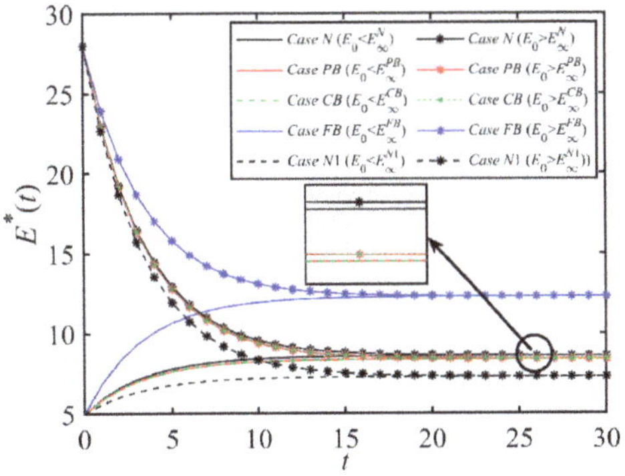

Figure 3. Trajectory diagram of emissions reductions level changing with t under different cases.

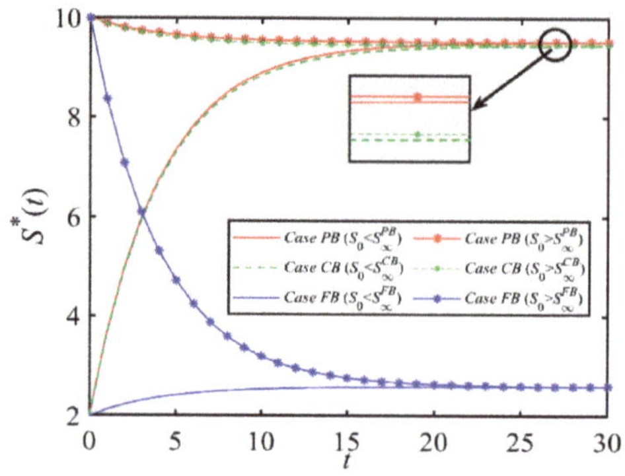

Figure 4. Trajectory diagram of service level changing with t under different cases.

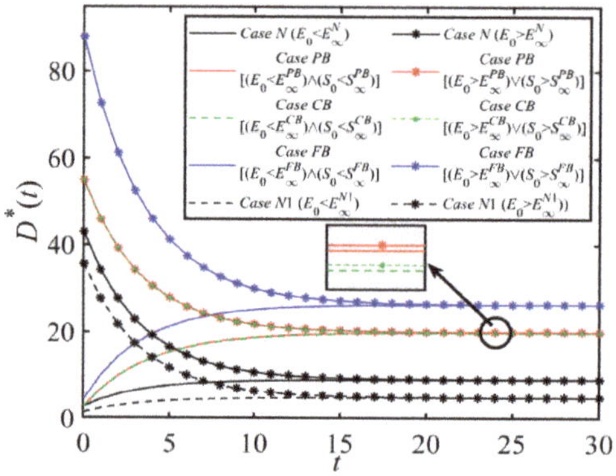

Figure 5. Trajectory diagram of shipping demand changing with t under different cases.

When $S_0 < S_\infty$, the shipping service level increases with time. Blockchain enhances information transparency and customs clearance efficiency, resulting in a smoother cargo transportation process. Customers can access cargo information more promptly, thereby improving their service experience. Meanwhile, ports and shipping companies improve shipping service levels by optimizing transportation processes through maintenance and upgrades of transportation equipment. In contrast, when $S_0 > S_\infty$, the shipping service level decreases with the increase of time. This may be because it is difficult to maintain a high service level at the initial stage for a long time. As business scales expand and market competition intensifies, failure to continuously innovate and optimize services can lead to a gradual decline in service levels until a steady state is reached.

When both $E_0 < E_\infty$ and $S_0 < S_\infty$ are satisfied, the shipping demand D increases over time; conversely, if either condition is violated, the demand decreases. In such cases, the enhancement of emissions reductions levels and the improvement in shipping service quality jointly elevate market competitiveness. This dual improvement aligns with consumers' growing emphasis on environmental protection and service quality, while the progress in emissions reductions meets societal demands for green development, thereby attracting environmentally conscious customers. Among the cases, *FB* had the fastest growth rate and the optimal strategy tended to a steady state with the evolution of time t. In Case *FB*, ports and shipping companies achieve information sharing and resource integration through their joint participation in the blockchain platform, fully demonstrating the synergistic effects of collaborative blockchain adoption.

To summarize, Figures 3–5 clearly demonstrate the changes in key indicators of the shipping supply chain across different scenarios, as well as blockchain technology' s critical role in enhancing emissions reduction levels and stimulating demand. These findings are consistent with the conclusions derived from Propositions 1–4, thereby providing robust support for decision-making processes in port and shipping enterprises.

Figures 6–8 show the trajectory of expected discounted profit of port company V_P, expected discounted profit of shipping company V_C, and expected discounted profit V_F of a shipping logistics blockchain platform changing over time t under five different scenarios. When both $E_0 < E_\infty$ and $S_0 < S_\infty$ are satisfied, V_P, V_C, and V_F are proportional to t; conversely, if either condition is violated, these profits decrease. From the port company' s perspective, under low initial emissions reduction levels and low initial shipping service levels, ports can effectively enhance customs clearance efficiency through blockchain technology investments over time. This improvement attracts more cargo owners to utilize their services, thereby boosting profitability. For shipping companies, under the same conditions, blockchain technology investments increase logistics transparency, enabling shippers to monitor cargo transportation status in real time. This transparency fosters trust, attracts additional business, increases shipping volume and freight revenue, and ultimately drives the growth of the expected discounted profit V_C. With joint participation in the shipping logistics blockchain platform, increased business volume elevates the platform' s utility value and revenue. Consequently, the expected discounted profit V_F rises proportionally as the platform' s adoption and operational scale expand.

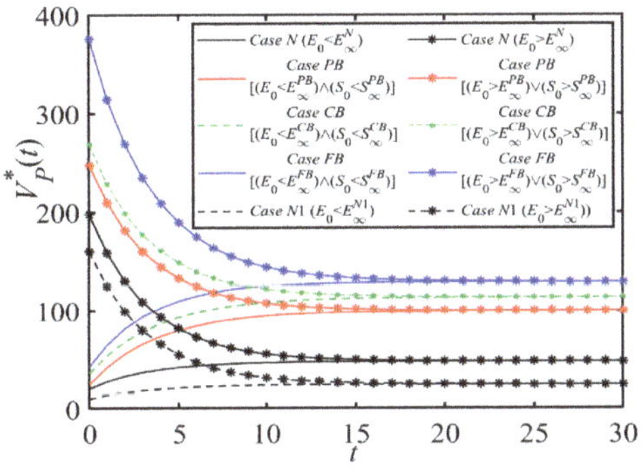

Figure 6. Trajectory diagram of port expected discounted profit changing with t.

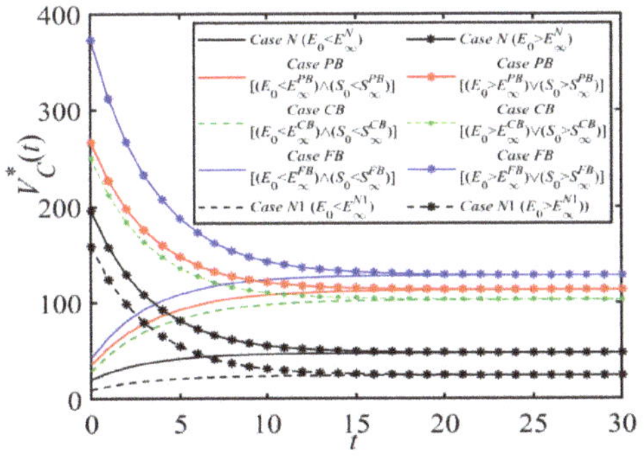

Figure 7. Trajectory diagram of shipping expected discounted profit changing with t.

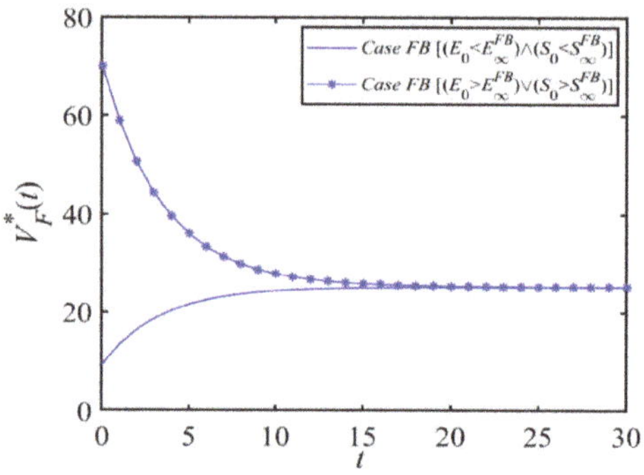

Figure 8. Trajectory diagram of blockchain platform expected discounted profit changing with t.

As time t increases, profits eventually stabilize toward a steady state. First, after an initial period of blockchain technology investment, the market gradually approaches saturation. The growth rate of business volume slows down, and profit growth for ports and shipping enterprises stabilizes. Second, although the early adoption of blockchain technology drives rapid profit growth, over time, the costs of technology investment, operations, and maintenance gradually rise. When cost growth rates align with revenue growth, profits stabilize. This dynamic aligns with the findings in Propositions 1–4, confirming that blockchain-enabled customer relationship management helps ports and shipping companies attract higher-quality clients, thereby demonstrating the long-term value of blockchain integration in the shipping supply chain.

7.2. The Influence of Key Parameters and the Comparison of Optimal Decision

In this section, the key parameters p, r, α, γ, β, φ, c_b are analyzed for sensitivity and the results obtained are shown in Figures 9–15.

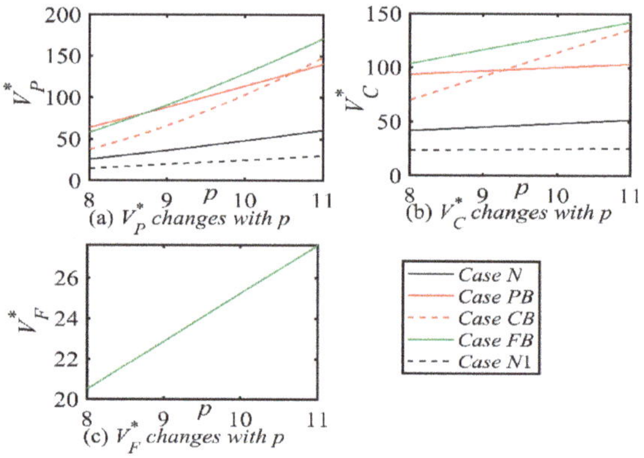

Figure 9. Trajectories of discounted profits under different models as a function of p.

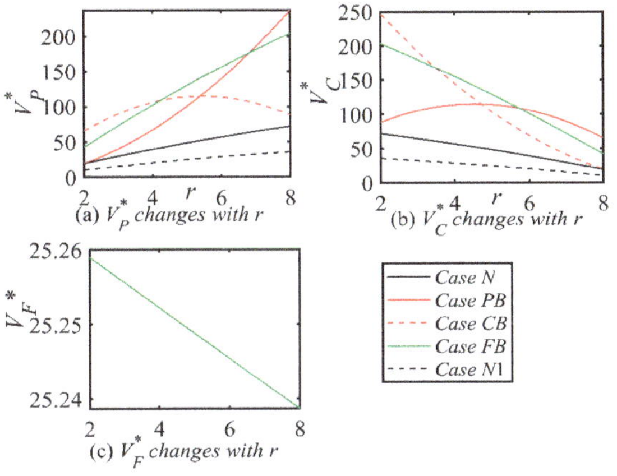

Figure 10. Trajectories of discounted profits under different models as a function of r.

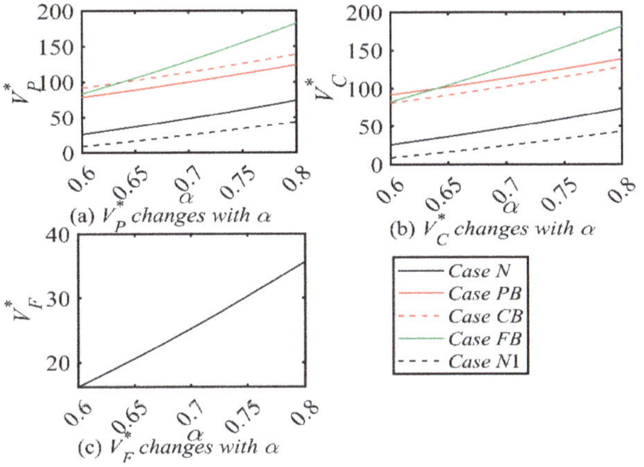

Figure 11. Trajectories of discounted profits under different models as a function of α.

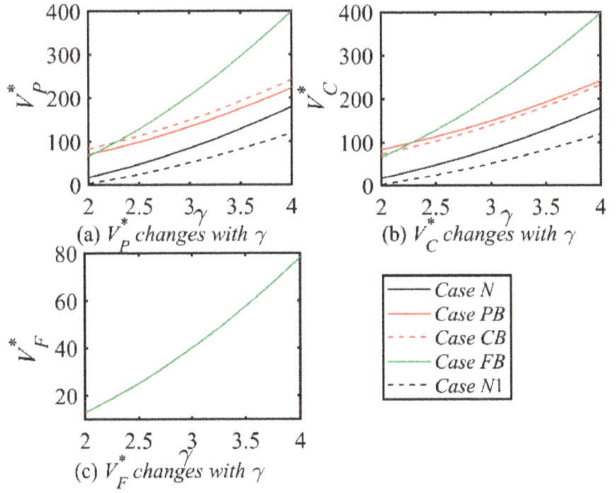

Figure 12. Trajectories of discounted profits under different models as a function of γ.

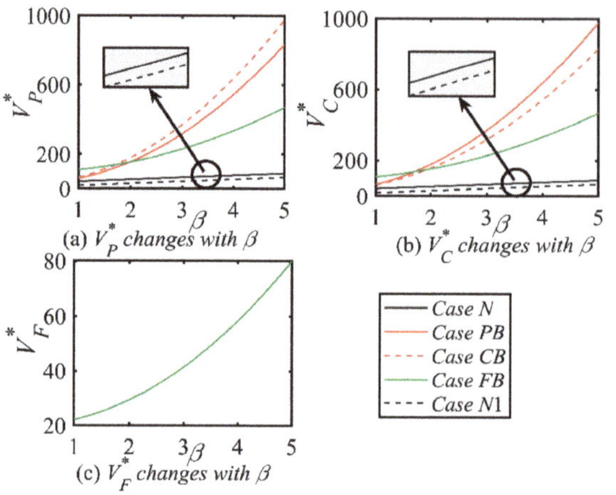

Figure 13. Trajectories of discounted profits under different models as a function of β.

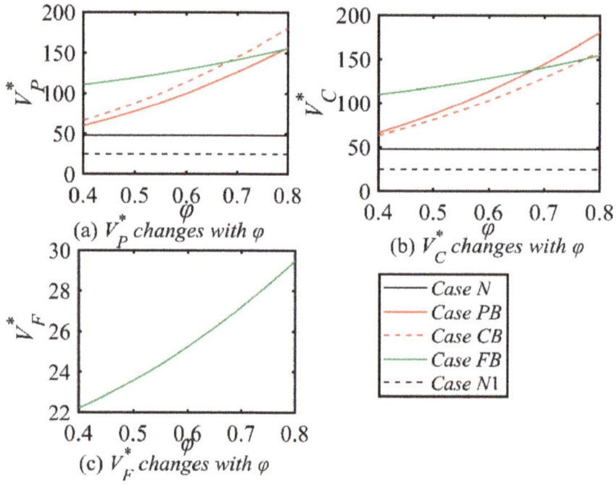

Figure 14. Trajectories of discounted profits under different models as a function of φ.

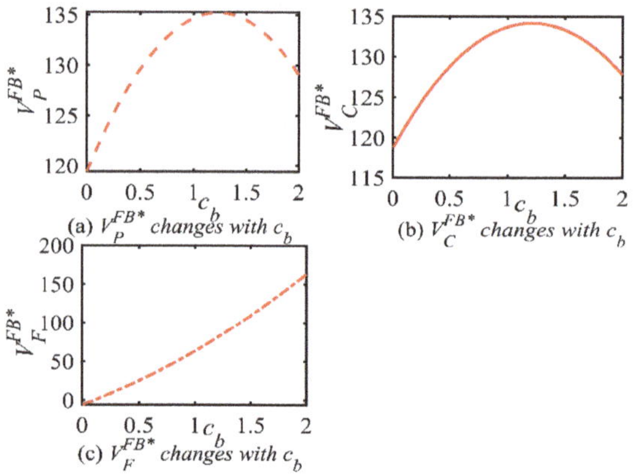

Figure 15. Trajectories of discounted profits under different models as a function of c_b.

Figure 9 represents the changes in V_P, V_C, V_F as the parameter p increases. Figure 9a shows that V_P increases with pp across all scenarios, with Case FB exhibiting the fastest growth rate and achieving the highest V_P value at any given p. Figure 9b reveals that V_C also increases with p; Case *CB* demonstrates the steepest upward trend. Shipping company-led scenarios are more adaptive when freight prices are high or fuel costs fluctuate dramatically. Shipping companies can optimize routes and adjust emissions reduction strategies in real time through the blockchain, amplifying service advantages in times of high returns and rapidly shrinking non-essential inputs in times of surging costs, reflecting the agile responsiveness of edge nodes to market changes. Figure 9c displays the relationship between V_F and p. Here, only the green solid line (Case *FB*) is plotted, indicating a linear growth pattern where V_F rises uniformly with p. This shows that the port obtains the fastest increase in profit when the port invests in blockchain, and the shipping company obtains the fastest profit when the shipping company invests in blockchain.

Figure 10 represents the variation in V_P, V_C, V_F as the parameter r increases. Figure 10a shows that only in Case *CB*, V_P first rises and then declines, peaking at approximately $r = 5$. Figure 10b indicates that in Case *PB*, V_C similarly exhibits a rise-and-fall pattern, reaching its maximum at $r = 4$. Figure 10c depicts a single green solid line (Case *FB*), demonstrating a linear decrease in V_F as r increases. This behavior reflects the strategic interaction between shipping companies and ports when blockchain technology is adopted by the former. Initially, as port service fees rise, shipping companies may tolerate the increase due to offsetting benefits from blockchain adoption (e.g., enhanced operational efficiency or market trust), allowing ports to capture higher profits. However, as fees continue to escalate, cost pressures on shipping companies intensify. Leveraging blockchain' s transparency, these companies can identify and switch to more cost-effective port services, eroding the port' s competitive advantage and ultimately reducing its discounted profit. The same is true when ports invest in blockchain. That is to say, the head port may consolidate its hub position through blockchain investment, squeezing the survival space of regional ports, needing an antitrust mechanism to prevent "winner-take-all".

Figures 11–13 represent the variation in V_P, V_C, V_F as the parameters α, β, γ increase. In Figures 11a, 12 and 13c, V_P, V_C, and V_F rise across all scenarios as α, β, and γ grow. This suggests that the profit growth potential of port companies, shipping companies, and shipping logistics blockchain platforms increases as the proportion of low-carbon preference shippers increases and the sensitivity of shippers to shipping services and the low-carbon preference of shippers strengthen. For port companies, addressing the needs of low-carbon-preference shippers may drive investments in green infrastructure, such as expanding shore power facilities to reduce carbon emissions during vessel port calls. Shipping companies, in turn, might adopt greener shipping technologies or optimize navigation routes to minimize emissions. Based on this, the government can provide blockchain investment tax credits for routes with a high percentage of low-carbon preferred shippers, avoiding the resource mismatch caused by "one-size-fits-all" subsidies. Concurrently, the shipping logistics blockchain platform enhances expected discounted profits for all stakeholders by documenting and transparently reporting emissions reduction efforts, thereby attracting environmentally conscious clients and fostering collaborative low-carbon initiatives.

Figure 14 represents the changes in V_P, V_C, V_F as the parameter φ increases. Figure 14a,b show that in scenarios without blockchain investment, V_P and V_C remain constant regardless of φ, since φ quantifies blockchain's direct impact on emissions reduction. In all other blockchain-enabled scenarios, V_P and V_C grow proportionally with φ. Figure 14c plots only the green solid line (Case *FB*), revealing a linear growth pattern where V_F increases uniformly with φ. These results confirm that blockchain adoption not only elevates emissions reductions efforts but also drives profit growth for all stakeholders. The alignment of profit incentives with sustainability goals underscores the dual benefits of blockchain integration in shipping logistics.

Figure 15 represents the variation in V_P, V_C, V_F with increasing parameter c_b. Figure 15a,b show that both V_P and V_C initially rise but subsequently decline with increasing c_b. Figure 15c demonstrates that V_F increases linearly with c_b. This suggests a significant short-term profit advantage for port-led scenarios when blockchain construction and operating costs are low. Ports can make up for technology investment by raising service fees while attracting customers who are not sensitive to low-carbon services, realizing a rapid cycle of "technology investment—efficiency improvement—profit growth". Ports, as the core nodes of the supply chain, can undertake blockchain investments. These investments have a natural advantage in reducing duplicate certification costs and enhancing regulatory compliance by improving customs clearance efficiency and quickly reducing information asymmetry among multiple parties. As blockchain usage fees increase further, a turning point in the cost-benefit balance is reached. When blockchain usage fees become too high, the increased costs for ports and shipping companies begin to outweigh the benefits of blockchain technology, at which point profits gradually diminish. The platform' s source of revenue is primarily the blockchain usage fees paid by port companies and shipping lines. All else being equal, higher fees mean that the platform can make more profit.

8. Conclusions

In this paper, we analyze four scenarios through a symmetry-aware dynamic model to investigate the impact of blockchain technology on shipping supply chain emissions reduction and operational strategies. Leveraging differential game theory and graph-theoretic principles, we frame ports as nodes and shipping firms as edges in a symmetrically interconnected network, constructing state equations for emissions reductions and service levels. By solving HJB equations, we derive optimal decisions under each scenario, revealing how structural symmetry (e.g., balanced port-shipping collaboration) and operational asymmetry (e.g., cost disparities) shape outcomes. Comparative and parametric analyses further demonstrate how blockchain's distributed symmetric architecture enhances information symmetry, reduces node–edge coordination inefficiencies, and improves network diagnosability (e.g., identifying emission-critical ports).

8.1. Key Findings

This study derives the principal findings as follows. We find that under a symmetry-driven dynamic framework, emissions reduction efforts, service levels, demand, and profits exhibit trajectories akin to graph-theoretic equilibria increased rapidly before stabilizing (Propositions 1–4). In the NB scenario, low initial emissions levels prompt ports (nodes) and shipping firms (edges) to enhance performance through green investments, while blockchain's distributed symmetric architecture optimizes node–edge collaboration by eliminating information asymmetry. Blockchain's symmetric transparency reshapes emission decisions by enhancing shippers' trust, indirectly improving performance through a low-carbon demand–investment–trust cycle (Propositions 5–8). Port- or shipping-led blockchain investments initially divert resources but long term, they enable node-level diagnosability (identifying emission-critical ports) and edge-level coordination. The port-led model is suitable for low-cost investment scenarios. When the blockchain operation cost is controlled within a reasonable range, the initial technology investment of the port will increase capital expenditure, but in the long run, it can realize profitability by improving customs clearance efficiency and attracting low-carbon cargo owners. Shipping company-led models are more valuable in high freight markets. A shipping company-owned blockchain platform could enhance customer trust by improving logistics transparency, allowing for service premiums and optimizing cost efficiency for abatement. Joint blockchain platforms achieve network-wide symmetry via multi-party data sharing, reducing regulatory costs through combinatorial optimization of emissions tracking. Threshold conditions for win–win outcomes depend on symmetry–asymmetry trade-offs between costs and benefits. Port-led investments thrive under cost symmetry (low blockchain operating costs), while shipping firms leverage asymmetric service premiums in high-freight environments (Propositions 9, 10 and 12). Joint platforms require synergistic symmetry between platform fees and trust, mirroring restricted connectivity optimization in multiprocessor systems (Propositions 11, 13, and 14). The core of the reason why blockchain platforms with joint participation can realize a "win–win" situation is that all parties have formed a stable cooperation mechanism of risk sharing and equal benefit sharing by reasonably sharing the cost of technological inputs and sharing the benefits of the data. In contrast, the stability of a single subject-led scenario (e.g., a port or shipping company building a blockchain alone) is highly dependent on whether the dominant party can control the cost of technological application within a reasonable range. If the cost borne by the dominant party is too high, it may lead to the withdrawal of the cooperating parties due to declining returns, destroying the balance of the system. Node–edge asymmetry dictates optimal blockchain leadership: ports (nodes) excel in cost control via customs efficiency and transparency, while shipping firms (edges) profit from demand-driven route optimization. Joint platforms, though constrained by multi-node costs, achieve resource symmetry through alliance chains (e.g., Shanghai Port's paperless platform), balancing logistics costs and emissions efficiency via graph neural network-inspired coordination.

From the perspective of symmetry, the shipping supply chain, with the help of the distributed blockchain architecture, has achieved a deep transformation from information asymmetric game to system symmetrical collaboration. This transformation has fundamentally reshaped the decision-making logic and benefit distribution mechanism. Under the traditional model, port and shipping enterprises were trapped in the predicament of local optima due to information barriers. Emissions reductions investment and service improvement worked independently, making it difficult to form a synergy effect. Then, distributed book blockchain technology broke the data island, enabling the parties to operate based on real-time sharing of a transparent information strategy, promoting efforts and green investment to move from isolated decision-making to joint optimization of resource allocation efficiency. This symmetric reconstruction is not only an upgrade of technological application but also an innovation of the underlying collaboration mechanism in the supply chain. It enables port and shipping enterprises to strike a balance between emissions reductions targets and economic goals, drive decision-making coordination through information symmetry, and ultimately achieve a win–win situation of economic and environmental benefits for the entire system, providing a new paradigm with both theoretical value and practical significance for the sustainable transformation of the global shipping industry.

Furthermore, the unique contribution of this study lies in optimizing the two shipping supply chain network structures (Structure A and Structure B), supported by blockchain, through differential game theory, and deeply coupling the node–edge dynamics in graph theory with the game equilibrium strategy. By analyzing the reconstruction effect of blockchain platform nodes on the network topology, we reveal how the distributed symmetric architecture drives the traditional hierarchical channel strategy to evolve towards multi-party collaborative equilibrium through node diagnosability, edge coordination, and global connectivity optimization, providing a dynamic framework with both theoretical strictness and practical adaptability for intelligent decision-making in shipping emissions reduction.

8.2. Managerial Insights

From these key findings, the following managerial implications emerge:

First, the government should actively promote the standardized application of blockchain technology in the shipping industry, such as establishing a unified data-sharing interface and green certification system. Simultaneously, the government should take the lead in or subsidize the construction of a "Shipping Blockchain Public Service Platform" to provide basic services and lower the technical threshold for small and medium-sized enterprises. For example, regional alliance chains could be established relying on the "Yangtze River Economic Belt" and the "Guangdong–Hong Kong–Macao Greater Bay Area," connecting hubs such as Shanghai Port and Ningbo–Zhoushan Port. These chains would enable real-time sharing and supervision of ship emission data, as well as blockchain-based processes for port charging, carbon trading, and other operations to enhance transparency.

Second, port enterprises should prioritize blockchain investment in low operating cost scenarios and attract low-carbon cargo owners by improving customs clearance efficiency (such as automatic customs declaration with smart contracts). Shipping companies should lead blockchain investment in scenarios with high sensitivity to market demand and improve service premium capabilities by optimizing route transparency (such as COSCO Shipping blockchain route tracking). At the same time, it should be noted that when ports or shipping companies build blockchain separately, they need to reserve sufficient cost buffer space in advance to cope with the increased cost of technical maintenance or service restoration caused by unexpected disruptions. If operating costs fluctuate greatly, shipping companies may consider building blockchain systems on their own in order to more flexibly adjust their transportation strategies in response to changes in costs, to maintain revenues by improving service transparency and efficiency during high-cost periods, and to expand their market share during low-cost periods. In addition, when investing in emissions reduction and blockchain technology, maritime companies must prioritize the equilibrium of cost containment and revenue management. By rationalizing shipping prices and port service charges, it ensures that the profitability of enterprises is maintained while the levels of emissions reductions and service are enhanced.

Third, shifting key parameters suggests an evolving port market landscape. In this case, port and shipping companies need to be keenly aware of these changes and optimize and adjust the cost of investing in blockchain technology in a timely way. Through continuous improvement, we can maximize the motivation of port enterprises to reduce emissions and enhance efficiency, so that they can maintain their competitiveness in the ever-changing market environment and achieve sustainable development.

8.3. Limitations and Future Research

This study has certain limitations. First, the model assumptions, although based on reality, are simplified and may not fully reflect the complexity of the shipping supply chain. For example, in reality, there are many participants with complex relationships, while the model only considers the case of one port and one shipping company. Second, this study only partially covers the factors that affect the decision to invest in and reduce emissions from blockchain technology. It ignores external factors such as macroeconomic fluctuations and policy instability, as well as internal factors such as management culture and the difficulty of technological integration within the enterprise. Third, the technical modeling of this study is based on the assumption of global interoperability of blockchain, but political and institutional constraints may significantly affect its applicability in reality. Future research needs to further internalize institutional variables such as multi-national data sovereignty rules and international carbon tariff games and construct a more politically flexible blockchain–emissions reduction collaborative model. In addition, the current work on blockchain-based shipping emissions reduction is still in the theoretical stage, with significant limitations, namely the lack of empirical-level validation. Future research needs to extend from theory to practice to promote blockchain technology to truly serve the realization of shipping emissions reduction goals, and fill the critical gap from theory to reality. Finally, this study examines how blockchain technology contributes to lowering carbon emissions, while also paving the way for future research into its broader applications across supply chain management systems.

Supplementary Materials: The following supporting information can be downloaded at https://www.mdpi.com/article/10.3390/sym17060817/sym17060817/s1: Supplementary S1. Proofs; Supplementary S2. Critical points.

Author Contributions: Conceptualization, Z.S., Y.X., B.S. and J.L.; Methodology, Y.X., B.S. and J.L.; Software, J.L.; Formal analysis, Z.S., Y.X. and B.S.; Writing—original draft, Z.S. and Y.X.; Writing—review & editing, Z.S. and Y.X.; Visualization, B.S.; Supervision, Z.S. and J.L.; Funding acquisition, Z.S. All authors have read and agreed to the published version of the manuscript.

Funding: This work was supported by the Humanities and Social Sciences Research Youth Foundation of Ministry of Education of China (Grant No. 23YJC630157).

Data Availability Statement: The original contributions presented in this study are included in the article/Supplementary Material. Further inquiries can be directed to the corresponding authors.

Acknowledgments: The authors are grateful to the Editor and anonymous reviewers for their very valuable comments and suggestions.

Conflicts of Interest: The authors declare no conflict of interests regarding the publication of this article.

References

1. Wang, X.T.; Liu, H.; Lv, Z.F.; Deng, F.Y.; Xu, H.L.; Qi, L.J.; Shi, M.S.; Zhao, J.C.; Zheng, S.X.; Man, H.Y.; et al. Trade-linked shipping CO_2 emissions. *Nat. Clim. Change* **2021**, *11*, 945–951. [CrossRef]
2. Ye, J.; Chen, J.H.; Shi, J.; Jiang, X.Y.; Zhou, S.R. Novel synergy mechanism for carbon emissions abatement in shipping decarbonization. *Transp. Res. Part D Transp. Environ.* **2024**, *127*, 104059. [CrossRef]
3. Huang, X.Y.; Liu, G.Y.; Zheng, P.J. Dynamic analysis of a low-carbon maritime supply chain considering government policies and social preferences. *Ocean Coast. Manag.* **2023**, *239*, 106564. [CrossRef]
4. Hoang, A.T.; Foley, A.M.; Nižetić, S.; Huang, Z.H.; Ong, H.C.; Ölçer, A.I.; Pham, V.V.; Nguyen, X.P. Energy-related approach for reduction of CO_2 emissions: A critical strategy on the port-to-ship pathway. *J. Clean. Prod.* **2022**, *355*, 131772. [CrossRef]
5. Chen, Y.T.; Li, D.F. Strategic Analysis of the Cooperation and Competition between the Shipping Logistics Blockchain Platform and Shipping Companies Considering Shippers' Information Preferences. *Chin. J. Manag. Sci.* **2024**, *41*, 1–12.
6. Yang, C.S. Maritime shipping digitalization: Blockchain-based technology applications, future improvements, and intention to use. *Transp. Res. Part E Logist. Transp. Rev.* **2019**, *131*, 108–117. [CrossRef]
7. Meng, L.P.; Liu, K.M.; He, J.L.; Han, C.F.; Liu, P.H. Carbon emission reduction behavior strategies in the shipping industry under government regulation: A tripartite evolutionary game analysis. *J. Clean. Prod.* **2022**, *378*, 134556. [CrossRef]
8. Chen, J.H.; Xu, J.H.; Zhou, S.R.; Liu, A. Slot co-chartering and capacity deployment optimization of liner alliances in containerized maritime logistics industry. *Adv. Eng. Inform.* **2023**, *56*, 101986. [CrossRef]
9. Liu, J.G.; Zhao, H.D.; Li, J. Research on the Investment Strategy of the Port-Shipping Supply Chain Based on Green Investment Efficiency. *Chin. J. Manag. Sci.* **2021**, *11*, 33–44. [CrossRef]
10. Liu, J.G.; Kong, Y.D.; Zhen, L. Research on Sustainable Investment in the Port-Shipping Supply Chain Considering Double Equilibrium. *Chin. J. Manag. Sci.* **2022**, *3*, 142–153.
11. Liang, J.; Zhang, L.; Liu, Y.X. Research on Emission Reduction Strategies of Port and Shipping Enterprises Considering Carbon Emission Policies. *J. Transp. Syst. Eng. Inf. Technol.* **2023**, *1*, 39–47.
12. Chen, Y.T.; Li, D.F. The Influence of Consumers' Information Preferences on Shipping Companies' Decision-making to Participate in Shipping Logistics Blockchain Platforms. *Control Decis.* **2024**, *8*, 2791–2800.
13. Zhang, Y.G.; Kuang, H.B.; Yu, F.P.; Wan, M.; Li, J.C. Research on Investment and Subsidy Decision-making of Port and Shipping Blockchain Electronic Delivery Platform. *Syst. Eng. Theory Pract.* **2024**, *44*, 1–20.

14. Liu, M.; Xin, X.; Wang, X.; Zhang, T.; Chen, K. Dual-channel slot sales strategy for container liner shipping companies with blockchain technology adoption. *Transp. Policy* **2025**, *162*, 200–220. [CrossRef]
15. Xu, X.; Liu, M.H.; Wang, X.L.; Chen, H.C.; Chen, K. Investment strategy for blockchain technology in a shipping supply chain. *Ocean Coast. Manag.* **2022**, *226*, 106263.
16. Li, H.J.; Gao, J.W.; Li, X. Blockchain adoption strategy of two-sided shipping platforms connecting forwarder and liner company. *Ocean Coast. Manag.* **2024**, *247*, 106932. [CrossRef]
17. Alahmadi, D.; Baothman, F.; Alrajhi, M.; Alshahrani, F.; Albalawi, H. Comparative analysis of blockchain technology to support digital transformation in ports and shipping. *J. Intell. Syst.* **2022**, *31*, 55–69. [CrossRef]
18. Chen, Y.; Yang, B. Cooperative Decision Making of Supply Chain Members of Shipping Logistics Services Under the Background of Blockchain. *Asia-Pac. J. Oper. Res.* **2021**, *39*, 2140018. [CrossRef]
19. Lorenz-Meyer, F.; Santos, V. Blockchain in the shipping industry: A proposal for the use of blockchain for SMEs in the maritime industry. *Procedia Comput. Sci.* **2023**, *219*, 807–814. [CrossRef]
20. Zhao, H.; Liu, J.; Hu, X. Servitization with blockchain in the maritime supply chain. *Ocean Coast. Manag.* **2022**, *225*, 106195. [CrossRef]
21. Wang, H.; Wang, C.C.; Li, M.; Xie, Y.L. Blockchain technology investment strategy for shipping companies under competition. *Ocean Coast. Manag.* **2023**, *243*, 106696. [CrossRef]
22. Wang, M.; Ren, Y.; Lin, Y.; Wang, S. The tightly super 3-extra connectivity and diagnosability of locally twisted cubes. *Am. J. Comput. Math.* **2017**, *7*, 127–144. [CrossRef]
23. Wang, M.; Lin, Y.; Wang, S. The nature diagnosability of bubble-sort star graphs under the PMC model and MM∗ model. *Int. J. Eng. Appl. Sci.* **2017**, *4*, 2394–3661.
24. Babaei, A.; Babaee Tirkolaee, E.; Ali, S.S. Assessing the viability of blockchain technology in renewable energy supply chains: A consolidation framework. *Renew. Sustain. Energy Rev.* **2025**, *212*, 115444. [CrossRef]
25. Henrichs, E.; Boller, M.L.; Stolz, J.; Krupitzer, C. Quantum of Trust: Overview of Blockchain Technology for Product Authentication in Food and Pharmaceutical Supply Chains. *Trends Food Sci. Technol.* **2025**, *157*, 104892. [CrossRef]
26. Heydari, M.; Shojaei, A. Blockchain applications in the construction supply chain. *Autom. Constr.* **2025**, *171*, 105998. [CrossRef]
27. Wang, J.; Li, X.; Chen, C.; Zhu, W.T. Proof of carbon reduction: A novel incentive mechanism in blockchain for carbon emissions reduction in construction. *Build. Environ.* **2025**, *272*, 112684. [CrossRef]
28. Vu, N.H.A. An Organizational Modeling for Developing Smart Contracts on Blockchain-based Supply Chain Finance Systems. *Procedia Comput. Sci.* **2024**, *239*, 3–10.
29. Wang, M.; Lin, Y.; Wang, S. The connectivity and nature diagnosability of expanded k-ary n-cubes. *RAIRO Theor. Inform. Appl.* **2017**, *51*, 71–89. [CrossRef]
30. Psaraftis, H.N.; Zis, T.; Lagouvardou, S. A comparative evaluation of market based measures for shipping decarbonization. *Mar. Transp. Res.* **2021**, *2*, 100019. [CrossRef]
31. Gao, F.; Souza, G.C. Carbon Offsetting with Eco-Conscious Consumers. *Manag. Sci.* **2022**, *68*, 7879–7897. [CrossRef]
32. Park, H.; Blanco, C.C.; Bendoly, E. Vessel sharing and its impact on maritime operations and carbon emissions. *Prod. Oper. Manag.* **2022**, *31*, 2925–2942. [CrossRef]
33. Pasha, J.; Dulebenets, M.A.; Fathollahi-Fard, A.M.; Tian, G.; Lau, Y.Y.; Singh, P.; Liang, B. An integrated optimization method for tactical-level planning in liner shipping with heterogeneous ship fleet and environmental considerations. *Adv. Eng. Inform.* **2021**, *48*, 101299. [CrossRef]
34. Chen, Y.; Ma, Y.; Wang, Y.; Sun, Z.; Han, Y. Impact of China's marine governance policies on the marine ecological environment–A case study of the Bohai rim. *Ocean Coast. Manag.* **2023**, *246*, 106913. [CrossRef]
35. Li, D.C.; Yang, H.L.; Xing, Y.W. Economic and emission assessment of LNG-fuelled ships for inland waterway transportation. *Ocean Coast. Manag.* **2023**, *246*, 106906. [CrossRef]
36. Ji, C.Y.; Chen, B.J.; Zhao, W.; Wang, X.Y.; Qian, W.Y. Selection of emission reduction modes for energy-intensive enterprises under the dynamic carbon cap-and-trade regulation. *Heliyon* **2025**, *11*, e42424. [CrossRef]
37. Wang, H.L.; Lang, X.; Mao, W.G. Voyage optimization combining genetic algorithm and dynamic programming for fuel/emissions reduction. *Transp. Res. Part D Transp. Environ.* **2021**, *90*, 102670. [CrossRef]
38. Wang, S.; Wang, Y.; Wang, M. Connectivity and matching preclusion for leaf-sort graphs. *J. Interconnect. Netw.* **2019**, *19*, 1940007. [CrossRef]
39. Zhu, C.; Ma, J.; Li, J. Dynamic production and carbon emission reduction adjustment strategies of the brand-new and the remanufactured product under hybrid carbon regulations. *Comput. Ind. Eng.* **2022**, *172*, 108517. [CrossRef]
40. Koohathongsumrit, N.; Chankham, W. Route selection in multimodal supply chains: A fuzzy risk assessment model-BWM-MARCOS framework. *Appl. Soft Comput.* **2023**, *137*, 110167. [CrossRef]
41. Zhang, L.L.; Ren, J.Q.; Zhang, G.Q. Optimal dynamic strategy for emission reduction and operation considering hybrid carbon policy with carbon tax and cap-and-trade. *Comput. Ind. Eng.* **2024**, *187*, 109820. [CrossRef]

42. Ma, S.; He, Y. Investment of Green Technology in a Tourism Supply Chain Under Competition. *IEEE Trans. Eng. Manag.* **2023**, *70*, 1199–1214. [CrossRef]
43. Wu, D.; Yang, Y. Study on the Differential Game Model for Supply Chain with Consumers' Low Carbon Preference. *Chin. J. Manag. Sci.* **2021**, *29*, 126–137.
44. Kang, Y.W.; Dong, P.W.; Ju, Y.B.; Zhang, T.Y. Differential game theoretic analysis of the blockchain technology investment and carbon reduction strategy in digital supply chain with government intervention. *Comput. Ind. Eng.* **2024**, *189*, 109953. [CrossRef]
45. Ma, X.L.; Zhao, Y.; Luo, Q.; Bai, Q.G. Preservation technology investment and carbon abatement strategies in a supplier-retailer cold chain based on a differential game. *Comput. Ind. Eng.* **2022**, *172*, 108540. [CrossRef]
46. Yang, L.; Cai, Y.; Wei, Y.; Huang, S. Choice of technology for emission control in port areas: A supply chain perspective. *J. Clean. Prod.* **2019**, *240*, 118105. [CrossRef]
47. Yu, W.; Wang, Y.; Feng, W.R.; Bao, L.; Han, R.Z. Low carbon strategy analysis with two competing supply chains considering carbon taxation. *Comput. Ind. Eng.* **2022**, *169*, 108203. [CrossRef]
48. Rashid, T.; Ali, A.; Chu, Y.-M. Hybrid BW-EDAS MCDM methodology for optimal industrial robot selection. *PLoS ONE* **2021**, *16*, e0246738. [CrossRef]
49. Chen, Y.; Li, L. Differential game model of carbon emission reduction decisions with two types of government contracts: Green funding and green technology. *J. Clean. Prod.* **2023**, *389*, 135847. [CrossRef]
50. Meng, L.; Wang, J.; Yan, W.; Han, C. A differential game model for emission reduction decisions between ports and shipping enterprises considering environmental regulations. *Ocean Coast. Manag.* **2022**, *225*, 106221. [CrossRef]
51. Yang, H.X.; Chen, W.B. Retailer-Driven Carbon Emission Abatement with Consumer Environmental Awareness and Carbon Tax: Revenue-Sharing Versus Cost-Sharing. *Omega* **2018**, *78*, 179–191. [CrossRef]
52. Zhou, H.Y.; Li, B.T. Analysis of Emission Reduction Decisions of Port and Shipping Enterprises under Carbon Tax and Customers' Low-Carbon Preferences. *Navig. China* **2022**, *3*, 72–79.
53. Zhou, H.N.; Liu, M.Q.; Tan, Y. Long-term emission reduction strategy in a three-echelon supply chain considering government intervention and consumers' low-carbon preferences. *Comput. Ind. Eng.* **2023**, *186*, 109697. [CrossRef]
54. Cheng, P.Y.; Ji, G.X.; Zhang, G.T.; Shi, Y.Y. A closed-loop supply chain network considering consumer's low-carbon preference and carbon tax under the cap-and-trade regulation. *Sustain. Prod. Consum.* **2022**, *29*, 614–635. [CrossRef]
55. Ghosh, S.K.; Seikh, M.R.; Chakrabortty, M. Analyzing a stochastic dual-channel supply chain under consumers' low carbon preferences and cap-and-trade regulation. *Comput. Ind. Eng.* **2020**, *149*, 106765. [CrossRef]
56. Cai, J.H.; Cao, Z.G.; Shang, J. Blockchain adoption in a green supply chain: Considering information asymmetry of consumers' privacy concern. *Int. J. Prod. Econ.* **2025**, *279*, 109459. [CrossRef]
57. Yu, T.Y.; Guan, Z.M.; Zhang, J.; Dong, J.Y. Blockchain adoption and contract coordination of poverty alleviation supply chain considering altruistic preference. *Comput. Ind. Eng.* **2024**, *188*, 109879. [CrossRef]
58. Xiao, L.; Chen, Z.S.; Hou, R.; Mardani, A.; Skibniewski, M.J. Greenness-based subsidy and dual credit policy to promote new energy vehicles considering consumers' low-carbon awareness. *Comput. Ind. Eng.* **2023**, *185*, 109620. [CrossRef]
59. Shi, Z.Y.; Cheng, J.W. How do government subsidies and consumers' low-carbon preference promote new energy vehicle diffusion? A tripartite evolutionary game based on energy vehicle manufacturers, the government and consumers. *Heliyon* **2023**, *9*, e14327. [CrossRef]
60. Nerlove, M.; Arrow, K.J. Optimal Advertising Policy under Dynamic Conditions. *Economica* **1962**, *29*, 129–142. [CrossRef]
61. Zhu, C.; Xi, X.; Goh, M. Differential game analysis of joint emission reduction decisions under mixed carbon policies and CEA. *J. Environ. Manag.* **2024**, *358*, 120913. [CrossRef] [PubMed]
62. Li, Z.; Wang, L.; Wang, G.; Xin, X.; Chen, K.; Zhang, T. Investment and subsidy strategy for low-carbon port operation with blockchain adoption. *Ocean Coast. Manag.* **2024**, *248*, 106966. [CrossRef]
63. Choi, T.M. Blockchain-technology-supported platforms for diamond authentication and certification in luxury supply chains. *Transp. Res. Part E Logist. Transp. Rev.* **2019**, *128*, 17–29. [CrossRef]
64. Sui, R.; Liu, M.; Liu, Y.; Zha, X. Two-sided dynamic pricing and value-added service investment strategies of competitive platforms considering indirect network effects. *Int. J. Prod. Econ.* **2024**, *272*, 109262. [CrossRef]
65. Liu, M.; Du, S.; Nie, T.; Zhu, Y. Pricing, channel design, and platform operations with buy-online-and-pick-up-in-store in online food delivery market. *Int. J. Prod. Econ.* **2024**, *274*, 109293. [CrossRef]
66. Xia, L.; Li, K.; Wang, J.; Xia, Y.; Qin, J. Carbon emission reduction and precision marketing decisions of a platform supply chain. *Int. J. Prod. Econ.* **2024**, *268*, 109104. [CrossRef]

67. Cai, J.; Jiang, F. Decision models of pricing and carbon emission reduction for low-carbon supply chain under cap-and-trade regulation. *Int. J. Prod. Econ.* **2023**, *264*, 108964. [CrossRef]
68. Jiang, Y.; Liu, C. Research on carbon emission reduction and blockchain investment under different dual-channel supply chains. *Environ. Sci. Pollut. Res.* **2022**, *29*, 65304–65321. [CrossRef]

symmetry

MDPI

Article

Graph-Symmetry Cognitive Learning for Multi-Scale Cloud Imaging: An Uncertainty-Quantified Geometric Paradigm via Hierarchical Graph Networks

Qing Xu, Zichen Zhang, Guanfang Wang and Yunjie Chen *

School of Mathematics and Statistics, Nanjing University of Information Science and Technology, Nanjing 210044, China
* Correspondence: priestcyj@nuist.edu.cn

Abstract

Cloud imagery analysis from terrestrial observation points represents a fundamental capability within contemporary atmospheric monitoring infrastructure, serving essential functions in meteorological prediction, climatic surveillance, and hazard alert systems. However, traditional ground-based cloud image segmentation methods have fundamental limitations, particularly their inability to effectively model the graph structure and symmetry in cloud data. To address this, we propose G-CLIP, a ground-based cloud image segmentation method based on graph symmetry. G-CLIP synergistically integrates four innovative modules. First, the Prototype-Driven Asymmetric Attention (PDAA) module is designed to reduce complexity and enhance feature learning by leveraging permutation invariance and graph symmetry principles. Second, the Symmetry-Adaptive Graph Convolution Layer (SAGCL) is constructed, modeling pixels as graph nodes, using cosine similarity to build a sparse discriminative structure, and ensuring stability through symmetry and degree normalization. Third, the Multi-Scale Directional Edge Optimizer (MSDER) is developed to explicitly model complex symmetric relationships in cloud features from a graph theory perspective. Finally, the Uncertainty-Driven Loss Optimizer (UDLO) is proposed to dynamically adjust weights to address foreground–background imbalance and provide uncertainty quantification. Extensive experiments on four benchmark datasets demonstrate that our method achieves state-of-the-art performance across all evaluation metrics. Our work provides a novel theoretical framework and practical solution for applying graph neural networks (GNNs) to meteorology, particularly by integrating graph properties with uncertainty and leveraging symmetries from graph theory for complex spatial modeling.

Keywords: graph symmetry; graph neural networks; cloud image segmentation; uncertainty quantification; permutation invariance; asymmetric attention mechanism

1. Introduction

With the acceleration of worldwide climatic shifts and the notable rise in severe atmospheric phenomena occurrences, accurate weather forecasting and climate monitoring have become critical requirements for the sustainable development of human society. According to a report by the American Meteorological Society, the number of weather-related natural disasters increased from 1383 incidents between 1980 and 1985 to 4020 incidents between 2013 and 2018, indicating a sharp upward trend in extreme weather events [1]. Ground-based cloud imagery provides valuable supplementary data for local nowcasting

https://doi.org/10.3390/sym17091477

and cloud physics research. While numerical weather prediction models and satellite data remain the primary tools for operational forecasting, ground-based observations offer unique high-resolution insights into local cloud dynamics and boundary layer processes that are particularly useful for short-term forecasting and research applications [2]. In this context, ground-based cloud image segmentation serves as a valuable supplementary technology in modern meteorological observation systems, providing high-resolution local details that complement broader-scale data sources such as satellites and radar [3]. However, segmenting ground-based cloud images presents distinct technical hurdles: the ambiguity arising from highly indistinct cloud edges, the difficulty of fusing visual cues due to clouds' intricate topological layouts, and the segmentation skew caused by severe foreground–background imbalance [4]. In typical ground-based cloud image datasets, the foreground region often accounts for only 5–10% of the total pixels [5]. These challenges require segmentation methods to not only handle spatial features in traditional image analysis but also effectively integrate the rich graph structure information contained in cloud image data.

Traditional cloud image segmentation methods have revealed numerous limitations when addressing modern meteorological observation requirements. The inherent blurriness of cloud boundaries makes threshold-based and edge detection methods inadequate, while the highly irregular shapes and complex textures of cloud layers exceed the expressive capabilities of traditional feature extraction methods [6]. More critically, traditional methods lack the ability to effectively utilize the graph structural information in cloud image data, failing to fully exploit the spatial relationships and topological characteristics between cloud layers [7].

Building on the preceding analysis, we introduce a graph-symmetry-driven approach for ground-based cloud-image segmentation,, which systematically addresses the limitations of existing methods through the collaborative work of four innovative modules:

- Prototype-Driven Asymmetric Attention (PDAA). This module uses the K-means algorithm for the dynamic clustering of features and employs an exponential moving average strategy to update cluster centers, thereby better capturing the feature distribution of cloud image data. Additionally, a permutation-invariant intra-group attention mechanism is designed to reduce computational complexity while enhancing the model's precision in focusing on cloud image features. This innovative design combines a combination clustering algorithm with graph symmetry principles to ensure graph node permutation invariance.
- Symmetry-Adaptive Graph Convolution Layer (SAGCL). This module models cloud image pixels as graph nodes, uses cosine similarity as a semantic distance metric, and constructs a sparse and discriminative graph structure. Symmetrization operations and degree normalization ensure the stability of the graph structure, enabling effective modeling of complex spatial relationships and topological characteristics between cloud layers. This module can further establish feature propagation and global contextual associations across cloud clusters based on the clustering attention mechanism.
- Multi-Scale Directional Edge Refiner (MSDER). Using multi-scale combined convolution decomposition technology, features are extracted and fused from multiple scales to more comprehensively capture cloud map information. Additionally, a gated feature fusion mechanism is designed to dynamically adjust the fusion process based on feature uncertainty, significantly improving the segmentation accuracy of thin fog boundaries and achieving the integration of graph attributes and uncertainty. This design models the complex symmetrical relationships of cloud map features from a graph theory symmetry perspective, enabling intelligent aggregation of multi-scale features and noise suppression.

- Uncertainty-Driven Loss Optimizer (UDLO). This optimizer uses CAM technology to generate activation maps highlighting foreground features, dynamically calculates hit rates for various categories, and uses an exponential decay function to adaptively adjust loss weights. This design enables the model to focus more on rare cloud types that are difficult to identify during training, significantly improving detection rates and enhancing the reliability of the entire network.

The synergistic design of these four modules not only addresses the key limitations of traditional methods and existing deep learning approaches but also provides a comprehensive solution for ground-based cloud map segmentation, with significant improvements in feature extraction, graph structure modeling, multi-scale fusion, and category balancing.

2. Related Work

This section provides a comprehensive review of existing approaches relevant to our proposed method, organized into three main areas: advances in graph neural networks for visual segmentation, symmetric graph theory applications, and U-Net-based segmentation methods. To facilitate understanding and comparison, we present both detailed discussions and summarized comparisons of key methods.

2.1. Advances in Graph Neural Networks for Visual Segmentation

Graph-based neural architectures have exhibited remarkable capabilities and substantial promise within visual parsing domains, offering new solutions to traditional convolutional neural network (CNN) methods. Traditional CNNs have limitations in exploring the structural relationships between image components. Researchers have proposed graph structure learning to enhance neural networks, utilizing the contextual information generated by CNNs as graph node features and constructing adjacency matrices through self-supervised graph generators [8]. Pan and colleagues introduced the HybridGNN architecture, which excels at processing intricate graph topologies through the combination of GATv2, GraphSAGE, and GIN components, enabling robust extraction of both localized nodal connections and overarching structural features [9]. It introduces a Jumping Knowledge (JK) mechanism to aggregate multi-layer network representations, enabling the utilization of both shallow and deep-level information. The methodology exhibits superior performance in processing hierarchically-organized visual information, utilizing mixed-precision computation alongside gradient accumulation strategies to enhance both memory efficiency and processing speed.

Currently, GNNs in visual segmentation are showing trends toward multimodal feature fusion and deepening self-supervised learning, effectively modeling complex spatial relationships and semantic dependencies among image pixels. They demonstrate significant advantages in segmentation tasks involving irregular shapes, blurry boundaries, and complex textures [10]. In the field of unsupervised image segmentation, methods combining pseudo-label generation and self-supervised learning have made significant progress, utilizing the inherent structure of graphs for unsupervised representation learning to reduce reliance on manually labeled data [11].

2.2. Symmetric Graph Theory and GNN Applications in Segmentation

Symmetry, as a core concept in graph theory, provides mathematical tools for handling complex network structures. Wang et al. systematically explored the symmetry properties of graphs, establishing a theoretical framework for g-good-neighbor connectivity and diagnosability, demonstrating that the symmetric structural characteristics of networks influence their fault tolerance and reliability, thereby providing a theoretical foundation for GNN applications in complex image data processing [12,13]. In the study of central k-ary n-cubes, it was proven that g-good-neighbor connectivity is 2n and g-extra connectivity is also 2n. These mathematical properties of symmetric structures provide insights for designing efficient graph neural network architectures [14]. Within both PMC and MM* frameworks, the diagnostic capability for g-good-neighbor configurations achieves a value of 2n + g, illustrating how exploiting symmetric characteristics in graphs can improve diagnostic precision and operational effectiveness in networks. Wang et al. proposed the Modified Comparison model (MC model), which integrates the advantages of classic algorithms to improve modern learning methods [15]. By embedding conventional graph-based algorithms as foundational knowledge within GNN learning procedures, this framework establishes a novel integration strategy that bridges classical computational approaches with contemporary neural network architectures.

The theoretical development of GNNs has undergone a significant shift from spectral graph convolutions to spatial graph convolutions, with the mathematical principles of graph attention mechanisms and graph pooling operations becoming increasingly refined. However, existing methods often neglect spatial symmetry information when processing image data with intrinsic geometric structures. Classic methods such as GraphSAGE are insufficient in preserving local geometric structures [16], while GAT, though achieving dynamic weight allocation, has high computational complexity and lacks symmetry guarantees. In computer vision applications, GNN methods incorporating symmetry constraints hold promise for significant roles in fields such as meteorological imagery. Key challenges include systematic studies of symmetry patterns in meteorological imagery, balancing graph structural representation capabilities with computational complexity and designing GNN architectures that balance symmetry and efficiency for small-scale datasets [17].

2.3. Segmentation Methods Based on U-Net and Its Variants

Models based on convolutional neural networks (CNNs) have made significant progress in semantic segmentation tasks. To bridge the semantic gap between the encoder and decoder, Ronneberger et al. [18] first proposed the skip-connection mechanism, which preserves more edge information and helps predict the detailed texture of the target region. Att-UNet [19] introduced a gating mechanism into skip connections, enabling the model to focus more efficiently on key regions.

Although CNNs excel at capturing local details and low-level features, their layer-wise extraction of local information limits their ability to model the global context, making it difficult to effectively handle remote semantic information connections. ViT [20] introduced the attention mechanism into computer vision, achieving breakthrough progress in tasks such as semantic segmentation through its global modeling capabilities. The deepest features of the visual transformer U-Net contain highly abstract high-level semantic information (such as cloud boundary shapes and positions), but traditional CNNs may lose global contextual information due to local convolution operations. Swin-UNet [21] introduces a hierarchical design and Shifted Window Attention, significantly improving global modeling efficiency and computational performance. Laplacian [22] designed a frequency attention mechanism with Gaussian kernels of different variances to enhance texture and edge detection capabilities. MA-SegCloud [23] introduced spatial attention and channel attention into cloud map segmentation to enhance strong feature extraction capabilities. CSWin-UNet [24] introduced Cross-Shaped Attention, where half the channels interact horizontally and half interact vertically, enhancing content-aware capabilities. Rolling-Unet [25] and UNeXt [26] capture long-range dependencies by rolling across the bottleneck layer, achieving the same computational efficiency as 3×3 convolutions without increasing computational overhead. A detailed comparative summary of existing methods and our proposed framework is provided in Supplementary Table S1.

3. Methods

3.1. Overall Framework

In our architecture design (shown in Figure 1), the U-Net bottleneck layer first performs preliminary semantic grouping and local attention enhancement of cloud image features through a clustering/grouping attention mechanism. This mechanism effectively identifies local cloud cluster structures in cloud images and groups pixels with similar features through clustering operations. However, the clustering attention mechanism primarily focuses on feature aggregation within local regions, and it still has limitations in modeling long-range semantic associations between cloud layers and global contextual information.

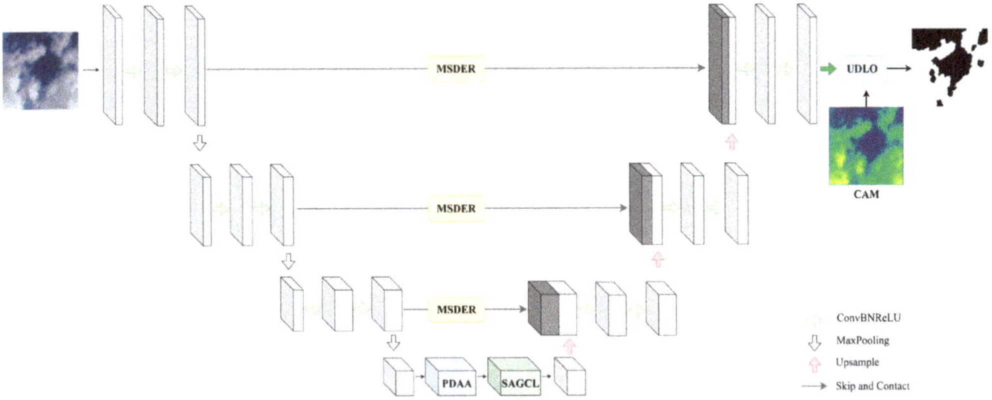

Figure 1. G-CLIP architecture: graph symmetry-driven cloud segmentation with PDAA, SAGCL, MSDER, and UDLO modules.

Cloud morphological features often exhibit global properties, and the correct identification of individual cloud blocks requires comprehensive consideration of contextual information across the entire sky region. Especially under complex weather conditions, discrimination between different cloud types (such as cumulus, stratus, cirrus, etc.) not only relies on local features after clustering and grouping but also necessitates the establishment of semantic dependency relationships between distant pixels. To further enhance the output features of the clustering attention mechanism, we have concatenated an adaptive graph convolutional network module based on k-nearest neighbors. This aims to construct global graph topological relationships based on grouped cloud features, enabling feature propagation and semantic association modeling across cloud clusters, thereby improving the accuracy and robustness of cloud image segmentation.

Figure 1 shows the complete architecture of the Ground-based Cloud Image Partitioning (G-CLIP) method based on graph symmetry, which uses an improved U-Net as the backbone network. The encoder part retains the traditional U-Net encoder structure, gradually extracting multi-scale features of the cloud image through multiple layers of convolution and pooling operations, covering high-resolution detail features to low-resolution semantic features. At the bottleneck layer of the U-Net, two key innovative modules are integrated: the PDAA module uses the K-means clustering algorithm to dynamically group features, employing a permutation-invariant intra-group attention mechanism to achieve efficient feature clustering and attention calculation; the SAGCL module models cloud pixels as graph nodes, constructs a sparse graph structure using cosine similarity, and employs symmetric operations and degree normalization to ensure graph structure stability, thereby modeling long-range semantic associations between cloud layers. The MSDER component integrates into U-Net's skip pathways, featuring both channel-wise adaptive mechanisms and multi-resolution directional edge enhancement modules. It employs 1 × 7- and 7 × 1-long kernel convolutions to capture horizontal and vertical boundary features, achieving intelligent multi-scale feature fusion. The decoder adopts the traditional U-Net upsampling and feature fusion structure but is equipped with the UDLO module, which dynamically adjusts loss weights using CAM technology to address the issue of extreme imbalance between foreground and background.

3.2. Prototype-Driven Asymmetric Attention (PDAA)

In the task of foundation cloud map segmentation, to overcome the issue of excessive computational complexity in traditional Transformer architectures when processing large-scale data and further enhance feature representation capabilities, this paper proposes an innovative clustering attention mechanism module (as shown in Figure 2) at the bottleneck layer of the U-Net-based algorithm. We aim to group similar features through a content-aware clustering process and perform efficient attention calculations within each group, thereby reducing computational complexity while enhancing the semantic consistency and discriminative power of features. PDAA employs the K-means algorithm for dynamic clustering of bottleneck layer features and designs group-internal attention that satisfies graph node permutation invariance, innovatively combining the combination clustering algorithm with graph symmetry principles.

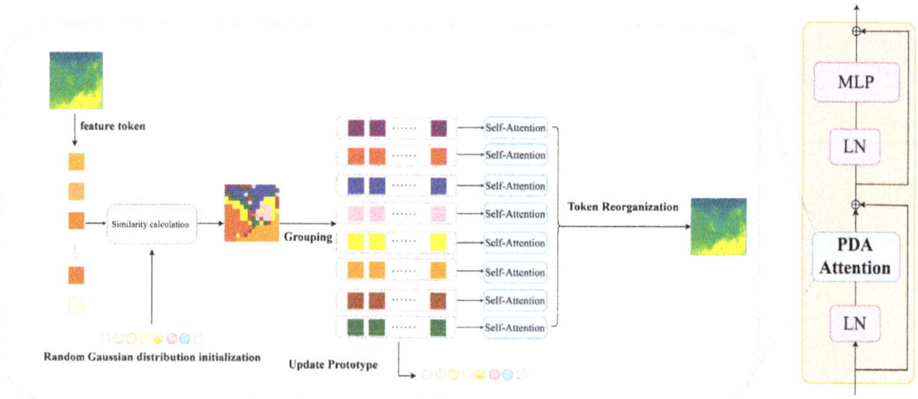

Figure 2. PDAA module structure diagram.

To establish the mathematical foundation for our clustering approach, we begin by defining the cluster initialization strategy. First, define the set of cluster centers as $M = \{m_1, m_2, \ldots, m_K\}$, where K represents the number of cluster centers. The initial cluster centers are defined as follows:

$$m_j^{(0)} = \frac{1}{B \cdot G} \sum_{i=1}^{B} \sum_{g=1}^{G} x_{i,g,j}, \tag{1}$$

where B represents the batch size and G represents the number of groups for each image. The cluster centers are initialized based on the average values of the batches and groups to ensure that the initial distribution covers different regions of the feature space. This initialization method enables the initial distribution of the cluster centers to cover different regions of the feature space as much as possible, providing a reasonable starting point for the subsequent clustering iterations. The double averaging operation $\frac{1}{B \cdot G}$ ensures the consistency of the initialization scale and avoids the instability of the values caused by changes in batch size or group number.

Building upon this initialization, we implement a dynamic updating mechanism to adapt to changing feature distributions during training. In order to enable the cluster centers to dynamically adapt to changes in the distribution of data features, we adopt the exponential moving average (EMA) strategy to update the cluster centers:

$$m_j^{(t)} = \alpha m_j^{(t-1)} + (1-\alpha)\tilde{m}_j^{(t)}, \tag{2}$$

where α represents the attenuation rate, which is used to control the weight of the historical clustering center and the estimated clustering center value $\tilde{m}_j^{(t)}$ obtained from the current batch calculation during the update process. When α approaches 1, learning is slow but stable, and when α is small, it can quickly adapt to data changes. The EMA mechanism inherently has a low-pass filtering characteristic, which can smooth the update process of the clustering center and avoid drastic oscillations, ensuring the convergence of the training process. In this way, the clustering center can gradually approach the essential structure of the data during the training process, enhancing the model's adaptability to the distribution of different ground-based cloud image data.

With the cluster centers established, we proceed to define the similarity computation mechanism that enables effective feature grouping. To calculate the similarity between the feature vector x and the clustering center, we first normalize the feature vector to prepare for the subsequent dot product similarity calculation, ensuring that the similarity mainly reflects the direction rather than the amplitude difference, thereby enhancing the stability of the similarity calculation:

$$x_{norm} = \frac{x}{||x||_2}, \tag{3}$$

Subsequently, the dot product similarity between the normalized feature vector and the normalized cluster center is calculated:

$$s_{i,j} = x_{norm,i} \cdot m_{norm,j}, \tag{4}$$

where $s_{i,j}$ represents the similarity between the ith feature vector and the jth cluster center. The dot product operation is more computationally efficient than the complex distance measures (such as Euclidean distance) and is suitable for linearly separable feature spaces. It is highly compatible with the linear projection operations of the Transformer architecture. Following the similarity computation, we implement the assignment strategy to group features based on their semantic relationships. Based on the magnitude of the similarity, each feature vector is assigned to the group corresponding to the cluster center that is most similar to it, as follows:

$$idx_i = \underset{j}{\text{argmax}} s_{i,j}, \tag{5}$$

where idx_i represents the clustering index to which the ith feature vector belongs. In this way, we can group vectors with similar semantic or spatial features together, providing a more meaningful feature grouping structure for subsequent intra-group attention calculations. The hard assignment ensures that each feature vector belongs to only one cluster, avoiding information confusion caused by ambiguous attribution, which is advantageous in meteorological applications with high requirements for cloud boundary clarity.

Having established the grouping mechanism, we now detail the intra-group attention computation that leverages these semantic clusters. After the features are grouped, the intra-group attention calculation stage begins. We divide the sorted and reorganized query, key, and value features into multiple groups, with each group having a size of S (group_size). For the features within the gth group, the attention score is first calculated:

$$a_{g,i,j} = \frac{q_{g,i} \cdot k_{g,j}^T}{\sqrt{d}}, \tag{6}$$

where d represents the size of the attention head. This formula calculates the attention score by multiplying the query vector with the transposed key vector and then dividing by the square root of the attention head size. After performing a softmax operation on the attention score, the attention weight $\alpha_{g,i,j}$ is obtained:

$$\alpha_{g,i,j} = \frac{\exp\left(a_{g,i,j}\right)}{\sum_{j'} \exp\left(a_{g,i,j'}\right)}, \tag{7}$$

Based on the obtained attention weights, calculate the intra-group context features:

$$c_{g,i} = \sum_j \alpha_{g,i,j} \cdot v_{g,j}. \tag{8}$$

The context features here are obtained by multiplying the attention weights with the corresponding value vectors and then summing them up, which can reflect the correlation and importance of the features within the group. Compared to the complexity of global attention, the complexity of intra-group attention achieves a significant efficiency improvement. Finally, the context features calculated within the group are restored to their original order and projected through the output linear layer to obtain the final attention output. This step converts the intra-group context features into output features with the same dimension as the input features so that subsequent network layers can perform further processing.

From the clustering results (Figure 3), it can be observed that cloud layer regions with similar texture features are classified into the same category, and even in the case of illumination changes, PDAA can accurately identify the essential features of the cloud layer. The clustering boundaries closely match the real cloud layer boundaries, which proves the superiority of PDAA in maintaining the integrity of the cloud layer. In the first row, the complex cloud layer structure is accurately segmented into different semantic regions, and each region maintains high consistency within itself; in the second row, the blue sky background and the cloud area are clearly separated, avoiding semantic confusion. The PDAA module successfully organizes the complex cloud map features into meaningful semantic regions. We not only effectively reduce the computational complexity but also improve the quality of feature representation, laying a solid foundation for the high performance of the entire segmentation system.

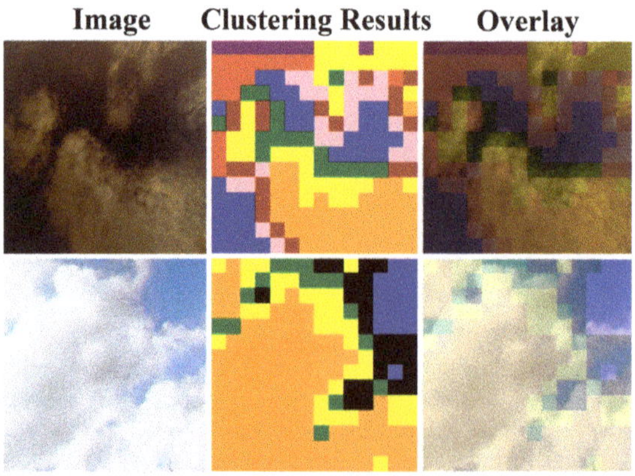

Figure 3. PDAA module clustering results display.

3.3. Symmetry-Adaptive Graph Convolution Layer (SAGCL)

After passing through the bottleneck layer clustering/grouping attention mechanism, the cloud image features have acquired certain local semantic grouping characteristics. Similar cloud areas exhibit stronger aggregation in the feature space. However, this clustering-based grouping mainly focuses on local similarities and is still limited in modeling the long-distance semantic associations between cloud layers. The distribution of cloud layers in ground-based cloud images shows significant spatial non-uniformity. The boundaries of cloud blocks often present a gradual transition rather than a clear demarcation, and there may be complex interrelationships between different cloud clusters.

To address these limitations, we adopt a graph-based approach that models pixel relationships more comprehensively. Therefore, we treat cloud pixels as graph nodes and model the semantic relationships between pixels by constructing an adaptive graph structure. Traditional convolution operations have limitations in capturing long-range dependencies between pixels. Graph convolutional networks can effectively model non-local dependencies between pixels, but standard GCNs face high computational complexity when processing large-scale data and struggle to adaptively capture the graph structure characteristics of different datasets. To address this, we propose a KNN-based symmetric adaptive graph convolutional module (as shown in Figure 4), which adds self-loops and symmetrization to meet graph symmetry requirements. This aims to construct an efficient pixel-to-pixel relationship graph and achieve adaptive feature aggregation and transformation through a learnable weight matrix, thereby enhancing the performance of ground-based cloud image segmentation.

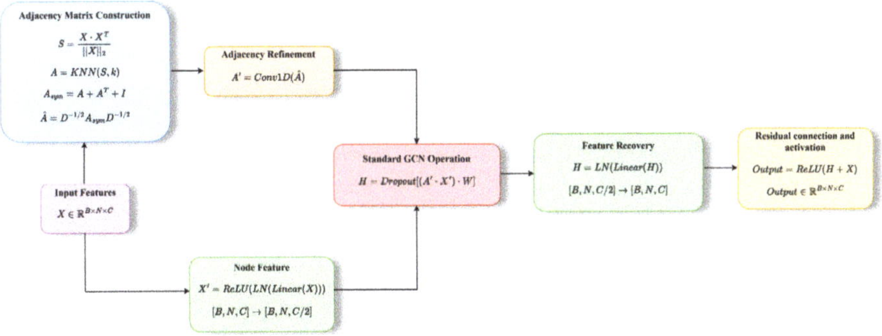

Figure 4. SAGCL module structure diagram.

The foundation of our graph construction relies on an appropriate similarity metric tailored to cloud image characteristics. Considering that similar cloud types in cloud maps may be spatially distant, we adopt cosine similarity as the semantic distance metric between nodes to capture cloud texture and intensity features, adapting to the feature distribution of cloud maps:

$$S_{i,j} = \frac{x_i^T x_j}{||x_i||_2 ||x_j||_2}, \tag{9}$$

where x_i and x_j represent the feature vectors of the ith and jth pixel positions, respectively. Compared to metrics such as Euclidean distance, cosine similarity is more computationally efficient in high-dimensional feature spaces and can effectively capture the semantic similarity of cloud layer features without being affected by the amplitude of the feature vectors. This is crucial for the identification of cloud patches with different brightness but the same texture in the cloud image. Through L2 norm normalization, this metric is robust to the scale changes of the feature vectors and avoids the interference of illumination changes on the similarity calculation.

Based on this similarity measure, we construct a sparse yet informative graph structure using the k-nearest neighbor approach. Given the significant differences in the size of cloud patches in the cloud image, we select k most similar neighbors for each pixel node to construct a sparse and discriminative graph structure:

$$A = kNN\left(S_{i,j}, k\right). \tag{10}$$

This strategy enables pixels belonging to the same cloud block to establish strong connections while maintaining appropriate separation between different cloud types, effectively enhancing the ability to identify cloud boundaries. By selecting only the k most similar neighbors, it effectively filters out weakly correlated connections, reduces the interference of weather noise and illumination changes on the graph structure, and improves the stability of cloud image segmentation. The selection of the k value directly affects the connection density of the graph, and the k value is usually set as a small proportion of the total number of nodes (in this paper, it is set as $\sqrt{N}$), which not only ensures effective information transmission but also controls the computational complexity.

To ensure robust graph properties that align with cloud morphological characteristics, we implement symmetrical operations and normalization. The morphology of clouds usually has certain symmetrical characteristics. We ensure the stability of the graph structure through symmetrical operations:

$$A_{sym} = \frac{1}{2}\left(A + A^T\right) + I_N. \tag{11}$$

The addition of self-loops ensures that each pixel retains its own cloud feature information, which is crucial for the precise positioning of cloud boundaries. The symmetric matrix has excellent spectral properties, with all eigenvalues being real and the eigenvectors being orthogonal, providing numerical stability guarantees for subsequent graph convolution operations. To balance information propagation across regions with varying cloud density, we apply degree normalization. Considering the differences in cloud density in different regions of the cloud image, we use degree normalization to balance information propagation:

$$\hat{A} = D^{-1/2} A_{sym} D^{-1/2}. \tag{12}$$

The degree matrix D is defined as follows:

$$D_{ii} = \sum\nolimits_{j=1}^{N} A_{sym,ij} \tag{13}$$

This normalization method ensures a balanced distribution of features in dense and sparse cloud regions, avoiding the biasing influence of cloud density on the segmentation results. At the same time, normalization limits the eigenvalues of the Laplacian matrix to the range of $[-1, 1]$, preventing the problem of gradient explosion and improving training stability. To further optimize the adjacency relationship representation of the cloud map, we introduce one-dimensional convolution operations to refine the normalized adjacency matrix, smooth the connection relationships of cloud boundaries, reduce the interference of weather noise and illumination changes on the graph structure, and improve the stability of cloud map segmentation.

With the graph structure established, we implement the core graph convolution operations that enable global feature aggregation. To ensure the details of the cloud map while improving computational efficiency, we first reduce the dimension of the cloud features output by the U-Net encoder and then apply LayerNorm and ReLU activation functions to enhance the discriminative ability of the cloud features. The core graph convolution propagation strictly follows the GCN theory, achieving global aggregation of cloud features, and through graph convolution operations, each pixel can aggregate feature information from similar cloud regions, significantly improving the accuracy of cloud boundary recognition and cloud-type classification. Considering the complexity and variability of ground-based cloud maps, we introduce Dropout operations to prevent model overfitting and restore the dimension of the cloud features after graph convolution to be consistent with the output of the U-Net encoder. To maintain the hierarchical features of U-Net and integrate the global information of graph convolution, we adopt residual connections. The fused features are reshaped to the original spatial dimensions and continue to participate in the upsampling and segmentation process of the U-Net decoder.

3.4. Multi-Scale Directional Edge Refiner (MSDER)

In the U-Net-based ground-based cloud map segmentation architecture, skip connections play a crucial role in fusing multi-scale features from the encoder with upsampled features from the decoder. However, traditional direct feature concatenation methods have significant limitations when handling the complex features of cloud maps. Ground-based cloud maps exhibit high irregularity and scale variability, with features at different levels often containing noise information and redundant representations. Direct fusion may lead to feature contamination and reduced segmentation accuracy.

To address these challenges from a theoretical perspective, we analyze the symmetry properties inherent in cloud image features. From the perspective of graph theory symmetry, cloud map features exhibit complex symmetry and asymmetry patterns across different scales and spatial positions. The morphological distribution of cloud layers exhibits both locally symmetric texture structures and globally asymmetric spatial layouts. Therefore, we need to design a skip-connection mechanism that can adaptively model these complex symmetry relationships. Stemming from this analysis, we propose our Multi-Scale Directional Edge Refiner, which treats feature fusion as a graph-based information propagation process. Based on this, we propose the Multi-Scale Directional Edge Refiner (MSDER), which (as shown in Figure 5) models the feature fusion process in skip connections as the propagation of symmetry information between graph nodes using graph neural network ideas, thereby achieving intelligent aggregation and noise suppression of multi-scale features in cloud images.

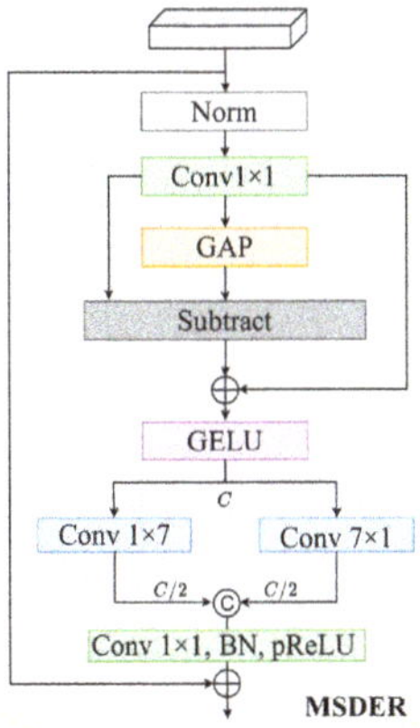

Figure 5. MSDER module structure diagram.

The core innovation of MSDER lies in its specialized handling of cloud boundary characteristics through directional processing. The Multi-Scale Directional Edge Refiner optimizes for the challenges of blurred cloud boundaries and irregular shapes in cloud image segmentation by introducing residual edge enhancement and multi-scale directional convolution mechanisms into the U-Net skip connection—the primary component focuses on enhancing local edge information while suppressing background interference. This module first highlights local edge texture information through residual edge enhancement operations—global average pooling (GAP) extracts the global background context information of the feature map, and subtracting the original features from this global pooling result effectively removes background interference and highlights local detail differences. These results are then added to the original features to form residual connections, which maintain feature integrity while enhancing edge response. Following edge enhancement, we apply directional feature extraction to capture the complex boundary patterns characteristic of cloud formations. Subsequently, asymmetric convolution kernels of 1×7 and 7×1 are applied to capture edge features in different directions on the enhanced features. Since cloud boundaries often exhibit complex directional features and lack clear geometric shape constraints and traditional symmetric convolution kernels struggle to effectively capture these subtle edge changes, this module employs a cascaded processing approach of first performing edge enhancement followed by directional feature extraction, enabling more accurate identification and preservation of the blurred boundaries between clouds and the sky, thereby significantly improving segmentation accuracy. For segmentation tasks involving non-rigid structural targets like cloud images, specialized edge enhancement mechanisms are required to address their boundary blurring issues.

3.5. Uncertainty-Driven Loss Optimizer (UDLO)

In the task of ground-based cloud image segmentation, the number of foreground (cloud feature) pixels is significantly different from that of background pixels. Traditional loss functions do not consider the difference in category importance, which often leads the model to predict the majority background category and ignore key foreground features. The inherent challenge in binary cloud image segmentation stems from the distinct characteristics of different regions: cloud areas contain rich textural information, while sky regions are relatively homogeneous, causing models to disproportionately focus on cloud features. This natural bias leads to severe false-positive problems, where the model's attention becomes heavily concentrated on textured cloud regions at the expense of accurate sky region identification.

To systematically mitigate this class imbalance challenge, we develop a dynamic weighting mechanism based on real-time model performance assessment. To address this issue, we utilize Score-Weighted Visual Explanations for Convolutional Neural Networks (Score-CAM) [27] to generate activation maps that can highlight the foreground features. CAM visualizations (Figure 6) serve a dual purpose: they not only reveal the model's current attention distribution but also provide clear evidence of the imbalanced classification scenario that necessitates dynamic intervention. These visualizations demonstrate how unweighted attention maps exhibit excessive focus on cloud regions while neglecting sky regions, thereby motivating our uncertainty-driven loss optimization approach.

Based on this map, we calculate the hit rate of each category and then dynamically adjust the weights of the loss function, enabling the model to focus more on the foreground category during training and providing an uncertainty quantification tool for the reliability analysis of meteorological networks. Our uncertainty quantification mechanism operates through periodic assessment; we calculate CAM every 5 epochs during training to evaluate the model's current attention distribution and confidence levels. These activation patterns inform the dynamic updating of uncertainty weights, transforming traditional static loss weighting into an adaptive, uncertainty-aware optimization strategy. This approach effectively counterbalances the model's natural tendency to over-attend to textured regions, thereby reducing false-positive rates and improving overall segmentation performance.

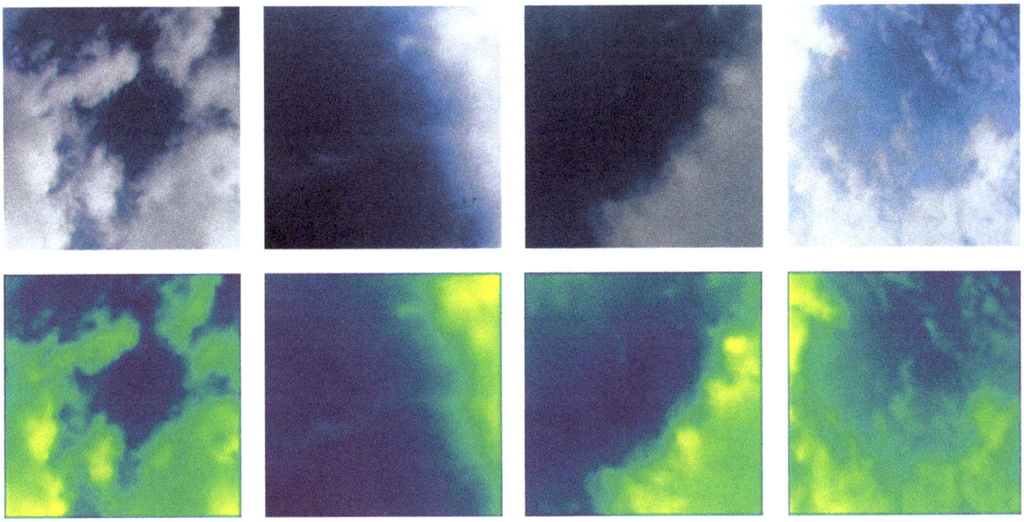

Figure 6. CAM visualizations.

Definition (Score-CAM) As illustrated in Figure 7, Score-CAM builds upon Grad-CAM's foundation by employing score-based gradients instead of logit-derived ones, enhancing the accuracy of spatial localization [28]. The core formula for Score-CAM (the structure diagram is shown in Figure 2) is the following:

$$\text{Score} - \text{CAM} = ReLU\left(\sum_k \alpha_k^c A_l^k\right), \tag{14}$$

$$\alpha_k^c = C\left(A_l^k\right), \tag{15}$$

where $C(\cdot)$ denotes the Channel-wise Increase of Confidence (CIC) for activation map A_l^k. CIC is defined as follows:

$$C\left(A_l^k\right) = f\left(X \circ H_l^k\right) - f(X_b), \tag{16}$$

where

$$H_l^k = s\left(Up\left(A_l^k\right)\right), \tag{17}$$

where $s(\cdot)$ is the normalization function that maps each element in the input matrix to [0, 1] and $Up\left(A_l^k\right)$ denotes the operation that upsamples A_l^k into the input size; X_b is the baseline, and X is the input.

Score-CAM extracts the features in Stage 1. Subsequently, the system applies each mask to the source image iteratively, computing corresponding class-specific scores. This second phase executes N iterations matching the count of active feature maps. The final output emerges from weighted combinations of scores and their corresponding activation maps. Both initial and secondary phases utilize a shared CNN architecture for feature extraction. Hereafter, Score-CAM will be abbreviated as 'CAM'.

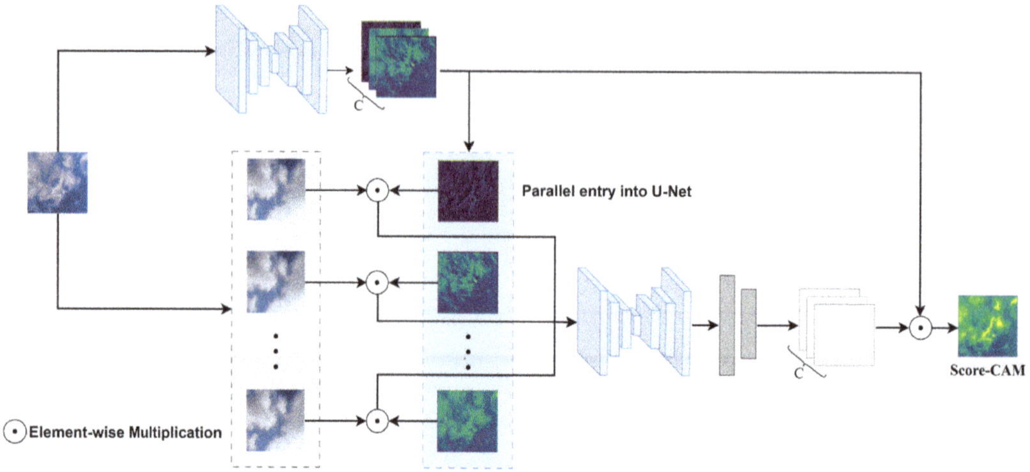

Figure 7. Score-CAM structure diagram.

The foundation of our approach is the quantitative measurement of model attention to different categories through hit-rate calculation. For each category $c \in \{0, 1, \ldots, C\}$, the hit rate is defined as follows:

$$HR_c = \frac{\sum_{(i,j)\in\Omega_c} CAM_{i,j}}{|\Omega_c|}, \tag{18}$$

where Ω_c represents the set of pixels belonging to category c and $CAM_{i,j}$ is the activation value at the spatial position (i, j). The *CAM* value dynamically reflects the model's sensitivity to different categories in the current training state, enabling the weight adjustment to respond in real time to the model's learning progress. Utilizing this hit-rate measurement, we design an adaptive weight calculation mechanism that inversely correlates with model confidence. Based on the hit rate of each category, the adaptive weight for each category is calculated using an exponential decay function:

$$\omega_c = \exp(-HR_c). \tag{19}$$

The negative exponent ensures that categories with higher hit rates receive lower weights, while those with lower hit rates receive higher weights, achieving the design goal of "paying attention to the weak categories". The exponential function nonlinearly amplifies small differences, enabling even minor differences in hit rates to produce significant weight adjustment effects, enhancing the model's sensitivity to class imbalance. The range of the number function avoids the extreme situation of zero weights, ensuring that all categories can receive certain training attention. For binary segmentation tasks, we implement a relative weighting scheme that maintains numerical stability. The relative weight ratio is the following:

$$\omega = \frac{\exp(-HR_0)}{\exp(-HR_1)}. \tag{20}$$

To ensure numerical stability and prevent extreme weight values, we apply weight truncation:

$$\omega_{final} = \max(\omega, 1.0). \tag{21}$$

Finally, we integrate these adaptive weights into the loss function to achieve end-to-end optimization. Applying the calculated weights to the *BCE* loss function, the updated loss function is as follows:

$$L_{BCE} = -\frac{1}{N}\sum_{i=1}^{N} [y_i \log(\hat{y}_i) + (1 - y_i) \log(1 - \hat{y}_i)] \cdot \omega_{final}, \quad (22)$$

where N represents the sample size and y_i and $\hat{y}_i$ represent the true label and the predicted probability, respectively. This weighted loss-function mechanism achieves a transformation from the "static category statistics" to the "dynamic attention distribution" weight adjustment paradigm. During the training process, it enables the model to pay more attention to the foreground category, thereby improving its segmentation performance for the key features of the cloud image.

This design achieves end-to-end optimization from the attention mechanism to the loss function, converting the internal attention distribution of the model into a guiding signal for the training process, providing theoretical support and practical solutions for the imbalance problem of foreground and background in cloud image segmentation. To create a robust training objective, we combine multiple loss components with complementary properties. We combine the binary cross-entropy (BCE) loss with Dice loss, which is calculated as follows:

$$L = \lambda L_{BCE} + (1 - \lambda)\, L_{DICE} \quad (23)$$

where λ is a hyperparameter. The Dice loss is not affected by the size of the foreground, and the *BCE* loss can play a guiding role for the Dice loss in the network learning process.

4. Experiments

To validate the superiority of the Uncertainty-Quantified Geometric Paradigm via Hierarchical Graph Networks (G-CLIP) proposed in this paper, we compare it with representative semi-supervised segmentation methods—U-Net [18], Att-UNet [19], Swin-Unet [21], Laplacian [22], MA-SegCloud [23], CSWin-UNet [24], Rolling-Unet [25], and UNeXt [26]—for a comprehensive comparison.

4.1. Datasets

We conducted experiments on four datasets: SWINSEG/SWIMSEG [29], TCDD [30], and HRC_WHU [31].

The SWIMSEG and SWINSEG datasets were developed by Nanyang Technological University, Singapore, for sky/cloud image segmentation research. SWIMSEG contains 1013 sky/cloud images captured using the ground-based Wide-Angle High-Resolution Sky Imaging System (WAHRSIS), equipped with a Canon EOS Rebel T3i (EOS 600D) (manufactured by Canon Inc., in Tokyo, Japan) camera body and a Sigma 4.5 mm F2.8 EX DC HSM Circular Fish-eye Lens (manufactured by Sigma Corporation, headquartered in Kawasaki, Kanagawa, Japan.) with a 180-degree field of view. The captured images undergo comprehensive preprocessing, including vignetting correction, color calibration using an 18-patch color checkerboard reference, and geometric distortion correction. The final undistorted images have dimensions of 600 × 600 pixels, with a 68-degree viewing angle. SWINSEG comprises 115 carefully selected diverse images captured between January and December 2016, representing various weather conditions, cloud coverage patterns, and seasonal variations. These images are processed to 500 × 500-pixel dimensions using ray-tracing techniques for distortion correction. Ground-truth annotations for both datasets were performed in collaboration with experts from the Singapore Meteorological Service, ensuring professional accuracy in cloud/sky segmentation labeling.

The TCDD (Tianjin Cloud Detection Database), released in 2023, encompasses 2300 ground-based cloud images collected over a one-year period (2019–2020) from nine provinces across China. This geographical diversity ensures comprehensive coverage of various climate zones and weather patterns. The dataset is divided into 1874 training images (first nine months) and 426 test images (last three months), maintaining temporal separation to prevent data leakage. Images are captured by visual sensors and stored in PNG format at 512 × 512-pixel resolution, with corresponding binary cloud masks jointly annotated by meteorologists and cloud detection researchers.

The HRC_WHU dataset provides 150 high-resolution satellite and aerial images, with spatial resolutions ranging from 0.5 to 15 m, collected from Google Earth across diverse global regions. The dataset covers five major land-cover types—water bodies, vegetation, urban areas, snow/ice surfaces, and barren land—ensuring robust evaluation across different surface backgrounds. Each RGB image is accompanied by precisely delineated cloud masks created using Adobe Photoshop's lasso and magic wand tools (tolerance: 5–30) by remote-sensing interpretation specialists. This dataset is particularly valuable for evaluating fine-grained segmentation capabilities and boundary preservation in high-resolution imagery, demonstrating the applications of multi-source optical data fusion.

4.2. Implementation Details

Experimental setup utilized Python version 3.10 with PyTorch 2.4.0 and CUDA 12.4. Model development and evaluation employed an NVIDIA RTX A6000 GPU with 48GB memory (Santa Clara, CA, USA). Training configurations for SWIMSEG, SWINSEG, TCDD, and HRC_WHU datasets included: starting learning rate of 5×10^{-4} with AdamW optimization, implementing cosine annealing to decrease the rate to 5×10^{-6} [M1] [xs2]; batch configuration of 4 samples across 100 epochs; input/output dimensions maintained at 224 × 224 pixels; stochastic Gaussian noise augmentation applied at 50% probability (Table 1). Binary cross-entropy served as the optimization criterion across all architectures. The framework automatically preserved optimal parameters whenever validation metrics showed improvement (Table 2).

Table 1. Performance comparison of various models in processing four images of size 224 × 224, measuring FLOPs, parameters, and GPU inference time across different model architectures.

Model	Param (M)	FLOPs (G)	GPU Inference Time (ms)
U-Net	34.53	50.191	16.29
Att-UNet	34.88	50.98	17.09
MA-SegCloud	35.72	16.247	14.4
Rollin-Unet (L)	28.33	25.179	122.58
Swin-UNet	27.17	5.949	7.64
Laplacian-Former	25.33	4.97	27.77
CSWin-UNet	23.57	4.723	22.91
UNeXt	1.47	0.45	3.01
Ours	107.4	26.783	19.66

Table 2. Hyperparameter settings of each model component and training configuration used in our experiments.

Component	Parameter	Value	Description
PDAA	K (clusters)	8	Number of cluster centers
	α (EMA decay)	0.999	Exponential moving average rate
	Group size (S)	128	Size of each attention group
	Iteration count	3	

Table 2. *Cont.*

Component	Parameter	Value	Description
SAGCL	k (neighbors)	64	Number of nearest neighbors
	Similarity metric	Cosine	Distance metric for graph construction
MSDER	Kernel sizes	$1 \times 7, 7 \times 1$	Directional convolution kernels
UDLO	CAM		Calculate the frequency of CAM
Training	λ (loss weight)	0.5	Balance between BCE and Dice loss
	Learning rate	0.0005	Initial learning rate
	Batch size	4	Training batch size
	Input size	224 × 224	Input image dimensions

4.3. Evaluation Metrics

To comprehensively evaluate the performance of our proposed method, we employ four widely-adopted evaluation metrics: recall, F1-score, error rate, and mean Intersection over Union (mIoU). These metrics provide complementary perspectives on model performance across different aspects of the prediction task.

Recall measures the proportion of actual positive instances that are correctly identified by the model. It is particularly important in scenarios where missing positive cases have significant consequences. Error rate quantifies the proportion of incorrect predictions made by the model, providing a straightforward measure of classification accuracy. The F1-score provides a harmonic mean of precision and recall, offering a balanced assessment of model performance when both false positives and false negatives are equally important. Mean Intersection over Union (mIoU) is used to evaluate pixel-level prediction accuracy. The metrics are defined as follows:

$$\text{Recall} = \frac{TP}{TP+FN}, \tag{24}$$

$$\text{Error Rate} = \frac{FP+FN}{TP+FP+TN+FN}, \tag{25}$$

$$\text{F1-score} = \frac{2TP}{2TP+FP+FN}, \tag{26}$$

$$\text{MIoU} = \frac{1}{N}\sum_{i=1}^{N} IOU_i, \tag{27}$$

where *TP* refers to the correctly identified foreground elements in the prediction output; *TN* corresponds to accurately recognized background elements; *FP* indicates regions mistakenly classified as foreground in the prediction but are actually background, as per the ground truth; conversely, *FN* denotes areas incorrectly labeled as background in the prediction, despite being foreground in the ground-truth annotation.

4.4. Comparison Experiments

The segmentation results from the SWIMSEG and SWINSEG datasets (Figure 8) demonstrate the superior performance of the proposed method under different lighting conditions: in terms of cloud boundary accuracy, the proposed method can more accurately identify cloud boundaries than other methods, especially in the complex cloud structure in the first row, avoiding the common over-segmentation issue in traditional methods; in terms of shape preservation, in the different cloud types in rows 2–4, the proposed method better preserves the intact shape of cloud layers, reducing fragmented segmentation; in terms of foreground–background balance, thanks to the UDLO module, it can still accurately identify rare cirrus clouds in scenes with fewer foreground cloud regions, avoiding the tendency to predict the background. Specifically, in the red-boxed region analysis, in the red box of the first row (complex cloud layer boundaries), the PDAA clustering attention mechanism effectively identifies local cloud cluster structures, avoiding incorrect segmentation at complex boundaries by other methods. SAGCL constructs a graph structure using cosine similarity, accurately modeling semantic relationships between cloud layers to achieve precise boundary localization. In the second row of red boxes (dense cloud regions), the SAGCL module constructs a sparse graph structure using k-nearest neighbors to handle complex connection relationships in dense cloud regions. Graph convolutions better propagate cloud layer feature information than traditional convolutions, reducing segmentation discontinuities. In the red box on lines 3–4 (blurred boundary regions), the MSDER multi-scale directional boundary refinement unit uses 1×7 and 7×1-long kernel convolutions to effectively capture weak boundary information in horizontal and vertical directions. The UDLO module dynamically adjusts loss weights to make the model focus more on difficult-to-identify boundary regions.

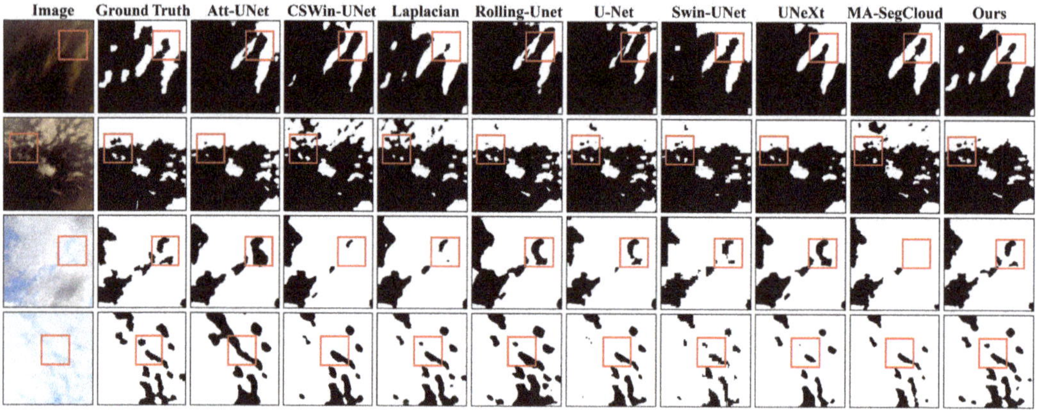

Figure 8. Comparison test results of SWIMSEG and SWINSEG datasets.

The experimental results from the TCDD dataset (Figure 9) demonstrate that the proposed method exhibits significant advantages in complex scenarios across multiple geographical environments. In terms of graph structure modeling, the SAGCL module effectively adapts to changes in cloud layer morphology across different geographical environments by constructing graph structures, establishing semantic dependencies between distant pixels, which is crucial for identifying large-scale cloud systems. It accurately captures the irregular shape features of cumulus clouds within complex structures, overcoming the limitations of traditional convolutional methods. Simultaneously, the clustering and grouping attention mechanism identifies texture consistency within cumulus clouds, reducing internal segmentation discontinuity issues and maintaining high-precision boundaries of cumulus clouds. In terms of detail preservation, the proposed method maintains clear segmentation boundaries, even in cases of thin clouds or cirrus clouds with blurred boundaries. The multi-scale directional boundary refinement units of the MSDER module capture the horizontal extension boundary features of stratus clouds through long kernel convolutions. The gated feature fusion mechanism dynamically adjusts the fusion process to enhance the accuracy of blurred boundary identification. Additionally, the graph structure establishes long-distance semantic associations, connecting similar stratus cloud regions and avoiding discontinuities at gradient boundaries. In terms of noise suppression, compared to other methods, the proposed method demonstrates stronger noise resistance when handling complex backgrounds.

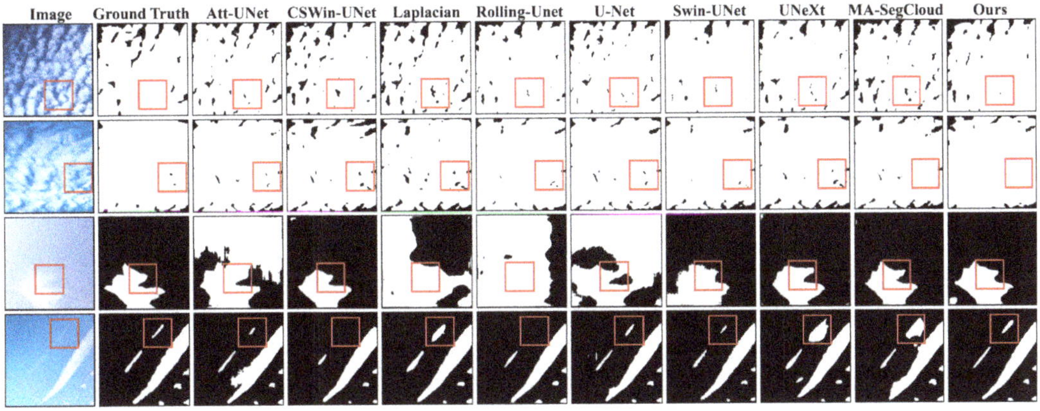

Figure 9. Comparison test results of TCDD dataset.

Furthermore, analyzing the red-boxed regions from the first to the fourth rows further highlights the advantages of each module. In scenarios with dense cloud clusters, the sparse graph structure of the SAGCL module effectively models the spatial relationships between cloud clusters, enabling accurate separation. The PDAA module enhances the consistency of internal features within cloud clusters, maintaining their integrity while accurately identifying boundaries. For cirrus cloud filament structures, the MSDER module's multi-directional long kernel convolution and channel-adaptive adjustment unit perform exceptionally well, making it suitable for processing the linear extension structures of cirrus clouds. It enhances the local difference features of filament boundaries, offering a natural advantage over traditional square convolution kernels. Meanwhile, the SAGCL module connects different parts of cirrus cloud filaments through graph structures to avoid fragmentation issues, and the UDLO module ensures the model adequately focuses on rare cirrus clouds. In contrast, methods such as Att-UNet and CSWin-UNet exhibit boundary blurring and shape distortion in cumulus red-box regions, while U-Net and Swin-UNet encounter boundary identification errors at the boundary between stratus clouds and the sky. Laplacian and Rolling-Unet produce segmentation fragmentation in densely clustered cloud regions, MA-SegCloud exhibits cloud cluster boundary confusion, and Transformer-based methods like UNeXt and CSWin-UNet perform poorly in handling cirrus cloud filament structures. Traditional U-Net series methods are limited by their receptive field and cannot effectively capture the long-distance continuity of cirrus clouds. Overall, whether in the dry northern environment or the humid southern conditions, the SAGCL module's adaptability effectively captures local cloud layer features, and the PDAA module's clustering/grouping mechanism adapts to differences in cloud layer feature distributions across various geographical environments. Additionally, the proposed method accurately identifies cumulus cloud block structures and clear boundaries, effectively handles the extensive coverage and gradual boundaries of stratus clouds, successfully separates dense cloud clusters while maintaining integrity, and accurately captures the filamentous structures and directional characteristics of cirrus clouds.

In the high-resolution scenes included in the HRC_WHU dataset (Figure 10), the MSDER module demonstrates significant multi-scale feature fusion capabilities in terms of fine boundary processing, effectively handling fine boundary information at resolutions ranging from 0.5 to 15 m. In terms of integrity preservation, the MSDER module achieves significantly superior performance in accurately locating cloud boundaries and maintaining integrity to the comparison methods. Analysis of the red-boxed regions shows that in high-resolution detail areas, the MSDER module's channel-adaptive adjustment unit (CAAU) and multi-scale directional boundary refinement unit (MSDBR) work synergistically to effectively process fine features in high-resolution images. From a graph theory symmetry perspective, this module models the complex symmetrical relationships between cloud map features at different scales, achieving intelligent feature aggregation.

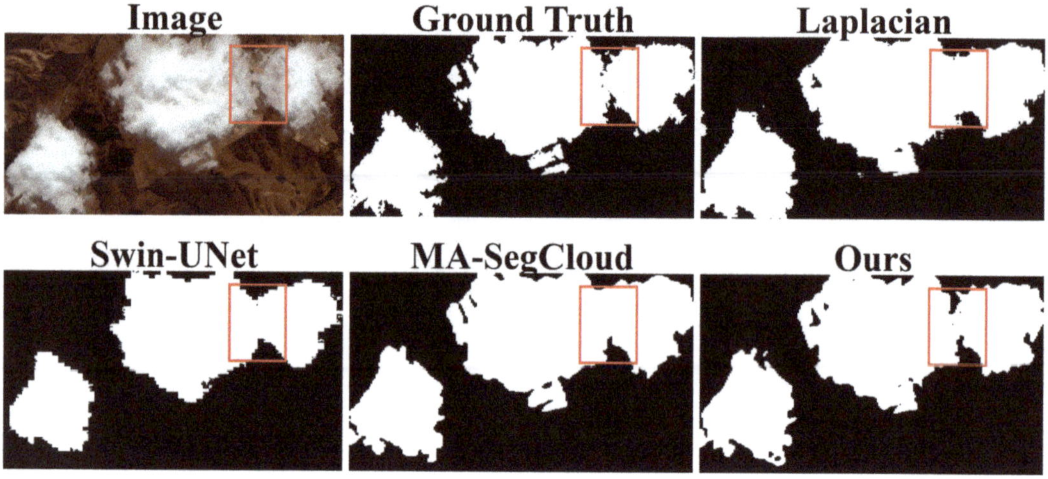

Figure 10. Comparison test results of HRC_WHU dataset.

As shown in Table 3, under daytime conditions, our method achieved the best performance in all evaluation metrics. The recall rate reached 93.08%, which is 3.30 percentage points higher than the 89.78% achieved by the second-best method, UNeXt. the F1-score reached 92.56%, surpassing UNeXt's 91.00% by approximately 1.56 percentage points; the error rate is reduced to 6.07%, a decrease of 1.24 percentage points compared to UNeXt's 7.31%; MIoU reached 87.32%, an improvement of 2.52 percentage points over UNeXt's 84.80%. This significant improvement is primarily attributed to the clustering and grouping attention mechanism of the PDAA module, which effectively identifies cloud cluster structures under daytime lighting conditions. Meanwhile, the SAGCL module accurately models the complex spatial relationships between cloud layers by constructing a graph structure based on cosine similarity.

Nighttime scene segmentation tasks are more challenging, but our method still maintains a leading advantage. Recall reached 86.76%, an improvement of 0.89 percentage points over the best comparison method, Swin-UNet's 85.87%; the F1-score is 88.02%, significantly surpassing Swin-UNet's 85.80% by approximately 2.22 percentage points; the error rate is reduced to 10.01%, a decrease of 1.26 percentage points compared to Swin-UNet's 11.27%; MIoU reached 79.62%, an improvement of 2.90 percentage points over Swin-UNet's 76.72%. The performance improvement under nighttime conditions is primarily attributed to the multi-scale directional boundary refinement capability of the MSDER module, which effectively captures weak boundary information under low-light conditions at night through 1×7- and 7×1-long kernel convolutions.

On a mixed dataset of daytime and nighttime scenes, our method demonstrates strong generalization capabilities, achieving a recall of 92.41%, an F1-score of 92.08%, an error rate of only 6.49%, and an MIoU of 86.51%. Compared to the next-best method, UNeXt, we achieved a 3.48 percentage-point improvement in recall, a 1.72 percentage-point improvement in F1-score, a 1.32 percentage-point reduction in error rate, and a 2.67 percentage-point improvement in MIoU. This comprehensive performance enhancement validates the effectiveness of the UDLO module in addressing foreground–background imbalance issues.

Table 3. Results of the comparison experiments on the SWINSEG and SWIMSEG dataset (best results are labeled in red, second in blue).

Type	Method	Recall ↑	F1-Score ↑	Error Rate ↓	MIoU ↑
Day	U-Net 2015 [19]	85.67%	88.85%	8.53%	81.92%
	Att-UNet 2018 [20]	87.23%	89.66%	8.17%	82.91%
	Swin-Unet 2021 [22]	88.82%	90.70%	7.60%	84.40%
	Laplacian 2023 [23]	89.37%	90.67%	7.58%	84.50%
	MA-SegCloud 2022 [24]	87.59%	90.45%	7.59%	84.20%
	CSWin-UNet 2025 [25]	88.05%	90.82%	7.82%	84.52%
	Rolling-Unet 2024 [26]	87.66%	90.27%	7.91%	83.69%
	UNeXt 2022 [27]	89.78%	91.00%	7.31%	84.80%
	Ours	93.08%	92.56%	6.07%	87.32%
Night	U-Net [19]	78.00%	82.13%	12.82%	71.96%
	Att-UNet [20]	78.74%	83.67%	12.65%	73.65%
	Swin-Unet [22]	85.87%	85.80%	11.27%	76.72%
	Laplacian [23]	76.69%	83.39%	12.56%	73.62%
	MA-SegCloud [24]	77.21%	82.77%	12.31%	72.70%
	CSWin-UNet [25]	71.26%	80.57%	13.16%	70.06%
	Rolling-Unet [26]	83.51%	83.69%	12.69%	74.33%
	UNeXt [27]	81.75%	84.98%	12.04%	75.71%
	Ours	86.76%	88.02%	10.01%	79.62%
Day + Night	U-Net [19]	84.86%	88.14%	8.98%	80.87%
	Att-UNet [20]	83.71%	87.91%	8.99%	80.60%
	Swin-Unet [22]	88.51%	90.19%	7.98%	83.59%
	Laplacian [23]	88.04%	89.91%	8.10%	83.36%
	MA-SegCloud [24]	86.23%	89.55%	8.22%	82.85%
	CSWin-UNet [25]	86.28%	89.74%	8.38%	83.00%
	Rolling-Unet [26]	87.22%	89.58%	8.41%	82.71%
	UNeXt [27]	88.93%	90.36%	7.81%	83.84%
	Ours	92.41%	92.08%	6.49%	86.51%

Table 4 presents the experimental results from the TCDD dataset. This dataset covers multiple geographical environments across nine provinces in China, featuring higher scene complexity and geographical diversity. Our method achieves state-of-the-art performance on key metrics: MIoU reaches 78.77%, an improvement of 1.62 percentage points over the second-best method, Att-UNet, which achieves 77.15%; the error rate was reduced to 7.98%, a decrease of 0.50 percentage points compared to the best comparison method, CSWin-UNet, which achieved 8.48%, and it tied with Rolling-Unet for the best performance on the recall metric, achieving 87.41%.

It is worth noting that on the TCDD dataset, the F1-score of the traditional U-Net method (83.22%) is higher than that of our method (82.47%), which may be related to the specific data distribution and annotation characteristics of this dataset. However, we still maintain a significant advantage in the more important MIoU metric, indicating that our method remains superior in overall segmentation quality. The SAGCL module plays a crucial role in handling the complex cloud layer topology across multiple geographical environments, effectively capturing the morphological characteristics of clouds under different geographical conditions through adaptive graph structure modeling.

Table 4. Results of the comparison experiments on the TCDD dataset (best results are labeled in red, second in blue).

Method	Recall ↑	F1-Score ↑	Error Rate ↓	MIoU ↑
U-Net [19]	87.29%	83.22%	9.30%	75.81%
Att-UNet [20]	85.57%	81.80%	8.75%	77.15%
Swin-Unet [22]	85.96%	82.87%	8.96%	75.12%
Laplacian [23]	83.33%	80.14%	9.60%	73.77%
MA-SegCloud [24]	86.72%	80.74%	11.80%	73.41%
CSWin-UNet [25]	83.95%	80.69%	8.48%	74.27%
Rolling-Unet [26]	87.41%	82.67%	9.30%	74.93%
UNeXt [27]	85.15%	80.96%	8.66%	75.17%
Ours	87.41%	82.47%	7.98%	78.77%

Table 5 shows the experimental results from the high-resolution HRC_WHU dataset. This dataset features high resolution ranging from 0.5 to 15 m, imposing higher demands on the method's ability to preserve details. Our method achieves the best performance across all evaluation metrics: recall reaches 92.12%, an improvement of 1.19 percentage points over the second-best method, Swin-UNet, which achieved 90.93%; the F1-score is 92.60%, surpassing the second-best method CSWin-UNet's 92.23% by approximately 0.37 percentage points; the error rate is reduced to 5.25%, approaching CSWin-UNet's 5.23%; and MIoU reaches 86.42%, an improvement of 0.54 percentage points over the second-best method CSWin-UNet's 85.88%.

Table 5. Results of the comparison experiments on the HRC_WHU dataset (best results are labeled in red, second in blue).

Method	Recall ↑	F1-Score ↑	Error Rate ↓	MIoU ↑
U-Net [19]	88.59%	91.36%	6.06%	84.36%
Att-UNet [20]	89.65%	91.90%	5.71%	85.34%
Swin-Unet [22]	90.93%	91.81%	5.64%	85.32%
Laplacian [23]	83.39%	84.98%	9.98%	75.23%
MA-SegCloud [24]	90.49%	91.95%	5.68%	85.34%
CSWin-UNet [25]	89.12%	92.23%	5.23%	85.88%
Rolling-Unet [26]	88.26%	90.38%	6.73%	82.91%
UNeXt [27]	89.38%	89.92%	6.85%	82.08%
Ours	92.12%	92.60%	5.25%	86.42%

The outstanding performance on high-resolution datasets is primarily attributed to the multi-scale feature fusion capability of the MSDER module. This module effectively processes fine boundary information in high-resolution images through the synergistic action of the channel-adaptive adjustment unit (CAAU) and the multi-scale directional boundary refinement unit (MSDBR), ensuring the accurate localization and integrity of cloud boundaries.

Based on the experimental results from the three datasets, our method achieves the best performance in the key metric MIoU, with an average improvement of 2–3 percentage points, demonstrating the universality and effectiveness of the method. From daytime to nighttime, from simple to complex scenes, and from low to high resolution, our method shows good adaptability and robustness. Qualitative analysis reveals that our method excels in handling complex cloud boundaries, particularly in cases of thin clouds or cirrus clouds with blurred boundaries, maintaining clear and accurate segmentation boundaries. Additionally, the PDAA module effectively reduces computational complexity while maintaining segmentation accuracy through its clustering-based attention mechanism, providing practical feasibility for real-world applications.

4.5. *Ablation Study*

The ablation experiment results (Table 6) clearly demonstrate the effectiveness and synergistic effects of the four innovative modules proposed in this paper. Specifically, the SAGCL module shows the most significant effect. Compared with the baseline U-Net, adding SAGCL alone significantly improves recall from 84.86% to 93.81% (+8.95%) and MIoU from 80.87% to 84.12% (+3.25%). This demonstrates the superiority of the symmetry-adaptive graph convolutional layer in modeling long-range semantic associations between cloud layers. By modeling cloud pixels as graph nodes and constructing a graph structure based on cosine similarity, it effectively captures the complex topological characteristics of cloud layers. The PDAA module achieves a balance between computational efficiency and performance. Using PDAA alone improves the F1-score to 90.04% (+1.90%) and MIoU to 84.12% (+3.25%). The clustering attention mechanism, which combines K-means dynamic clustering and intra-group attention calculation, effectively enhances feature representation quality while reducing computational complexity. The MSDER module introduces relatively moderate improvements; adding MSDER alone only increases MIoU by 1.26% to 82.13%, but it lays the foundation for subsequent module combinations. The uncertainty-aware gate fusion module primarily optimizes the feature fusion process in skip connections, with its effects becoming more pronounced when combined with other modules.

Table 6. Ablation study on the four datasets.

	Recall ↑	F1-Score ↑	Error Rate ↓	MioU ↑
U-Net	84.86%	88.14%	8.98%	80.87%
U-Net + SAGCL	93.81%	90.68%	8.03%	84.12%
U-Net + PDAA	88.54%	90.04%	8.17%	84.12%
U-Net + MSDER	84.57%	89.09%	8.66%	82.13%
U-Net + SAGCL + PDAA	89.46%	91.28%	7.26%	85.20%
U-Net + SAGCL + PDAA + MSDER	91.43%	91.76%	6.85%	86.00%
U-Net + SAGCL + PDAA + MSDER + UDLO	92.41%	92.08%	6.49%	86.51%

The SAGCL + PDAA combination demonstrates good synergy, with the two modules combined achieving an F1-score of 91.28% and an error rate of 7.26%, validating the design approach of "clustering and grouping followed by graph convolution". Clustering and grouping provide a better local feature foundation for graph convolution, while graph convolution further establishes global associations across cloud clusters. After combining the three modules (SAGCL + PDAA + MSDER), the F1-score reached 91.76%, MIoU improved to 86.00%, and the error rate dropped to 6.85%. This indicates that the uncertainty-aware gated fusion module plays a crucial role in multi-scale feature integration, enhancing overall performance through intelligent aggregation and noise suppression. When all four modules are enabled, all metrics reach optimal levels: recall 92.41%, F1-score 92.08%, error rate 6.49%, and MIoU 86.51%. UDLO effectively addresses the foreground–background imbalance issue through CAM technology and adaptive weight adjustment, enabling the model to focus more on difficult-to-identify cloud-type features during training.

5. Conclusions

This work establishes a novel paradigm for graph symmetry-driven ground-based cloud image segmentation through the proposed G-CLIP framework, which systematically integrates four modules—PDAA, SAGCL, MSDER, and UDLO—to address core challenges in graph structure modeling, uncertainty quantification, and diagnostic reliability within meteorological imaging systems. The key theoretical advances are rooted in graph theory and symmetry principles, offering a cohesive architecture for handling complex cloud formations.

The SAGCL module achieves symmetry-adaptive graph modeling by incorporating graph symmetrization and degree normalization into a sparse graph built via cosine similarity, effectively capturing topological relationships among cloud structures and contributing to a significant gain of 8.95% in recall. Complementing this, the PDAA module leverages permutation invariance to reduce computational complexity from $O(N^2)$ to $O(N{\cdot}S)$ through dynamic clustering and group-level attention, ensuring efficient and semantically consistent feature grouping. Further enhancing the framework, the MSDER and UDLO modules introduce multi-scale directional refinement and uncertainty-aware optimization. MSDER employs asymmetric convolutions to model directional symmetries in cloud boundaries, while UDLO utilizes CAM-driven loss reweighting to handle class imbalance and quantify prediction uncertainty.

The design of the four modules follows a principled hierarchical flow that combines local feature clustering, global graph reasoning, multi-scale feature fusion, and uncertainty propagation. Specifically, local groupings generated by PDAA provide structured inputs to SAGCL, which in turn establishes robust long-range dependencies through symmetric graph operations. MSDER then refines the multi-level features with emphasis on directional edges, and UDLO aggregates uncertainty signals across the network to adaptively guide the training process. This synergistic integration is empirically validated through comprehensive ablation studies, where the full model achieves a 92.08% F1-score, outperforming any partial combination of modules and underscoring the complementary roles of each component.

Extensive validation on multiple datasets—including TCDD, which spans nine Chinese provinces—confirms the robustness and state-of-the-art performance of G-CLIP across diverse geographic and climatic conditions. The model achieved a notable +1.62% improvement in mIoU on the TCDD dataset, consistent gains in recall and F1-score on SWINSEG and SWIMSEG under both daytime and nighttime conditions, and strong results on high-resolution HRC_WHU imagery, demonstrating effective generalization across scales and sensor types. Despite these advancements, several challenges remain open for future work. These include extending the symmetry-aware framework to spatio-temporal cloud evolution modeling, integrating cross-sensor data from ground-based, satellite, and radar sources, developing end-to-end uncertainty quantification across the full pipeline, optimizing graph computations for real-time application, and improving domain adaptation for varying climate regions.

In conclusion, G-CLIP provides a unified and scalable framework that bridges graph theory symmetry with practical meteorological applications. By integrating principles from graph neural networks, uncertainty quantification, and multi-scale feature learning, this research offers a robust foundation for next-generation cloud analysis systems and promotes cross-disciplinary advances in computational meteorology.

Supplementary Materials: The following supporting information can be downloaded at: https://www.mdpi.com/article/10.3390/sym17091477/s1, Table S1: Comparison of Existing Methods and the Proposed Framework.

Author Contributions: Conceptualization, Q.X. and Z.Z.; methodology, Z.Z.; software, Y.C.; validation, Q.X., Y.C. and Z.Z.; formal analysis, G.W.; investigation, Y.C.; resources, Z.Z.; data curation, Q.X.; writing—original draft preparation, Z.Z.; writing—review and editing, Y.C.; visualization, Z.Z.; supervision, Q.X.; project administration, Y.C.; funding acquisition, Q.X. All authors have read and agreed to the published version of the manuscript.

Funding: This research received no external funding.

Data Availability Statement: The raw data supporting the conclusions of this article will be made available by the authors on request.

Conflicts of Interest: The authors declare no conflicts of interest.

References

1. Brunet, G.; Parsons, D.B.; Ivanov, D.; Lee, B.; Bauer, P.; Bernier, N.B.; Bouchet, V.; Brown, A.; Busalacchi, A.; Flatter, G.C.; et al. Advancing Weather and Climate Forecasting for Our Changing World. *Bull. Amer. Meteor. Soc.* **2023**, *104*, E909–E927. [CrossRef]
2. Nie, B.; Lu, Z.; Han, J.; Chen, W.; Cai, C.; Pan, W. Investigation on Ground-Based Cloud Image Classification and Its Application in Photovoltaic Power Forecasting. *IEEE Trans. Instrum. Meas.* **2025**, *74*, 1–11. [CrossRef]
3. Xu, Q.; Zhang, Z.; Wang, G.; Chen, Y. Physics-Guided Multi-Representation Learning with Quadruple Consistency Constraints for Robust Cloud Detection in Multi-Platform Remote Sensing. *Remote Sens.* **2025**, *17*, 2946. [CrossRef]
4. Xu, Q.; Zhang, Z.; Wang, G.; Chen, Y. Explainable Multi-Scale CAM Attention for Interpretable Cloud Segmentation in Astro-Meteorological Applications. *Appl. Sci.* **2025**, *15*, 8555. [CrossRef]
5. Li, K.; Ma, N.; Sun, L. Cloud detection of multi-type satellite images based on spectral assimilation and deep learning. *Int. J. Remote Sens.* **2023**, *44*, 3106–3121. [CrossRef]
6. Mohamadzadeh, S.; Ghayedi, M.; Pasban, S.; Shafiei, A.K. Algorithm of Predicting Heart Attack with using Sparse Coder. *Int. J. Eng.* **2023**, *36*, 2190–2197. [CrossRef]
7. Zhang, C.; Weng, L.; Ding, L.; Xia, M.; Lin, H. CRSNet: Cloud and Cloud Shadow Refinement Segmentation Networks for Remote Sensing Imagery. *Remote Sens.* **2023**, *15*, 1664. [CrossRef]
8. Liu, J.; Zhang, Z. Graph Structure Learning Boosted Neural Network for Image Segmentation. In Proceedings of the 2022 18th IEEE International Conference on Advanced Video and Signal Based Surveillance (AVSS), Madrid, Spain, 29 November–2 December 2022; pp. 1–8. [CrossRef]
9. Pan, C.-H.; Qu, Y.; Yao, Y.; Wang, M.-J.-S. HybridGNN: A Self-Supervised Graph Neural Network for Efficient Maximum Matching in Bipartite Graphs. *Symmetry* **2024**, *16*, 1631. [CrossRef]
10. Kovvuri, S.; Reddy, G.; Saran, B.; Adityaja, A.M.; Shigwan, S.J.; Kumar, N. UnSegGNet: Unsupervised Image Segmentation using Graph Neural Networks. *arXiv* **2024**. [CrossRef]
11. Kovvuri, R.; Saran, B.; Adityaja, A.; Saurabh, S.; Nitin, K.; Snehasis, K. UnSeGArmaNet: Unsupervised Image Segmentation using Graph Neural Networks with Convolutional ARMA Filters. *arXiv* **2024**. [CrossRef]
12. Wang, S.; Wang, Y.; Wang, M. Connectivity and matching preclusion for leaf-sort graphs. *J. Interconnect. Netw.* **2019**, *19*, 1940007. [CrossRef]
13. Wang, M.; Xiang, D.; Qu, Y.; Li, G. The diagnosability of interconnection networks. *Discret. Appl. Math.* **2024**, *357*, 413–428. [CrossRef]
14. Wang, M.; Wang, S. Connectivity and diagnosability of center k-ary n-cubes. *Discret. Appl. Math.* **2021**, *294*, 98–107. [CrossRef]
15. Wang, M.-J.; Xiang, D.; Hsieh, S.-Y. G-good-neighbor diagnosability under the modified comparison model for multiprocessor systems. *Theor. Comput. Sci.* **2025**, *1028*, 115027. [CrossRef]
16. Hamilton, W.; Ying, Z.; Leskovec, J. Inductive Representation Learning on Large Graphs. Advances in Neural Information Processing Systems. *arXiv* **2017**. [CrossRef]
17. Veličković, P.; Cucurull, G.; Casanova, A.; Romero, A.; Lio, P.; Bengio, Y. Graph Attention Networks. In Proceedings of the International Conference on Learning Representations, Vancouver, BC, Canada, 30 April–3 May 2018. [CrossRef]
18. Ronneberger, O.; Fischer, P.; Brox, T. U-Net: Convolutional Networks for Biomedical Image Segmentation. In *Medical Image Computing and Computer-Assisted Intervention—MICCAI 2015. MICCAI 2015*; Lecture Notes in Computer Science; Navab, N., Hornegger, J., Wells, W., Frangi, A., Eds.; Springer: Cham, Switzerland, 2015; Volume 9351. [CrossRef]
19. Oktay, O.; Schlemper, J.; Folgoc, L.L.; Lee, M.J.; Heinrich, M.P.; Misawa, K.; Mori, K.; McDonagh, S.G.; Hammerla, N.Y.; Kainz, B.; et al. Attention U-Net: Learning Where to Look for the Pancreas. *arXiv* **2018**, arXiv:1804.03999. [CrossRef]
20. Dosovitskiy, A.; Beyer, L.; Kolesnikov, A.; Weissenborn, D.; Zhai, X.; Unterthiner, T.; Dehghani, M.; Minderer, M.; Heigold, G.; Gelly, S.; et al. An image is worth 16 $\times$ 16 words: Transformers for image recognition at scale. *arXiv* **2020**, arXiv:2010.11929v2. [CrossRef]
21. Cao, H.; Wang, Y.; Chen, J.; Jiang, D.; Zhang, X.; Tian, Q.; Wang, M. Swin-Unet: Unet-Like Pure Transformer for Medical Image Segmentation. In *Computer Vision—ECCV 2022 Workshops, Proceedings of Part III, Tel Aviv, Israel, 23–27 October 2022*; Springer: Berlin, Heidelberg, 2022; pp. 205–218. [CrossRef]
22. Azad, R.; Kazerouni, A.; Azad, B.; Aghdam, E.K.; Velichko, Y.; Bagci, U.; Merhof, D. Laplacian-Former: Overcoming the Limitations of Vision Transformers in Local Texture Detection. *Med. Image Comput. Comput. Assist. Interv.* **2023**, *14222*, 736–746. [CrossRef] [PubMed]

23. Zhang, L.; Wei, W.; Qiu, B.; Luo, A.; Zhang, M.; Li, X. A Novel Ground-Based Cloud Image Segmentation Method Based on a Multibranch Asymmetric Convolution Module and Attention Mechanism. *Remote Sens.* **2022**, *14*, 3970. [CrossRef]
24. Liu, X.; Gao, P.; Yu, T.; Wang, F.; Yuan, R.-Y. CSWin-UNet: Transformer UNet with cross-shaped windows for medical image segmentation. *Inf. Fusion* **2025**, *113*, 102634. [CrossRef]
25. Liu, Y.; Zhu, H.; Liu, M.; Yu, H.; Chen, Z.; Gao, J. Rolling-Unet: Revitalizing MLP's Abil-ity to Efficiently Extract Long-Distance Dependencies for Medical Image Segmentation. In Proceedings of the AAAI Conference on Artificial Intelligence, Vancouver, BC, Canada, 20–27 February 2024; pp. 3819–3827. [CrossRef]
26. Valanarasu, J.M.J.; Oza, P.; Hacihaliloglu, I.; Patel, V.M. Medical Transformer: Gated Axial-Attention for Medical Image Segmentation. In *Medical Image Computing and Computer Assisted Intervention—MICCAI 2021*; Lecture Notes in Computer Science; de Bruijne, M., Cattin, P.C., Cotin, S., Padoy, N., Speidel, S., Zheng, Y., Essert, C., Eds.; Springer: Cham, Switzerland, 2021; Volume 12901. [CrossRef]
27. Wang, H.; Wang, Z.; Du, M.; Yang, F.; Zhang, Z.; Ding, S.; Mardziel, P.; Hu, X. Score-CAM: Score-Weighted Visual Explanations for Convolutional Neural Networks. In Proceedings of the IEEE/CVF Conference on Computer Vision and Pattern Recognition Workshops, Seattle, WA, USA, 14–19 June 2020; pp. 24–25.
28. Selvaraju, R.R.; Cogswell, M.; Das, A.; Vedantam, R.; Parikh, D.; Batra, D. Grad-CAM: Visual Explanations from Deep Networks via Gradient-Based Localization. In Proceedings of the 2017 IEEE International Conference on Computer Vision (ICCV), Venice, Italy, 22–29 October 2017; pp. 618–626.
29. Dev, S.; Nautiyal, A.; Lee, Y.H.; Winkler, S. CloudSegNet: A Deep Network for Nychthemeron Cloud Image Segmentation. *IEEE Geosci. Remote Sens. Lett.* **2019**, *16*, 1814–1818. [CrossRef]
30. Zhang, Z.; Yang, S.; Liu, S.; Xiao, B.; Cao, X. Ground-Based Cloud Detection Using Multiscale Attention Convolutional Neural Network. *IEEE Geosci. Remote Sens. Lett.* **2022**, *19*, 1–5. [CrossRef]
31. Li, Z.; Shen, H.; Cheng, Q.; Liu, Y.; You, S.; He, Z. Deep learning based cloud detection for medium and high resolution remote sensing images of different sensors. *ISPRS J. Photogramm. Remote Sens.* **2019**, *150*, 197–212. [CrossRef]

symmetry

MDPI

Article

S-ResGCN-I: A Symmetry-Enhanced Residual Graph Convolutional Network for MRI-Based Brain Tumor Classification

Qiujing Gan, Yingzhou Bi *, Jiangtao Huang, Leigang Huo, Shanrui Liu and Kairui Xiong

School of Artificial Intelligence, Nanning Normal University, Nanning 530199, China; ganqiujing@email.nnnu.edu.cn (Q.G.); jiangtao@nnnu.edu.cn (J.H.); huoleigang@nnnu.edu.cn (L.H.); liushanrui@email.nnnu.edu.cn (S.L.)

* Correspondence: byz@nnnu.edu.cn

Abstract

Early and accurate detection of brain tumors is critical for MRI-based diagnosis. Conventional convolutional neural networks often struggle to capture fine-grained details, small or boundary-ambiguous lesions, and hemispheric symmetry patterns. To address these limitations, we propose S-ResGCN, a symmetry-aware framework integrating hierarchical feature extraction, attention mechanisms, and graph-based classification. S-ResGCN employs a ResNet50 backbone to extract multi-level features, with Convolutional Block Attention Modules applied to intermediate and deep layers to enhance key information and discriminative features. Furthermore, we introduce a novel self-paired regularization to enforce feature consistency between original and horizontally flipped images, improving sensitivity to bilateral symmetric structures. Extracted features are converted into nodes and modeled as a small graph, and a graph convolutional network captures inter-node relationships to generate symmetry-aware predictions. Evaluation on three publicly available brain tumor MRI datasets demonstrates that S-ResGCN achieves average accuracies of 99.83%, 99.37% and 99.26% ± 0.16, with consistently high precision, recall, and F1-scores. These results indicate that S-ResGCN effectively captures fine-grained and symmetric tumor characteristics often overlooked by conventional models, providing a robust and efficient tool for automated, graph convolutional network.

Keywords: MRI; brain tumor; symmetry; ResNet50; self-paired regularization; multi-level attention modules; graph convolutional network

1. Introduction

Brain tumors are among the most common and aggressive malignancies of the central nervous system, typically arising from the abnormal proliferation of glial or meningeal cells. They pose a severe threat to neurological function and patient survival. Epidemiological studies indicate that brain tumors rank among the leading causes of mortality and disability in neurological disorders, particularly when lesions occur in critical brain regions where they can profoundly impair speech, motor, and cognitive functions. In addition to their heterogeneous and irregular morphologies, brain tumors often exhibit locally symmetric growth patterns, which complicates accurate identification and precise boundary delineation. Consequently, early detection and timely intervention are essential for improving survival rates, delaying disease progression, and optimizing patient outcomes. Prompt tumor identification not only reduces surgical risks but also prevents irreversible neurological damage.

Magnetic resonance imaging (MRI) [1], with its superior soft-tissue contrast, non-ionizing nature, and multi-sequence imaging capability, has become an indispensable modality for clinical brain tumor diagnosis. MRI enables clear visualization of abnormal brain structures, providing reliable evidence for tumor detection, localization, and grading. However, the interpretation of MRI scans is highly dependent on radiologists' expertise and subjective judgment. This dependence can prolong diagnostic time and introduce variability due to differences in clinical experience or visual fatigue, ultimately reducing diagnostic consistency and accuracy. To address these challenges, traditional computer-aided diagnosis (CAD) [2] methods have been extensively applied to brain MRI analysis. Such approaches rely on handcrafted feature extraction—commonly including texture descriptors (e.g., gray-level co-occurrence matrices, local binary patterns), shape features, and statistical measures—followed by classification using machine learning algorithms such as support vector machines (SVM) [3], random forests (RF) [4], or k-nearest neighbors (KNN) [5]. Although these methods achieved early success, their labor-intensive feature engineering, subjectivity, and limited generalization ability hinder their effectiveness for the complex, diverse, and locally symmetric morphological characteristics of brain tumors.

In recent years, deep learning has emerged as the dominant paradigm for medical image analysis, with convolutional neural networks (CNNs) [6] demonstrating remarkable performance in brain tumor classification tasks. For example, Musa et al. [7] constructed a ResNet50-based detection model that effectively assisted radiologists in identifying abnormal regions and improving diagnostic accuracy. Ahmed et al. [8] proposed an optimized CNN architecture that significantly enhanced classification performance while maintaining manageable model complexity. Other studies have incorporated pretrained networks to improve generalization; Nizamli et al. [9] used a fixed-weight VGG-19 network to convert MRI images into high-level feature representations combined with an SVM classifier, achieving shorter training times without compromising accuracy. Similarly, Haq et al. [10] integrated CNNs with long short-term memory networks to capture both spatial and temporal information, further improving performance through data augmentation. However, these approaches often rely heavily on global features and fail to explicitly capture fine local details and symmetry-related structures, resulting in reduced sensitivity to small, blurred, or irregular lesions—critical for precise clinical diagnosis.

To design deep learning architectures that are robust and sensitive to local symmetry, insights from graph theory and complex network analysis can be particularly valuable. Previous studies—such as those by Wang et al. [11], Wang et al. [12,13] and Jiang et al. [14]—have systematically investigated the connectivity and diagnosability of locally twisted cubes, leaf-sort graphs, and maximally 4-restricted edge-connected graphs. Additionally, the connectivity and diagnosability of leaf-sort graphs were further explored in a separate study by Wang et al. [15]. The diagnosability of interconnection networks was discussed by Xiang et al. [16], and the connectivity of m-ary n-dimensional hypercubes was investigated in [17–19]. These studies highlight the importance of information-flow reliability, fault tolerance, and node-level symmetry in complex networks, providing a conceptual foundation for developing deep learning architectures capable of capturing local structural and symmetric patterns in brain MRI. Zarenia et al. [20] further combined data augmentation techniques with a hierarchical mul-ti-scale deformable attention module (MS-DAM) to effectively capture irregular and complex tumor patterns, thereby significantly enhancing the model's classification performance.

Motivated by these considerations, we propose S-ResGCN, a symmetry-aware framework for brain tumor classification. Compared with conventional approaches, the main contributions of S-ResGCN are: (1) Using a ResNet50 backbone for hierarchical feature extraction, with Convolutional Block Attention Modules (CBAM) [21] applied to intermediate and deep layers to enhance key information and discriminative features. (2) Inspired by consistency regularization approaches [22], we introduce a novel self-paired regularization (SPR) loss, which enforces feature consistency between original and horizontally flipped images, improving sensitivity to bilateral structures. (3) Constructing node features via global average pooling and modeling inter-node relationships with a graph convolutional network (GCN) [23] head, enabling symmetry-aware predictions for robust detection of complex and symmetric lesions.

2. Materials and Methods

2.1. Dataset

We retrospectively collected a total of 7023 MRI images from the Brain Tumor MRI Dataset [24] and 3264 MRI images from the Brain Tumor MRI Dataset [25]. As shown in Figure 1, both datasets encompass four tumor categories. Dataset I comprises 2000 images of No Tumor, 1757 images of Pituitary Tumor, 1621 images of Glioma, and 1645 images of Meningioma. Dataset II contains 500 images of No Tumor, 900 images of Pituitary Tumor, 926 images of Glioma, and 937 images of Meningioma. Dataset III was provided by the General Hospital and Nanfang Hospital of Tianjin Medical University and was publicly released online by Cheng, Jun et al. [26]. It contains a total of 3064 MRI images covering three types of brain tumors: 708 images of meningioma, 1426 images of glioma, and 930 images of pituitary tumors.These images cover a wide spectrum of tumor types and patient demographics and were carefully curated to ensure sufficient quality for subsequent analyses.

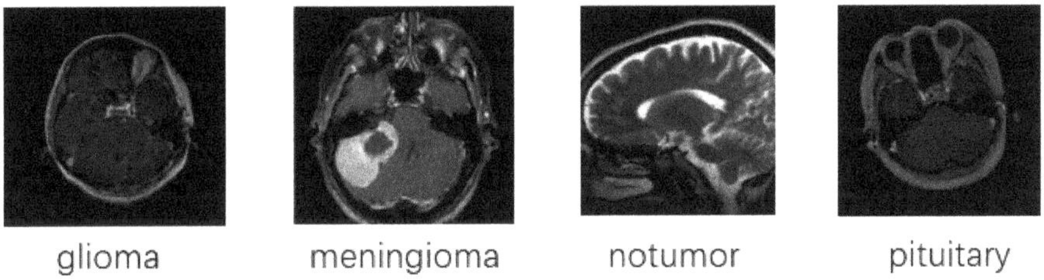

Figure 1. Brain tumor types: glioma, meningioma, no tumor, and pituitary.

2.2. S-ResGCN Model

The S-ResGCN model, illustrated in Figure 2, utilizes a standard ResNet50 backbone to extract hierarchical feature representations from input MRI images, effectively capturing low-level textures and edge information. Convolutional Block Attention Modules (CBAMs) are integrated after the second and fourth residual blocks to enhance both channel-wise and spatial attention, emphasizing symmetric and discriminative features. Finally, a graph convolutional network (GCN) classification head is applied to the extracted features, incorporating information from both the original and horizontally flipped images to achieve symmetry-aware classification.

Initially, the input MRI images underwent systematic preprocessing and data augmentation to enhance model generalization and reinforce symmetry-aware feature learning. The augmentation pipeline included random rotations, flips, color jittering, and affine transformations. Specifically, each image was randomly rotated within $\pm 30^\circ$, randomly flipped along both horizontal and vertical axes to preserve spatial symmetry, subjected to brightness and contrast adjustments for color jittering, and transformed via translation and scaling. For each original image, five augmented variants were generated, and all images were resized to a uniform dimension of 224×224 pixels.

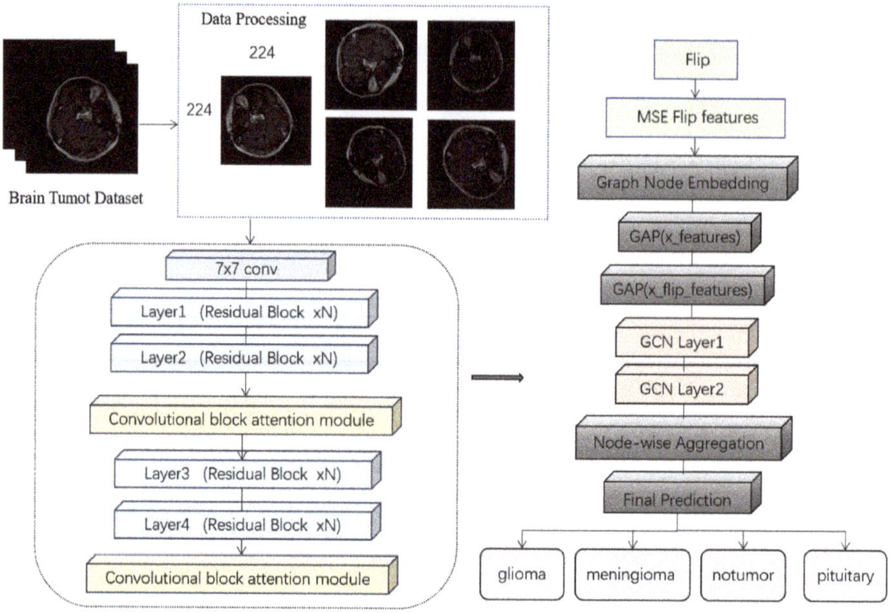

Figure 2. S-ResGCN Model Architecture.

For an input image X_{input}, local convolutional features are first extracted to generate a feature map $X \in \mathbb{R}^{C\times H\times W}$, where C denotes the number of channels, and H and W denote the height and width, respectively. The original 7×7 convolution in the first layer (conv1) followed by batch normalization and ReLU activation, and a 3×3 max-pooling layer produces an initial feature map:

$$X_1 = \text{MaxPool}\Big(\text{ReLU}\left(\text{BN}(\text{Conv}_{7\times 7}(X_{\text{input}}))\right)\Big). \tag{1}$$

where $\text{Conv}_{7\times 7}(\cdot)$ represents a 7×7 convolution operation, $\text{BN}(\cdot)$ denotes batch normalization, $\text{ReLU}(\cdot)$ is the rectified linear unit activation function, and $\text{MaxPool}(\cdot)$ refers to a 3×3 max-pooling operation.

The feature map X_1 is then propagated through the first residual block (layer1), generating:

$$X_2 = \text{Layer}_1(X_1). \tag{2}$$

Next, as shown in Figure 3, the CBAM was integrated after the second and fourth residual blocks, while the first and third residual blocks were not selected. Features in the first residual block mainly capture low-level information such as edges and textures, with limited semantic content; applying attention at this stage may not significantly enhance discriminative capability. The third residual block, although containing more semantic information, has reduced spatial resolution, resulting in partial loss of local details, which limits the effectiveness of attention for refining boundaries and fine structures. After the second residual block, the feature maps already contain some semantic information while retaining rich spatial details. At this stage, CBAM applies channel attention and spatial attention to recalibrate the feature maps: channel attention adaptively adjusts the importance of each feature channel, enabling the network to focus on channels carrying discriminative information, while spatial attention highlights key regions and suppresses irrelevant background. This mechanism enhances sensitivity to local details, facilitating precise tumor boundary detection and the capture of left–right symmetry features. After the fourth residual block, the feature maps become more abstract and semantically rich. At this stage, the CBAM primarily strengthens global discriminative capability: channel attention emphasizes feature channels that are globally informative, and spatial attention highlights critical regions across the entire image, helping the model more effectively differentiate between tumor types and healthy tissue. By applying attention at different network depths, the CBAM balances local detail and global semantic understanding, enabling the model to capture fine-grained boundary information while comprehending overall structural patterns, thereby improving classification performance and generalization.

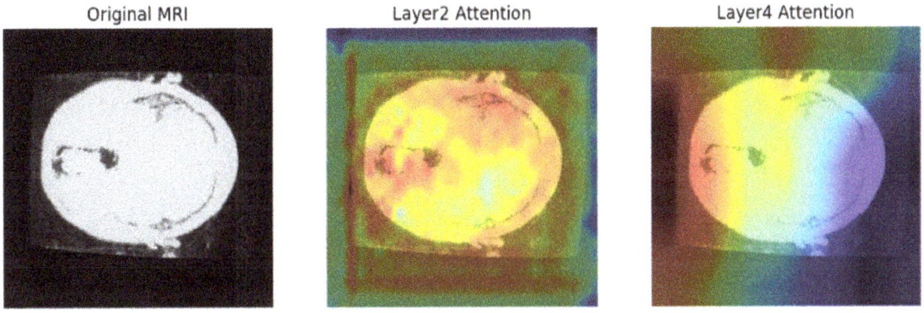

Figure 3. Convolutional Block Attention Module Heatmap.

The second residual block is applied, followed by the CBAM to emphasize symmetric and discriminative features:

$$X_3 = \mathrm{CBAM}_2(\mathrm{Layer}_1(X_2)), \tag{3}$$

where Layer_k denotes the k-th residual layer, and CBAM_k represents the attention module in that stage.

The CBAM sequentially applies channel and spatial attention to emphasize symmetric and discriminative features. As shown in Figure 4, the channel attention mechanism refines the input feature by aggregating spatial information through global average pooling and max pooling, followed by a shared multi-layer perceptron to generate a channel attention map. The channel attention is computed as:

$$A_{\mathrm{channel}} = \sigma\Big(W_2\ \mathrm{ReLU}(W_1 \cdot \mathrm{GAP}(X_2))\Big), \tag{4}$$

where $\mathrm{GAP}(\cdot)$ represents global average pooling, W_1 and W_2 are learnable weight matrices of the shared multi-layer perceptron, $\sigma(\cdot)$ is the sigmoid activation function, and A_{channel} is the resulting channel attention map.

Spatial attention is computed as:

$$A_{\mathrm{spatial}} = \sigma\Big(\mathrm{Conv}([\mathrm{GAP}(X_2), \mathrm{MaxPool}(X_2)])\Big), \tag{5}$$

The CBAM-enhanced feature map is then obtained by:

$$X_3' = X_3 \cdot A_{\mathrm{channel}} \cdot A_{\mathrm{spatial}} + X_3, \tag{6}$$

where $\cdot$ denotes element-wise multiplication, and X_3' is the CBAM-enhanced feature map.

Similarly, the feature map is propagated through layer3:

$$X_4 = \mathrm{Layer}_1(X_3'), \tag{7}$$

$$X_5 = \text{CBAM}_4(\text{Layer}_1(X_4)). \tag{8}$$

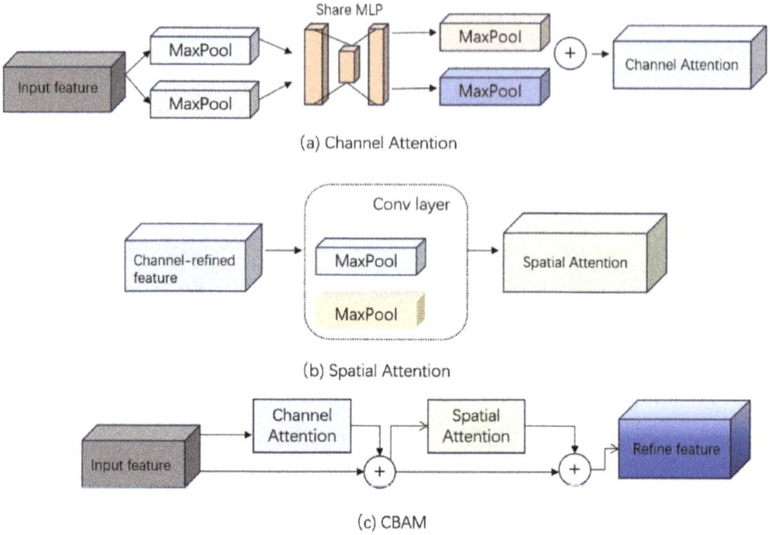

Figure 4. (**a**) Channel Attention Module, which uses an MLP to highlight important feature channels. (**b**) Spatial Attention Module, which focuses on key regions in the feature map using a convolutional layer. (**c**) Convolutional Block Attention Module (CBAM), which sequentially applies the channel and spatial attention mechanisms from (**a**,**b**) to refine the input features, combining both for enhanced feature representation.

To reinforce symmetry-aware feature learning, each input image was horizontally flipped to obtain X_{flip}, and its feature map was extracted through the backbone network:

$$X_{\text{flip\_features}} = Backbone(X_{\text{flip}}) \tag{9}$$

The self-paired regularization (SPR) loss enforces symmetry consistency between the original and flipped features, as illustrated in Figure 5. Encouraging the network to be sensitive to symmetric structures commonly observed in brain tumors. To prevent redundancy or potential data leakage during training, explicit controls are applied: flips for data augmentation are randomly applied to input images to improve model generalization, whereas flips for SPR are performed at the feature-map level to compute a symmetry loss between original and mirrored features. These operations occur at different levels, avoiding direct reuse of the same data. Furthermore, the SPR loss is applied only during training for regularization and does not introduce information from the validation or test sets; mirrored features participate only within the current mini-batch, ensuring no leakage of label information. The SPR loss is computed as:

$$L_{\text{SPR}} = \frac{1}{B}\sum_{b=1}^{B}\left\| X_5^{(b)} - X_{\text{flip\_features}}^{(b)} \right\|_2^2 \tag{10}$$

where B is the batch size, $X_5^{(b)}$ denotes the backbone feature map of the b-th original image (after CBAM), and $X_{\text{flip\_features}}^{(b)}$ denotes the corresponding flipped feature map. The squared L2 norm $\|\cdot\|_2^2$ measures the discrepancy between symmetric feature representations.

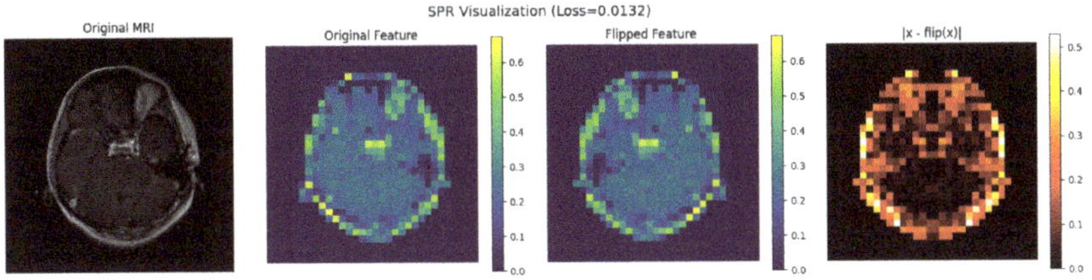

Figure 5. Visualization of the Self-Paired Regularization (SPR) loss. The figure illustrates how SPR enhances symmetry-aware feature learning in brain MRI. The first panel presents the original MRI image, while the second and third panels show the feature maps extracted by the backbone network from the original and horizontally flipped images, respectively. The fourth panel visualizes the absolute difference $|x - \text{flip}(x)|$ between the two feature maps, highlighting regions where symmetry is not fully preserved.

Finally, the feature maps of the original and flipped images are aggregated via Global Average Pooling:

$$Node_0 = GAP(X_5), \quad Node_1 = GAP(X_{\text{flip\_features}}) \tag{11}$$

Graph nodes are constructed as:

$$X_{\text{nodes}} = [Node_0, Node_1] \tag{12}$$

The GCN processes node features to produce node-level predictions:

$$H_1 = GCNLayer_1(X_{\text{nodes}}), \quad H_2 = GCNLayer_2(H_1) \tag{13}$$

The final prediction aggregates the outputs of original and flipped nodes:

$$\hat{y} = softmax\Big(\tfrac{1}{2}(H_2[:,0,:] + H_2[:,1,:])\Big) \tag{14}$$

where $Node_0$ and $Node_1$ denote the global average pooled feature vectors of the original and horizontally flipped images, respectively. X_{nodes} is the resulting node matrix, and H_2 is the intermediate node embeddings generated by the first and second GCN layers. $[:,0,:]$ and $[:,1,:]$ denote the feature vectors corresponding to the original and horizontally flipped nodes, respectively. Here, ":" indicates all elements along the batch or feature dimension, 0 and 1 select the first (original) and second (flipped) nodes, and the final $softmax$ converts the averaged node embeddings into a class probability vector $\hat{y}$.

2.3. Experiment

In this study, Datasets I and II were partitioned into training and test sets at a 4:1 ratio to ensure sufficient diversity for model training. Dataset III was further evaluated using five-fold cross-validation, whereby the dataset was randomly divided into five equal subsets. In each fold, four subsets were used for training and the remaining subset for validation. This procedure was repeated five times, and the average performance across all folds was computed to comprehensively assess the model's robustness and generalization capability.

We implemented an enhanced SymmetryResNet50 architecture (see Table 1) based on the PyTorch version 2.7.1 with CUDA 11.8 support deep learning framework, integrating multiple collaborative modules to strengthen feature representation and enforce structural symmetry constraints. All training and validation were conducted on a local workstation equipped with an NVIDIA GeForce RTX 3070 GPU (8 GB VRAM) under a CUDA 11.3 environment. The SymmetryResNet50GCN model contains approximately 25.5 million trainable parameters, including the ResNet50 backbone, CBAMs, and the GCN head. Self-Paired Regularization (SPR) imposes a mean-squared-error-based constraint between the original and horizontally flipped feature maps, with a regularization coefficient of $\lambda = 0.05$. This regularization is applied only during training and does not affect validation or testing. The total loss is defined as the weighted sum of the cross-entropy loss and the SPR loss. Optimization is performed using AdamW with an initial learning rate of 5×10^{-5} and a weight decay of 1×10^{-4}, combined with a cosine-annealing learning rate scheduler over 200 epochs. The batch size is set to 16. Peak GPU memory usage during training is approximately 6–8 GB, while inference requires roughly 2–3 GB of GPU memory.

Table 1. SymmetryResNet50GCN Network Architecture and Output Sizes.

Stage/Layer	Output Size	Notes
Input	[B, 3, 224, 224]	RGB MRI image
conv1 + bn + relu	[B, 64, 112, 112]	7×7 convolution, stride 2
maxpool	[B, 64, 56, 56]	3×3 max pooling, stride 2
layer1	[B, 256, 56, 56]	3 × Bottleneck blocks (each block: 3 conv layers)
layer2 → CBAM2	[B, 512, 28, 28]	4 × Bottleneck blocks, CBAM applied after layer2
layer3	[B, 1024, 14, 14]	6 × Bottleneck blocks
layer4 → CBAM4	[B, 2048, 7, 7]	3 × Bottleneck blocks, CBAM applied after layer4
AdaptiveAvgPool → Flatten	[B, 2048, 1, 1] → [B, 2048]	Pool × and flipped separately
GCN input → output	[B, 2, 2048] → [B, num_classes]	2 GCN layers: 2048→256→n

Model performance was systematically evaluated using four standard metrics: Accuracy, Precision, Recall, and F1-score. Accuracy quantifies the overall classification correctness and is defined as:

$$\text{Accuracy} = \frac{TP + TN}{TP + TN + FP + FN} \tag{15}$$

where TP denotes the number of true positives, TN the number of true negatives, FP the number of false positives, and FN the number of false negatives.

Precision measures the proportion of correctly predicted positive samples for a given class:

$$\text{Precision} = \frac{TP}{TP + FP} \tag{16}$$

Recall evaluates the model's ability to identify actual positive samples:

$$\text{Recall} = \frac{TP}{TP + FN} \tag{17}$$

The F1-Score provides a harmonic mean of Precision and Recall, balancing the trade-off between them:

$$\text{F1 Score} = \frac{2 \times (\text{Precision} \times \text{Recall})}{\text{Precision} + \text{Recall}} \tag{18}$$

These metrics collectively provide a multi-dimensional assessment of the model's classification performance across different tumor categories.

3. Results

3.1. Overall Performance

As shown in Figures 6 and 7, the proposed S-ResGCN model exhibits outstanding performance on the four-class brain tumor classification task across both Dataset I and Dataset II. For all categories—including meningioma, glioma, no tumor, and pituitary—the model achieved Precision, Recall, and F1-Score values exceeding 98%, with the no tumor category in Dataset II reaching 100%, demonstrating exceptional robustness and highly consistent discriminative capability. In addition, as shown in Figure 8, the five-fold cross-validation results on Dataset III further demonstrate the stability and generalization capability of the proposed S-ResGCN model with minimal variation across folds, indicating highly consistent performance. All tumor categories—including glioma, meningioma, and pituitary—exhibited high precision, recall, and F1-scores, reflecting the model's balanced discrimination across different classes.

The accuracy curves in Figures 9 and 10 indicate that training accuracy increased rapidly during the initial iterations and stabilized above 99%, while validation accuracy converged to 99.83% for Dataset I and 99.37% for Dataset II. Furthermore, as shown in Figure 11, the five-fold average results on Dataset III indicate that the model exhibits high stability during both training and validation phases. The training accuracy becomes stable after approximately 100 epochs, while the validation accuracy continues to improve and remains around 99.26% ± 0.16. For all three datasets, both training and validation losses show a sharp decline in the early stages and minimal fluctuations later, suggesting good convergence and no evident overfitting. Overall, these results demonstrate that the proposed model achieves stable learning behavior and excellent generalization performance across different data partitions.

As illustrated in Figures 12 and 13, the proposed model demonstrates stable and superior classification performance across the four brain tumor categories: glioma, meningioma, pituitary tumor, and no tumor. On Dataset I, the model correctly classifies 1624 glioma, 1688 meningioma, 1992 no-tumor, and 1707 pituitary images, with only a few misclassifications mainly occurring between meningioma and pituitary. Similarly, on Dataset II, the model achieves comparable results, correctly identifying 930 glioma, 913 meningioma, 406 no-tumor, and 891 pituitary images, with minimal confusion observed between glioma and meningioma. The strong diagonal dominance observed in both confusion matrices highlights the model's excellent discriminative capability, high sensitivity, and robust generalization across different datasets.

Figure 14 illustrates the predictive performance of the model on the brain tumor classification task using Dataset III under five-fold cross-validation. The confusion matrix for each fold evaluates the three tumor classes: glioma, meningioma, and pituitary. Overall, the model achieves high classification accuracy across most folds, with particularly stable performance in distinguishing pituitary tumors. Some degree of confusion between glioma and meningioma is observed, especially in folds 4 and 5, where a portion of glioma samples were misclassified as meningioma. This suggests that these two tumor types may share highly similar imaging features, making boundary cases more challenging for the model. Nevertheless, the overall misclassification rate remains low, indicating that the model possesses strong capability and robustness in feature extraction and class discrimination.

Collectively, these results confirm that the S-ResGCN model not only achieves high classification accuracy but also maintains robust stability and generalization, effectively handling MRI images with diverse tumor types and varying levels of complexity.

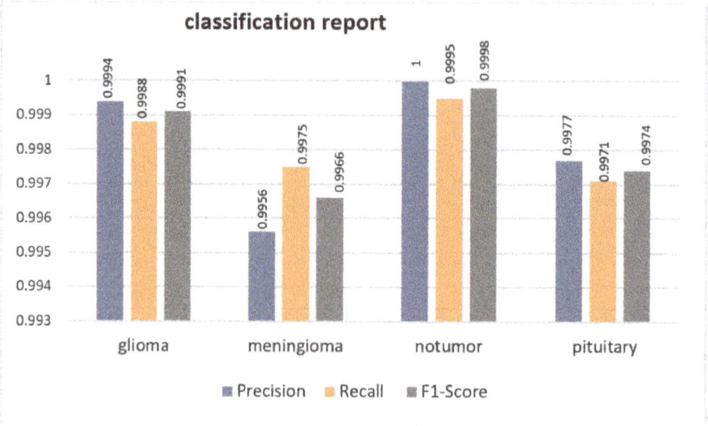

Figure 6. Classification report on dataset I.

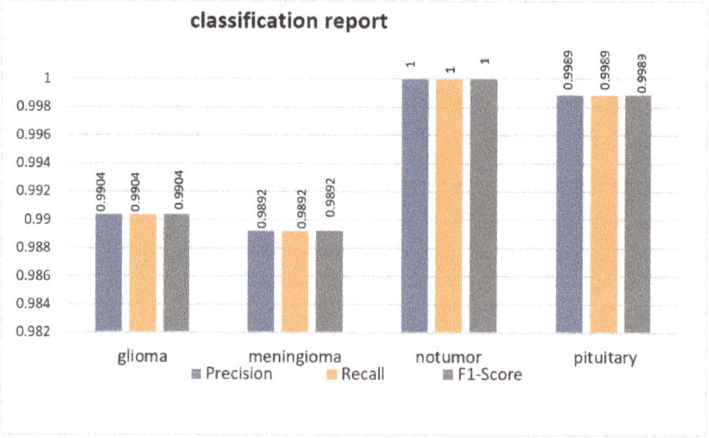

Figure 7. Classification report on dataset II.

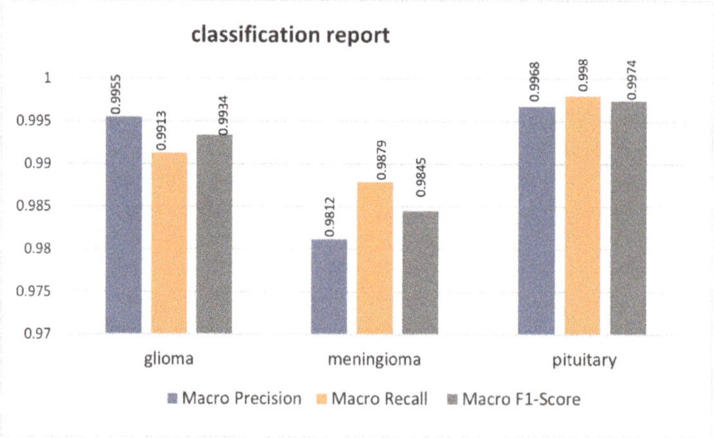

Figure 8. Classification report on dataset III.

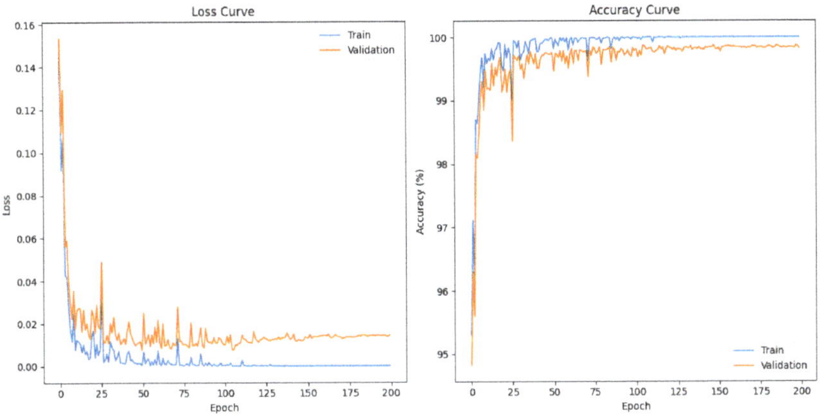

Figure 9. Loss and accuracy curves on dataset I.

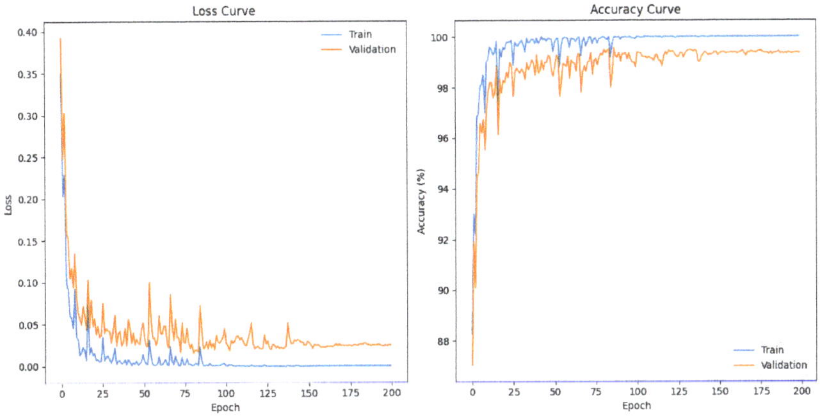

Figure 10. Loss and accuracy curves on dataset II.

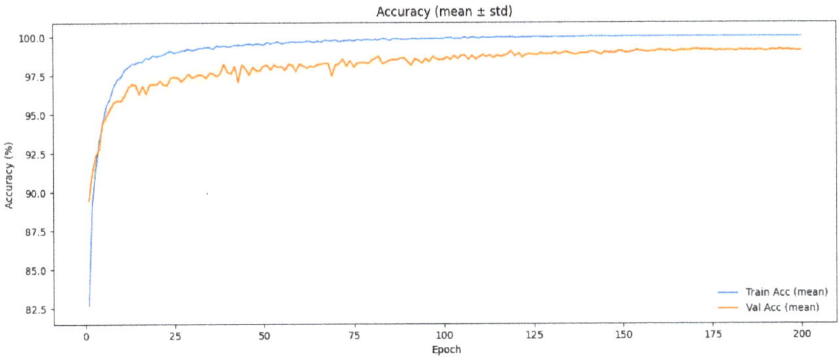

Figure 11. *Cont.*

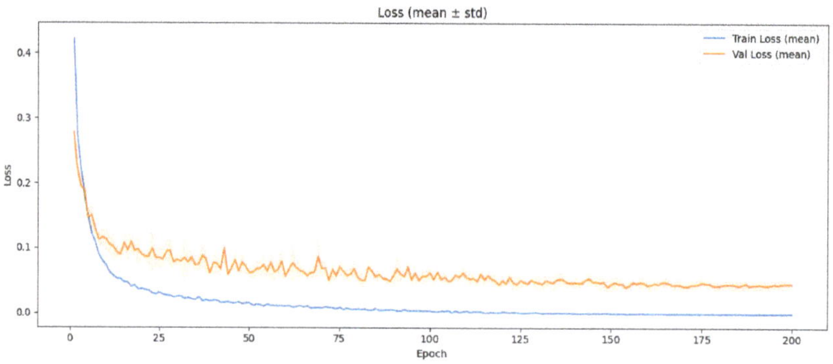

Figure 11. Mean Loss and accuracy curves on dataset III.

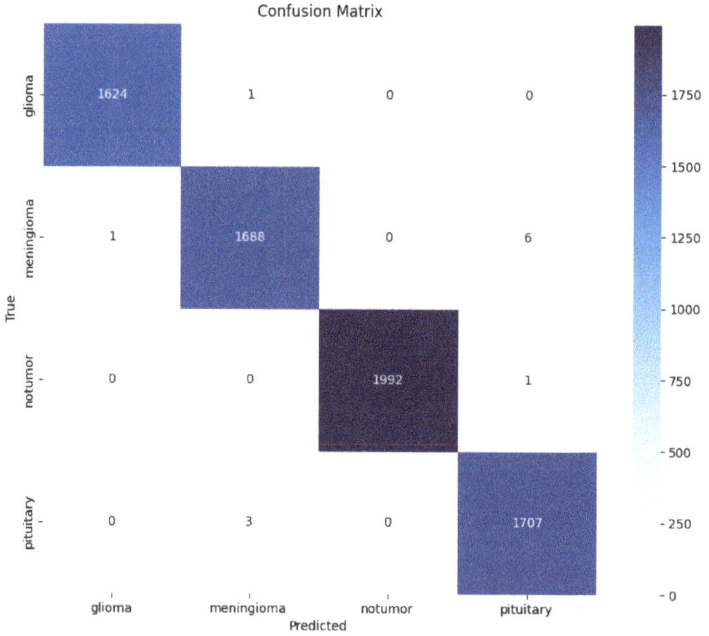

Figure 12. The results of the confusion matrix model on dataset I.

3.2. Comparison with Baseline Methods

The proposed S-ResGCN was evaluated on Brain Tumor MRI Dataset I, with its performance summarized in Table 2, and compared against a range of representative models, including lightweight networks, classic CNNs, attention-enhanced architectures, multi-scale networks, and Transformer-based approaches. MobileNetV2 and ResNet-18 achieved moderate accuracies of 84.45% and 86.59%, respectively, while VGG16 improved to 94.97%. The incorporation of attention mechanisms further enhanced performance, as demonstrated by CBAM-CNN with an accuracy of 96.70%. Deeper or multi-scale architectures, such as Inception V3, Pat-GridMask, and Custom CNN, achieved 97–98% accuracy, whereas the Transformer-based FTVT-132 reached 98.70%.

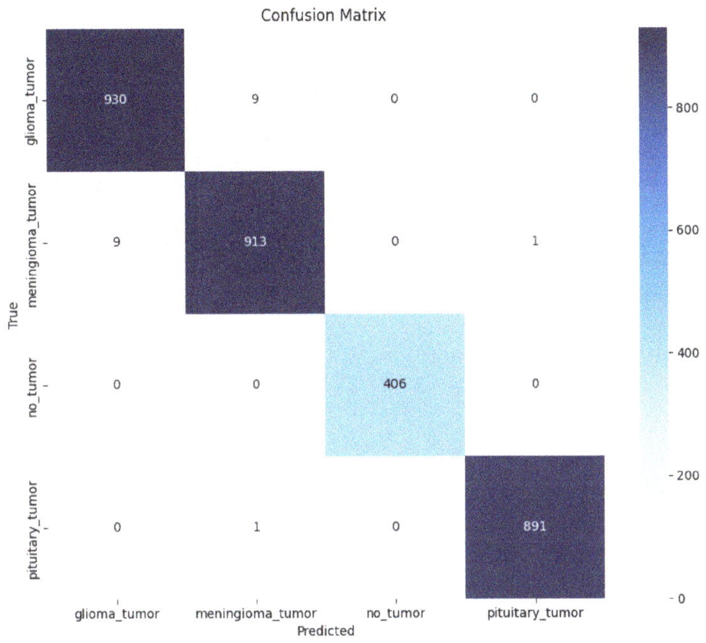

Figure 13. The results of the confusion matrix model dataset II.

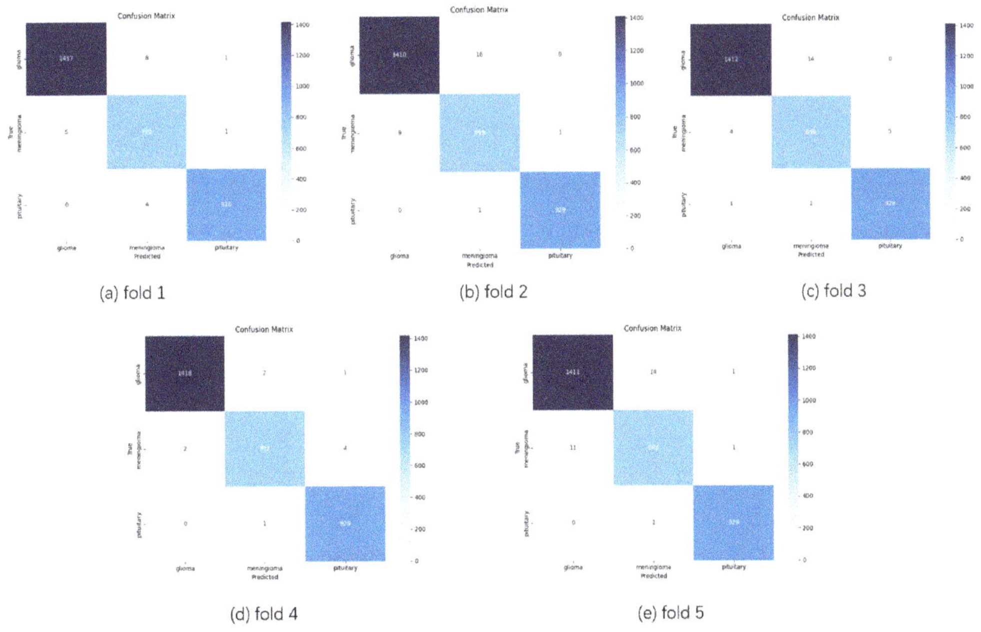

Figure 14. The results of the confusion matrix model dataset III.

In contrast, S-ResGCN attained 99.83% across all evaluation metrics, including accuracy, precision, recall, and F1-score, outperforming all baseline methods. This result highlights the effectiveness of hierarchical feature extraction, self-paired regularization, and graph convolutional modeling in capturing fine-grained and symmetric tumor characteristics, which are often overlooked by conventional models.

Table 2. Experimental Results for Brain Tumor MRI Dataset I.

Methods	Accuracy	Precision	Recall	F1-Score
MobileNetV2 [27]	0.8445	0.8498	0.8445	0.8431
ResNet-18 [27]	0.8659	0.8658	0.8659	0.8635
VGG16 [27]	0.9497	0.9495	0.9497	0.9494
CBAM-CNN [28]	0.9670	0.9675	0.9650	0.9675
Inception V3 [29]	0.9712	0.9797	–	–
Pat-GridMask [30]	0.9774	–	–	0.9775
Custom CNN [31]	0.9809	0.9820	0.9810	0.9815
FTVT-132 [32]	0.9870	0.9870	0.9870	0.9870
S-ResGCN	0.9983	0.9982	0.9982	0.9982

Table 3 presents the classification results on Brain Tumor MRI Dataset II. The proposed S-ResGCN achieved an accuracy of 99.37%, with mean precision, recall, and F1-score all reaching 99.46%, substantially outperforming baseline methods such as Swin Transformer (88.88%), MSCNN (91.20%), HDL2BT (92.13%), and a conventional CNN (93.30%). It also surpassed advanced architectures including EfficientNet-B7 (95.00%), CustomEfficientNet (97.00%), and TLAEN (97.00%), as well as the previously best-performing Innovation CNN (98.20%), achieving nearly 1% higher accuracy while maintaining superior robustness across all metrics. These results indicate that S-ResGCN exhibits remarkable capability in capturing fine-grained features, precise boundary delineation, and minority-class recognition.

Table 3. Experimental Results on Brain Tumor MRI Dataset II.

Methods	Accuracy	Precision	Recall	F1-Score
Swin Transformer [33]	0.8888	0.8600	0.7500	0.8700
MSCNN [34]	0.9120	0.9200	0.9070	0.9100
HDL2BT [35]	0.9213	0.9213	–	–
CNN [36]	0.9330	–	0.9113	–
EfficientNet B7 [37]	0.9500	0.9300	0.9200	0.9300
CustomEfficientNet [38]	0.9700	0.9600	0.9600	0.9600
TLAEN [39]	0.9700	0.9700	0.9700	0.9700
Innovation CNN [40]	0.9820	–	–	–
S-ResGCN	0.9937	0.9946	0.9946	0.9946

The superior performance of S-ResGCN arises from its combination of hierarchical feature extraction, attention-enhanced symmetric feature learning via CBAM, self-paired regularization to enforce symmetry consistency, and a GCN-based head that captures inter-node relationships, collectively enabling more robust and fine-grained brain tumor classification than baseline models.

As shown in Table 4, compared with traditional convolutional neural networks such as InceptionV3 and DenseNet201, S-ResGCN exhibits a significant improvement in both classification accuracy and result stability. This advantage mainly stems from the Symmetry-aware Residual Graph Convolution, which jointly captures local spatial details and inter-hemispheric structural relationships, enhancing the model's ability to discriminate lesions with blurred boundaries or similar morphology. In addition, the Attention-guided Feature Refinement module adaptively emphasizes tumor-relevant channels and suppresses redundant information, leading to more discriminative and robust feature representations that conventional CNNs often fail to achieve.

Furthermore, compared with the densely connected VGG16-NADE and the lightweight fusion-based MobDenseNet, S-ResGCN incorporates a Self-Paired Regularization (SPR) strategy that constrains bilateral brain feature consistency at the representation level, effectively reducing overfitting to asymmetric lesions during training. By enforcing structural symmetry consistency in the latent space, SPR further enhances the model's generalization and stability across different subjects and scanning conditions.

Table 4. Experimental Results on Brain Tumor MRI Dataset III.

Methods	Accuracy	Precision	Recall	F1-Score
InceptionV3 [41]	0.9286	0.9270	0.9170	0.9200
DenseNet201 [41]	0.9481	0.9400	0.9400	0.9360
VGG16-NADE [42]	0.9601	0.9572	0.9564	0.9568
CNN [43]	0.9727	–	0.9113	–
MobDenseNet [44]	0.9840	0.9860	0.9840	0.9850
Innovation CNN [41]	0.9870	0.9830	0.9860	0.9860
S-ResGCN	0.9926 ± 0.16	0.9912	0.9924	0.9918

3.3. Ablation Studies

An ablation study on Brain Tumor MRI Dataset II (Table 5) was conducted to evaluate the individual and combined contributions of S-ResGCN's core components. The baseline ResNet50 backbone achieved an accuracy of 95.73%, indicating limited capability in detecting small or poorly defined lesions. Incorporating the GCN head increased accuracy to 96.99%, demonstrating that graph-based relational modeling effectively strengthens spatial reasoning by aggregating features from both the original and horizontally flipped images. Adding CBAM further improved accuracy to 97.47%, highlighting its capacity to adaptively emphasize informative channels and spatial regions critical for tumor localization. Employing SPR loss alone yielded 96.84% accuracy, confirming that enforcing symmetry consistency enhances robustness to subtle and symmetric tumor structures.

Table 5. Impacts of CBAM, SPR and GCN on Classification Accuracy.

Exp	CBAM	SPR	GCN	Accuracy	Precision	Recall	F1-Score
1				0.9573	0.9504	0.9642	0.9565
2			✓	0.9699	0.9695	0.9729	0.9710
3	✓			0.9747	0.9763	0.9785	0.9772
4		✓		0.9684	0.9635	0.9699	0.9665
5	✓		✓	0.9810	0.9827	0.9828	0.9827
6		✓	✓	0.9794	0.9683	0.9805	0.9740
7	✓	✓		0.9842	0.9847	0.9836	0.9841
8	✓	✓	✓	0.9937	0.9946	0.9946	0.9946

Combining two components resulted in additional performance gains. The combination of the CBAM and GCN achieved 98.10% accuracy by effectively integrating attention-guided feature selection with graph-based relational modeling. CBAM combined with SPR reached 97.94% accuracy, leveraging the synergy between attention mechanisms and symmetry-aware regularization to improve lesion detection. The combination of GCN and SPR achieved 98.42% accuracy, reinforcing both spatial reasoning and symmetry consistency to better discriminate small lesions. The full integration of CBAM, GCN, and SPR achieved the highest accuracy of 99.37%, demonstrating that attention mechanisms, graph-based modeling, and symmetry regularization are complementary, jointly delivering substantial improvements in classification accuracy and the recognition of fine-grained tumor structures.

4. Conclusions

In this study, we proposed S-ResGCN, a symmetry-aware framework for brain tumor MRI classification that integrates hierarchical feature extraction, self-paired regularization, and a graph convolutional head. By jointly leveraging original and horizontally flipped images, the model enhances sensitivity to symmetric and discriminative tumor structures, while Convolutional Block Attention Module (CBAM) modules effectively emphasize critical lesion regions. Experiments on two public MRI datasets demonstrated consistently high accuracy, precision, recall, and F1-scores, particularly for complex and symmetric lesions. These findings highlight S-ResGCN's robustness and its potential as a foundation for automated, symmetry-sensitive diagnostic systems.

However, the network design of S-ResGCN has certain limitations. First, the model relies on 2D MRI slices during training and evaluation, which may limit its ability to capture complex 3D tumor morphology. Second, the benefits of SPR are more pronounced for tumors with strong symmetry, while irregularly shaped tumors see comparatively less improvement. Moreover, the multi-branch structure and GCN head increase computational complexity, posing challenges for real-time processing on large-scale clinical datasets. Clearly stating these limitations helps readers better understand the framework's applicability and potential areas for improvement.In the future, we plan to extend S-ResGCN to multi-modal MRI data and cross-center datasets to improve generalization under diverse imaging conditions. Further exploration of semi-supervised learning may reduce dependence on labeled data, while optimizing computational efficiency could enable real-time clinical deployment. Additionally, incorporating 3D volumetric inputs may enhance its effectiveness for tumor monitoring and treatment planning.

Author Contributions: Conceptualization, Q.G. and Y.B.; Methodology, Q.G., Y.B. and L.H.; Validation, Q.G., Y.B., J.H. and S.L.; Formal analysis, J.H.; Investigation, Q.G., Y.B., J.H., L.H. and S.L.; Resources, K.X.; Data curation, Q.G., Y.B., J.H., L.H. and S.L.; Writing—original draft, Q.G. and L.H.; Writing—review & editing, Q.G., Y.B., J.H. and K.X.; Project administration, K.X. All authors have read and agreed to the published version of the manuscript.

Funding: This research was funded by the National Natural Science Foundation of China, grant number 62067007, and the Guangxi Graduate Education and Teaching Reform Project, grant number JGY2023236.

Data Availability Statement: The data that support the findings of this study are publicly available. Dataset I, the Brain Tumor MRI Dataset containing 7023 images, can be accessed at https://www.kaggle.com/datasets/masoudnickparvar/brain-tumor-mri-dataset (accessed on 1 December 2023). Dataset II, the Brain Tumor MRI Dataset containing 3264 images, is available at https://www.dilitanxianjia.com/13366/ (accessed on 1 December 2023). Brain Tumor MRI Dataset containing 3064 images, is available at https://figshare.com/articles/dataset/brain_tumor_dataset/1512427 (accessed on 12 November 2024).

Conflicts of Interest: The authors declare no conflicts of interest.

References

1. Katti, G.; Ara, S.A.; Shireen, A. Magnetic resonance imaging (MRI)—A review. *Int. J. Dent. Clin.* **2011**, *3*, 65–70.
2. Doi, K. Computer-aided diagnosis in medical imaging: Historical review, current status and future potential. *Comput. Med. Imaging Graph.* **2007**, *31*, 198–211. [CrossRef]
3. Jakkula, V. *Tutorial on Support Vector Machine (Svm)*; School of EECS, Washington State University: Pullman, WA, USA, 2006; Volume 37, p. 3.
4. Fang, K.; Wu, J.; Zhu, J.; Xie, B. Review of random forest methods. *Stat. Inf. BBS* **2011**, *26*, 32–38.

5. Guo, G.; Wang, H.; Bell, D.; Bi, Y.; Greer, K. KNN model-based approach in classification. In *OTM Confederated International Conferences "On the Move to Meaningful Internet Systems"*; Springer: Berlin/Heidelberg, Germany, 2003; pp. 986–996.
6. O'shea, K.; Nash, R. An introduction to convolutional neural networks. *arXiv* **2015**, arXiv:1511.08458. [CrossRef]
7. Musa, M.N. MRI-based brain tumor classification using resnet-50 and optimized softmax regression. *J. Infotel* **2024**, *16*, 598–614. [CrossRef]
8. Ahmed, G.; Er, M.J.; Fareed, M.M.S.; Zikria, S.; Mahmood, S.; He, J.; Asad, M.; Jilani, S.F.; Aslam, M. Dad-net: Classification of alzheimer's disease using adasyn oversampling technique and optimized neural network. *Molecules* **2022**, *27*, 7085. [CrossRef]
9. Nizamli, Y.A.; Filatov, A.Y. Improving transfer learning performance for abnormality detection in brain MRI images using feature optimization techniques. In Proceedings of the 2024 XXVII International Conference on Soft Computing and Measurements (SCM), St. Petersburg, Russia, 22–24 May 2024; pp. 432–435.
10. Haq, A.U.; Li, J.P.; Agbley, B.L.Y.; Khan, A.; Khan, I.; Uddin, M.I.; Khan, S. IIMFCBM: Intelligent integrated model for feature extraction and classification of brain tumors using MRI clinical imaging data in IoT-healthcare. *IEEE J. Biomed. Health Inform.* **2022**, *26*, 5004–5012. [CrossRef]
11. Wang, M.; Ren, Y.; Lin, Y.; Wang, S. The tightly super 3-extra connectivity and diagnosability of locally twisted cubes. *Am. J. Comput. Math.* **2017**, *7*, 127–144. [CrossRef]
12. Wang, S.; Wang, Y.; Wang, M. Connectivity and matching preclusion for leaf-sort graphs. *J. Interconnect. Netw.* **2019**, *19*, 1940007. [CrossRef]
13. Wang, M.; Xiang, D.; Qu, Y.; Li, G. The diagnosability of interconnection networks. *Discret. Appl. Math.* **2024**, *357*, 413–428. [CrossRef]
14. Jiang, J.; Wu, L.; Yu, J.; Wang, M.; Kong, H.; Zhang, Z.; Wang, J. Robustness of bilayer railway-aviation transportation network considering discrete cross-layer traffic flow assignment. *Transp. Res. Part D Transp. Environ.* **2024**, *127*, 104071. [CrossRef]
15. Wang, M.; Xiang, D.; Wang, S. Connectivity and diagnosability of leaf-sort graphs. *Parallel Process. Lett.* **2020**, *30*, 2040004. [CrossRef]
16. Xiang, D.; Hsieh, S.Y. G-good-neighbor diagnosability under the modified comparison model for multiprocessor systems. *Theor. Comput. Sci.* **2025**, *1028*, 115027.
17. Wang, M.; Lin, Y.; Wang, S. The connectivity and nature diagnosability of expanded *k*-ary *n*-cubes. *RAIRO-Theor. Inform. Appl.-Inform. Théor. Appl.* **2017**, *51*, 71–89. [CrossRef]
18. Wang, M.; Lin, Y.; Wang, S. The nature diagnosability of bubble-sort star graphs under the PMC model and MM* model. *Int. J. Eng. Appl. Sci.* **2017**, *4*, 55–56.
19. Wang, M.; Wang, S. Connectivity and diagnosability of center k-ary n-cubes. *Discret. Appl. Math.* **2021**, *294*, 98–107. [CrossRef]
20. Zarenia, E.; Akhlaghi Far, A.; Rezaee, K. Automated multi-class MRI brain tumor classification and segmentation using deformable attention and saliency mapping. *Sci. Rep.* **2025**, *15*, 8114. [CrossRef]
21. Woo, S.; Park, J.; Lee, J.Y.; Kweon, I.S. Cbam: Convolutional block attention module. In Proceedings of the European Conference on Computer Vision (ECCV), Munich, Germany, 8–14 September 2018; pp. 3–19.
22. Rahman, Z.; Zhang, R.; Bhutto, J.A. A symmetrical approach to brain tumor segmentation in MRI using deep learning and threefold attention mechanism. *Symmetry* **2023**, *15*, 1912. [CrossRef]
23. Zhang, S.; Tong, H.; Xu, J.; Maciejewski, R. Graph convolutional networks: A comprehensive review. *Comput. Soc. Netw.* **2019**, *6*, 11. [CrossRef]
24. Nickparvar, M. *Brain Tumor MRI Dataset*; Kaggle: San Francisco, CA, USA, 2021.
25. Sayedgomaa, S. Brain Tumor. Kaggle Notebook. 2022. Available online: https://www.kaggle.com/code/sayedgomaa/brain-tumor/notebook (accessed on 21 December 2022).
26. Cheng, J. Brain Tumor Dataset. 2017. Available online: https://figshare.com/articles/dataset/brain_tumor_dataset/1512427 (accessed on 20 October 2025).
27. Liu, X.; Wang, Z. Deep learning in medical image classification from mri-based brain tumor images. In Proceedings of the 2024 IEEE 6th International Conference on Power, Intelligent Computing and Systems (ICPICS), Shenyang, China, 26–28 July 2024; pp. 840–844.
28. Binish, M.; Raj, R.S.; Thomas, V. Brain tumor classification using multi-resolution averaged spatial attention features with CBAM and convolutional neural networks. In Proceedings of the 2024 1st International Conference on Trends in Engineering Systems and Technologies (ICTEST), Kochi, India, 11–13 April 2024; pp. 1–7.
29. Gómez-Guzmán, M.A.; Jiménez-Beristaín, L.; García-Guerrero, E.E.; López-Bonilla, O.R.; Tamayo-Perez, U.J.; Esqueda-Elizondo, J.J.; Palomino-Vizcaino, K.; Inzunza-González, E. Classifying brain tumors on magnetic resonance imaging by using convolutional neural networks. *Electronics* **2023**, *12*, 955. [CrossRef]
30. Lee, J.H.; Chae, J.W.; Cho, H.C. Improved classification of different brain tumors in mri scans using patterned-gridmask. *IEEE Access* **2024**, *12*, 40204–40212. [CrossRef]

31. Khan, M.A.; Auvee, R.B.Z. Comparative Analysis of Resource-Efficient CNN Architectures for Brain Tumor Classification. In Proceedings of the 2024 27th International Conference on Computer and Information Technology (ICCIT), Cox's Bazar, Bangladesh, 20–22 December 2024; pp. 639–644.
32. Reddy, C.K.K.; Reddy, P.A.; Janapati, H.; Assiri, B.; Shuaib, M.; Alam, S.; Sheneamer, A. A fine-tuned vision transformer based enhanced multi-class brain tumor classification using MRI scan imagery. *Front. Oncol.* **2024**, *14*, 1400341. [CrossRef] [PubMed]
33. Zahoor, A.; Irfan, M.; Usman, M.; Haider, W. Brain tumor detection in magnetic resonance images using swin transformer. *Conclus. Med.* **2025**, *1*, 1–5. [CrossRef]
34. Yazdan, S.A.; Ahmad, R.; Iqbal, N.; Rizwan, A.; Khan, A.N.; Kim, D.H. An efficient multi-scale convolutional neural network based multi-class brain MRI classification for SaMD. *Tomography* **2022**, *8*, 1905–1927. [CrossRef]
35. Khan, A.H.; Abbas, S.; Khan, M.A.; Farooq, U.; Khan, W.A.; Siddiqui, S.Y.; Ahmad, A. Intelligent model for brain tumor identification using deep learning. *Appl. Comput. Intell. Soft Comput.* **2022**, *2022*, 8104054. [CrossRef]
36. Mahmud, M.I.; Mamun, M.; Abdelgawad, A. A deep analysis of brain tumor detection from mr images using deep learning networks. *Algorithms* **2023**, *16*, 176. [CrossRef]
37. Wibowo, M.P.; Al Fayyadl, M.B.; Azhar, Y.; Sari, Z. Classification of brain tumors on mri images using convolutional neural network model efficientnet. *J. RESTI (Rekayasa Sist. Teknol. Informasi)* **2022**, *6*, 538–547. [CrossRef]
38. Ishaq, A.; Ullah, F.U.M.; Hamandawana, P.; Cho, D.J.; Chung, T.S. Improved EfficientNet architecture for multi-grade brain tumor detection. *Electronics* **2025**, *14*, 710. [CrossRef]
39. SHARMA, P.; SHUKLA, A.P. Transfer learning approach using efficientnet architecture for brain tumor classification in Mri images. *Adv. Appl. Math. Sci.* **2022**, *21*, 7091–7106.
40. Ramadhani, M.R.; Soesanti, I.; Hidayah, I. Brain Tumor Classification Based on Deep Learning Algorithms. In Proceedings of the 2024 4th International Conference on Electronic and Electrical Engineering and Intelligent System (ICE3IS), Yogyakarta, Indonesia, 7–8 August 2024; pp. 81–86.
41. Ait Amou, M.; Xia, K.; Kamhi, S.; Mouhafid, M. A novel MRI diagnosis method for brain tumor classification based on CNN and Bayesian Optimization. *Healthcare* **2022**, *10*, 494. [CrossRef]
42. Sowrirajan, S.R.; Balasubramanian, S.; Raj, R.S.P. MRI brain tumor classification using a hybrid VGG16-NADE model. *Braz. Arch. Biol. Technol.* **2022**, *66*, e23220071. [CrossRef]
43. Sadr, H.; Nazari, M.; Yousefzade-Chabok, S.; Emami, H.; Rabiei, R.; Ashraf, A. Enhancing brain tumor classification in MRI images: A deep learning-based approach for accurate classification and diagnosis. *Image Vis. Comput.* **2025**, *159*, 105555. [CrossRef]
44. Afroj, M.; Mondal, M.R.H.; Hassan, M.R.; Akter, S. MobDenseNet: A Hybrid Deep Learning Model for Brain Tumor Classification Using MRI. *Array* **2025**, *26*, 100413. [CrossRef]

symmetry

MDPI

Article

Temporal Convolutional and LSTM Networks for Complex Mechanical Drilling Speed Prediction

Yang Huang [1], Wu Yang [1], Junrui Hu [2,3,*] and Yihang Zhao [4]

[1] School of Architectural Engineering, Chongqing Industry Polytechnic University, Chongqing 401120, China
[2] Faculty of Economics, L.N. Gumilyov Eurasian National University, 010008 Astana, Kazakhstan
[3] China Chemicalgeology and Mine Bureau, Beijing 100020, China
[4] CEC Technical & Economic Consulting Center of Power Construction, Electric Power Development Research Institute Co., Ltd., Beijing 100053, China
* Correspondence: 18795938858@163.com

Abstract

Accurate prediction of drilling speed is essential in mechanical drilling operations, as it improves operational efficiency, enhances safety, and reduces overall costs. Traditional prediction methods, however, are often constrained by delayed responsiveness, limited exploitation of real-time parameters, and inadequate capability to model complex temporal dependencies, ultimately resulting in suboptimal performance. To overcome these limitations, this study introduces a novel model termed CTLSF (CNN-TCN-LSTM with Self-Attention), which integrates multiple neural network architectures within a symmetry-aware framework. The model achieves architectural symmetry through the coordinated interplay of spatial and temporal learning modules, each contributing complementary strengths to the prediction task. Specifically, Convolutional Neural Networks (CNNs) extract localized spatial features from sequential drilling data, while Temporal Convolutional Networks (TCNs) capture long-range temporal dependencies through dilated convolutions and residual connections. In parallel, Long Short-Term Memory (LSTM) networks model unidirectional temporal dynamics, and a self-attention mechanism adaptively highlights salient temporal patterns. Furthermore, a sliding window strategy is employed to enable real-time prediction on streaming data. Comprehensive experiments conducted on the Volve oilfield dataset demonstrate that the proposed CTLSF model substantially outperforms conventional data-driven approaches, achieving a low Mean Absolute Error (MAE) of 0.8439, a Mean Absolute Percentage Error (MAPE) of 2.19%, and a high coefficient of determination (R^2) of 0.9831. These results highlight the effectiveness, robustness, and symmetry-aware design of the CTLSF model in predicting mechanical drilling speed under complex real-world conditions.

Keywords: energy exploration; time series prediction; mechanical drilling; LSTM; temporal convolutional networks

1. Introduction

In the oil and gas industry, real-time prediction of drilling speed is a fundamental aspect of intelligent operational management. Accurate rate of penetration (ROP) forecasting plays a crucial role in improving operational efficiency, reducing costs, and ensuring drilling safety. Drilling operations are inherently complex, time-consuming, and expensive, with daily expenditures reaching up to 500,000 USD [1], which underscores the importance

 https://doi.org/10.3390/sym17111962

of precise ROP prediction. Reliable drilling speed forecasting not only enables the optimization of drilling parameters and supports informed decision-making but also minimizes non-productive time, thereby reducing overall operational costs [2,3]. However, traditional prediction methods based on simplified physical models or empirical formulas are often inadequate for capturing the nonlinear, time-dependent, and strongly coupled dynamics of drilling processes [4–7]. To address these limitations, symmetry-based modeling approaches have recently been introduced. By exploiting the inherent symmetrical patterns within drilling data, these methods enhance model robustness and predictive accuracy. Despite these advances, achieving a balance between prediction accuracy and real-time computational performance remains a persistent technical challenge in modern oilfield engineering [8,9].

The rapid advancement of artificial intelligence (AI) has profoundly reshaped various industries, particularly the oil and gas sector, where AI-driven techniques have brought remarkable improvements in automation and decision-making efficiency [10–13]. Intelligent oilfield development has become a prominent research focus, leveraging AI's capabilities in data processing, feature extraction, and pattern recognition to optimize operational workflows and enhance predictive accuracy [14–16]. As a key subfield of AI, machine learning (ML) has demonstrated strong potential in predicting essential oilfield parameters, such as drilling speed, production rate, and reservoir characteristics [17]. By integrating symmetry-aware learning algorithms that account for the underlying symmetrical structures in drilling data, researchers are developing more adaptive and accurate ML-based models. These advancements further improve the reliability and real-time performance of predictive systems in increasingly complex drilling environments.

Deep learning models, particularly those combining Convolutional Neural Networks (CNNs) and Long Short-Term Memory Networks (LSTMs), have emerged as powerful tools for geological data analysis and prediction [18,19]. Hegde [20] developed an enhanced drilling penetration prediction model based on a data-driven machine learning framework, demonstrating the capability of machine learning in addressing complex geological challenges. Li [21] further proposed a comprehensive workflow encompassing data acquisition, preprocessing, model construction, and performance evaluation, which significantly improved the accuracy of drilling efficiency prediction and achieved notable advantages over traditional approaches. In a related study, Skrobek [22] tackled the problem of predicting the performance of fixed-bed and fluidized-bed adsorption systems by introducing a deep learning framework integrating LSTM, BiLSTM, and GRU architectures. Experiments with silica gel composite adsorbents achieved high prediction precision, with an R^2 value exceeding 0.97, thereby enhancing the efficiency of adsorption cooling systems. Similarly, Alsaihati [23] developed an integrated hybrid model that combines a random forest meta-model with artificial neural networks and adaptive neuro-fuzzy inference systems as base learners. Validation using real well data revealed that this approach substantially outperformed both its individual base learners and conventional empirical models, achieving a low absolute mean percentage error of 7.8% and a high coefficient of determination (R^2) of 0.94. Despite these advances, deep learning-based models still face several practical limitations. Their performance often depends on the availability of large volumes of high-quality data, extensive training durations, and significant computational resources. Such requirements may hinder their scalability and robustness in real-time industrial applications, leading to imbalances in model performance and resource utilization.

Beyond model selection, data preprocessing and optimization strategies play a crucial role in enhancing predictive accuracy. Gan [24] proposed a rate of penetration (ROP) prediction framework that integrates wavelet filtering, mutual information-based variable optimization, and a hybrid bat algorithm, effectively improving the performance of support vector regression through hyperparameter optimization. Ashrafi [25] introduced a hybrid learning model by coupling four evolutionary algorithms with artificial neural networks, demonstrating superior capability in managing nonlinear features and noise interference, thereby improving the robustness and adaptability of drilling speed prediction. Moreover, Khalifa [26] proposed a machine learning-based rock type classification approach that enables real-time identification of lithology using drilling data. By integrating nine drilling parameters and employing the open Volve oilfield dataset, the model ensured dataset impartiality through feature selection and sample balancing techniques, achieving a testing accuracy of 95%. However, the computational complexity and intensive parameter tuning associated with these methods may restrict their applicability in large-scale real-time data environments, where rapid response and model efficiency are essential.

In the context of real-time prediction and dynamic model adaptability, Soares [27] developed a real-time learning framework that enhances model stability and prediction accuracy under varying operational conditions. By continuously capturing and integrating drilling process data, this method improves the flexibility and responsiveness of traditional analytical models. Subsequent studies have demonstrated that real-time data feedback and continuous learning mechanisms not only enhance predictive accuracy but also expand model applicability and adaptability across diverse drilling environments [28,29]. In the domain of drilling operation optimization and control, Gan [30] introduced a dynamic ROP prediction model based on a moving window strategy. By incorporating correlation analysis among drilling parameters, this approach provides robust support for intelligent drilling optimization and real-time decision-making. Nevertheless, real-time learning methods impose substantial demands on data transmission speed, computational hardware capability, and model update efficiency, which may limit their scalability when dealing with highly dynamic and complex industrial data streams.

Beyond real-time adaptability, the interpretability of models has emerged as an equally critical yet challenging research focus. Model interpretability and predictive performance are inherently interdependent, and achieving a suitable balance between the two remains a central issue in intelligent drilling modeling. Pei [31] improved the interpretability of fully connected neural networks (FNNs), thereby facilitating more effective optimization of drilling parameters and enhancing decision-making transparency. Similarly, Caicedo [32] proposed an innovative computational strategy for rock strength estimation, enabling improved prediction of drill bit performance and offering valuable insights for enhancing drilling efficiency and cost reduction. Despite these advancements, achieving a balance between interpretability and high predictive accuracy continues to be a major challenge, particularly in the context of complex, data-intensive drilling operations [33].

Unlike conventional hybrid models that typically combine modules in a generic manner, the proposed CNN-TCN-LSTM with Self-Attention (CTLSF) model is designed with a task-specific architecture tailored for drilling speed prediction. It integrates CNN, TCN, LSTM, and a self-attention mechanism in a coordinated and purposeful way. Specifically, CNN is used to extract localized spatial features from sequential drilling data. The TCN module then applies dilated convolutions and residual connections to effectively capture long-range dependencies while maintaining computational efficiency. The LSTM module further models the temporal dynamics of the sequence in a forward direction, capturing how drilling conditions evolve over time. To enhance the model's focus on critical time steps, a self-attention mechanism is applied after the LSTM layer, allowing the model to adaptively assign greater importance to the most informative temporal features. This carefully designed architecture, combined with dimensionality reduction through global pooling and compact fully connected layers, sets CTLSF apart from existing hybrid models. It is specifically developed to address the challenges of multivariate, nonlinear, and strongly time-dependent drilling parameter prediction, offering high task relevance and practical value.

Firstly, as shown in Figure 1, the historical drilling data and current moment data are saved to the drilling database according to the measurement equipment, and then, each parameter is transmitted from the database to the subnetwork and, finally, jointly passed into the data-driven model for ROP prediction. For specific details of the model, please refer to Table 1. This study also systematically outlines the experimental workflow, and Figure 2 illustrates the detailed experimental framework of the method. The proposed symmetry-aware architecture balances feature extraction across different network paths, ensuring stable gradient propagation and reducing bias toward specific feature patterns. This design enhances learning efficiency and helps the model capture important patterns in complex drilling data, improving both stability and generalization.

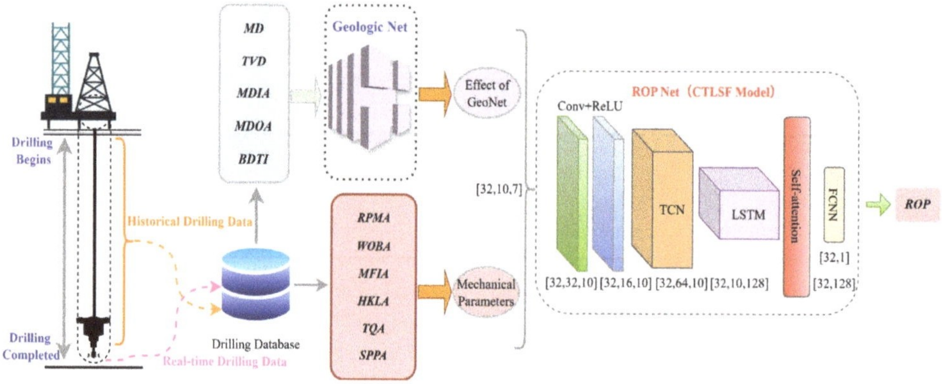

Figure 1. The proposed model, the structure of a real-time mechanical drilling speed prediction method.

Table 1. CTLSF model architecture and tensor shapes.

Layer	Shape
Input	[32, 10, 7]
Permute	[32, 7, 10]
CNN-1	[32, 32, 10]
CNN-2	[32, 16, 10]
TCN	[32, 64, 10]
Permute	[32, 10, 64]
LSTM	[32, 10, 128]
Self-Attentional	[32, 10, 128]
Mean	[32, 128]
FCNN	[32, 1]

- Z-score standardization and outlier removal were performed on oilfield drilling data, and the data from different wells were divided into training data and test data at a ratio of 3:1.
- Combine graph modeling techniques to analyze the correlation of different parameters in drilling data. Based on the data-driven method, a geologic subnetwork is constructed to extract the strong correlation parameters and train the neural network, so as to obtain the geologic fusion influence factor.

- Construction of the CNN-TCN-LSTM with Self-Attention (CTLSF) drilling speed prediction model was started to determine the hyperparameters, such as maximum number of iterations, hidden layer dimensions, learning rate, and batch size.
- The CTLSF model is trained, and the weights and bias values are optimized based on the output error of each iteration.
- The identified CTLSF models were tested with the test dataset, and the corresponding Mean Absolute Error (MAE), Mean Absolute Percentage Error (MAPE), Mean Squared Error (MSE), Root Mean Squared Error (RMSE), and the Coefficient of Determination (R^2) evaluation metric values were calculated, and the model hyperparameters were appropriately adjusted according to the metric values.
- The data-driven model of this study was used to compare and analyze with the current mainstream predictive models, which ultimately led to the study's conclusions.

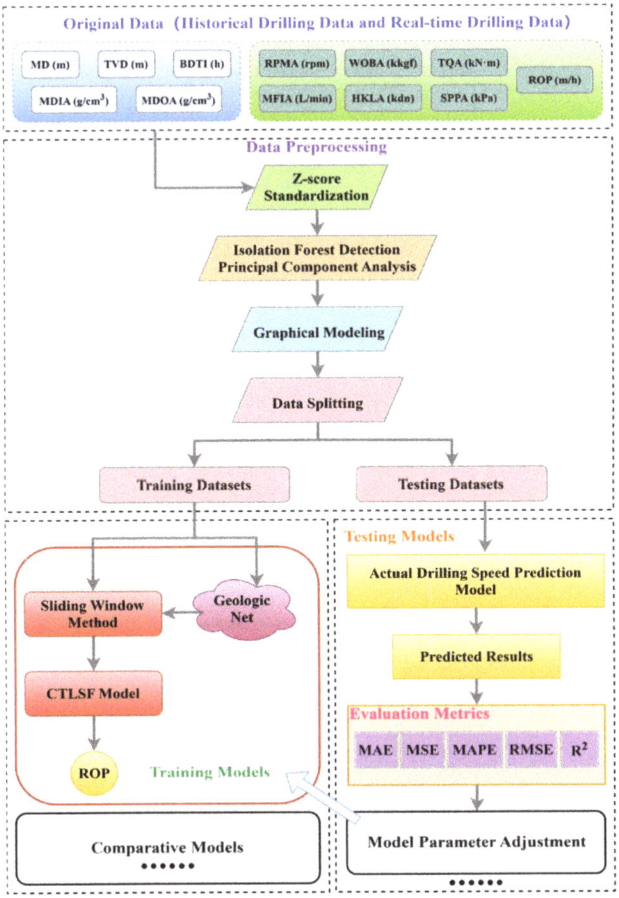

Figure 2. Data-driven modeling research process.

It is important to note that this study was conducted under several simplifying assumptions. Specifically, it was assumed that all wells were drilled using similar equipment, including rig type and bit condition (e.g., wear). This assumption helps minimize data variability caused by equipment differences and ensures consistency across the dataset. Based on this methodology and experimental procedure, the study successfully developed an efficient and accurate drilling speed prediction model, which provides practical technical support for real-time drilling speed forecasting in oilfield operations.

2. Materials and Methods

In the following sections, the basic principles and important functions of the CNN, TCN, LSTM, and SAM are mainly briefly introduced. At the end of the section, an overview of the composition and implementation process of the CTLSF oilfield drilling speed prediction model proposed in this study is presented.

2.1. CNN

Convolutional Neural Network (CNN) is a deep learning model architecture first proposed by Yann LeCun et al. in 1998. It has been widely used in computer vision tasks such as image recognition, target detection, and image segmentation [34]. The basic structure of a Convolutional Neural Network includes a convolutional layer, a pooling layer, and a fully connected layer [35], as shown in Figure 3. CNN is able to automatically learn and recognize local patterns and features in time series data by means of local perception, demonstrating a powerful feature extraction capability, which is especially suitable for processing complex and time series input data.

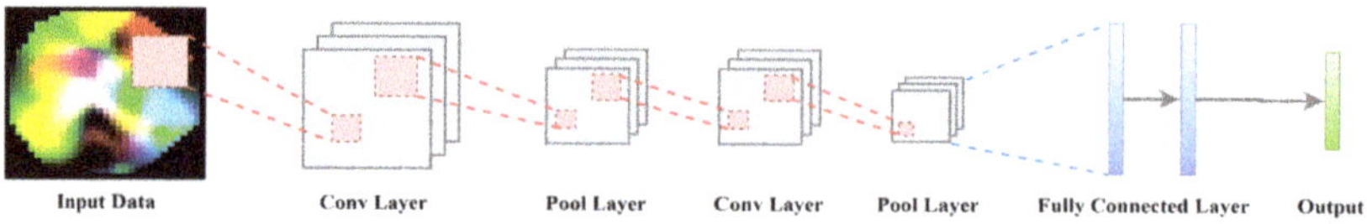

Figure 3. CNN basic structure diagram.

2.2. TCN

Temporal convolutional network is a deep learning architecture. The model has shown excellent performance in the field of sequence modeling by virtue of the advantages of recurrent neural networks in capturing long-term dependencies in sequences [36]. The core innovation of TCN is the introduction of causal convolution, extended convolution, and residual connectivity modules. Among them, causal convolution ensures the causal nature of the network, i.e., the output at the current moment depends only on the current and past inputs, avoiding information leakage. Its mathematical form is described as follows:

$$y_t = f(x_1, x_2, \ldots, x_t) \tag{1}$$

where x_t is the input at the current time step of the sequence, y_t is the output at the current time step, and f represents the function that establishes the relationship between the output and the input. Dilated convolution builds upon traditional convolution by introducing a dilation factor that expands the receptive field of the convolution operation. The mathematical expression for the *s-th* neuron in a dilated convolution is as follows:

$$F(s) = (x \times df)(s) = \sum_{i=0}^{k-1} f(i) \cdot x_{s-d \cdot i} \tag{2}$$

$$R = activation(x + F(x)) \tag{3}$$

where s represents the input sequence information, d is the dilation factor, $\times$ denotes the convolution operation, k is the size of the convolution kernel, and $s - d \cdot i$ indicates the past direction in time. Figure 4a illustrates an example of dilated convolution. As the dilation factor d increases, the receptive field of the TCN expands, allowing for the reception of more information. To mitigate the vanishing gradient problem in deep networks, TCN incorporates residual connections. As shown in Figure 4b, each residual block consists of a convolutional layer, ReLU activation function, weight normalization, and a dropout layer. The mathematical representation of the residual block is as follows:

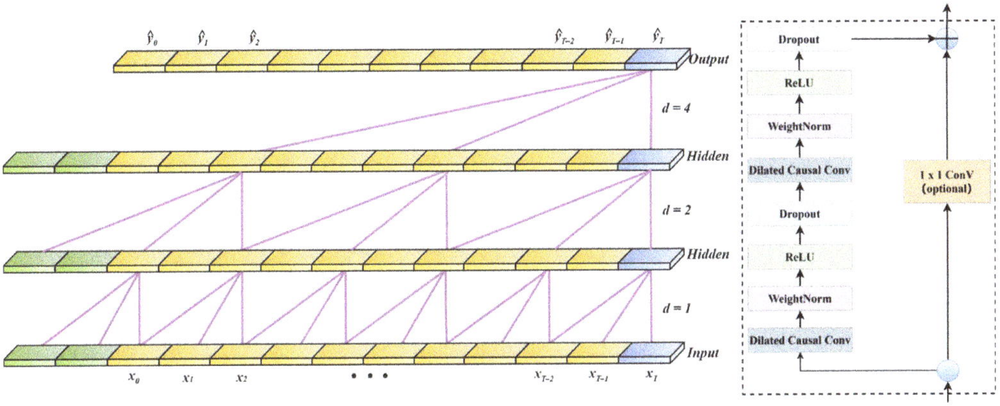

(a) (b)

Figure 4. (**a**) TCN network extended convolutional map; (**b**) residual module.

2.3. LSTM

The Long Short-Term Memory (LSTM) network is a specialized type of recurrent neural network (RNN) designed to effectively address the limitations of traditional RNNs in capturing long-term dependencies [37]. Conventional RNNs often suffer from vanishing or exploding gradient problems during the modeling of long sequences, which significantly reduces their ability to represent long-range dependencies. In contrast, LSTM Networks introduce memory cells and gating mechanisms, substantially improving their capacity and stability in modeling long-term sequences, both theoretically and empirically [38]. As shown in Figure 5, the LSTM Network is composed of multiple LSTM subunits arranged in a hierarchical structure, with each subunit consisting of a forget gate, an input gate, and an output gate.

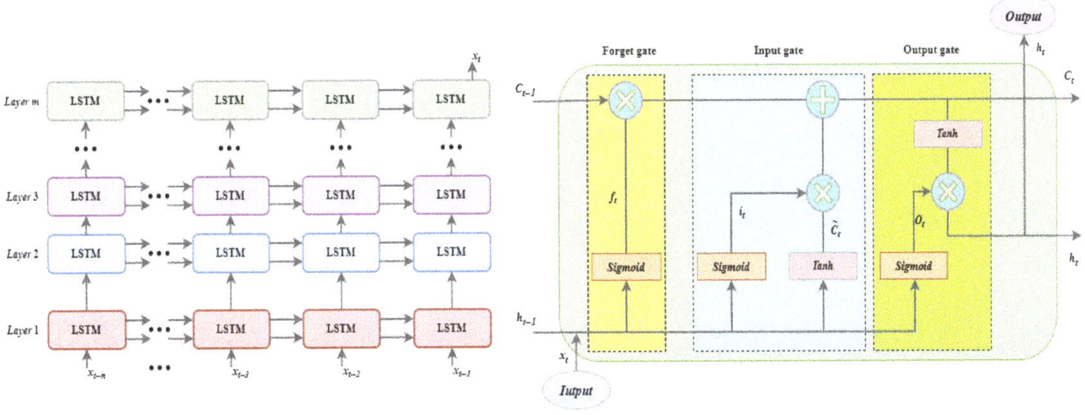

Figure 5. LSTM Network structure and logical structure of LSTM Network subunits.

The forget gate determines which information in the memory cell of the current time step should be forgotten or discarded.

Its activation value is represented as

$$f_t = \sigma\left(W_f \cdot [h_{t-1}, x_t] + b_f\right) \tag{4}$$

The input gate controls the influence of the input information at the current time step on the memory cell state, determining how new information is stored in the cell state.

Its computation is represented as

$$i_t = \sigma(W_i \cdot [h_{t-1}, x_t] + b_i) \tag{5}$$

$$\widetilde{c}_t = tanh(W_c \cdot [h_{t-1}, x_t] + b_c) \tag{6}$$

$$c_t = f_t \odot c_{t-1} + i_t \odot \widetilde{c}_t \tag{7}$$

The output gate determines the hidden state h_t at the current time step by extracting information from the cell state and passing it to the next layer or output of the network.

Its calculation is expressed as

$$o_t = \sigma(W_o \cdot [h_{t-1}, x_t] + b_o) \tag{8}$$

$$h_t = o_t \odot tanh(c_t) \tag{9}$$

2.4. Self-Attentional Mechanism

The self-attention mechanism (SAM) is a method used to calculate the dependencies between elements in a sequence, making it particularly effective for processing long sequences of data [39]. It generates weighted representations for each element by calculating its relevance to all other elements in the sequence. The computation process of the self-attention mechanism involves three key components: queries, keys, and values. As shown in Figure 6, the process begins by calculating the dot product between the query vector Q and the key vector K to evaluate the relevance between each pair of elements in the sequence. Next, the softmax function is applied to normalize the resulting relevance, transforming them into a probability distribution. Finally, the normalized weights are used to perform a weighted sum of the value vector V, generating the final representation. The computation is expressed as

$$Q = XW_Q \tag{10}$$

$$K = XW_K \tag{11}$$

$$V = XW_V \tag{12}$$

$$a_i = Softmax\left(\frac{QK^T}{\sqrt{d_k}}\right)V \tag{13}$$

In the equation, W_K, W_Q, and W_V are the weight matrices learned during training, which are used to transform the input X into the query, key, and value vectors, respectively, with C representing the final output.

2.5. CTLSF Model

The core idea of the proposed CTLSF model lies in leveraging the collaborative effect of multiple modules to fully extract multi-level feature information from the data. First, the CNN module performs initial feature extraction on the input time series data through dual convolution operations. The convolutional layers capture local spatial features, extract low-level features from the data, and smooth the time series signals, thereby reducing the complexity of the raw data. Next, TCN utilizes dilated convolution to gradually expand the receptive field while maintaining computational efficiency, enabling the model to handle longer time steps without increasing computational costs. On this basis, a bidirectional LSTM is employed to capture contextual information from both directions of the input sequence, enabling the model to fully learn bidirectional dependencies and further improve prediction accuracy. Additionally, self-attention computes the weight relationships between different time steps, empowering the model to selectively focus on the most critical parts of the input sequence.

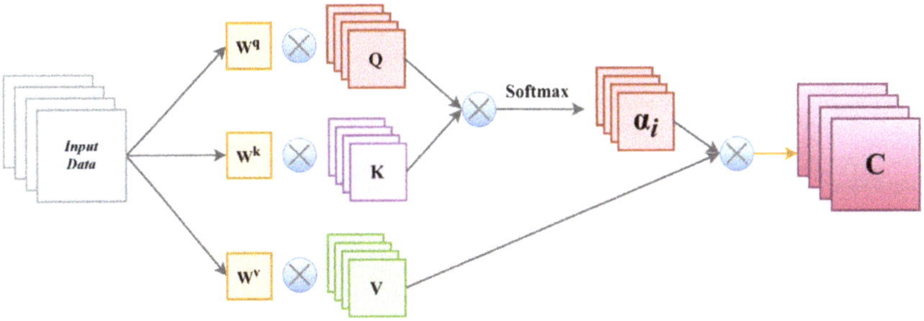

Figure 6. Structure of the self-attention mechanism.

Compared with traditional single-network models, CTLSF demonstrates superior feature fusion capabilities in processing time series data and excels at capturing long-term dependencies, significantly enhancing the accuracy and robustness of oilfield mechanical drilling rate prediction. Therefore, the proposed CTLSF model offers a novel approach for time series forecasting tasks and holds great potential for a wide range of applications.

3. Related Preparations

This section focuses on the data preprocessing phase, aiming to improve the data quality by systematically handling outliers and missing values. A graph-based modeling approach is employed to explore the correlations among multidimensional oilfield drilling data, constructing subnetworks for highly correlated attributes. A sliding window mechanism is then applied to input the geological influence factor and drilling data into the prediction model in chronological order. This ensures that the prediction model is fully trained on representative data, thereby enhancing its generalization capability for unseen samples. This step plays a critical role in reducing data noise, optimizing model performance, and improving the overall prediction accuracy.

3.1. Data Preparation

In this study, the available Volve dataset released by Equinor was utilized. This dataset originates from the Volve oilfield in the Norwegian Continental Shelf of the North Sea. Due to its high accessibility and comprehensive nature, the dataset serves as a valuable resource for external validation and cross-domain comparative studies, making it an ideal choice for evaluating and validating the proposed model.

3.1.1. Datasets Overview and Parameter Distribution

Among the numerous open-access wells in the Volve oilfield of the North Sea, the data completeness and the distribution ranges of various drilling attributes vary significantly across wells. Therefore, this study selected drilling data from four wells with complete observational records as the data source for drilling rate prediction. The selected wells are labeled as W4, W5, W6, and W7. Specifically, W4, W5, and W6 were used as the training dataset to capture the overall drilling process patterns, while W7 was used as the test dataset to evaluate the model's accuracy in predicting mechanical-specific energy. This selection ensures that the experimental dataset not only represents the geological diversity within the oilfield but also includes a wide range of operational data. Preserving complete well data for testing better simulates real-world drilling scenarios where models must predict the ROP for entirely new wells, and this partitioning strategy effectively validates the model's generalization capability across geological heterogeneity. The diversity and comprehensiveness of these data are critical for ensuring the accuracy and reliability of prediction modeling and analysis. Table 2 summarizes the depth range and data volume of each well.

Table 2. Drilling data information.

Well	Depth Start, m	Depth End, m	Data Entries	Category
W4	269.1	899.9	8377	Train
W5	309.1	451.2	2113	Train
W6	300.9	633.5	2886	Train
W7	923.6	1360.8	2397	Test

As shown in Table 3, each well contains a variety of attributes essential for oilfield drilling operations. These attributes collectively provide a comprehensive understanding of the drilling activities and geological features. Taking the W4 well data as an example, a detailed overview of the range and values of these modeling parameters is provided in Table 3.

Table 3. W4 drilling parameter information.

Features	Abbreviation	Units	Max	Min	Mean	Median
Measured Depth	MD	m	899.95	269.10	605.86	625.52
True Vertical Depth	TVD	m	889.91	269.11	602.68	622.82
Rotary Per Minute of Annulus	RPMA	rpm	189.0	68.0	145.57	145.0
Weight On Bit Average	WOBA	kkgf	9.03	0.58	4.74	4.75
Mud Flow In Average	MFIA	L/min	4496.43	2085.15	3961.18	3781.82
Mud Density In Annulus	MDIA	g/cm^3	1.27	1.27	1.27	1.27
Mud Density Out Annulus	MDOA	g/cm^3	1.15	1.15	1.15	1.15
Hook Load Average	HKLA	kdn	114.63	91.63	100.17	98.55
Torque Average	TQA	kN·m	9.60	0.01	4.01	4.76
Stand Pipe Pressure Average	SPPA	kPa	16502.0	4572.0	11,368.66	10,416.99
Bit Drill Time	BDTI	h	55,330.75	3523.60	31,694.50	31,432.41
Rate of Penetration	ROP	m/h	99.61	2.93	50.89	52.18

3.1.2. Z-Score Standardization

Z-score normalization is a commonly used data preprocessing method that eliminates the impact of differences in scale and magnitude between features.

This is achieved through the following formulas:

$$x' = \frac{x - \mu}{\sigma} \tag{14}$$

$$\sigma = \sqrt{\frac{1}{N}\sum_{i=1}^{N}(x_i - \mu)^2} \tag{15}$$

$$\mu = \frac{1}{N}\sum_{i=1}^{N} X_i \tag{16}$$

where x is the raw data, σ is the standard deviation, and μ is the mean of the data. In this study, Z-score normalization was applied to all parameters, ensuring a more uniform distribution of the input data in the feature space. This improved both the model's convergence speed and prediction accuracy. The effects of the normalization are shown in Figure 7. Z-score normalization was applied independently to each feature dimension to ensure comparability across features.

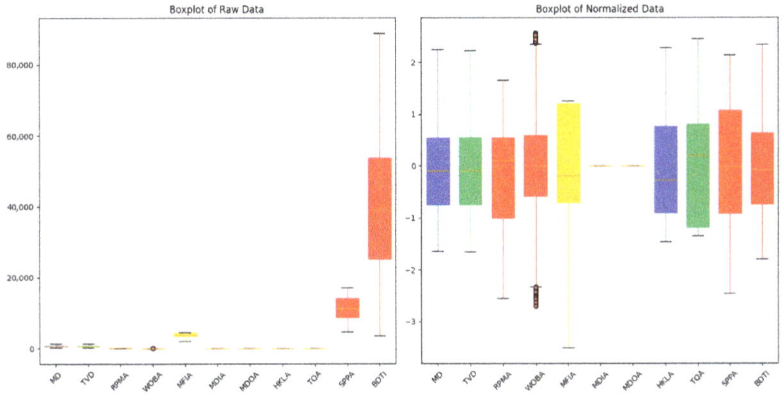

Figure 7. Comparison of numerical standardization for drilling.

3.1.3. Outlier Detection

To ensure data quality, further detection and processing of outliers in the dataset were performed. Outliers may arise from measurement errors, data acquisition noise, or extreme conditions and can negatively impact the stability and generalization performance of the model. In this section, the Isolation Forest algorithm was employed for anomaly detection to identify outliers in the data. Isolation Forest is an unsupervised machine learning algorithm specifically designed for anomaly detection, which isolates outliers by randomly partitioning the feature space. In the algorithm design, the contamination parameter was set to 0.05, indicating that approximately 5% of the data points were considered outliers. The algorithm labels each data point, where −1 denotes an outlier and 1 denotes a normal point. Finally, representative features such as MD, WOBA, and RPMA were selected to construct a 3D scatterplot, with colors indicating outliers and normal points, as shown in Figure 8.

3.2. Sliding Window Size Analysis

The sliding window is an important preprocessing step in time series analysis, used to extract local features from continuous data while preserving the temporal information. As shown in Figure 9, a sliding window of length L is applied to process the data sequence. As new samples arrive, the sliding window moves forward along the sequence. At each window update, the model is trained multiple times using the data within the window, thereby predicting the next ROP value. In this study, different window sizes were set and experiments were conducted to analyze the impact of window size on model performance. As shown in Table 4, set the window size to 5, 10, and 20, respectively, for the experiment, and the results indicate that smaller windows retain more fine-grained information but increase the computational complexity, while larger windows reduce the capture of detailed features but improve computational efficiency and model robustness. Ultimately, a window size of 10 was selected, as it exhibited the best balance between prediction accuracy and computational complexity, providing a reliable basis for further model optimization.

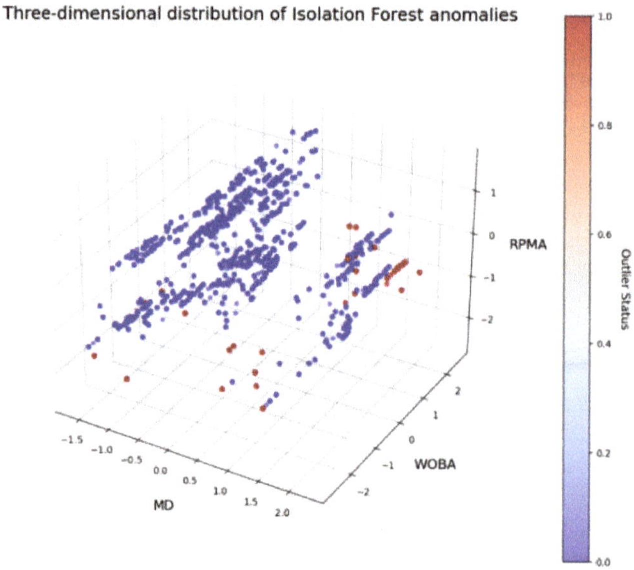

Figure 8. Three-dimensional distribution of anomalies.

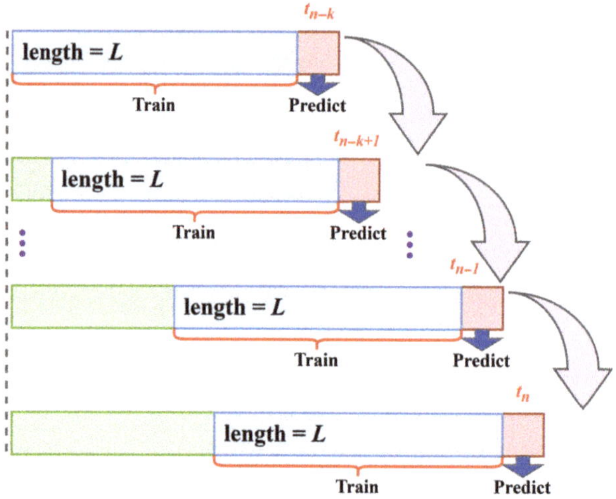

Figure 9. Schematic diagram of the sliding window method.

Table 4. Window size experiment.

Case	Epoch	lr	Length	MAE	MAPE	MSE	RMSE	R^2	Time (s)
case 1	1000	0.0001	5	1.3347	3.22%	10.0707	3.1734	0.9723	1698
case 2	1000	0.0001	10	1.3332	3.22%	9.4178	3.0688	0.9741	1643
case 3	1000	0.0001	20	1.3926	3.36%	9.9968	3.1618	0.9725	1603

3.3. Correlation Analysis

To thoroughly analyze the impact of drilling parameters on the rate of penetration (ROP), this study employed mutual information to quantitatively assess 11 parameters, aiming to reveal the correlation between each input feature and the target variable ROP. As shown in Figure 10, parameters such as MD, TVD, and BDTI exhibit a strong influence on ROP, whereas MDOA, MFIA, and MDIA have a relatively limited impact.

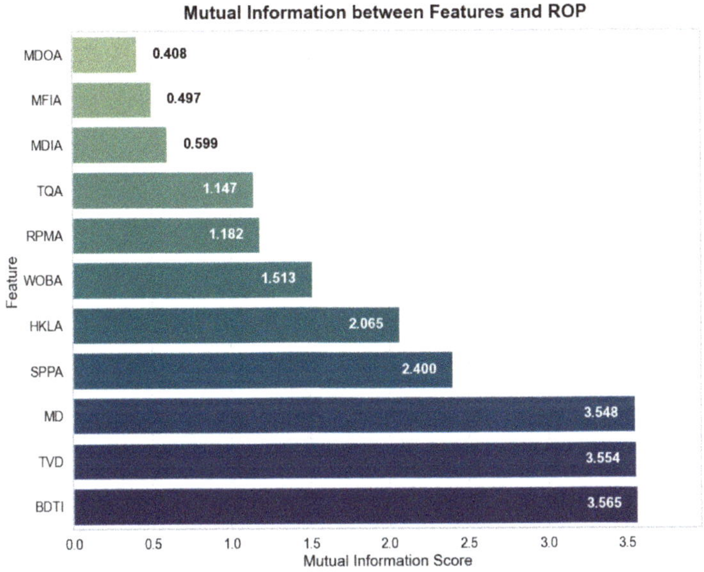

Figure 10. Mutual information scores barplot between features and ROP.

The drilling rate is influenced by a variety of complex factors, and there exists a certain degree of correlation between the input parameters. Therefore, careful selection of the input features is crucial in the construction of data-driven models. Correlation analysis, as one of the common methods for feature selection, provides a scientific basis for quantitatively characterizing the relationships between variables. In this study, graphical modeling techniques are employed to represent variables as nodes in a network, with edges indicating their correlations. The Pearson correlation coefficient is used to construct the correlation matrix, which quantitatively describes the linear relationships between the variables. Furthermore, a heatmap is used to visualize the correlation matrix, with a color gradient clearly illustrating the strength and direction of the correlations. Strongly correlated parameters are more prominently displayed in the heatmap, revealing potential key relationships.

Applying this method to dataset W4, the analysis results are shown in Figure 11. Among the 11 input parameters under study, the correlation experiment indicates that MD, TVD, MDIA, MDOA, and BDTI exhibit strong correlations. Therefore, a geological subnetwork can be constructed based on these highly correlated parameters, and these parameters can be incorporated as input features into the neural network model. This enables the training of a comprehensive influence factor, providing more accurate and effective data support for the prediction of the mechanical drilling rate.

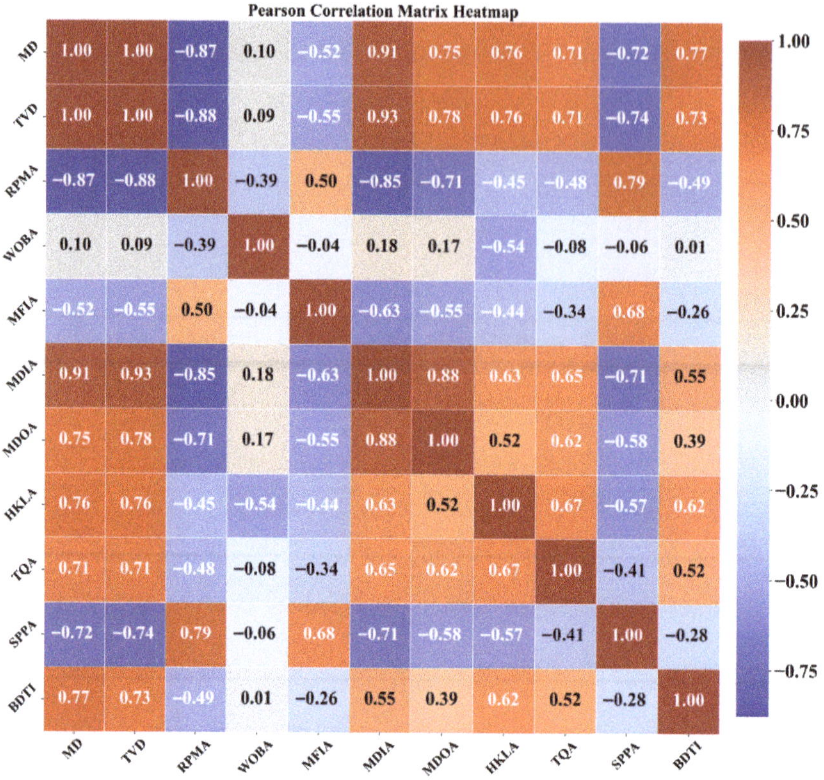

Figure 11. Pearson correlation matrix heatmap.

3.4. Subnetwork Construction

As shown in Figure 12, the geological subnetwork is designed not merely as a standard MLP for dimensionality reduction or fusion, but as a domain-guided module tailored to extract deep representations from strongly correlated geological inputs. While it employs a fully connected neural network structure—including an input layer, two hidden layers, and an output layer—the novelty lies in its dedicated role and selective input mechanism within the entire model framework. Specifically, based on Pearson correlation analysis and geological domain knowledge, we select five highly interrelated parameters (MD, TVD, MDLA, MDOA, and BDTI) that characterize subsurface structural and lithological information. These are processed independently in this subnetwork to preserve internal correlations and enhance their semantic contribution, before being fused with dynamic drilling signals in the later stages of the model. This modular and hierarchical fusion design allows the network to mitigate multi-collinearity risks and avoid the curse of dimensionality that often occurs when high-dimensional static parameters are directly mixed with time-varying features.

Furthermore, the geological subnetwork provides an interpretable latent representation, serving as a compact geological influence factor for subsequent multi-source coupling in drilling rate prediction. Thus, the originality of this subnetwork lies not in its architectural complexity but in its task-specific, geologically informed functional design that contributes to both prediction accuracy and interpretability.

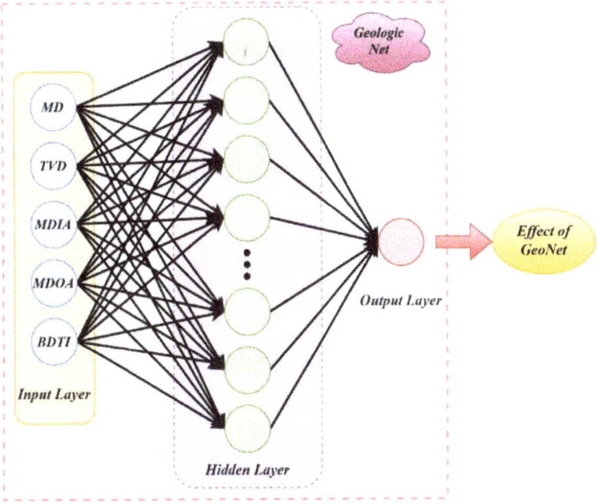

Figure 12. Geologic network structure.

3.5. Model Evaluates Metrics

To evaluate the performance of the proposed oilfield drilling rate prediction model, this study employs several commonly used regression evaluation metrics, including the *MAE*, *MAPE*, *MSE*, *RMSE*, and the R^2.

The definitions and explanations of these metrics are as follows:

$$MAE = \frac{1}{n}\sum_{i=1}^{n}|y_i - \hat{y}_i| \tag{17}$$

$$MAPE = \frac{1}{n}\sum_{i=1}^{n}\left|\frac{y_i - \hat{y}_i}{y_i}\right| \times 100\% \tag{18}$$

$$MSE = \frac{1}{n}\sum_{i=1}^{n}(y_i - \hat{y}_i)^2 \tag{19}$$

$$RMSE = \sqrt{\frac{1}{n}\sum_{i=1}^{n}(y_i - \hat{y}_i)^2} \tag{20}$$

$$R^2 = 1 - \frac{\sum_{i=1}^{n}(y_i - \hat{y}_i)^2}{\sum_{i=1}^{n}(y_i - \overline{y}_i)^2} \tag{21}$$

where y_i represents the actual drilling rate in the oilfield, $\hat{y}_i$ denotes the predicted drilling rate, and n is the total number of drilling data points in the experimental dataset. The model with the lowest values for these metrics is considered the best predictive model.

4. Results and Discussion

This section aims to provide a systematic evaluation of the predictive performance of the proposed CTLSF model. Specifically, the evaluation focuses on four key performance metrics: the *MAE*, *MAPE*, *MSE*, *RMSE*, and R^2. Based on the validation results for both raw and filtered datasets, the performance of the CTLSF model is compared with that of the current mainstream data-driven models, providing a comprehensive quantification of the model's strengths and weaknesses. Furthermore, to further validate the accuracy and robustness of the CTLSF model, experiments were conducted under different dataset conditions to deeply analyze the model's performance, uncovering its potential advantages and limitations in prediction tasks and laying a solid foundation for its further application and optimization.

To ensure fair comparison and result stability, all experiments were conducted in the same computing environment: an AMD Ryzen9 7945 processor, NVIDIA GeForce RTX 4060 (8G), CPU clock speed of 2.5 GHz, and 32.0 GB of RAM. In addition, the specifics of the parameter configuration of the CTLSF model are shown in Table 5.

Table 5. Model parameterization.

Model	Model Parameter	Description
CTLSF	hidden_dim: 64	Hidden layer dimension
	num_layers: 2	Number of layers
	cnn_kernel_size: 3	Convolutional kernel size
	cnn_nn.ReLU()	Activation function for convolution
	tcn_layers: 3	3 residual blocks
	dilation: 2**i	Exponential growth (1, 2, 4) (** is the power operator, used to compute a specified power of a number.)
	batch_size: 32	Number of samples per batch
	optim.Adam	Optimizer
	num_epochs: 10,000	Training rounds
	lr: 1×10^{-4}	Learning rate
	sws_length: 10	Sliding window size
	nn.MSELoss()	Loss function
	weight_norm	Anti overfitting technology
	Dropout: 0.5	50% neuron dropout

4.1. Model Capability Analysis

To evaluate the predictive performance of the data-driven model, this study applied the aforementioned preprocessing methods to filter the W4, W5, W6, and W7 drilling datasets and incorporated geological influence factor to construct the final filtered dataset for experimentation. Meanwhile, the raw datasets for all four wells were retained to assess the model's robustness under noisy conditions. The experimental results for the CTLSF model are shown in Figures 13 and 14.

Under the influence of noise in the raw dataset, the predictive accuracy of the data-driven model was significantly lower than that observed in the filtered dataset. This phenomenon is primarily due to the presence of outliers and large fluctuations in the raw data, which conventional prediction models find challenging to adapt to the complex drilling process and extreme conditions. As shown in Figure 12, the horizontal coordinate x-axis represents the sample training time sequence, i.e., the beginning sample point to the end of the consecutive sample points, and the vertical coordinate y-axis represents the ROP value corresponding to the current sample point; in addition, the yellow solid line represents the real sample point, and the blue dotted line represents the ROP value corresponding to the current sample point predicted by the data-driven model. The figure includes subplots for the four different datasets, each illustrating the model's performance in different drilling areas. From the overall trend, the measured and predicted values are closely aligned, indicating that the model designed in this study can effectively capture the drilling rate variation patterns, demonstrating a certain level of robustness. However, in regions with significant drilling rate fluctuations or intense oscillations, some deviations between the predicted and measured values still exist, which may reflect the model's insufficient adaptability when handling high-frequency fluctuations.

In the final experimental dataset constructed for this study, the performance metrics of the CTLSF model showed significant improvement, with the predicted ROP values closely aligning with the measured values, demonstrating the outstanding predictive capability of the data-driven model. Compared to the raw data, the model's *MAE* on the processed W4 dataset was significantly reduced to 0.8439, and the *MAPE* decreased by 8.8%. This result indicates that data preprocessing and the analysis of correlations between model parameters played a crucial role in improving the prediction accuracy.

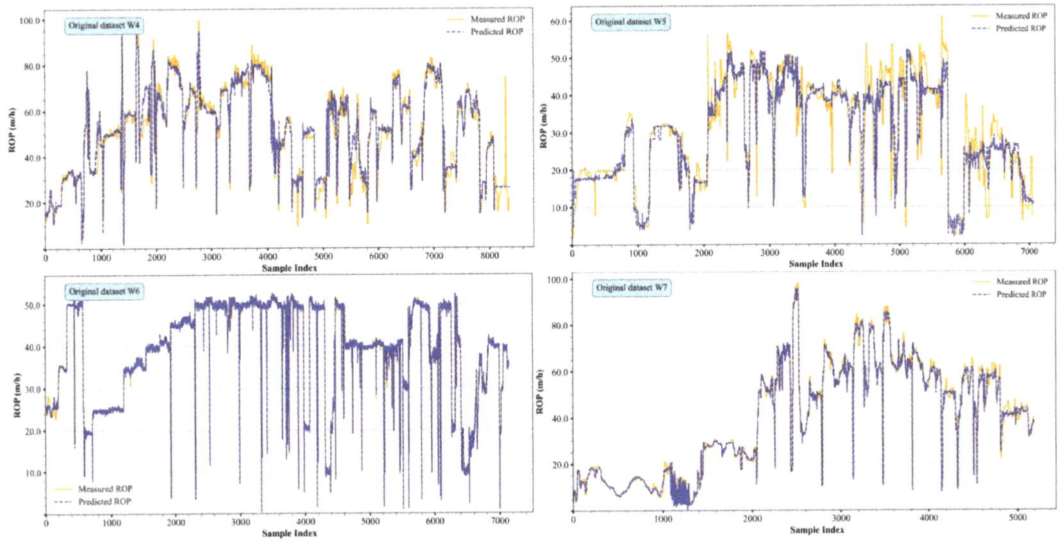

Figure 13. Test results of the CTLSF model with the original dataset.

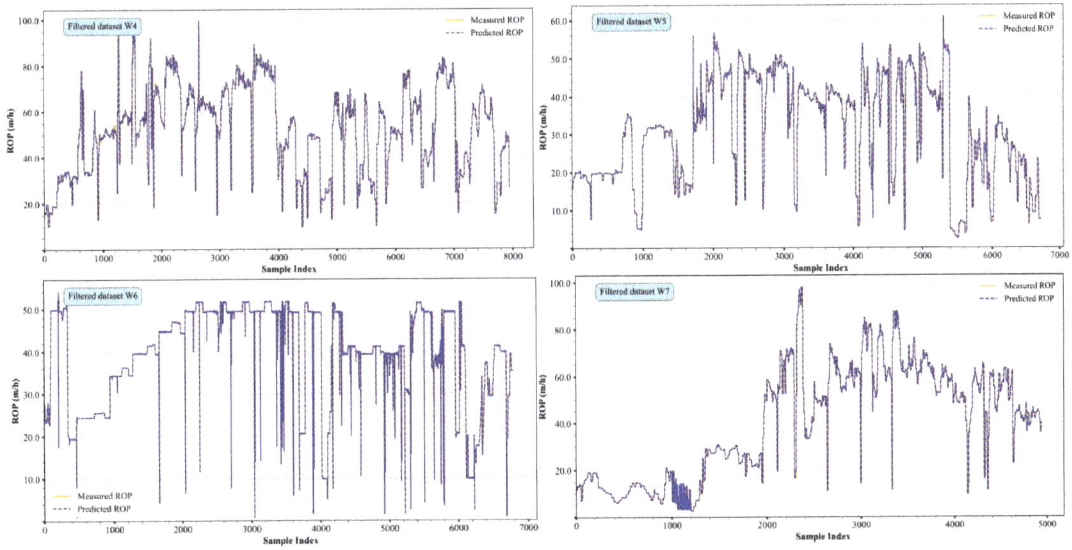

Figure 14. Test results of the CTLSF model with filtered datasets.

For the raw datasets of W4 and W5, the prediction errors are more apparent. Specifically, the W4 data showed a *MAE* value of 3.8947 and a *MAPE* value of 10.99% in a single test, while the W5 data showed a *MAE* value of 3.6534 and a *MAPE* value of 18.56%. The drilling rate fluctuations in these datasets were relatively large, posing a greater challenge for the model. In contrast, the model performed significantly better on the W6 dataset, with a *MAE* value of 0.5311 and a *MAPE* value of 1.77%, demonstrating a strong ability to capture the abrupt changes in the actual ROP.

As shown in Figure 15, the scatterplots of the measured and predicted values for the four wells clearly illustrate the predictive performance of the CTLSF model across different drilling rate ranges. The data points exhibited tight clustering along the 1:1 ideal prediction line (slope = 1, intercept = 0), with over 90% of the predictions falling within ±10% of the measured value, and only a very small number of points were not accurately predicted to be farther from the ideal prediction line. Most of the data points are closely distributed around the ideal prediction line, indicating that the model can accurately capture the variation trends of the actual drilling rate within these ranges. The predicted values closely align with the measured values, highlighting the model's superior predictive ability across the majority of the drilling rate intervals.

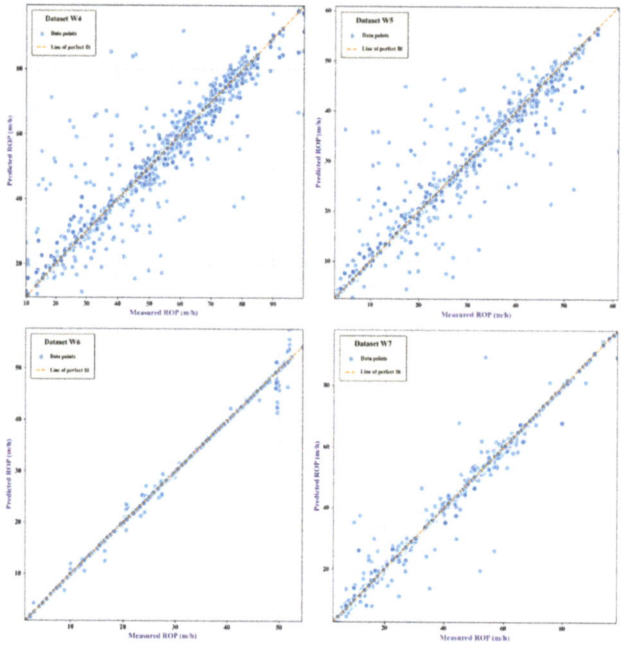

Figure 15. Scatterplot relationship between the predicted ROP and measured ROP.

4.2. Model Comparison

To evaluate the advantages of the proposed CTLSF prediction model over the current mainstream models, we compared it with models such as LSTM, SA-LSTM, and CNN-LSTM and tested each model's noise robustness on the raw data. As shown in Table 6, although the CTLSF model, by incorporating dual convolution and TCN structures, has a larger number of parameters than the other mainstream models—resulting in a longer per-epoch computation time—it outperforms the other models in both raw noisy data and filtered data. In the filtered data, the CTLSF model achieves an R^2 value of 0.9831 and a *MAE* of only 0.8439, significantly outperforming the other comparison models. This demonstrates that the CTLSF model holds significant research value in drilling rate prediction, as it can more effectively handle noise interference and provide accurate predictions. It is important to note that *MAPE* calculates the relative error percentage.

Table 6. Performance of each model under the test set.

Input Data	Model	MAE	MAPE	MSE	RMSE	R^2	Time (s)
Original Data (Unfiltered Data)	CTLSF	3.8947	10.99%	40.9358	6.3981	0.8970	1.97
	LSTM	5.9786	17.39%	87.1792	9.3370	0.7806	0.59
	SA-LSTM	5.7092	16.23%	78.5864	8.8649	0.8022	0.91
	CNN-LSTM	3.9076	11.67%	43.6644	6.6079	0.8901	0.93
Filtered Data	CTLSF	0.8439	2.19%	7.9509	2.8197	0.9831	1.87
	LSTM	1.0144	2.44%	8.2299	2.8688	0.9774	0.55
	SA-LSTM	1.0880	2.64%	8.3897	2.8965	0.9769	0.72
	CNN-LSTM	1.2930	3.17%	8.9220	2.9870	0.9754	0.63

The data from Table 6 were visualized in a radar chart, generating Figure 16. Each model is evaluated based on the five aforementioned metrics, with the orange area representing the model's performance on the raw noisy data, and the purple area reflecting the model's performance on the filtered data. From the four subplots, it is clearly evident that the area of the purple region is significantly smaller than that of the orange region. This indicates that data preprocessing, parameter correlation analysis, and subnetwork partitioning play crucial roles in enhancing the model's performance, effectively improving its ability to perform well on filtered data. Among all models, the CTLSF model performed the best, demonstrating its stronger modeling capabilities for complex time series data. In contrast, the LSTM and CNN-LSTM models had higher errors on unfiltered data and were significantly affected by noise in the raw data. Although SA-LSTM showed some improvement over traditional LSTM, it still fell short of CTLSF in terms of overall performance across all metrics. It is important to note here that *MSE* is a large value, and to show it clearly, we divide the value of *MSE* by 10 to visualize the expression.

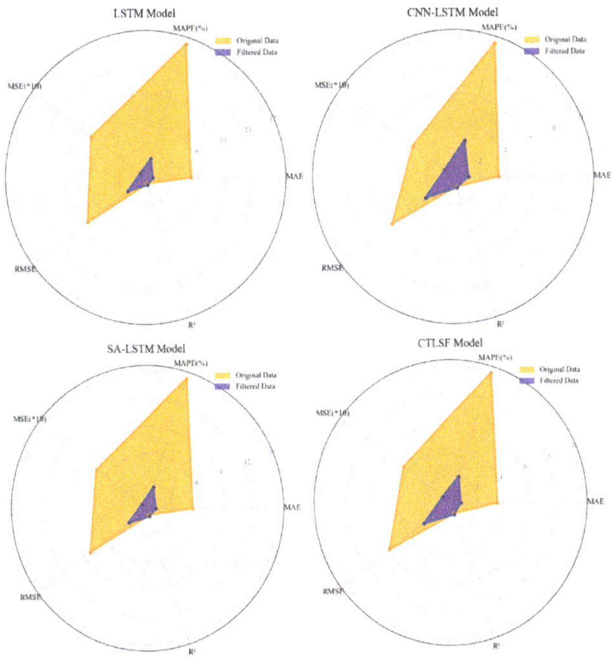

Figure 16. Radar plots of the predictive performance of each model with raw and filtered data.

Furthermore, based on the W4 drilling dataset, we compared the predicted values of each model, with different colors representing different prediction models. As shown in Figure 17, the predicted curve of the CTLSF model closely follows the actual measurement curve, showing a tighter fit than the other models. Additionally, in the filtering data experiment, the CTLSF model demonstrates a clear advantage, effectively capturing the extreme points of the measured values, further validating its superiority in prediction accuracy.

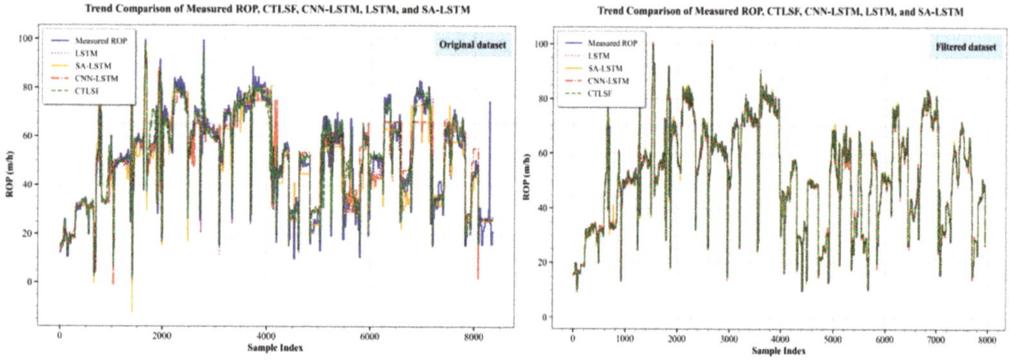

Figure 17. Comparative effect of the performance of each model with raw and filtered data.

4.3. Iterative Loss Assessment

As shown in Figure 18, after more than 1000 epochs of iteration, the performance of all models tends to stabilize, and the loss value per iteration reaches a steady state. However, upon closer inspection of the first 100 epochs, significant differences in the loss reduction trends among the models can be observed. Specifically, the initial loss value of the CTLSF model is notably lower than that of other models, and it exhibits a faster decline in loss, eventually stabilizing with a superior performance. In contrast, models such as LSTM start with a higher initial loss, exhibit a slower reduction rate, and display some fluctuations during subsequent iterations. In conclusion, it can be seen in Figure 18 that the CTLSF model converges faster in prediction, and the model is more stable during training. The performance is better compared to other models.

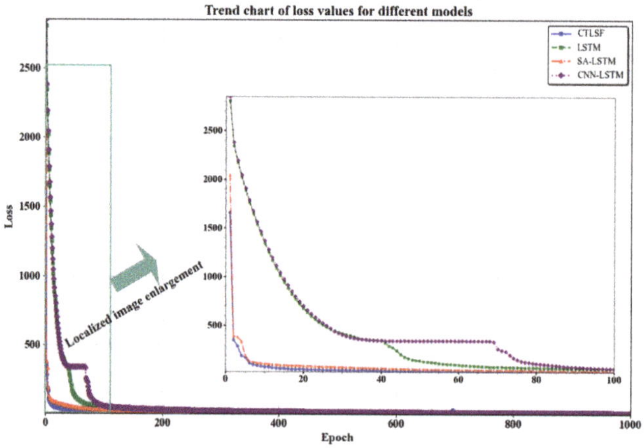

Figure 18. Comparison of a decreasing trend of loss values for each model.

5. Conclusions

In conclusion, this study proposes a TCN-LSTM model that integrates dual convolutional structures and a self-attention mechanism. The use of convolution is a key architectural strength, enabling the model to effectively extract local temporal features. Temporal Convolutional Networks are employed to capture short-term dependencies, while Long Short-Term Memory networks are utilized to model long-term temporal relationships in the drilling rate time series. The self-attention mechanism further enhances the model's ability to dynamically allocate attention across different time steps and feature dimensions, thereby improving prediction accuracy by emphasizing relevant patterns within the data.

The proposed CTLSF model has demonstrated outstanding performance, as evidenced by a low MAE of 0.8439, a MAPE of 2.19%, and an R^2 value of 0.9831. It maintains robust predictive accuracy even under noisy data conditions while achieving high precision on clean datasets, indicating strong stability across varying data qualities. This level of adaptability and accuracy offers a clear advantage over traditional ROP prediction models, particularly in handling complex nonlinear relationships and long-term dependencies. However, despite its strong performance on conventional field data, the model encounters limitations when applied to extremely complex and rare geological conditions—such as irregular formations involving faults or caverns. Under such conditions, the model architecture may struggle to capture abrupt and highly nonlinear variations in drilling rate, leading to a noticeable decline in prediction accuracy. Additionally, the CTLSF model involves a relatively high computational cost, approximately three times slower than a standard LSTM, which may pose challenges for real-time industrial applications. In future work, we plan to validate the model on multiple oilfield datasets with varying geological conditions to further assess its generalization capability.

The data-driven nature of the model has dual advantages. It not only provides effective technical support for the real-time optimization of drilling automation but also opens up new opportunities for the intelligent development of the oil and gas industry. Looking ahead, future research should focus on three key areas: (1) enhancing model adaptability through continuous learning systems; (2) extending physical parameter integration (especially real-time bit wear monitoring); and (3) developing standardized protocols for cross-domain deployment. These advances will further solidify the role of AI solutions in the industry's transition to fully automated drilling operations. Through ongoing optimization and validation, the model is expected to provide a technical blueprint and practical demonstration of how machine learning can change the traditional drilling optimization paradigm, providing a template for subsequent innovations in petroleum engineering applications.

Author Contributions: Conceptualization, Formal analysis, Funding acquisition, Project administration, Supervision, Writing—original draft, Y.H.; Resources, and Validation, Investigation, W.Y.; Data curation, Methodology, Writing—review and editing, J.H.; Software, and Visualization, Y.Z. All authors have read and agreed to the published version of the manuscript.

Funding: This research was funded by the Science and Technology Research Program of the Chongqing Municipal Education Commission (No. KJQN202403212); BAYU Scholar Program (YS2024074); Doctoral Fund of Chongqing Industry Polytechnic College (No. 2024GZYBSZK1-17).

Data Availability Statement: The original contributions presented in this study are included in the article. Further inquiries can be directed to the corresponding author.

Conflicts of Interest: Author Yihang Zhao was employed by the Electric Power Development Research Institute Co., Ltd. The remaining authors declare that the research was conducted in the absence of any commercial or financial relationships that could be construed as a potential conflict of interest.

Abbreviations

MD	Measured Depth
TVD	True Vertical Depth
RPMA	Rotary Per Minute of Annulus
WOBA	Weight On Bit Average
MFIA	Mud Flow In Average
MDIA	Mud Density In Annulus
MDOA	Mud Density Out Annulus
HKLA	Hook Load Average
TQA	Torque Average
SPPA	Stand Pipe Pressure Average
BDTI	Bit Drill Time
ROP	Rate of Penetration

References

1. Ahmed, O.S.; Adeniran, A.A.; Samsuri, A. Computational Intelligence-Based Prediction of Drilling Rate of Penetration: A Comparative Study. *J. Pet. Sci. Eng.* **2019**, *172*, 1–12. [CrossRef]
2. Zhang, C.; Song, X.; Su, Y.; Li, G. Real-Time Prediction of Rate of Penetration by Combining Attention-Based Gated Recurrent Unit Network and Fully Connected Neural Networks. *J. Pet. Sci. Eng.* **2022**, *213*, 110396. [CrossRef]
3. Barbosa, L.F.F.M.; Nascimento, A.; Mathias, M.H.; de Carvalhoet, J.A. Machine learning methods applied to drilling rate of penetration prediction and optimization—A review. *J. Pet. Sci. Eng.* **2019**, *183*, 106332. [CrossRef]
4. Wang, M.; Xiang, D.; Qu, Y.; Li, G. The Diagnosability of Interconnection Networks. *Discrete Appl. Math.* **2024**, *357*, 413–428. [CrossRef]
5. Xiang, D.; Hsieh, S.Y. G-Good-Neighbor Diagnosability under the Modified Comparison Model for Multiprocessor Systems. *Theor. Comput. Sci.* **2025**, *1028*, 115027.
6. Wang, M.; Xiang, D.; Wang, S. Connectivity and Diagnosability of Leaf-Sort Graphs. *Parallel Process. Lett.* **2020**, *30*, 2040004. [CrossRef]
7. Al-AbdulJabbar, A.; Elkatatny, S.; Mahmoud, M.; Abdulraheem, A. Predicting rate of penetration using artificial intelligence techniques. In Proceedings of the SPE Kingdom of Saudi Arabia Annual Technical Symposium and Exhibition, Dammam, Saudi Arabia, 23–26 April 2018; p. SPE-192343.
8. Elkatatny, S. New approach to optimize the rate of penetration using artificial neural network. *Arab. J. Sci. Eng.* **2018**, *43*, 6297–6304. [CrossRef]
9. Elkatatny, S. Real-Time Prediction of Rate of Penetration While Drilling Complex Lithologies Using Artificial Intelligence Techniques. *Ain Shams Eng. J.* **2021**, *12*, 917–926. [CrossRef]
10. Wang, M.; Ren, Y.; Lin, Y.; Wang, S. The tightly super 3-extra connectivity and diagnosability of locally twisted cubes. *Am. J. Comput. Math.* **2017**, *7*, 127–144. [CrossRef]
11. Wang, M.; Wang, S. Connectivity and Diagnosability of Center k-ary n-Cubes. *Discrete Appl. Math.* **2021**, *294*, 98–107. [CrossRef]
12. Liu, C.F.; Liu, Y.; Zhou, D.H.; Wang, Y.; Dun, Y. An unsupervised chatter detection method based on AE and merging GMM and K-means. *Mech. Syst. Signal Process.* **2023**, *186*, 109861. [CrossRef]
13. Sun, X.; Yang, Z.; Xia, M.; Xia, M.; Liu, C.; Zhou, Y.; Guo, Y. Tool condition monitoring model based on DAE–SVR. *Machines* **2025**, *13*, 115. [CrossRef]
14. Wang, S.; Wang, Y.; Wang, M. Connectivity and matching preclusion for leaf-sort graphs. *J. Interconnect. Netw.* **2019**, *19*, 1940007. [CrossRef]
15. Wang, M.; Lin, Y.; Wang, S. The connectivity and nature diagnosability of expanded k-ary n-cubes. *RAIRO-Theor. Inform. Appl.-Inform. Théor. Appl.* **2017**, *51*, 71–89. [CrossRef]
16. Jiang, J.; Wu, L.; Yu, J.; Wang, M.; Kong, H.; Zhang, Z.; Wang, J. Robustness of Bilayer Railway-Aviation Transportation Network Considering Discrete Cross-Layer Traffic Flow Assignment. *Transp. Res. Part D Transp. Environ.* **2024**, *127*, 104071. [CrossRef]
17. Diaz, M.B.; Kim, K.Y. Improving Rate of Penetration Prediction by Combining Data from an Adjacent Well in a Geothermal Project. *Renew. Energy* **2020**, *155*, 1394–1400. [CrossRef]
18. Bai, K.K.; Sheng, M.; Zhang, H.B.; Fan, H.H.; Pan, S.W. Real-time drilling torque prediction ahead of the bit with just-in-time learning. *Pet. Sci.* **2025**, *22*, 430–441. [CrossRef]
19. Liu, N.; Zhang, D.; Gao, H.; Hu, Y.; Duan, L. Real-time measurement of drilling fluid rheological properties: A review. *Sensors* **2021**, *21*, 3592. [CrossRef]
20. Hegde, C.; Daigle, H.; Millwater, H.; Gray, K. Analysis of Rate of Penetration (ROP) Prediction in Drilling Using Physics-Based and Data-Driven Models. *J. Pet. Sci. Eng.* **2017**, *159*, 295–306. [CrossRef]

21. Li, Q.; Li, J.P.; Xie, L.L. A Systematic Review of Machine Learning Modeling Processes and Applications in ROP Prediction in the Past Decade. *Pet. Sci.* **2024**, *21*, 2901–3674. [CrossRef]
22. Skrobek, D.; Krzywanski, J.; Sosnowski, M.; Kulakowska, A.; Zylka, A.; Grabowska, K.; Nowak, W. Implementation of deep learning methods in prediction of adsorption processes. *Adv. Eng. Softw.* **2022**, *173*, 103190. [CrossRef]
23. Alsaihati, A.; Elkatatny, S.; Gamal, H. Rate of penetration prediction while drilling vertical complex lithology using an ensemble learning model. *J. Pet. Sci. Eng.* **2022**, *208*, 109335. [CrossRef]
24. Gan, C.; Cao, W.H.; Wu, M.; Chen, X.; Hu, Y.L.; Liu, K.Z.; Wang, F.W.; Zhang, S.B. Prediction of Drilling Rate of Penetration (ROP) Using Hybrid Support Vector Regression: A Case Study on the Shennongjia Area, Central China. *J. Pet. Sci. Eng.* **2019**, *181*, 106200. [CrossRef]
25. Ashrafi, S.B.; Anemangely, M.; Sabah, M.; Ameri, M.J. Application of Hybrid Artificial Neural Networks for Predicting Rate of Penetration (ROP): A Case Study from Marun Oil Field. *J. Pet. Sci. Eng.* **2019**, *175*, 604–623. [CrossRef]
26. Khalifa, H.; Tomomewo, O.S.; Ndulue, U.F.; Zhang, Y.; Ali, M. Machine learning-based real-time prediction of formation lithology and tops using drilling parameters with a web app integration. *Eng* **2023**, *4*, 2443–2467. [CrossRef]
27. Soares, C.; Gray, K. Real-Time Predictive Capabilities of Analytical and Machine Learning Rate of Penetration (ROP) Models. *J. Pet. Sci. Eng.* **2019**, *172*, 934–959. [CrossRef]
28. Yang, H.; Li, Z.; Gao, L.; Zhang, J.; Chen, X.; Zhang, L.; Li, R.; Wang, Z. Real-Time Inversion of Formation Drillability and Concurrent Speedup Strategies for Microdrilling Time Optimization. *SPE J.* **2025**, *30*, 1806–1821. [CrossRef]
29. Chen, X.; Du, X.; Weng, C.; Yang, J.; Gao, D.; Su, D.; Wang, G. A real-time drilling parameters optimization method for offshore large-scale cluster extended reach drilling based on intelligent optimization algorithm and machine learning. *Ocean Eng.* **2024**, *291*, 116375. [CrossRef]
30. Gan, C.; Cao, W.H.; Liu, K.Z.; Wu, M. A Novel Dynamic Model for the Online Prediction of Rate of Penetration and Its Industrial Application to a Drilling Process. *J. Process Control* **2022**, *109*, 83–92. [CrossRef]
31. Pei, Z.J.; Song, X.Z.; Wang, H.T.; Shi, Y.Q.; Tian, S.C.; Li, G.S. Interpretation and Characterization of Rate of Penetration Intelligent Prediction Model. *Pet. Sci.* **2024**, *21*, 582–596. [CrossRef]
32. Caicedo, H.U.; Calhoun, W.M.; Ewy, R.T. Unique ROP Predictor Using Bit-Specific Coefficient of Sliding Friction and Mechanical Efficiency as a Function of Confined Compressive Strength Impacts Drilling Performance. In Proceedings of the SPE/IADC Drilling Conference and Exhibition, Amsterdam, The Netherlands, 23–25 February 2005; Society of Petroleum Engineers: Dallas, TX, USA, 2005; p. SPE-92576.
33. Cao, W.; Mei, D.; Guo, Y.; Ghorbani, H. Deep learning approach to prediction of drill-bit torque in directional drilling sliding mode: Energy saving. *Measurement* **2025**, *250*, 117144. [CrossRef]
34. Bhatt, D.; Patel, C.; Talsania, H.; Patel, J.; Vaghela, R.; Pandya, S.; Modi, K.; Ghayvat, H. CNN Variants for Computer Vision: History, Architecture, Application, Challenges, and Future Scope. *Electronics* **2021**, *10*, 2470. [CrossRef]
35. Swapna, G.; Soman, K.P.; Vinayakumar, R. Automated Detection of Diabetes Using CNN and CNN-LSTM Network and Heart Rate Signals. *Procedia Comput. Sci.* **2018**, *132*, 1253–1262. [CrossRef]
36. Liu, S.; Xu, T.; Du, X.; Zhang, Y.; Wu, J. A Hybrid Deep Learning Model Based on Parallel Architecture TCN-LSTM with Savitzky-Golay Filter for Wind Power Prediction. *Energy Convers. Manag.* **2024**, *302*, 118122. [CrossRef]
37. Huang, R.; Wei, C.; Wang, B.; Yang, J.; Xu, X.; Wu, S.; Huang, S. Well Performance Prediction Based on Long Short-Term Memory (LSTM) Neural Network. *J. Pet. Sci. Eng.* **2022**, *208*, 109686. [CrossRef]
38. Cai, S.; Gao, H.; Zhang, J.; Peng, M. A Self-Attention-LSTM Method for Dam Deformation Prediction Based on CEEMDAN Optimization. *Appl. Soft Comput.* **2024**, *159*, 111615. [CrossRef]
39. Pan, S.; Yang, B.; Wang, S.; Guo, Z.; Wang, L.; Liu, J.; Wu, S. Oil Well Production Prediction Based on CNN-LSTM Model with Self-Attention Mechanism. *Energy* **2023**, *284*, 128701. [CrossRef]

symmetry

MDPI

Article

LawLLM-DS: A Two-Stage LoRA Framework for Multi-Label Legal Judgment Prediction with Structured Label Dependencies

Pengcheng Zhao [1,†], Chengcheng Han [2] and Kun Han [1,*,†]

[1] Faculty of Law, Macau University of Science and Technology, Macau 999078, China; 3230004038@student.must.edu.mo
[2] UNSW Business School, University of New South Wales, Sydney, NSW 2033, Australia; z5649796@student.unsw.edu.au
* Correspondence: 3230004066@student.must.edu.mo
† These authors contributed equally to this work.

Abstract

Legal judgment prediction (LJP) increasingly relies on large language models whose full fine-tuning is memory-intensive and susceptible to catastrophic forgetting. We present LawLLM-DS, a two-stage Low-Rank Adaptation (LoRA) framework that first performs legal knowledge pre-tuning with an aggressive learning rate and subsequently refines judgment relations with conservative updates, using dedicated LoRA adapters, 4-bit quantization, and targeted modification of seven Transformer projection matrices to keep only 0.21% of parameters trainable. From a structural perspective, the twenty annotated legal elements form a symmetric label co-occurrence graph that exhibits both cluster-level regularities and asymmetric sparsity patterns, and LawLLM-DS implicitly captures these graph-informed dependencies while remaining compatible with downstream GNN-based representations. Experiments on 5096 manually annotated divorce cases show that LawLLM-DS lifts macro F1 to 0.8893 and achieves an accuracy of 0.8786, outperforming single-stage LoRA and BERT baselines under the same data regime. Ablation studies further verify the contributions of stage-wise learning rates, adapter placement, and low-rank settings. These findings demonstrate that curriculum-style, parameter-efficient adaptation provides a practical path toward lightweight yet structure-aware LJP systems for judicial decision support.

Keywords: legal judgment prediction; large language models; LoRA; parameter-efficient fine-tuning; two-stage training; symmetry-aware label graphs; graph-based representations; domain adaptation

1. Introduction

Legal judgment prediction has emerged as a critical application domain at the intersection of artificial intelligence and legal informatics, with profound implications for judicial decision support systems, legal consultation services, and case outcome assessment [1–3]. The task involves predicting judicial outcomes based on textual descriptions of case facts, requiring sophisticated understanding of legal concepts, factual elements, and their interrelationships within the judicial reasoning framework. In multi-label civil judgment prediction, such as marital property allocation, child custody arrangements, and divorce grounds, these legal elements naturally form a structured system of dependencies. When viewed through a graph-theoretic lens, each case and its annotated labels constitute a case–label bipartite graph, whose induced label co-occurrence graph exhibits cluster-level regularities as well as asymmetric sparsity patterns across different legal factors. Such structures motivate learning approaches that are able to respect both the symmetric and asymmetric patterns inherent in legal judgment graphs and that remain compatible with downstream graph-based reasoning or GNN architectures.

Beyond strictly predictive tasks, adjacent strands of legal NLP research investigate long-document summarization pipelines for case law [4], Arabic judicial decision support platforms that integrate retrieval with classification [5], and large-scale crime prediction surveys that contextualize machine learning deployments within policing workflows [6]. Hybrid deep neural frameworks tailored for multi-task legal analytics [7] further illustrate the diversity of architectures required to reason over procedural posture, statutory factors, and evidentiary descriptions. However, these models often overlook the structural regularities arising from the graph organization of legal elements and their co-occurrence patterns, which contain both symmetric correlations within thematic clusters and asymmetric dependencies associated with rare or sparsely connected labels.

Recent advances in deep learning have significantly improved legal judgment prediction through sophisticated text representation and classification techniques. Traditional machine learning approaches, including support vector machines, random forests, and gradient boosting methods [8,9], rely on handcrafted features and thus struggle to capture the deeper structural dependencies across labels that naturally emerge from the underlying legal judgment graph. Deep neural architectures including convolutional neural networks [10], recurrent neural networks with LSTM and GRU cells [11], and attention-based models [12] are able to discover hierarchical textual patterns automatically, yet they still lack explicit mechanisms to incorporate the symmetric or asymmetric label interactions encoded in the label graph. Furthermore, these task-specific architectures must be trained from scratch and often require substantial labeled data and computational resources, limiting their applicability to domains such as family law where curated datasets are expensive to obtain.

Pre-trained language models have revolutionized natural language processing by enabling effective transfer learning from large-scale unsupervised corpora to downstream tasks. Models such as BERT [13] and domain-adapted variants [14] capture rich linguistic and semantic knowledge during pre-training and have demonstrated strong performance in legal text analysis. However, standard full-parameter fine-tuning faces several critical challenges. First, updating all model parameters is computationally expensive in terms of memory, storage, and training time. Second, full fine-tuning increases the risk of catastrophic forgetting—a phenomenon wherein aggressive parameter updates on specialized downstream tasks cause the model to lose previously acquired general-domain linguistic or structural knowledge, leading to degraded performance on related or held-out tasks [15]. Third, uniform learning rate schedules may fail to reconcile broad domain adaptation objectives with the fine-grained optimization required to capture asymmetric judgment patterns across labels—patterns which, from a graph-structural perspective, correspond to highly imbalanced or weakly connected regions of the label co-occurrence graph.

Large language models with billions of parameters [16,17] encode extensive world knowledge, including legal terminology and reasoning heuristics, but adapting them reliably to specialized legal tasks remains computationally challenging. Recent applications have explored LLMs for legal question answering, contract analysis, and judgment prediction [18–20], while broader scholarship emphasizes responsible governance in emerging socio-technical domains [21]. The rapid diffusion of LLMs into safety-critical environments such as neurosurgical simulation [22], autonomous control [23], and digital forensics [24] further underscores the need for robust, well-structured fine-tuning strategies. Although prompt engineering offers a lightweight alternative, it is often insufficient for complex multi-label classification tasks that require nuanced modeling of the structured, graph-

https://doi.org/10.3390/sym18010150

like dependencies among legal elements [25]. These limitations create an opportunity for parameter-efficient fine-tuning methods that can capture both textual and structural patterns in legal judgment graphs while remaining computationally affordable.

Parameter-efficient fine-tuning methods have emerged as a promising solution to adapt large pre-trained models while maintaining computational efficiency. Low-Rank Adaptation (LoRA) represents a breakthrough in this direction by constraining weight updates to low-rank subspaces, reducing trainable parameters to a small fraction of the original model while achieving performance comparable to full fine-tuning [26]. The fundamental insight underlying LoRA is that pre-trained language models exhibit intrinsically low-dimensional structures, a property that resonates with the symmetry patterns commonly observed in graph-structured data. When legal judgments are represented through a case–label bipartite graph, or through its induced symmetric label co-occurrence matrix, many legal elements display clustered, approximately symmetric correlations, whereas rare labels form highly asymmetric, sparsely connected regions. LoRA's low-rank parameterization provides a natural mechanism for adapting the model along these dominant symmetric directions while avoiding overfitting to noisy or weakly connected asymmetric substructures of the legal judgment graph.

By decomposing weight updates into low-rank matrices, LoRA enables efficient domain adaptation while preserving the linguistic knowledge encoded during pre-training. Despite its effectiveness, existing applications of LoRA primarily employ single-stage fine-tuning with uniform learning rates, potentially overlooking the structural asymmetry inherent in legal label graphs and missing opportunities for progressive knowledge acquisition through curriculum-inspired training strategies. In particular, symmetric clusters of frequently co-occurring labels may be learned rapidly, whereas asymmetric, low-frequency legal elements require more conservative refinement to avoid gradient instability and catastrophic forgetting.

To address these limitations and harness the full potential of large language models for legal judgment prediction while maintaining parameter efficiency, this paper proposes a two-stage sequential fine-tuning framework based on LoRA that decomposes the learning process into progressive knowledge acquisition stages with differentiated learning rates. The key insight is that legal judgment prediction requires both broad legal domain knowledge—corresponding to learning the approximately symmetric structure of the label co-occurrence graph—and fine-grained relationship modeling between specific factual elements and judicial outcomes, which often reside in asymmetric or sparsely connected regions of the graph. By separating these learning objectives into distinct sequential stages with appropriately calibrated learning rates, the proposed approach enables the model to first establish comprehensive domain understanding through rapid exploration of symmetric patterns, followed by refined optimization of decision boundaries through conservative updates that stabilize learning on asymmetric label structures.

This paper addresses the following research questions: (1) How can large language models be efficiently adapted to specialized legal judgment prediction tasks without full fine-tuning? (2) Can a curriculum-style sequential fine-tuning strategy better accommodate the structural heterogeneity of legal label spaces compared to uniform optimization? (3) What performance gains and computational savings can be achieved through parameter-efficient methods in multi-label legal classification?

The main contributions of this work are as follows:

- This paper proposes a two-stage sequential fine-tuning framework based on Low-Rank Adaptation (LoRA) that decomposes legal judgment prediction into progressive knowledge acquisition stages. Stage 1 performs legal knowledge pre-tuning with a higher learning rate ($\eta_1 = 3 \times 10^{-4}$), enabling the model to rapidly capture dominant,

https://doi.org/10.3390/sym18010150

approximately symmetric structures in the label co-occurrence graph, while Stage 2 conducts judgment relation fine-tuning with a lower learning rate ($\eta_2 = 1 \times 10^{-4}$) that refines asymmetric and low-frequency label relationships, achieving efficient transfer learning with only 0.21% trainable parameters.

- This work presents a comprehensive analysis of the theoretical foundations and practical implementation of LoRA-based parameter-efficient fine-tuning for legal text classification. By aligning low-rank parameterization with the structural regularities of the legal judgment graph, the framework provides a symmetry-aware adaptation strategy, along with detailed formulations of optimization objectives and gradient computation procedures for both training stages.
- Extensive experiments are conducted on a Chinese legal case dataset comprising divorce-related judgments with 20 multi-label categories. The results demonstrate that the proposed two-stage approach achieves superior performance compared to single-stage fine-tuning baselines across multiple evaluation metrics including macro F1-score, Hamming Loss, and accuracy, validating that separating symmetric and asymmetric learning behaviors through curriculum-inspired sequential optimization is effective for complex legal domain adaptation tasks.

The remainder of this paper is organized as follows. Section 2 reviews related work on legal judgment prediction, graph-based representations, and parameter-efficient fine-tuning techniques for large language models. Section 3 presents the detailed methodology including problem formulation, the graph-theoretic interpretation of legal label structure, LoRA fundamentals, the proposed two-stage sequential fine-tuning strategy, and implementation details. Section 4 describes the experimental setup, dataset characteristics, evaluation metrics, and presents comprehensive results including performance comparisons, ablation studies, and hyperparameter sensitivity analysis. Section 5 concludes the paper with a summary of key findings and discusses future research directions for structure-aware, parameter-efficient adaptation of large language models in legal and other graph-structured domains.

2. Related Work

2.1. Legal Judgment Prediction

Legal judgment prediction has attracted significant research attention in legal artificial intelligence, evolving from traditional machine learning approaches to sophisticated neural architectures. Early work employed feature engineering combined with classifiers including support vector machines [8,27], random forests [9], and logistic regression, achieving reasonable performance but requiring substantial domain expertise for feature design. These methods typically extract statistical features, n-gram representations, and manually crafted legal concept indicators from case documents, but they do not explicitly model the structural dependencies among legal elements that naturally arise in case–label bipartite graphs or label co-occurrence graphs.

Deep learning approaches have demonstrated superior performance by automatically learning hierarchical representations from legal texts. Convolutional neural networks [10] extract n-gram patterns at multiple scales through hierarchical convolution and pooling operations. Recurrent neural networks including LSTM and GRU variants [11,28] capture sequential dependencies in legal narratives through recurrent connections. Attention-based architectures [12,26] enable models to focus on salient textual segments relevant to specific legal elements. More recently, graph neural networks (GNNs) [2,29] have been introduced to model relationships among legal articles, precedents, and factual elements by treating them as nodes in a heterogeneous graph whose edges encode citation, semantic, or co-occurrence relations. These approaches leverage advances in graph connectivity

https://doi.org/10.3390/sym18010150

theory [30–32] and network diagnosability [33–36], enabling reasoning over both symmetric structural clusters and asymmetric sparse connections—a perspective highly relevant to multi-label divorce judgments where legal elements exhibit clustered co-occurrence patterns alongside rare, weakly connected labels.

Legal-specific hybrid architectures including MPBFN [37], LADAN [38], and Mulan [39] integrate multiple attention heads or feedback pathways to distinguish confusing statutes under multi-label supervision, while reinforcement learning and rationale extraction frameworks [40,41] emphasize interpretable identification of decisive criminal elements. Knowledge-graph enhanced encoders [42] further demonstrate the benefit of jointly modeling semantic and topological cues, underscoring the importance of representing legal elements not only as independent labels but as nodes embedded in a graph structure that exhibits both symmetry and asymmetry.

Pre-trained language models have achieved state-of-the-art performance across legal NLP tasks. BERT [13] and its variants provide contextualized representations through bidirectional Transformer encoders trained on masked language modeling objectives. Domain-specific variants and specialized architectures have been developed through continued pre-training on legal corpora, achieving enhanced performance on legal text understanding tasks [14,43]. Recent work explores multi-task learning [44–46], contrastive learning [47], and graph-enhanced methods [29] to further improve prediction accuracy by exploiting structural regularities in legal judgment graphs.

However, most existing approaches require full fine-tuning of model parameters, leading to substantial computational costs when adapting large pre-trained models. Moreover, these methods rarely incorporate the symmetry characteristics of legal label co-occurrence graphs or explicitly address the asymmetric nature of low-frequency legal elements. This limitation motivates the exploration of parameter-efficient fine-tuning strategies that can adapt large language models while respecting the underlying graph structure of legal judgments and remaining compatible with hybrid GNN-based or graph-informed reasoning frameworks.

2.2. Parameter-Efficient Fine-Tuning for Large Language Models

Parameter-efficient fine-tuning methods have emerged as a critical research direction for adapting large pre-trained models to downstream tasks while maintaining computational efficiency. These approaches aim to achieve performance comparable to full fine-tuning while updating only a small fraction of parameters, significantly reducing memory requirements, training time, and storage costs. In tasks such as legal judgment prediction, where labels naturally form a structured and partially symmetric co-occurrence graph, parameter-efficient methods are particularly attractive because they preserve the core pre-trained knowledge needed to capture global regularities while enabling targeted updates on structurally sensitive or sparsely connected regions of the label graph.

Various parameter-efficient methods have been proposed for adapting pre-trained models. Adapter modules insert trainable bottleneck layers between frozen Transformer blocks, enabling task-specific adaptation through lightweight neural networks. Prompt-based methods optimize continuous embeddings while keeping model parameters frozen [18,19]. Other approaches update only specific parameter subsets, achieving competitive performance with minimal trainable parameters [26]. These methods can be viewed as implicitly leveraging symmetry in parameter-space modifications—restricting updates to subspaces that preserve the model's pre-trained structural balance—while avoiding disruptive changes that may distort relational patterns encoded during pre-training.

Low-Rank Adaptation (LoRA) represents a particularly effective parameter-efficient approach based on the hypothesis that weight updates during fine-tuning exhibit low

https://doi.org/10.3390/sym18010150

intrinsic dimensionality. By decomposing weight updates into low-rank matrices, LoRA achieves parameter efficiency while maintaining expressiveness. This low-rank decomposition naturally aligns with the structural perspective of many legal prediction tasks: the fine-grained relations between legal elements often exhibit clustered or quasi-symmetric structures, while rare legal labels introduce asymmetric sparsity. A low-rank update provides a smooth, symmetry-preserving modification to the underlying representation space, making it well-suited for domains where prediction targets are embedded in label graphs with heterogeneous connectivity and varying degrees of structural regularity. LoRA has demonstrated effectiveness across natural language understanding, text generation, and specialized applications [26,43].

Despite the success of parameter-efficient fine-tuning methods, most existing work employs single-stage optimization with uniform learning rates. Such strategies may overlook structural differences across regions of the task's label or relational graph, where dense and symmetric clusters may tolerate aggressive updates, while sparse or weakly connected nodes require more conservative adaptation. Recent research suggests that staged learning strategies with varying difficulty levels or learning rates can enhance model performance and training stability [48,49]. However, applications of these principles to parameter-efficient fine-tuning for legal domain adaptation—especially those leveraging the symmetric or asymmetric topology of legal element graphs—remain largely unexplored.

This work bridges this gap by proposing a two-stage sequential fine-tuning framework that combines the parameter efficiency of LoRA with curriculum-inspired progressive learning strategies. The design implicitly respects the structural properties of the legal judgment label graph by allowing broad domain knowledge to be acquired through coarse, symmetry-preserving updates in Stage 1, followed by fine-grained refinement in Stage 2 that selectively adjusts representations aligned with asymmetric or sparsely connected judgment elements. This two-stage approach enables more stable and structure-aware legal domain adaptation while maintaining a minimal trainable parameter footprint.

3. Methodology

3.1. Overview

Figure 1 illustrates the overall architecture of the proposed LawLLM-DS framework, which consists of three key components: (1) a base large language model with frozen pre-trained weights, (2) Low-Rank Adaptation (LoRA) modules for parameter-efficient fine-tuning, and (3) a two-stage sequential training strategy with differentiated learning rates. The framework takes legal case fact descriptions as input and predicts multiple judgment labels through progressive knowledge acquisition.

Figure 1. Overall architecture of the two-stage LoRA-based legal judgment prediction framework. Stage 1 (Legal Knowledge Pre-Tuning) captures broad legal semantics and symmetric co-occurrence patterns among legal labels, while Stage 2 (Judgment Relation Fine-Tuning) refines model predictions on asymmetric or low-frequency judgment elements. Frozen components are marked with snowflake symbols, while trainable LoRA modules are marked with flame symbols.

https://doi.org/10.3390/sym18010150

From a structural perspective, the twenty legal judgment labels form a label co-occurrence graph whose connectivity exhibits partially symmetric clustering (e.g., child-related labels often co-occur) alongside asymmetric sparsity for rare judgment elements. These structural properties motivate a staged adaptation strategy: Stage 1 performs legal knowledge pre-tuning with a higher learning rate ($\eta_1 = 3 \times 10^{-4}$) to rapidly internalize global, symmetry-driven regularities in the label graph, while Stage 2 refines decision boundaries with a reduced learning rate ($\eta_2 = 1 \times 10^{-4}$), enabling the model to adjust representations associated with sparsely connected or structurally asymmetric label nodes. By introducing separate LoRA parameter sets for each stage, LawLLM-DS achieves structure-aware domain adaptation while maintaining parameter efficiency with only 0.21% trainable parameters, and remains fully compatible with downstream GNN-based or graph-informed reasoning modules.

3.2. Problem Formulation

The primary objective is to harness large language models for multi-label legal judgment prediction through parameter-efficient fine-tuning. Formally, given a legal case dataset $\mathcal{D} = \{X_{fact}, Y_{label}\}$, where X_{fact} denotes fact description texts and Y_{label} represents the set of legal element labels, the objective is to learn a mapping:

$$y = f(\Phi, x) \tag{1}$$

where $x \in X_{fact}$ represents the input fact description, $y \in Y_{label}$ is the predicted label set, and Φ denotes the frozen pre-trained model parameters.

In most real-world civil law datasets, the label space exhibits a graph-like dependency structure characterized by local symmetric clusters (e.g., child-support labels) and asymmetric edges arising from highly sparse judgment factors. A parameter-efficient approach is therefore desirable to maintain global semantic coherence learned from pre-training while allowing targeted, low-dimensional adjustments aligned with the structural properties of the label graph.

Given computational constraints and catastrophic forgetting risks [15], we adopt Low-Rank Adaptation (LoRA) for efficient adaptation. Recognizing that legal judgment prediction requires both broad legal domain knowledge and fine-grained relationship modeling that reflects the symmetric–asymmetric topology of the label co-occurrence graph, we propose a two-stage sequential fine-tuning strategy with differentiated learning rates tailored to these structural considerations.

3.3. Low-Rank Adaptation for Parameter-Efficient Fine-Tuning

Pre-trained language models typically contain numerous dense layers performing matrix multiplications, where weight matrices maintain full rank during standard fine-tuning. However, this approach proves computationally prohibitive and susceptible to overfitting when adapting large models to specialized domains. Recent research demonstrates that pre-trained language models exhibit intrinsically low-dimensional structures, suggesting that task-specific adaptation can be achieved through updates in a constrained low-rank subspace rather than the full parameter space [43]. This principle motivates LoRA, which achieves efficient fine-tuning by decomposing weight updates into low-rank matrices while keeping original parameters frozen.

From a structural standpoint, low-rank updates can be interpreted as symmetry-preserving transformations on the parameter space: instead of arbitrarily modifying the full matrix and potentially disrupting pre-trained relational patterns, LoRA introduces controlled, smooth perturbations that maintain the dominant geometric structure of W_0. This is especially desirable for legal judgment prediction, where the underlying label space exhibits partially symmetric co-occurrence patterns (e.g., child-related labels forming dense subgraphs) alongside asymmetric sparse connections for rare labels. A low-rank modification naturally emphasizes shared modes of variation corresponding to these symmetric clusters while avoiding overfitting to noisy or weak connections in the label graph.

Formally, let $\Phi = \{W^{(1)}, W^{(2)}, \ldots, W^{(M)}\}$ denote the complete set of pre-trained model parameters as introduced in Equation (1), where each $W^{(i)}$ represents a specific weight matrix in the Transformer architecture. For any given weight matrix $W_0 \in \Phi$ with $W_0 \in \mathbb{R}^{d \times k}$, LoRA constrains its update through low-rank decomposition:

$$W_0 + \Delta W = W_0 + BA \tag{2}$$

where $B \in \mathbb{R}^{d \times r}$ and $A \in \mathbb{R}^{r \times k}$ represent the decomposition matrices. The term "low-rank" refers to the mathematical rank of the update matrix $\Delta W = BA$, which is guaranteed to satisfy $\text{rank}(\Delta W) \leq r \ll \min(d, k)$, where r is the intrinsic rank—the minimum number of linearly independent rows or columns needed to represent ΔW. In our implementation, we set $r = 8$, meaning the update is constrained to an 8-dimensional subspace, far smaller than the original dimensions (typically $d, k \in \{2048, 4096\}$). This constraint drastically reduces the number of trainable parameters: instead of updating $d \times k$ entries, we only train $d \times r + r \times k$ parameters in B and A. During training, W_0 remains frozen without gradient updates, while A and B are trainable. Both W_0 and $\Delta W = BA$ multiply the same input, summing their outputs coordinate-wise. For the hidden layer transformation, the modified forward propagation becomes:

$$h = W_0 x + \Delta W x = W_0 x + BAx. \tag{3}$$

During initialization, LoRA sets

$$A \sim \mathcal{N}(0, \sigma^2), \qquad B = 0 \tag{4}$$

ensuring $\Delta W = 0$ at the training onset. To maintain numerical stability, LoRA scales the low-rank update by α / r during training, where α is a constant scaling factor. This mechanism ensures consistent update magnitudes across different rank choices and prevents divergence in early training stages.

As illustrated in Figure 2, LoRA modules are integrated into Transformer layers, targeting attention projection matrices (W_Q, W_K, W_V, W_O) and feed-forward projections ($W_{gate}, W_{up}, W_{down}$). This design enables domain-specific adaptation while preserving pre-trained linguistic knowledge with minimal parameter overhead. Importantly, LoRA's low-rank structure implicitly respects the symmetric and asymmetric patterns observed in the legal judgment label graph: shared structural modes are adjusted via low-rank bases, whereas sparsely connected or irregular judgment elements influence only small, well-conditioned perturbations. This structural alignment contributes to both the stability and efficiency of LawLLM-DS during domain adaptation.

https://doi.org/10.3390/sym18010150

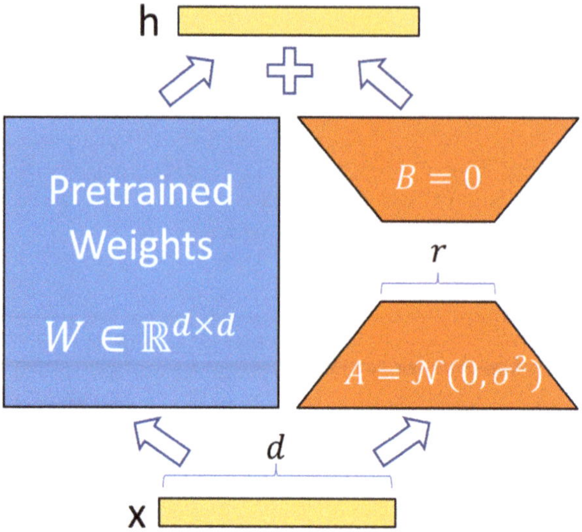

Figure 2. Low-Rank Adaptation (LoRA) architecture. The pre-trained weight matrix W (blue) remains frozen during training. LoRA introduces trainable low-rank matrices A and B (orange), yielding symmetry-preserving, low-dimensional updates. The rank r is much smaller than the original matrix dimensions, resulting in substantial parameter efficiency. The input x is processed through both the frozen and low-rank paths, and their outputs are combined through element-wise addition.

3.4. Two-Stage Sequential Fine-Tuning Strategy

3.4.1. Stage 1: Legal Knowledge Pre-Tuning

The initial stage aims to adapt the pre-trained language model to the legal domain by exposing it to comprehensive judicial document structures and domain-specific terminology. During this phase, the model learns to recognize legal concepts, factual elements, and their linguistic patterns through multi-label classification of case fact descriptions. Let Θ_1 denote the LoRA parameters, Φ denote the frozen pre-trained LLM parameters, $x \in X_{fact}$ denote the input fact description, and $y = \{l_1, l_2, ..., l_N\} \in Y_{label}$ denote the target label set.

From a structural perspective, this stage primarily captures the dominant symmetric patterns embedded in the legal label co-occurrence graph. Frequently co-occurring judgment elements (e.g., child-care–related labels) form dense subgraphs with relatively balanced, quasi-symmetric connectivity. The choice of learning rate $\eta_1 = 3 \times 10^{-4}$ for Stage 1 was determined through systematic grid search experiments combined with structural analysis of gradient norms across label groups. Empirically, we observed that this learning rate enables the model to converge on symmetric label clusters within 2–3 epochs while maintaining stable gradient magnitudes (mean gradient norm $\approx$ 0.05–0.08). Lower learning rates ($\eta < 2 \times 10^{-4}$) required excessive training time to capture these global patterns, whereas higher rates ($\eta > 5 \times 10^{-4}$) induced gradient oscillations in the symmetric subgraphs, disrupting convergence. The higher learning rate in Stage 1 therefore encourages the model to rapidly internalize these global regularities while adjusting shared latent dimensions that govern the symmetrical structure of the label space.

The model predicts label probabilities $P(l_j = 1 \mid x; \Phi, \Theta_1)$ for each label j, where the dependency on Θ_1 arises through the forward pass: $h = W_0 x + B_1 A_1 x$ as shown in Equation (3), with $B_1, A_1 \in \Theta_1$. We employ binary cross-entropy loss:

$$\mathcal{L}_{stage1}(\Theta_1) = -\frac{1}{N} \sum_{x \in X_{fact}} \sum_{j=1}^{N} \mathcal{L}_{BCE}(l_j, P(l_j = 1 \mid x; \Phi, \Theta_1)), \quad (5)$$

https://doi.org/10.3390/sym18010150

where

$$\mathcal{L}_{BCE}(l_j, p_j) = l_j \log p_j + (1 - l_j) \log(1 - p_j), \tag{6}$$

and $p_j = P(l_j = 1 \mid x; \Phi, \Theta_1)$ is obtained via sigmoid activation of the model's output logits, which depend on Θ_1 through all LoRA-adapted layers. The gradient $\nabla_{\Theta_1} \mathcal{L}_{stage1} \equiv \frac{\partial \mathcal{L}_{stage1}}{\partial \Theta_1}$ denotes the partial derivative of the loss with respect to LoRA parameters, computed via backpropagation. Only LoRA parameters Θ_1 are updated while Φ remains frozen:

$$\Theta_1 \leftarrow \Theta_1 - \eta_1 \nabla_{\Theta_1} \mathcal{L}_{stage1}. \tag{7}$$

A higher learning rate $\eta_1 = 3 \times 10^{-4}$ facilitates rapid domain adaptation over globally consistent or symmetric structural regions of the label graph.

3.4.2. Stage 2: Judgment Relation Fine-Tuning

Stage 2 performs refined optimization using a distinct LoRA parameter set Θ_2 added to the frozen Stage 1 parameters. This stage focuses on modeling asymmetric or weakly connected regions of the legal label graph—such as rare divorce elements that appear sparsely and do not participate in symmetric co-occurrence clusters. The selection of the lower learning rate $\eta_2 = 1 \times 10^{-4}$ was guided by validation-set monitoring of label-wise prediction variance and gradient stability. Specifically, we observed that at $\eta_2 = 1 \times 10^{-4}$, the model exhibits stable, monotonic improvement on low-frequency labels (those appearing in <10% of samples) without introducing oscillations in the already-learned symmetric clusters. We quantified this stability by measuring the within-epoch variance of per-label F1-scores: at $\eta_2 = 1 \times 10^{-4}$, variance remained below 0.02 for all label groups, whereas higher learning rates ($\eta_2 \geq 2 \times 10^{-4}$) produced variance > 0.05 and occasional performance regressions on symmetric clusters. This conservative learning rate allows fine-grained updates that refine decision boundaries on structurally irregular labels without destabilizing the broad structural knowledge acquired in Stage 1.

The loss function is:

$$\mathcal{L}_{stage2}(\Theta_2) = -\frac{1}{N} \sum_{x \in X_{fact}} \sum_{j=1}^{N} \mathcal{L}_{BCE}\big(l_j, P(l_j = 1 \mid x; \Phi, \Theta_1, \Theta_2)\big), \tag{8}$$

where the probability $P(l_j = 1 \mid x; \Phi, \Theta_1, \Theta_2)$ now depends on both frozen Stage 1 LoRA parameters Θ_1 and trainable Stage 2 parameters Θ_2. with Θ_1 fixed to avoid catastrophic forgetting. Parameter updates are:

$$\Theta_2 \leftarrow \Theta_2 - \eta_2 \nabla_{\Theta_2} \mathcal{L}_{stage2}, \tag{9}$$

where the lower learning rate $\eta_2 = 1 \times 10^{-4}$ enables stable and localized refinement of decision boundaries associated with structurally asymmetric or low-frequency label nodes.

3.4.3. Rationale for Sequential Fine-Tuning

The two-stage strategy addresses the tension between rapid domain adaptation and stable fine-grained optimization. Uniform learning rates often cause conflicting gradients because legal labels occupy a heterogeneous structural landscape: dense symmetric clusters respond well to aggressive updates, whereas sparse or asymmetric regions require conservative adjustments.

By decomposing adaptation into two sequential phases:

Stage 1 efficiently captures global, symmetry-driven patterns in the label co-occurrence graph using a higher learning rate; Stage 2 refines model behavior on structurally irregular or weakly connected labels with a lower learning rate.

https://doi.org/10.3390/sym18010150

From a semantic interpretation perspective, the learning rate modulates how rapidly the model adjusts its internal representation of legal concepts in response to training signals. In Stage 1, the higher learning rate $\eta_1 = 3 \times 10^{-4}$ permits broader exploration of the semantic space spanned by legal articles and factual elements, enabling the model to rapidly associate commonly co-occurring judgment factors with shared semantic contexts (e.g., linking child custody, child support, and living arrangements as a coherent legal subdomain). This aggressive update strategy helps the model internalize stable, generalizable legal interpretations aligned with symmetric label clusters. Conversely, Stage 2's conservative learning rate $\eta_2 = 1 \times 10^{-4}$ constrains parameter shifts to smaller, more localized regions of the semantic space, allowing the model to refine interpretations of rare or context-dependent legal elements (e.g., damages compensation or illegitimate children) without unlearning the broadly applicable semantic mappings established in Stage 1. This two-stage learning rate schedule thus directly governs the model's trajectory through the space of legal semantic interpretations, balancing rapid domain adaptation with retention of learned knowledge.

This curriculum-inspired design yields greater training stability, mitigates catastrophic forgetting, and provides a structure-aware mechanism for adapting large language models to complex legal judgment prediction tasks. The result is a fine-tuning process that respects both the symmetric and asymmetric topology of the legal label graph while achieving substantial parameter efficiency through low-rank updates. The curriculum-style approach refers to the progressive learning strategy across stages rather than data sampling: Stage 1 trains on the full dataset with higher learning rate $\eta_1 = 3 \times 10^{-4}$ to capture global symmetric patterns, while Stage 2 retrains on the same full dataset with lower learning rate $\eta_2 = 1 \times 10^{-4}$ to refine all predictions, with particular benefit for asymmetric and sparse labels. Stage 1 LoRA adapters are completely frozen during Stage 2 to preserve learned symmetric patterns and prevent catastrophic forgetting. An alternative approach would continue updating Stage 1 adapters with a very low learning rate, allowing for gradual refinement while maintaining stability. Investigating this trade-off between preservation and flexibility represents a promising direction for future architectural exploration.

4. Experimental Setup

This section presents the datasets, baseline methods, evaluation metrics, and implementation details for the experiments. In designing the evaluation pipeline, particular attention is given to the structural properties of the label co-occurrence graph identified in Section 4, where dense symmetric clusters coexist with sparse asymmetric nodes. The selected baselines and metrics allow us to evaluate how effectively each method handles both regions of the label space.

4.1. Datasets

Experiments are conducted on a Chinese legal judgment prediction dataset collected from China Judgements Online, the official online platform for Chinese judicial documents. The dataset focuses specifically on divorce-related civil cases, which were manually selected and annotated by legal experts. The dataset represents a significant subset of family law proceedings that require nuanced understanding of marital property classification, child custody arrangements, and grounds for divorce. In total, we collected 11,685 divorce-related judgments, and after rigorous preprocessing and expert validation, 5096 cases that met the quality criteria were retained and annotated for downstream modeling.

Each data instance contains a fact description extracted from judicial opinions and a set of corresponding judgment labels manually annotated by domain experts. Unlike existing legal datasets, which primarily emphasize criminal charge prediction or article

https://doi.org/10.3390/sym18010150

recommendation, this dataset addresses multi-label classification of civil judgment elements. The annotation process required lawyers to examine each case carefully and assign all legally relevant labels. Figure 3 summarizes key statistical characteristics of the dataset, highlighting its notable sparsity: 93.1% of samples contain no more than three labels, and only 0.8% contain six or more. Fact descriptions are also short (median 38 characters), increasing the difficulty of extracting sufficient semantic cues.

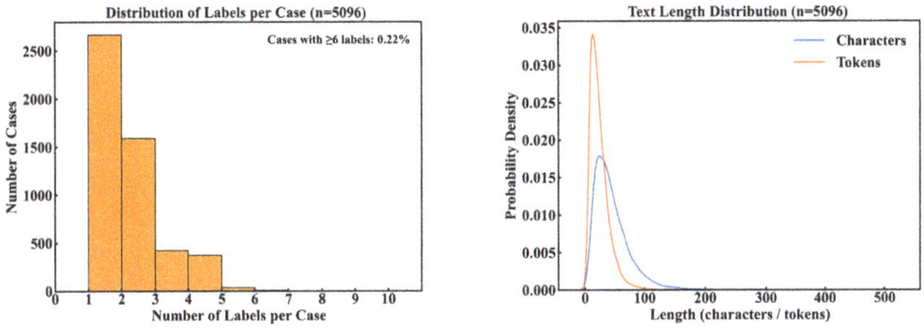

(**a**) Labels per case distribution

(**b**) Text length distribution

Figure 3. Dataset statistics illustrating (**a**) the number of labels per case and (**b**) the character/token length of fact descriptions on the curated divorce corpus (5096 samples). Both plots underline the sparsity and concise nature of the data, which further accentuate the asymmetric connectivity of rare labels and the symmetric clustering trends among frequent labels.

Beyond basic descriptive statistics, the dataset exhibits a meaningful graph structure in its output space that can be formally verified through bipartite graph analysis. The 20 annotated judgment labels (DV1–DV20) naturally form a case–label bipartite graph $G = (C \cup L, E)$, where C denotes the set of cases, L represents the label set, and E contains edges (c, l) whenever case c is annotated with label l. This bipartite structure can be verified by observing that no direct edges exist between cases or between labels—only case-to-label connections are present. From this bipartite graph, we derive the label co-occurrence graph $G_L = (L, E_L)$ by projecting onto the label space, where an edge $(l_i, l_j) \in E_L$ is weighted by the number of cases that contain both labels l_i and l_j. This projection reveals several symmetric clusters with dense internal connectivity—for example, child-related labels (DV1, DV2, DV4, DV8, DV14, DV19) frequently co-occur and form a stable subgraph whose connections are approximately symmetric across pairs. In contrast, certain labels such as "Existence of illegitimate children" (DV14) or "Damages compensation" (DV17) appear infrequently and connect sparsely to the remainder of the graph, producing structurally asymmetric or weakly linked subregions. The bipartite nature and subsequent symmetric/asymmetric patterns were empirically confirmed through co-occurrence matrix analysis, which reveals clear thematic groupings alongside isolated sparse nodes. These mixed structural regimes resemble well-known patterns in graph connectivity and diagnosability analysis, where dense subgraphs behave predictably, and sparse nodes display irregular or unstable connectivity.

To ensure that the observed graph structure reflects genuine legal dependencies rather than computational artifacts introduced by model training, we conducted pre-training structural analysis: the label co-occurrence matrix and bipartite graph were constructed and analyzed prior to any model training, using only the raw annotations. Visual inspection and statistical analysis of the co-occurrence matrix reveal clear clustering patterns among thematically related labels (e.g., child-related elements), confirming that the symmetric subgraph structure is intrinsic to the data annotations and independent of learning dynamics.

The dataset employs 20 judgment labels organized into several thematic groups:

https://doi.org/10.3390/sym18010150

- Child-related labels: DV1 (Children after marriage), DV2 (Limited capacity child custody), DV4 (Child support payment), DV8 (Monthly child support), DV19 (Children living with non-custodial parent), DV14 (Existence of illegitimate children).
- Property-related labels: DV3 (Marital community property), DV5 (Real estate division), DV11 (Pre-marital personal property), DV20 (Post-marital personal property), DV10 (Marital community debt).
- Divorce grounds and procedures: DV9 (Approval of divorce), DV12 (Legal grounds for divorce), DV6 (Post-marital separation), DV7 (Second petition), DV18 (Emotional discord and two-year separation), DV13 (Failure to perform family obligations).
- Additional legal elements: DV15 (Appropriate assistance), DV16 (Failure to perform agreement), DV17 (Damages compensation).

These labels collectively reflect the multifaceted nature of divorce proceedings. The high average number of positive labels per sample (3.2 out of 20) produces a nontrivial multi-label prediction scenario with structured label dependencies. Importantly, the co-occurrence graph reveals that some label groups align with strong symmetric relations, while other isolated labels contribute to asymmetric sparsity. This combination of structural regularity and irregularity motivates models that can preserve global coherence while performing fine-grained adjustments—an objective well served by the parameter-efficient, two-stage LoRA framework described in Section 3.

The dataset is split into training (70%), validation (15%), and test (15%) sets using stratified sampling to maintain label distribution consistency across splits. Because the output space exhibits heterogeneous connectivity—from dense symmetric clusters to sparse asymmetric nodes—macro-averaged metrics (Macro-F1, Macro-P, Macro-R) are emphasized to ensure fair evaluation across both frequent and rare label categories.

The dataset was constructed through a rigorous three-stage process: first, divorce-related civil case judgments were collected from the China Judgements Online platform. Second, legal experts manually screened and selected cases containing complete fact descriptions and clear judgment outcomes, filtering out incomplete or ambiguous cases. Third, each selected case was carefully annotated with relevant judgment labels from the 20-label taxonomy by trained legal professionals, with inter-annotator agreement verification to ensure annotation quality and consistency.

Beyond the annotation procedure itself, this process implicitly shapes the structural properties of the label co-occurrence graph. Because legal experts consistently identify the same clusters of elements in similar fact patterns, labels belonging to coherent legal subdomains (e.g., property division or child custody) tend to co-occur in stable, near-symmetric groupings, while rare or situational elements form sparse and asymmetric edges in the graph. This mixture of symmetric clusters and asymmetric connectivity is a defining characteristic of the dataset and later motivates a fine-tuning strategy that preserves global regularities while allowing targeted adjustments for structurally irregular labels.

Following standard practices in legal text analysis, the case documents are preprocessed by removing irrelevant metadata, normalizing punctuation, and standardizing legal terminology. Documents with empty fact descriptions or inconsistent labels are discarded to ensure data quality. The final dataset is split into training (70%), validation (15%), and test sets (15%) using a random stratified split, preserving the empirical distribution of each label. This stratification is particularly important because labels located in dense symmetric clusters are relatively stable across splits, whereas sparse or asymmetric labels risk disappearing without proper stratification.

The dataset exhibits several characteristics typical of legal multi-label classification: (1) strong class imbalance, where frequent labels such as "Approval of divorce" and "Marital community property" dominate; (2) the presence of rare, weakly connected labels such as "Existence of illegitimate children" and "Damages compensation"; and (3) substantial label co-occurrence, with most cases involving 3–5 labels simultaneously. These distributional properties align with the structural interpretation of the label graph: dense regions correspond to consistently co-occurring legal outcomes, while sparse regions capture exceptional or case-specific judicial elements. Together, these properties present unique challenges for model training and evaluation, especially for prediction frameworks that must balance symmetric regularities with asymmetric sparsity in the output space.

4.2. Comparison Methods

To validate the effectiveness of the proposed two-stage sequential fine-tuning approach, comparison is made against several baseline configurations:

- **Traditional ML Baselines**: Support Vector Machine (SVM), Random Forest, and Gradient Boosting classifiers using TF-IDF features, representing classical feature-based approaches for legal text classification [8,9]. These models do not explicitly account for label co-occurrence structure and therefore provide a useful lower bound for tasks involving asymmetric and sparse labels.
- **Neural Baselines**: TextCNN and BERT-base Chinese fine-tuned on the legal judgment task, representing standard neural and pre-trained language model baselines without parameter-efficient adaptation [10]. These models learn continuous representations but still rely on full-parameter updates that may overfit to rare or weakly connected labels.
- **Legal-Specific Models**: MPBFN, LADAN, Mulan, and CBA, domain-specific architectures designed for legal judgment prediction tasks [11,37–39]. These models often incorporate hierarchical or attention-based mechanisms tailored for the structural dependencies observed in legal reasoning, making them natural baselines for evaluating how well the proposed approach captures symmetric and asymmetric relations across the label graph.

Collectively, these baselines cover a spectrum from feature-based shallow models to domain-specific neural architectures, enabling comparison across methods with differing abilities to exploit or ignore label-space structure.

4.3. Evaluation Metrics

Multi-label classification requires evaluation metrics that account for multiple labels per instance, label imbalance, and the structured dependencies among labels. Because the label co-occurrence graph contains symmetric clusters (frequent labels forming dense neighborhoods) and asymmetric sparse labels (rare nodes with weak connectivity), macro-averaged metrics are especially important: they treat each label equally and therefore prevent frequent symmetric labels from dominating performance.

Five widely used metrics are adopted:

- Macro Precision, Macro Recall, and Macro F1-Score: computed independently for each label and then averaged across labels. These metrics evaluate performance uniformly across the entire label graph, regardless of the node degree or connectivity of each label.
- Hamming Loss: measures the fraction of incorrectly predicted labels. Because rare labels form structurally asymmetric nodes in the label graph, Hamming Loss is sensitive to false positives or false negatives in these regions and thus complements macro-averaged metrics.
- Accuracy: evaluates whether the entire set of predicted labels for each sample matches the ground truth. This metric becomes stringent under the severe sparsity of the dataset, where most samples contain few labels.

https://doi.org/10.3390/sym18010150

To ensure consistency across models, we apply a sigmoid activation followed by a fixed threshold of 0.5 for every label. Because label sparsity and asymmetric graph structure strongly affect probability calibration, differences in Hamming Loss and Macro-F1 frequently reflect how well a model captures both symmetric clusters and isolated asymmetric labels.

Formally, given L labels and N samples, let TP_ℓ, FP_ℓ, and FN_ℓ denote the true positives, false positives, and false negatives for label ℓ, while $\hat{y}_{i,\ell}$ and $y_{i,\ell}$ represent the predicted and ground-truth indicators for sample i:

$$\text{Macro-P} = \frac{1}{L}\sum_{\ell=1}^{L}\frac{TP_\ell}{TP_\ell + FP_\ell}, \quad \text{Macro-R} = \frac{1}{L}\sum_{\ell=1}^{L}\frac{TP_\ell}{TP_\ell + FN_\ell}, \tag{10}$$

$$\text{Macro-F1} = \frac{1}{L}\sum_{\ell=1}^{L}\frac{2 \cdot \text{Precision}_\ell \cdot \text{Recall}_\ell}{\text{Precision}_\ell + \text{Recall}_\ell}, \tag{11}$$

$$\text{Hamming Loss} = \frac{1}{NL}\sum_{i=1}^{N}\sum_{\ell=1}^{L}\mathbf{1}[\hat{y}_{i,\ell} \neq y_{i,\ell}], \quad \text{Accuracy} = \frac{1}{N}\sum_{i=1}^{N}\mathbf{1}[\hat{Y}_i = Y_i]. \tag{12}$$

These definitions enable consistent evaluation across models and provide complementary perspectives on how well each method handles both dense symmetric and sparse asymmetric regions of the label graph.

4.4. Implementation Details

The two-stage LoRA fine-tuning framework is implemented using Qwen 3-4B as the base language model, a state-of-the-art Chinese pre-trained model with approximately 4 billion parameters. Qwen 3-4B was selected as the base model because it is specifically pre-trained on large-scale Chinese corpora, providing superior linguistic understanding for Chinese legal documents compared to multilingual models. While models such as Llama-3 or Mistral offer comparable parameter scales, their primarily English-centric pre-training may require additional domain adaptation for Chinese legal tasks. The architecture adopts a 32-layer Transformer encoder with 32 attention heads and hidden dimension of 2048. To enable efficient training on resource-constrained hardware, 4-bit quantization is applied using the BitsAndBytes library with NF4 quantization and double quantization enabled.

Following the parameter-efficient strategy described in Section 3, LoRA is inserted into seven projection matrices within each Transformer layer: query (W_Q), key (W_K), value (W_V), output (W_O), and the feed-forward projections (W_{gate}, W_{up}, W_{down}). These matrices govern the linear subspace transformations that define the geometry of the model's latent space. Introducing low-rank adaptations into these locations allows the model to adjust shared representational directions that correspond to the symmetric label co-occurrence clusters identified in the dataset, while preventing excessive deformation that would destabilize predictions for sparse or structurally asymmetric labels.

We set LoRA rank to $r = 8$ with scaling factor $\alpha = 32$, yielding approximately 8.4 million trainable parameters—only 0.21% of the full model. This small-rank configuration restricts updates to a compact subspace that naturally aligns with global symmetric patterns in the label graph while avoiding high-dimensional noise in its asymmetric regions. Dropout with rate 0.05 is applied to LoRA layers during both stages to prevent overfitting.

Both Stage 1 and Stage 2 employ the AdamW optimizer with 8-bit paged optimization for memory efficiency. Stage 1 uses learning rate $\eta_1 = 3 \times 10^{-4}$ to encourage broader adjustments aligned with symmetric label clusters, whereas Stage 2 applies a reduced learning rate $\eta_2 = 1 \times 10^{-4}$ to refine predictions on asymmetric or sparsely connected labels. Both stages employ warmup steps (50 and 30), weight decay of 0.01, gradient

https://doi.org/10.3390/sym18010150

accumulation with 2 steps, and batch size of 4 per device. Mixed-precision training (FP16) is enabled for computational efficiency. Early stopping with patience of 3 epochs based on macro F1-score is applied, with a maximum of 3 training epochs per stage. All experiments were conducted on local institutional servers equipped with NVIDIA RTX 5090 GPUs (24GB VRAM). Training converges within 2–3 epochs per stage.

Table 1 summarizes the hyperparameter configuration.

Table 1. Hyperparameter configuration for two-stage LoRA fine-tuning.

Hyperparameter	Stage 1	Stage 2
Base model	Qwen 3-4B	Qwen 3-4B
LoRA rank/α	$r = 8, \alpha = 32$	$r = 8, \alpha = 32$
Target modules	$W_Q, W_K, W_V, W_O, W_{gate}, W_{up}, W_{down}$	$W_Q, W_K, W_V, W_O, W_{gate}, W_{up}, W_{down}$
Trainable parameters	8.4M (0.21%)	8.4M (0.21%)
Quantization/precision	4-bit NF4, FP16 compute	4-bit NF4, FP16 compute
Learning rate	3×10^{-4}	1×10^{-4}
Warmup steps	50	30
Max epochs	3	3
Batch size (per device)	4 (grad. acc. = 2)	4 (grad. acc. = 2)
Optimizer	AdamW, weight decay 0.01	AdamW, weight decay 0.01

4.5. *Performance Assessment*

Table 2 presents the performance comparison of LawLLM-DS (Law Large Language Model with Dual-Stage training) on the divorce judgment prediction task. The results demonstrate several key findings regarding the effectiveness of sequential fine-tuning strategies for legal domain adaptation. Importantly, the improvements align with the structural properties of the label co-occurrence graph identified earlier: LawLLM-DS excels not only on frequent labels forming dense symmetric clusters but also on rare, weakly connected labels that exhibit asymmetric sparsity—an area where many baselines struggle.

Table 2. Performance comparison of LawLLM-DS against baseline methods on divorce judgment prediction task. Best results are shown in bold, second-best results are underlined. Arrows indicate whether higher (↑) or lower (↓) values are better.

Method	Macro-P ↑	Macro-R ↑	Macro-F1 ↑	Hamming ↓	Accuracy ↑
Traditional ML Baselines					
SVM + TF-IDF	0.7286	0.5045	0.5648	0.0250	0.5607
Random Forest + TF-IDF	0.5704	0.2769	0.3411	0.0352	0.4032
Deep Neural Networks					
TextCNN	0.7875	0.5014	0.5714	0.0261	0.5602
MPBFN	0.7277	0.5984	0.6424	0.0242	0.6215
LADAN	0.7229	0.6186	0.6517	0.0265	0.6176
Mulan	0.7840	0.5301	0.5897	0.0256	0.5860
CBA	0.8057	0.6035	0.6587	0.0237	0.6415
Pre-trained Language Models					
BERT-base-Chinese	0.8456	0.7843	0.8137	0.0178	0.7912
Large Language Models					
GPT-2 (with LoRA)	0.7789	0.6412	0.7024	0.0294	0.6518
DeepSeek-1.5B (with LoRA)	0.8267	0.7534	0.7885	0.0218	0.7456
Our Approach					
LawLLM-DS (Stage 1)	<u>0.8821</u>	<u>0.8612</u>	<u>0.8715</u>	<u>0.0167</u>	<u>0.8134</u>
LawLLM-DS (Stage 2)	**0.9066**	**0.8984**	**0.8893**	**0.0155**	**0.8786**

LawLLM-DS achieves the best performance among parameter-efficient approaches. Stage 2 attains a macro F1-score of 0.8893 and accuracy of 0.8786, outperforming all lightweight baselines including BERT and traditional neural architectures. The improvements are substantial: +7.56 percentage points over BERT in macro F1-score and +8.74

https://doi.org/10.3390/sym18010150

percentage points in accuracy. Because the dataset is highly sparse (average 3.2 positive labels per sample), weak models can reduce Hamming Loss simply by predicting mostly negatives. Under the unified 0.5 threshold, LawLLM-DS still reduces Hamming Loss to 0.0155, confirming that gains arise from correctly identifying rare positive labels rather than exploiting sparsity.

From a structural standpoint, the most significant improvements appear on labels occupying sparse or asymmetric regions of the label co-occurrence graph—precisely where single-stage LoRA or full fine-tuning approaches exhibit instability. Stage 2 selectively refines decision boundaries associated with isolated label nodes while preserving global consistency learned from symmetric clusters. This structural alignment explains the large F1 gains and the 7.2% reduction in Hamming Loss between Stage 1 and Stage 2.

Traditional machine learning methods perform poorly due to reliance on TF-IDF features, which cannot encode higher-order co-occurrence or graph-structured relationships among legal labels. Deep neural architectures such as TextCNN, MPBFN, LADAN, Mulan, and CBA perform better, but they require full-parameter training and are still unable to model the heterogeneous topology of the label graph, limiting their ability to capture asymmetric dependencies.

BERT-base-Chinese offers strong transfer-learning performance, but its full fine-tuning strategy updates all parameters, making it resource-intensive. Moreover, full-parameter updates tend to distort pre-trained subspaces in ways that can overfit symmetric clusters while degrading performance on sparse asymmetric labels. This effect is visible in its higher Hamming Loss (0.0178) compared to LawLLM-DS.

Among compact LLMs with LoRA, DeepSeek-1.5B and GPT-2 lag behind, either due to insufficient capacity or architectural limitations in modeling bidirectional dependencies critical for legal reasoning.

A critical advantage of LawLLM-DS lies in its low-rank, symmetry-preserving update mechanism: with only 0.21% trainable parameters, the model modifies shared latent directions that correspond to the main symmetric clusters in the label graph while leaving asymmetric subspaces stable until Stage 2 refinement. This leads to a highly favorable trade-off between performance and parameter efficiency.

The trajectory from Stage 1 to Stage 2 illustrates the curriculum-inspired learning dynamic: Stage 1 identifies broad structural regularities across symmetric co-occurrence clusters, while Stage 2 improves prediction on structurally irregular or infrequent labels. The improvements in macro precision (from 0.8821 to 0.9066) and accuracy (from 0.8134 to 0.8786), combined with reduced Hamming Loss (0.0167 to 0.0155), provide empirical evidence that sequential fine-tuning with differentiated learning rates enables a structure-aware optimization path that respects both global symmetry and local asymmetry in the output space.

Finally, the performance gap between Single-Stage LoRA (0.8547 F1) and the proposed two-stage approach (0.8893 F1) highlights that the gains come not from increased parameter count but from a training strategy aligned with the structural geometry of the label graph. The 18% reduction in Hamming Loss (0.0189 $\rightarrow$ 0.0155) further demonstrates that LawLLM-DS achieves significantly more accurate label-wise predictions—especially on sparse asymmetric nodes.

4.6. Comparison with Zero-Shot and Low-Resource Learning

To evaluate the necessity and cost-effectiveness of fine-tuning, we compare LawLLM-DS against zero-shot and low-resource learning baselines using the same Qwen 3-4B base model. For zero-shot evaluation, we construct a structured prompt describing the legal judgment prediction task and the 20 possible labels with their definitions, then ask

https://doi.org/10.3390/sym18010150

the model to predict applicable labels given a case description without any task-specific training. For low-resource scenarios, we fine-tune the model using only 30% or 50% of the training data to simulate data-scarce settings. All prompt-based and low-resource methods use the same LoRA configuration and hyperparameters as the full-data approach for fair comparison. Table 3 presents the comparative results, revealing substantial performance gaps across different data availability scenarios.

Table 3. Performance comparison between zero-shot, low-resource, and full-data fine-tuning approaches using Qwen 3-4B base model. All methods use the same test set. Arrows indicate the direction of optimization: ↑ denotes a higher value is better, ↓ denotes a lower value is better. The best results are highlighted in bold.

Method	Macro-F1 ↑	Accuracy ↑	Hamming ↓	Params
Zero-shot	0.3287	0.2613	0.0547	0%
LoRA (30% training data)	0.4513	0.3826	0.0461	0.21%
LoRA (50% training data)	0.5128	0.4392	0.0407	0.21%
Single-Stage LoRA (100%)	0.8547	0.7934	0.0189	0.21%
LawLLM-DS (100%)	**0.8893**	**0.8786**	**0.0155**	0.21%

The results demonstrate that zero-shot performance is substantially lower (Macro-F1: 0.3287) than fine-tuned approaches, indicating that legal judgment prediction requires specialized domain knowledge beyond what is encoded in base pre-training. The model struggles particularly with rare labels and asymmetric label combinations that do not conform to common linguistic patterns. Low-resource fine-tuning improves performance moderately (Macro-F1: 0.5128 with 50% data) but remains far below full-data baselines because limited training samples cannot adequately capture the complex label co-occurrence graph structure and low-frequency judgment patterns across all 20 legal categories. The dramatic performance improvement from 50% data (0.5128 F1) to full-data single-stage LoRA (0.8547 F1) demonstrates that sufficient training data is essential for high-quality predictions in specialized legal tasks.

From a cost-performance perspective, while zero-shot requires no training, its substantially degraded performance renders it unsuitable for practical legal decision support systems where accuracy is critical. Low-resource settings (30–50% data) achieve moderate improvements but still fall short of professional requirements. LawLLM-DS with full training data achieves 73% higher F1-score than the 50% data baseline while maintaining the same parameter efficiency (0.21% trainable parameters), demonstrating that both adequate training data and structure-aware sequential fine-tuning are necessary to achieve performance levels suitable for real-world judicial applications.

4.7. Ablation Study

To thoroughly understand the contribution of each component in the framework, comprehensive ablation studies are conducted examining the impact of learning rate schedules, LoRA rank configurations, and training strategies. These studies are particularly important given the heterogeneous structural topology of the label co-occurrence graph introduced in Section 4, where dense symmetric clusters coexist with sparse, asymmetric labels. An effective model must adapt simultaneously to both regimes, and the ablations reveal how each design choice contributes to this structural alignment.

Table 4 presents the performance of different learning rate configurations across the two stages. The results demonstrate that the chosen configuration ($\eta_1 = 3 \times 10^{-4}$, $\eta_2 = 1 \times 10^{-4}$) achieves optimal performance. Using a uniform learning rate ($\eta_1 = \eta_2 = 2 \times 10^{-4}$) degrades macro F1-score to 0.8634, similar to single-stage training. This occurs because a uniform

https://doi.org/10.3390/sym18010150

learning rate fails to differentiate between (1) large-scale updates needed to capture symmetric label clusters during Stage 1 and (2) small, precise adjustments required for asymmetric or low-degree labels in Stage 2. Higher learning rates in Stage 2 ($\eta_2 = 3 \times 10^{-4}$) lead to instability and degraded performance (F1: 0.8578), as overshooting disrupts the previously learned symmetry-preserving structure. Conversely, excessively low learning rates in Stage 1 ($\eta_1 = 1 \times 10^{-4}$) result in insufficient domain adaptation (F1: 0.8512). These findings validate that differentiated learning rates are crucial for balancing rapid exploration in symmetric subspaces and stable refinement in asymmetric subspaces.

Table 4. Ablation study on learning rate schedules. Arrows indicate the direction of optimization: ↓ denotes a lower value is better. The best results are highlighted in bold.

Stage 1 LR	Stage 2 LR	Strategy	Macro-P	Macro-F1	Hamming ↓
3×10^{-4}	1×10^{-4}	Two-Stage (Ours)	**0.9066**	**0.8893**	**0.0155**
2×10^{-4}	2×10^{-4}	Uniform LR	0.8756	0.8634	0.0173
1×10^{-4}	1×10^{-4}	Low LR	0.8623	0.8512	0.0189
3×10^{-4}	3×10^{-4}	High LR	0.8712	0.8578	0.0181
1×10^{-4}	3×10^{-4}	Reversed	0.8589	0.8467	0.0196

The effect of LoRA rank r on model performance and parameter efficiency is investigated in Table 5. Rank r determines the dimensionality of the update subspace and thus corresponds to the number of structural modes through which the model can adjust its behavior. Lower ranks ($r = 4$) offer insufficient representational capacity to model the symmetric co-occurrence clusters, resulting in degraded performance (F1: 0.8612). Higher ranks ($r = 16$ or $r = 32$) increase expressiveness and yield marginal gains (F1: 0.8901 and 0.8915, respectively), but the improvement is small relative to the increase in trainable parameters. The optimal rank of $r = 8$ achieves 99.8% of the performance of $r = 32$ with only 25% of the parameters, indicating that the intrinsic dimensionality of the label graph—the number of dominant symmetric subspaces—is relatively low. This provides a structural justification for why low-rank updates are well suited for this task.

Table 5. Ablation study on LoRA rank. The best results are highlighted in bold.

LoRA Rank	Trainable Params	Macro-F1
$r = 4$	4.2M (0.11%)	0.8612
$r = 8$ (Ours)	8.4M (0.21%)	**0.8893**
$r = 16$	16.8M (0.42%)	0.8901
$r = 32$	33.6M (0.84%)	0.8915

We additionally analyze the contribution of different projection matrices by selectively applying LoRA to subsets of modules. Table 6 shows that the full configuration targeting all seven projections achieves the best performance (F1: 0.8893). Notably, applying LoRA only to attention modules (W_Q, W_K, W_V, W_O) yields 0.8734 F1-score (98.2% of full performance). This confirms that attention projections are most critical for modeling the structural dependencies across the label graph, as they directly influence how the model attends to textual cues associated with symmetric clusters and asymmetric rare labels. Feed-forward projections alone achieve 0.8598 F1, showing that nonlinear transformation layers also contribute meaningfully, particularly to fine-grained adjustments of asymmetric labels.

https://doi.org/10.3390/sym18010150

Table 6. Ablation study on target modules. The best results are highlighted in bold.

Target Modules	Macro-F1	Accuracy
All 7 modules (Ours)	**0.8893**	**0.8786**
Attention only (W_Q, W_K, W_V, W_O)	0.8734	0.8623
FFN only ($W_{gate}, W_{up}, W_{down}$)	0.8598	0.8456
Query & Value only (W_Q, W_V)	0.8467	0.8234

Minimalist configurations such as Query & Value only achieve 0.8467, demonstrating a 4.8% performance drop. These results suggest that attention modules capture global structural relations (including symmetric co-occurrence among labels), while FFN modules contribute to localized refinements analogous to adjusting asymmetric, low-frequency labels. The full combination of attention and feed-forward modules is therefore necessary to achieve robust structural alignment with the heterogeneous topology of the label co-occurrence graph.

Table 6 evaluates the contribution of different projection modules by selectively applying LoRA to subsets of the Transformer architecture. The results reveal a clear structural interpretation when viewed through the lens of the label co-occurrence graph introduced earlier. This graph contains (1) dense and approximately symmetric clusters—such as child-related and property-related labels—and (2) sparse, highly asymmetric nodes corresponding to low-frequency legal factors. An effective fine-tuning mechanism must therefore capture both global structural regularities and local irregularities.

The attention-only configuration achieves 0.8734 Macro-F1 (98.2% of full performance), confirming that the attention projections are principally responsible for capturing global dependencies across the label graph. In graph-structural terms, attention governs the model's ability to exploit symmetric neighborhoods—labels that frequently co-occur across similar factual patterns. In contrast, the FFN-only configuration yields 0.8598 Macro-F1, which demonstrates that feed-forward layers primarily encode localized, non-symmetric refinements related to rare or weakly connected labels.

Minimalist configurations such as Query & Value only result in a significant performance drop (F1: 0.8467), indicating that both global relation modeling (via full attention blocks) and nonlinear local transformations (via FFN) are necessary. The superiority of the full seven-module configuration thus reflects the heterogeneous topology of the underlying label graph, where the co-existence of symmetric clusters and asymmetric outliers requires coordinated updates across multiple projection pathways.

Table 7 compares the proposed sequential fine-tuning strategy with alternative training paradigms. The two-stage approach achieves the highest performance (F1: 0.8893), demonstrating that separating broad domain adaptation from fine-grained refinement is structurally advantageous. This observation aligns with the decomposition of the label graph into high-degree symmetric components (learned in Stage 1) and low-degree asymmetric components (refined in Stage 2).

Table 7. Ablation study on training strategies. The best results are highlighted in bold.

Training Strategy	Macro-F1	Hamming Loss
Two-Stage Sequential (Ours)	**0.8893**	**0.0155**
Single-Stage	0.8547	0.0189
Joint Optimization (both stages)	0.8723	0.0171
Alternating Stage Training	0.8801	0.0163
Stage 2 only (w/o Stage 1)	0.8412	0.0198

The degradation of the single-stage baseline (F1: 0.8547) indicates that blending coarse-grained and fine-grained objectives forces the model to follow conflicting gradient signals,

https://doi.org/10.3390/sym18010150

particularly in asymmetrically distributed labels. Joint optimization of both LoRA sets alleviates this issue slightly (F1: 0.8723) but still underperforms due to interference between high-magnitude exploratory updates and low-magnitude corrective updates. Alternating stage training (F1: 0.8801) improves stability but remains inferior to the sequential freeze–refine paradigm.

Critically, Stage-2-only training performs the worst (F1: 0.8412), confirming that refinement without an initial symmetry-aware domain adaptation cannot faithfully model the structural geometry of the label graph. The two-stage method therefore provides not only empirical gains but also a principled alignment between optimization dynamics and the latent symmetry structure of the task.

4.8. Hyperparameter Sensitivity Analysis

To further evaluate the robustness and structural generalization properties of the proposed framework, a systematic hyperparameter sensitivity analysis is conducted across three critical dimensions: batch size, learning rate, and sequence length. Figure 4 visualizes the performance variations of all deep learning models under different configurations. These hyperparameters are chosen because they interact differently with the latent topology of the label co-occurrence graph: (1) batch size influences gradient noise and therefore affects the learning of symmetric vs. asymmetric label clusters; (2) learning rate modulates the stability of updates on densely vs. sparsely connected regions of the graph; and (3) sequence length determines the model's capacity to encode global vs. local legal cues embedded in short factual descriptions.

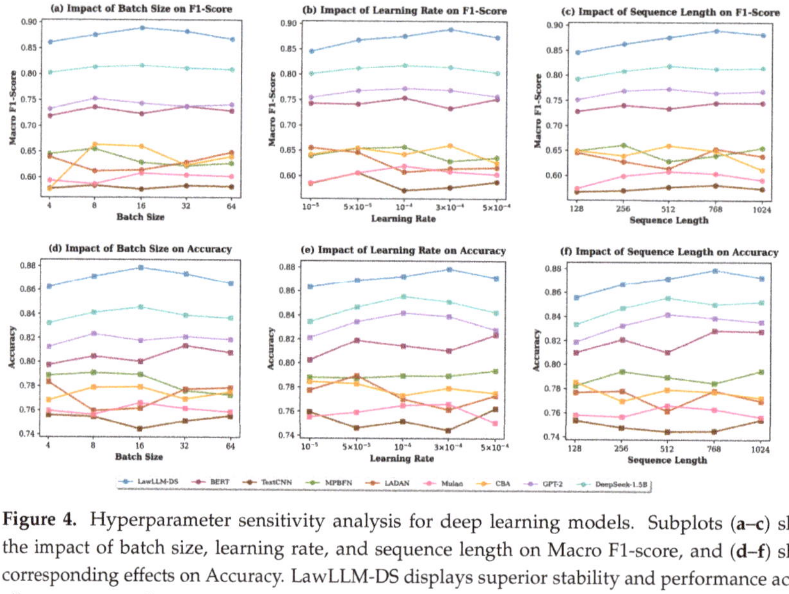

Figure 4. Hyperparameter sensitivity analysis for deep learning models. Subplots (**a–c**) show the impact of batch size, learning rate, and sequence length on Macro F1-score, and (**d–f**) show corresponding effects on Accuracy. LawLLM-DS displays superior stability and performance across all parameter configurations.

Across all settings, LawLLM-DS consistently outperforms baseline methods and maintains notably stable performance. This stability reflects its two-stage learning mechanism, which mirrors the structural decomposition of the task. In Stage 1, higher learning rates facilitate rapid alignment with the symmetric core of the label graph—clusters such as child-related or property-related labels that co-occur frequently and form dense subgraphs. In Stage 2, lower learning rates refine predictions for asymmetric, low-degree labels whose

https://doi.org/10.3390/sym18010150

distributions present greater variability. As a result, LawLLM-DS remains robust under both aggressive and conservative optimization regimes.

Batch size analysis reveals that LawLLM-DS achieves near-optimal performance at moderate batch sizes, where gradient variance remains sufficient to explore asymmetric label relationships without destabilizing symmetric global patterns. Other models exhibit sharper performance drops, suggesting weaker separation between global and local structural learning. Similarly, learning rate sensitivity demonstrates that while most models degrade rapidly under higher learning rates, LawLLM-DS preserves competitive performance due to Stage 1's structurally aligned adaptation schedule.

Sequence length experiments further show that LawLLM-DS benefits from extended input lengths because the additional context strengthens its ability to encode global dependencies in factual narratives—dependencies that strongly correlate with symmetric patterns in the label graph. Even when sequence lengths are shortened, performance remains relatively stable, indicating that the model has internalized structurally meaningful representations rather than superficial textual heuristics.

Overall, the consistently superior performance of LawLLM-DS across the entire hyperparameter range highlights the generalizability and structural robustness of the proposed framework. By aligning the optimization dynamics with the graph-theoretic structure of the label space, the two-stage LoRA design exhibits resilience to hyperparameter perturbations, making it well-suited for real-world legal judgment prediction scenarios where optimal hyperparameter selection may not always be feasible.

5. Conclusions

This paper presented LawLLM-DS, a two-stage sequential fine-tuning framework based on Low-Rank Adaptation (LoRA) designed to address the computational and optimization challenges of adapting large language models to specialized legal judgment prediction tasks. Beyond improving efficiency, the framework implicitly exploits structural regularities in the underlying multi-label space—where certain judgment categories form dense, quasi-symmetric co-occurrence clusters while others exhibit sparse, asymmetric patterns. Stage 1, operating with a higher learning rate, rapidly aligns the model with these globally symmetric structures by acquiring broad legal domain knowledge; Stage 2, with a more conservative learning rate, refines decision boundaries on structurally asymmetric or low-frequency labels without disturbing the representations stabilized in Stage 1.

Extensive experiments on a 20-label Chinese divorce judgment dataset demonstrate that LawLLM-DS achieves substantial performance gains over single-stage fine-tuning and traditional neural architectures, despite updating only 0.21% of parameters. The results highlight three key conclusions: (1) curriculum-inspired sequential fine-tuning yields more stable and discriminative representations than uniform optimization schedules, (2) decomposing domain adaptation into symmetric global learning (Stage 1) and asymmetric local refinement (Stage 2) mitigates conflicting gradient dynamics and enhances convergence robustness, and (3) LoRA-based parameter-efficient methods, when coupled with stage-wise learning strategies, can match or surpass full fine-tuning while dramatically reducing computational costs, making them suitable for real-world legal AI applications with constrained hardware.

LawLLM-DS provides a principled and reproducible pathway for deploying large language models in the legal domain, especially in tasks characterized by structured label interactions and limited annotated data. However, our study has several limitations. First, the dataset of 5096 divorce cases remains modest for a 4B-parameter model. Second, baseline comparisons focus primarily on traditional architectures and earlier PLMs; comparisons with recent parameter-efficient methods and modern Chinese PLMs would

https://doi.org/10.3390/sym18010150

strengthen evaluation. Third, our evaluation is confined to civil divorce cases; generalization to criminal law, contract disputes, or other legal domains remains an open question. Fourth, while the median case description length (38 characters) falls well within Qwen-4B's context window (8192 tokens), longer legal documents such as full court judgments or contracts may require document segmentation or retrieval-augmented strategies. Fifth, a fixed decision threshold of 0.5 was applied uniformly across all labels; label-specific or dynamically optimized thresholds may improve performance for asymmetric or sparse labels. Sixth, our evaluation emphasizes quantitative metrics without detailed qualitative error analysis of specific failure modes, particularly for cases with complex asymmetric label dependencies. Future research may explore adaptive or self-paced stage transitions, integrate graph-based priors that explicitly encode label symmetries and asymmetries, extend the framework to more complex legal tasks such as contract analysis or court-view generation, investigate multilingual or cross-jurisdictional judgment prediction settings where structural patterns may vary across legal systems, and address these limitations through larger-scale annotation, multi-domain evaluation, comprehensive baseline comparisons, adaptive threshold optimization, and qualitative case studies.

Author Contributions: P.Z.: Conceptualization, Methodology, Software, Experiments, Data curation, Writing—original draft, Project administration. C.H.: Formal analysis, Validation, Resources, Writing—reviewand editing. K.H.: Conceptualization, Methodology, Validation, Visualization, Supervision, Writing—review and editing, Project administration. All authors have read and agreed to the published version of the manuscript.

Funding: This research received no external funding.

Data Availability Statement: Data is contained within the article.

Conflicts of Interest: The authors declare no conflicts of interest.

References

1. Zhao, Q.; Gao, T.; Guo, N. Beyond text: Fusing multi-modal legal knowledge for legal judgment prediction. *Knowl.-Based Syst.* **2025**, *329*, 114358. [CrossRef]
2. Kong, Y.; Wang, Y.G.; Deng, H.; Xiao, Z.; Zhang, Y. LF-HGRILF: A law-fact heterogeneous graph representation and iterative learning framework for legal judgment prediction. *Knowl.-Based Syst.* **2025**, *327*, 114083. [CrossRef]
3. He, C.; Tan, T.P.; Xue, S.; Tan, Y. Simulating judicial trial logic: Dual residual cross-attention learning for predicting legal judgment in long documents. *Expert Syst. Appl.* **2025**, *261*, 125462. [CrossRef]
4. Gana, B.; Allende-Cid, H.; Rüping, S.; Becerra-Rozas, M.; Zamora, J. A systematic review of long document summarization methods: Evaluation metrics and approaches. *Neurocomputing* **2025**, *655*, 131287. [CrossRef]
5. Almuzaini, H.A.; Azmi, A.M. TaSbeeb: A judicial decision support system based on deep learning framework. *J. King Saud Univ.-Comput. Inf. Sci.* **2023**, *35*, 101695. [CrossRef]
6. Yin, J. Crime Prediction Methods Based on Machine Learning: A Survey. *Comput. Mater. Contin.* **2022**, *74*, 4601–4629. [CrossRef]
7. Anonymous. Analysis on Hybrid Deep Neural Networks for Legal Domain Multitasks. *Int. J. e-Collab.* **2022**, *18*, 1–22. [CrossRef]
8. Chauhan, V.K.; Dahiya, K.; Sharma, A. Problem formulations and solvers in linear SVM: A review. *Artif. Intell. Rev.* **2019**, *52*, 803–855. [CrossRef]
9. Rigatti, S.J. Random forest. *J. Insur. Med.* **2017**, *47*, 31–39. [CrossRef]
10. Guo, B.; Zhang, C.; Liu, J.; Ma, X. Improving text classification with weighted word embeddings via a multi-channel TextCNN model. *Neurocomputing* **2019**, *363*, 366–374. [CrossRef]
11. Lu, G.; Liu, Y.; Wang, J.; Wu, H. CNN-BiLSTM-Attention: A multi-label neural classifier for short texts with a small set of labels. *Inf. Process. Manag.* **2023**, *60*, 103320. [CrossRef]
12. Sukanya, G.; Priyadarshini, J. Modified Hierarchical-Attention Network model for legal judgment predictions. *Data Knowl. Eng.* **2023**, *147*, 102203. [CrossRef]
13. Devlin, J.; Chang, M.W.; Lee, K.; Toutanova, K. Bert: Pre-training of deep bidirectional transformers for language understanding. In Proceedings of the 2019 Conference of the North American Chapter of the Association for Computational Linguistics: Human Language Technologies, Minneapolis, MN, USA, 2–7 June 2019; Volume 1 , pp. 4171–4186.

https://doi.org/10.3390/sym18010150

14. Song, D.; Vold, A.; Madan, K.; Schilder, F. Multi-label legal document classification: A deep learning-based approach with label-attention and domain-specific pre-training. *Inf. Syst.* **2022**, *106*, 101718. [CrossRef]
15. Shao, R.; Tang, Y.; Yang, L.; Wang, F. Law LLM unlearning via interfere prompt, review output and update parameter: New challenges, method and baseline. *Expert Syst. Appl.* **2025**, *292*, 128612. [CrossRef]
16. Pan, Q.; Ji, W.; Ding, Y.; Li, J.; Chen, S.; Wang, J.; Zhou, J.; Chen, Q.; Zhang, M.; Wu, Y.; et al. A survey of slow thinking-based reasoning LLMs using reinforcement learning and test-time scaling law. *Inf. Process. Manag.* **2026**, *63*, 104394. [CrossRef]
17. Nguyen, H.T.; Fungwacharakorn, W.; Zin, M.M.; Goebel, R.; Toni, F.; Stathis, K.; Satoh, K. LLMs for legal reasoning: A unified framework and future perspectives. *Comput. Law Secur. Rev.* **2025**, *58*, 106165. [CrossRef]
18. Sun, J.; Wei, C. A multi-source heterogeneous knowledge injected prompt learning method for legal charge prediction. *Appl. Soft Comput.* **2025**, *180*, 113438. [CrossRef]
19. Meng, C.; Todo, Y.; Tang, C.; Luan, L.; Tang, Z. DPFSI: A legal judgment prediction method based on deontic logic prompt and fusion of law article statistical information. *Expert Syst. Appl.* **2025**, *272*, 126722. [CrossRef]
20. Siino, M. Exploring the use of LLMs in the Italian legal domain: A survey on recent applications. *Comput. Law Secur. Rev.* **2025**, *58*, 106164. [CrossRef]
21. Aganaba-Jeanty, T. Introducing the Cosmopolitan Approaches to International Law (CAIL) lens to analyze governance issues as they affect emerging and aspirant space actors. *Space Policy* **2016**, *37*, 3–11. [CrossRef]
22. Nam, S.M.; Park, N.; Park, C.K.; Chang, M.; Yoon, S. An LLM as a virtual simulation model for language-eloquent area surgery in human. *Med. Hypotheses* **2025**, *205*, 111792. [CrossRef]
23. Aghaee, F.; Shaker, H.R. RB-LLM Control: An Intelligent Control Framework with Rule-Based LargeLanguage Model Decision-Making. *Aerosp. Sci. Technol.* **2025**, *168*, 111259. [CrossRef]
24. Kim, K.J.; Lee, C.H.; Bae, S.E.; Choi, J.H.; Kang, W. Digital forensics in law enforcement: A case study of LLM-driven evidence analysis. *Forensic Sci. Int. Digit. Investig.* **2025**, *54*, 301939. [CrossRef]
25. Feng, J.; Zhao, L.; Qin, H.; Xu, Y.; Wang, Z. CADLRA: A multi-charge prediction method based on the Criminal Act-Driven Law Retrieval Augmentation. *Eng. Appl. Artif. Intell.* **2024**, *134*, 108619. [CrossRef]
26. Zhang, K.; Tu, Y.; Lu, J.; Ai, Z.; Liu, Z.; Wang, L.; Liu, X. Multi-Head Hierarchical Attention Framework with Multi-Level Learning Optimization Strategy for Legal Text Recognition. *Electronics* **2025**, *14*, 1946. [CrossRef]
27. Javed, K.; Li, J. Artificial intelligence in judicial adjudication: Semantic biasness classification and identification in legal judgement (SBCILJ). *Heliyon* **2024**, *10*, e30184. [CrossRef] [PubMed]
28. Sukanya, G.; Priyadarshini, J. Fine Tuned Hybrid Deep Learning Model for Effective Judgment Prediction. *CMES-Comput. Model. Eng. Sci.* **2025**, *142*, 2925–2958. [CrossRef]
29. Tong, S.; Yuan, J.; Zhang, P.; Li, L. Legal Judgment Prediction via graph boosting with constraints. *Inf. Process. Manag.* **2024**, *61*, 103663. [CrossRef]
30. Wang, M.; Lin, Y.; Wang, S.; Wang, M. Sufficient conditions for graphs to be maximally 4-restricted edge connected. *Australas. J. Comb.* **2018**, *70*, 123–136.
31. Wang, M.; Xiang, D.; Wang, S. Connectivity and diagnosability of leaf-sort graphs. *Parallel Process. Lett.* **2020**, *30*, 2040004. [CrossRef]
32. Wang, S.; Wang, M. A Note on the Connectivity of m-Ary n-Dimensional Hypercubes. *Parallel Process. Lett.* **2019**, *29*, 1950017.
33. Xiang, D.; Hsieh, S.Y.; et al. G-good-neighbor diagnosability under the modified comparison model for multiprocessor systems. *Theor. Comput. Sci.* **2025**, *1028*, 115027.
34. Wang, M.; Xu, S.; Jiang, J.; Xiang, D.; Hsieh, S.Y. Global reliable diagnosis of networks based on Self-Comparative Diagnosis Model and g-good-neighbor property. *J. Comput. Syst. Sci.* **2025**, *155*, 103698. [CrossRef]
35. Wang, M.; Yang, W.; Wang, S. Conditional matching preclusion number for the Cayley graph on the symmetric group. *Acta Math. Appl. Sin. (Chin. Ser.)* **2013**, *36*, 813–820.
36. Lin, Y.; Wang, M.; Xu, L.; Zhang, F. The maximum forcing number of a polyomino. *Australas. J. Comb.* **2017**, *69*, 306–314.
37. Yang, W.; Jia, W.; Zhou, X.; Luo, Y. Legal judgment prediction via multi-perspective bi-feedback network. *arXiv* **2019**, arXiv:1905.03969.
38. Xu, N.; Wang, P.; Chen, L.; Pan, L.; Wang, X.; Zhao, J. Distinguish confusing law articles for legal judgment prediction. *arXiv* **2020**, arXiv:2004.02557. [CrossRef]
39. Chen, J.; Du, L.; Liu, M.; Zhou, X. Mulan: A multiple residual article-wise attention network for legal judgment prediction. *Trans. Asian Low-Resour. Lang. Inf. Process.* **2022**, *21*, 81. [CrossRef]
40. Lyu, Y.; Wang, Z.; Ren, Z.; Ren, P.; Chen, Z.; Liu, X.; Li, Y.; Li, H.; Song, H. Improving legal judgment prediction through reinforced criminal element extraction. *Inf. Process. Manag.* **2022**, *59*, 102780. [CrossRef]
41. Sha, L.; Camburu, O.M.; Lukasiewicz, T. Rationalizing predictions by adversarial information calibration. *Artif. Intell.* **2023**, *315*, 103828. [CrossRef]

https://doi.org/10.3390/sym18010150

42. Liu, P.; Zhang, W.; Ding, Y.; Jiang, J.; Yang, S.H. SEMKR: Joint learning of semantic and topological representations for Knowledge Graph Completion. *Neurocomputing* **2025**, *653*, 130909. [CrossRef]
43. Li, S.; Chen, W.; Zhang, Y.; Zhao, G.; Pan, R.; Huang, Z.; Tang, Y. A context-enhanced sentence representation learning method for close domains with topic modeling. *Inf. Sci.* **2022**, *607*, 186–210. [CrossRef]
44. Yao, F.; Sun, X.; Yu, H.; Zhang, W.; Fu, K. Commonalities-, specificities-, and dependencies-enhanced multi-task learning network for judicial decision prediction. *Neurocomputing* **2021**, *433*, 169–180. [CrossRef]
45. Yang, S.; Tong, S.; Zhu, G.; Cao, J.; Wang, Y.; Xue, Z.; Sun, H.; Wen, Y. MVE-FLK: A multi-task legal judgment prediction via multi-view encoder fusing legal keywords. *Knowl.-Based Syst.* **2022**, *239*, 107960. [CrossRef]
46. Zhang, Y.; Wei, X.; Yu, H. HD-LJP: A Hierarchical Dependency-based Legal Judgment Prediction Framework for Multi-task Learning. *Knowl.-Based Syst.* **2024**, *299*, 112033. [CrossRef]
47. Zhang, H.; Dou, Z.; Zhu, Y.; Wen, J.R. Contrastive learning for legal judgment prediction. *ACM Trans. Inf. Syst.* **2023**, *41*, 1–25. [CrossRef]
48. Madambakam, P.; Sarma, H. Integrated dual-level dependency analysis framework for multi-task judicial decision prognosis in murder cases. *Eng. Appl. Artif. Intell.* **2025**, *160*, 112002. [CrossRef]
49. Yao, F.; Sun, X.; Yu, H.; Yang, Y.; Zhang, W.; Fu, K. Gated hierarchical multi-task learning network for judicial decision prediction. *Neurocomputing* **2020**, *411*, 313–326. [CrossRef]

https://doi.org/10.3390/sym18010150

symmetry

MDPI

Article

Target-Guided Asymmetric Path Modeling in Equipment Maintenance Knowledge Graphs

Meng Chen [1,2] and Yuming Bo [1,*]

[1] School of Automation, Nanjing University of Science and Technology, Nanjing 210094, China; cmeng@njust.edu.cn
[2] Shanghai Donghu Machinery Factory, Shanghai 200439, China
* Correspondence: byming@mail.njust.edu.cn

Abstract

Knowledge graph completion via link prediction is critical for intelligent equipment maintenance systems to support accurate fault diagnosis and maintenance decision making. However, existing approaches struggle to simultaneously capture local structural dependencies and perform effective multi-hop reasoning due to limited receptive fields or inefficient path exploration mechanisms. Traditional path-based methods implicitly assume path symmetry, treating all reasoning chains equally without considering their task-specific relevance. To address this issue, we propose a Graph Attention Network (GAT)-guided semantic path reasoning framework that breaks this symmetry through attention-driven asymmetric weighting, integrating local structural encoding with global multi-hop inference. The key innovation lies in a target-guided biased path sampling strategy, which transforms GAT attention weights into probabilistic transition biases, enabling adaptive exploration of high-quality semantic paths relevant to specific prediction targets. GATs learn importance-aware local representations, which guide biased random walks to efficiently sample task-relevant reasoning paths. The sampled paths are encoded and aggregated to form global semantic context representations, which are then fused with local embeddings through a gating mechanism for final link prediction. Experimental evaluations on FB15k-237, WN18RR, and a real-world equipment maintenance knowledge graph demonstrate that the proposed method consistently outperforms state-of-the-art baselines, achieving an MRR of 0.614 on the maintenance dataset and 0.485 on WN18RR. Further analysis shows that the learned path attention weights provide interpretable asymmetric reasoning evidence, enhancing transparency for safety-critical maintenance applications.

Keywords: knowledge graph completion; graph attention networks; link prediction; semantic path reasoning; graph neural networks; attention mechanism

1. Introduction

Equipment maintenance knowledge graphs have emerged as fundamental infrastructures for modern intelligent manufacturing and maintenance systems, providing structured representations of complex relationships among faults, components, maintenance activities, diagnostic procedures, and specialized tools [1,2]. By organizing maintenance domain knowledge into graph-structured formats where entities represent real-world objects and edges capture semantic relationships, these knowledge graphs enable intelligent systems to perform sophisticated reasoning for diagnostic support, predictive maintenance, and maintenance solution recommendation [3,4]. However, despite their increasing adoption in industrial applications, knowledge graphs inherently suffer from incompleteness—a significant portion of valid relationships remain unrecorded due to the limitations of manual curation, the dynamic nature of equipment systems, and the sparsity of maintenance records for rare fault scenarios [5]. This incompleteness severely constrains the effectiveness of downstream applications such as augmented reality (AR)-based maintenance guidance systems [6], intelligent fault diagnosis [7], and proactive maintenance scheduling [8,9].

Knowledge graph completion through link prediction—the task of automatically inferring missing relationships between entities [10]—has thus become a critical challenge in equipment maintenance informatics. The objective is to develop computational models that can predict whether a relationship exists between a given entity pair, thereby enriching the knowledge graph with previously unknown but semantically valid connections. For instance, given a specific fault symptom and a maintenance procedure, a link prediction model should determine whether the procedure is applicable to that fault, even if such an association has not been explicitly documented in historical maintenance records. Successful link prediction not only enhances knowledge graph completeness but also enables more accurate knowledge recommendation, more comprehensive fault correlation analysis, and more reliable maintenance decision support.

However, knowledge associations in the equipment maintenance domain exhibit unique characteristics that pose significant challenges to existing link prediction approaches. First, maintenance knowledge encompasses both tight local neighborhood relationships and complex multi-hop path dependencies. Local relationships, such as the direct causation between a specific component failure and its observable symptoms, require models to effectively capture fine-grained structural patterns within immediate neighborhoods. Conversely, many critical maintenance associations involve indirect, multi-hop reasoning paths—for example, the transitive logic chain "fault symptom → affected subsystem → responsible component → required maintenance activity → specialized tool" requires traversing multiple intermediate entities. Second, the importance and reliability of different paths vary significantly: some paths represent strong causal relationships grounded in engineering principles, while others may reflect spurious correlations arising from data artifacts. Third, the maintenance domain exhibits high relation heterogeneity, with diverse relation types (causal, compositional, temporal, functional) requiring differentiated modeling strategies.

Traditional knowledge graph link prediction methods struggle to adequately address these domain-specific challenges. Embedding-based models map entities and relations into low-dimensional vector spaces and define scoring functions to measure triple plausibility [11]. While these methods excel at capturing direct binary relationships and demonstrate high computational efficiency, their representational capacity is fundamentally limited to local patterns. They lack explicit mechanisms for modeling multi-hop reasoning paths, making them inadequate for capturing the transitive dependencies prevalent in maintenance knowledge. Graph neural network (GNN)-based approaches address this limitation by aggregating information from multi-hop neighborhoods through iterative message passing. These methods generate entity representations that are contextualized by their local topological structures, thereby improving their ability to capture complex relational patterns. However, traditional GNN architectures are constrained by limited receptive fields—even with multiple layers, they struggle to effectively propagate information across long paths, and deeper architectures often suffer from over-smoothing and gradient vanishing issues.

To explicitly incorporate multi-hop semantic information, recent research has explored path-based and subgraph-based reasoning methods that encode sequences of relations connecting entity pairs and integrate path semantics into scoring functions. These methods enhance interpretability and generalization to unseen entities. Despite these advances,

https://doi.org/10.3390/sym18030439

existing path-based methods face critical limitations in path sampling efficiency and quality. Random walk strategies, while computationally tractable, suffer from high blindness—they sample paths uniformly without considering their semantic relevance to the prediction task, leading to the inclusion of many uninformative paths. Meta-path methods, which constrain walks to predefined path templates, require extensive domain expertise and manual specification of path schemas, limiting their flexibility and generalization across diverse maintenance scenarios.

More recent work has attempted to integrate advanced architectures from deep learning and policy learning, employing learnable message passing and global self-attention mechanisms to overcome the locality constraints of traditional methods. While these advanced methods demonstrate state-of-the-art performance on benchmark datasets such as FB15k-237 [12] and WN18RR [13], they typically require substantial computational resources and large-scale training data, which may not be readily available in specialized domains like equipment maintenance. Furthermore, they often lack explicit mechanisms for leveraging domain-specific structural priors, such as the hierarchical organization of maintenance procedures or the causal nature of fault propagation.

To address the aforementioned limitations and unlock effective multi-hop reasoning for equipment maintenance knowledge graphs while maintaining computational tractability, this paper proposes an attention-aware path reasoning model that synergistically integrates local structure encoding via graph attention networks with global semantic reasoning via path-based inference. From a graph symmetry perspective, traditional random walk and path reasoning methods implicitly assume path equivalence, treating all reasoning chains connecting entity pairs as equally important regardless of their semantic relevance or structural significance. This symmetry assumption fails to capture the inherent heterogeneity in knowledge graphs, where different paths vary substantially in their informativeness for specific prediction tasks.

In the context of knowledge graph reasoning, we refer to path-level symmetry as the implicit assumption made by traditional path-based methods (e.g., uniform random walks or fixed meta-paths) that all paths of a given length or schema are equally informative for a prediction task. This treats reasoning chains as structurally equivalent, neglecting their inherent heterogeneity in semantic relevance and reliability. Our framework breaks this symmetry by introducing an asymmetric, task-dependent weighting mechanism. Specifically, the transition probability in our biased random walk is determined by two asymmetric factors: the locally non-uniform attention weights from GAT, and the global, target-specific similarity. Consequently, paths are no longer treated equally; those that are both locally salient and directed toward the prediction target receive higher sampling probability, leading to an asymmetric and adaptive utilization of the graph structure.

The key contribution of this work lies in a novel integration framework designed to break this symmetry through a principled attention-guided mechanism for the equipment maintenance domain. We propose a target-guided biased path sampling strategy that transforms attention weights learned by GAT into probabilistic transition biases, enabling adaptive, asymmetric path selection that prioritizes high-quality, task-relevant semantic paths. Unlike blind random walks that maintain path-level symmetry or manually defined meta-paths that require extensive domain expertise, the proposed approach automatically learns to distinguish and emphasize edges that are both locally important (as indicated by GAT attention) and globally relevant (as measured by similarity to target entities). This learned asymmetric weighting reflects the true structural importance and task-specific utility of different reasoning trajectories, which is particularly crucial for sparse and heterogeneous maintenance knowledge graphs. More precisely, the symmetry discussed here pertains to the structural equivalence of reasoning paths. In knowledge graphs, struc-

https://doi.org/10.3390/sym18030439

turally equivalent nodes with similar connectivity patterns can lead traditional, unbiased path sampling methods to treat all paths of comparable length as equally important—an implicit assumption of symmetry at the path level. Our approach breaks this symmetry via attention-driven asymmetric weighting. The attention weights α_{ij} from the GAT encoder capture the local, non-uniform importance of edges, while the target-similarity term $\mathrm{Sim}(e_{\mathrm{next}}, t)$ introduces a global, query-specific bias. Consequently, the transition probability prioritizes edges and paths that are both locally salient and directed toward the prediction target, enabling a task-adaptive and asymmetric utilization of semantic paths. The sampled paths are then encoded using bidirectional recurrent neural networks and aggregated via an attention mechanism, generating rich path context representations that capture the most salient reasoning chains. These global path representations are fused with local node embeddings learned by GAT through a gating mechanism, enabling the model to balance complementary information sources. Finally, a DistMult-based scoring function produces triple plausibility scores for link prediction. This symmetry-breaking design not only improves prediction accuracy by focusing computational resources on informative paths, but it also enhances model interpretability by revealing which asymmetric structural patterns contribute most strongly to each prediction.

The main contributions of this work can be summarized as follows:

- A novel GAT-guided path reasoning framework that seamlessly integrates local graph attention encoding with global multi-hop reasoning, specifically tailored for equipment maintenance knowledge graphs with sparse dependencies and heterogeneous relations.
- An innovative target-guided biased random walk strategy that transforms GAT attention weights into probabilistic transition biases, enabling adaptive sampling of high-quality semantic paths without manual path schema specification.
- An attention-based path aggregation mechanism that provides interpretable reasoning evidence by dynamically weighting different sampled paths, enhancing transparency for safety-critical maintenance scenarios.
- Comprehensive experimental validation demonstrating consistent improvements over state-of-the-art baselines on both benchmark datasets and a real-world maintenance knowledge graph, with practical deployment in an AR-based maintenance assistance system.

The remainder of this paper is organized as follows. Section 2 reviews related work on knowledge graph link prediction methods and equipment maintenance applications. Section 3 presents the technical details of the proposed attention-aware path reasoning model. Section 4 describes comprehensive experimental evaluation on benchmark datasets and domain-specific knowledge graphs. Section 5 showcases the practical deployment in an intelligent knowledge push system for AR-assisted equipment maintenance. Finally, Section 6 concludes the paper and outlines future research directions.

2. Related Work

2.1. Knowledge Graph Link Prediction Methods

The research paradigm of knowledge graph link prediction has undergone significant evolution from embedding-based representation learning to structure-aware models. Early representative works such as TransE [14], RESCAL [15], and DistMult [16] map entities and relations into low-dimensional vector spaces and measure the plausibility of triples through designed scoring functions. ComplEx [17] extends these approaches by introducing complex-valued embeddings to model asymmetric and inverse relations. Although these methods have advantages of computational efficiency and parameter simplicity,

https://doi.org/10.3390/sym18030439

their modeling capability is mainly limited to local binary relations, making it difficult to effectively capture complex multi-hop semantic associations between entities.

To overcome these limitations, graph neural networks [18] have been introduced into knowledge graph representation learning. Relational graph convolutional networks aggregate multi-hop neighborhood information through message passing mechanisms, generating node representations that are aware of local topological structures. The study of graph connectivity and structural properties [19–21] provides theoretical foundations for understanding information propagation in graph-based models. Building on this foundation, graph attention networks [22] further introduce attention mechanisms to dynamically characterize the importance differences of different neighbor nodes, thereby improving the modeling capability for heterogeneous relations. Advanced GNN architectures such as SACN [23] integrate weighted graph convolutional networks with Conv-TransE for end-to-end structure-aware modeling, while CompGCN [24] employs composition-based operations to jointly embed entities and relations. Tensor factorization methods like TuckER [25] leverage Tucker decomposition to model three-way interactions for knowledge graph completion. Research on graph fault tolerance and diagnostic properties [26–30] provides insights into the robustness and reliability of graph-based structures, which is particularly relevant for critical applications such as equipment maintenance systems. However, traditional graph neural network models, limited by their restricted receptive fields, still show insufficient capability in modeling long-range dependencies.

To explicitly model multi-hop semantic associations between entities, reasoning methods based on paths and subgraph structures have gradually attracted attention. PTransE [31] and similar models encode path sequences connecting entity pairs and integrate path semantics into the link prediction scoring process. SEAL [32] and GraIL [33] transform the link prediction problem into a local subgraph classification task centered on target node pairs, enhancing model interpretability while also improving generalization ability to unseen entities. Convolutional approaches such as ConvE [13] and InteractE [34] leverage 2D convolutions on entity–relation embeddings to capture expressive interaction patterns. However, these methods still face challenges in path sampling efficiency and quality: random walk strategies often lack targeting, while meta-path methods such as those previously explored rely heavily on domain-prior knowledge.

A critical limitation of traditional path-based methods lies in their implicit symmetry assumption regarding path importance. Most existing approaches treat all paths of similar length or structure as equally informative, either through uniform random sampling or predefined path templates. This path-level symmetry fails to capture the inherent heterogeneity in knowledge graphs, where different reasoning chains vary significantly in their semantic relevance and reliability. Breaking this symmetry through adaptive, task-dependent path weighting remains an open challenge that requires principled mechanisms to distinguish high-quality semantic paths from spurious correlations without extensive manual schema engineering.

In recent years, researchers have attempted to integrate policy learning and Transformer architectures into knowledge graph reasoning. For example, NBFNet [35] borrows from the generalized Bellman–Ford algorithm to explicitly model information propagation on all possible paths in a learnable manner; graph structure Transformers such as Graphormer [36] and TGformer [37] overcome the locality limitation of traditional GNNs through global self-attention mechanisms, significantly enhancing the model's perception capability for long-range dependencies and complex structural patterns. These advances provide new ideas and methodological support for deep semantic reasoning in knowledge graphs.

https://doi.org/10.3390/sym18030439

2.2. Application Background in Equipment Maintenance

Modern equipment maintenance is rapidly developing toward intelligence and precision. Augmented reality (AR)-based maintenance assistance systems provide intuitive operation guidance for technicians by overlaying virtual information onto real-world scenes [6]. However, the effectiveness of such systems highly depends on precise knowledge supply from the back-end. Most current systems still adopt keyword or rule-based knowledge push methods, making it difficult to perform deep semantic reasoning and associated knowledge recommendation based on dynamic maintenance contexts (such as fault phenomena and operational steps) [1].

Recent advances in equipment maintenance have demonstrated the growing importance of intelligent technologies. AI-driven predictive maintenance frameworks [7,38] enable early detection of equipment failures through real-time sensor data analysis. IoT-based reliability analysis approaches [8] enhance system reliability through interconnected monitoring. Maintenance optimization strategies [39–41] integrate degradation modeling, spare parts management, and scheduling to balance cost efficiency with equipment reliability. Temporal knowledge graph methods [42] capture dynamic evolution of maintenance events for predictive decision making. Advanced optimization frameworks [43,44] employ multi-objective approaches and data-driven priority scoring for maintenance resource allocation. Intelligent maintenance strategies also encompass specialized domains, including medical equipment [45], remote maintenance equipment [46], industrial process equipment [47], data center cooling systems [9], distribution grid equipment [48], unsupervised fault classification [49], warranty optimization for second-hand equipment [50], condition-based maintenance with queuing systems [51], and sustainable port maintenance [52]. Furthermore, digital-twin-embedded approaches [53] enable self-evolving operational paradigms through cognitive agents and virtual–real co-evolution, representing the frontier of intelligent maintenance methodologies.

However, effectively integrating deep reasoning capabilities into practical maintenance systems remains challenging due to several factors: knowledge sparsity in rare fault scenarios, dynamic evolution of equipment states, and the need for real-time, interpretable recommendations that adapt to specific maintenance contexts.

To address these challenges, this research is situated within an intelligent maintenance platform construction project for specific equipment types, aiming to build an auxiliary system with knowledge graph–AR dual-end collaboration [3]. In this system, the knowledge graph component undertakes the core reasoning task, responsible for analyzing the current maintenance process and proactively pushing highly relevant knowledge (such as related fault cases, specialized tools, safety tips, etc.) to the AR terminal for visual presentation [2], as illustrated in Figure 1.

This paper focuses on a key technology in this system—link prediction in equipment maintenance knowledge graphs. Its goal is to break through the inherent incompleteness limitations of knowledge graphs, automatically discover potential semantic associations between entities, thereby providing powerful reasoning capability support for upper-layer knowledge push services [4,5] and achieving an intelligent transformation from "people finding knowledge" to "knowledge finding people".

https://doi.org/10.3390/sym18030439

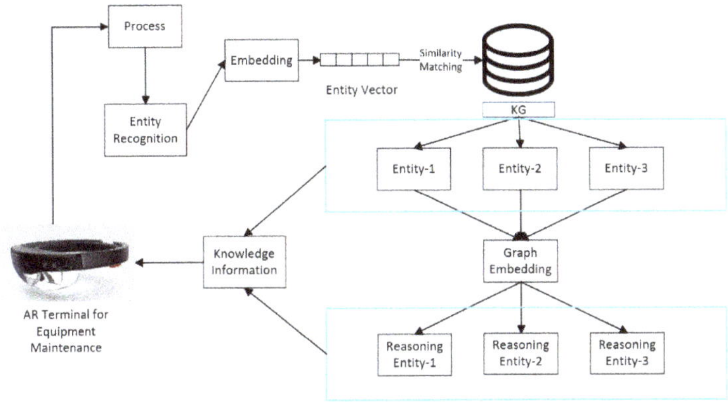

Figure 1. Knowledge graph and AR-based maintenance assistance system showing the integration of process recognition, entity embedding, graph reasoning, and knowledge delivery to AR terminals. The entities within the blue frame will serve as the source of knowledge.

3. Methodology

This section presents the technical details of the proposed attention-aware path reasoning model for equipment maintenance knowledge graphs. The problem is first defined, followed by an overview of the overall framework and detailed descriptions of each key module.

3.1. Problem Definition

This paper defines a knowledge graph as $G = (E, R, T)$, where E represents the entity set, R represents the relation set, and $T = \{(h, r, t) | h, t \in E, r \in R\}$ is the set of known facts (triples). The task of link prediction is defined as: given a query $(h, r, ?)$ or $(?, r, t)$, the model needs to predict the missing entity, i.e., find the most likely t or h from all candidate entities. This paper mainly focuses on the $(h, r, ?)$ prediction scenario. The model's objective is to learn a scoring function $\phi(h, r, t) \in \mathbb{R}$ that assigns high scores to true triples and low scores to false triples.

In the equipment maintenance domain, entities E can be instantiated as {fault phenomenon F_1, core component C_1, maintenance activity A_1, and maintenance tool $T_1, \ldots$}, and relations R can be instantiated as {causes, requires, uses, located_at} and other maintenance-specific relations.

3.2. Framework Overview

The overall workflow of the proposed approach is illustrated in Figure 2, which depicts the end-to-end pipeline from knowledge graph input through attention-guided path reasoning to knowledge delivery in AR-based maintenance systems.

The proposed model framework, as shown in Figure 3, adopts a unified architecture that synergistically integrates local structural encoding with global semantic path reasoning. At its foundation, the Graph Attention Encoder learns vector representations that fuse local neighborhood information for all entities and relations, capturing fine-grained relational patterns within the knowledge graph structure. Building upon these attention-aware embeddings, the Target-Guided Path Sampler leverages GAT attention weights as sampling bias to discover meaningful semantic paths between entity pairs, thereby focusing computational resources on high-value reasoning trajectories. The sampled variable-length paths are then processed by the Path Encoding and Aggregator, which encodes them into fixed-length vectors and synthesizes a unified path context representation through attention-weighted aggregation.

https://doi.org/10.3390/sym18030439

Finally, the Fusion and Prediction Module integrates the local neighborhood representations with global path context through a gating mechanism and produces final link prediction scores via a scoring function, enabling the model to make informed predictions by considering both immediate structural cues and long-range semantic dependencies.

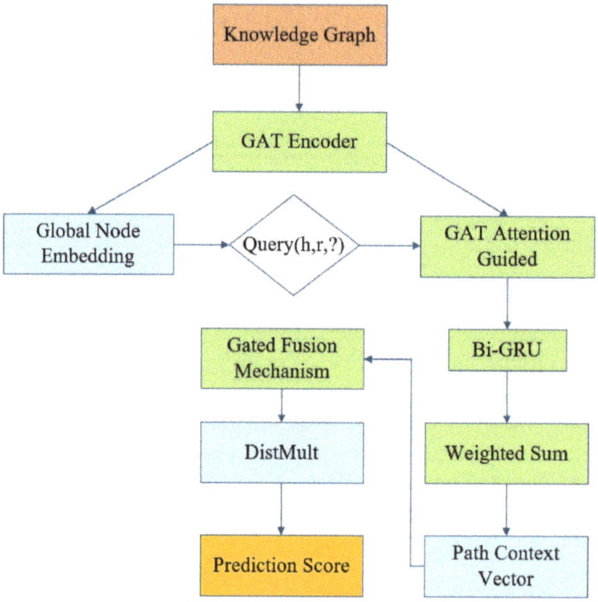

Figure 2. Overall workflow diagram showing the knowledge graph-based maintenance knowledge push system architecture. The system begins with equipment maintenance knowledge graph construction, proceeds through entity recognition and graph embedding, performs reasoning via the proposed attention-guided path model to complete missing links, and finally delivers actionable knowledge to AR terminals for maintenance technicians.

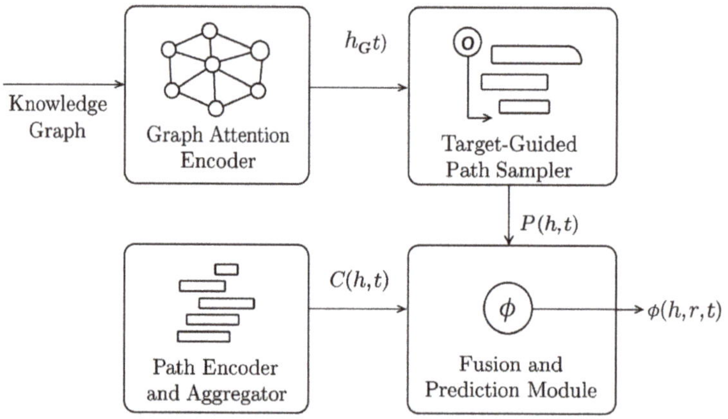

Figure 3. Proposed model framework. The model consists of four main components: Graph Attention Encoder for local structure encoding, Target-Guided Path Sampler for semantic path discovery, Path Encoder and Aggregator for path representation learning, and Fusion and Prediction Module for final scoring. The path information $P(h,t)$ and context vector $C(h,t)$ flow through the system to generate predictions $\phi(h,r,t)$.

https://doi.org/10.3390/sym18030439

The workflow of the model can be briefly described as follows: First, the entire knowledge graph is input to the GAT encoder to obtain embeddings h^{GAT} for all nodes. For each training triple (h, r, t), using the attention weights provided by the trained GAT, target-guided random walks are performed from h to t to sample a path set $P_{(h,t)}$. Subsequently, the path encoder maps each path to a vector, and the path aggregator aggregates these path vectors into a global path context vector $c_{(h,t)}$ through attention weights. Finally, the GAT embedding h_h^{GAT} of head entity h is fused with $c_{(h,t)}$, and together with the relation r embedding and tail entity t GAT embedding, they are input to the scoring function to calculate the score $\phi(h, r, t)$.

3.3. Graph Attention Encoder

This paper employs multi-head graph attention networks to encode local neighborhood information of nodes, whose structure is shown in Figure 4. For each entity v_i, its input feature is the initial feature vector x_i. After passing through one GAT layer, its output feature h_i' is obtained by weighted summation of neighbor node features:

$$\alpha_{ij} = \frac{\exp(\text{LeakyReLU}(a^T[Wx_i \| Wx_j]))}{\sum_{k\in N(i)} \exp(\text{LeakyReLU}(a^T[Wx_i \| Wx_k]))} \quad (1)$$

$$h_i' = \sigma\left(\sum_{j\in N(i)} \alpha_{ij} W x_j\right) \quad (2)$$

where α_{ij} is the attention coefficient of node i to neighbor node j, $N(i)$ is the neighbor set of node i, W is a shared weight matrix, a is the parameter vector of the attention mechanism, $\|$ denotes concatenation operation, and σ is a nonlinear activation function. To stabilize the learning process, a multi-head attention mechanism is adopted, concatenating or averaging the outputs of K heads as the final GAT embedding h^{GAT} of nodes. These learned attention weights $\{\alpha_{ij}\}$ are used for subsequent path sampling strategies. The architecture is illustrated in Figure 4.

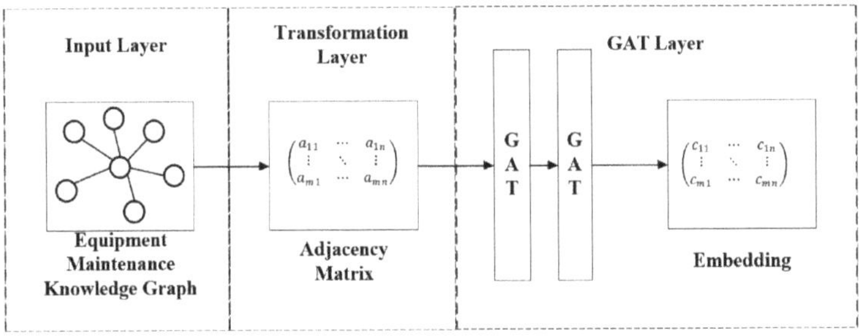

Figure 4. Graph attention network (GAT) architecture for equipment maintenance knowledge graph. The GAT processes the input knowledge graph through transformation layers and multi-head attention mechanisms to generate node embeddings.

3.4. Target-Guided Path Sampling Strategy

Traditional random walk sampling strategies have high blindness. To solve this problem, this paper designs a target-guided biased random walk strategy, whose core is to use the attention weights α_{ij} learned by the GAT as the bias for walk transitions.

For a given head–tail entity pair (h, t), the path sampling algorithm is as follows: Starting from h, at each step, let the current entity be e_{curr}. First, obtain all outgoing edge neighbors $N(e_{\text{curr}})$ of e_{curr}. Then, calculate the unnormalized probability $s(e_{\text{curr}}, e_{\text{next}})$ of transitioning to each neighbor $e_{\text{next}} \in N(e_{\text{curr}})$:

$$s(e_{\text{curr}}, e_{\text{next}}) = \alpha_{e_{\text{curr}}, e_{\text{next}}} + \lambda \cdot \text{Sim}(e_{\text{next}}, t) \tag{3}$$

where $\alpha_{e_{\text{curr}}, e_{\text{next}}}$ is the attention weight provided by the GAT. $\text{Sim}(e_{\text{next}}, t)$ is a function measuring the similarity between e_{next} and target t. This paper adopts their cosine similarity in the GAT embedding space:

$$\text{Sim}(e_{\text{next}}, t) = \cos(h_{e_{\text{next}}}^{(GAT)}, h_t^{(GAT)}) \tag{4}$$

λ is a hyperparameter controlling the strength of target guidance. Finally, $s(e_{\text{curr}}, e_{\text{next}})$ is normalized to obtain the transition probability distribution, and the next entity is sampled according to this distribution.

To illustrate this process with a simplified example, consider current entity e_{curr} with three candidate next entities $\{v_1, v_2, v_3\}$. Suppose the GAT attention weights are $\alpha = [0.1, 0.7, 0.2]$, and their cosine similarities to the target t are $\text{Sim} = [0.3, 0.8, 0.1]$. Using $\lambda = 0.5$, the unnormalized scores are $s = [0.1 + 0.5 * 0.3, 0.7 + 0.5 * 0.8, 0.2 + 0.5 * 0.1] = [0.25, 1.1, 0.25]$. The resulting transition probabilities after softmax normalization would heavily favor v_2 (probability ≈ 0.67), as it scores high on both local importance and target guidance. This demonstrates how the sampling bias effectively combines both signals.

To ensure the reproducibility of our approach, we provide the following implementation specifications. Specifically, during the biased random walk, cycles are prevented by disallowing immediate traversal back to the previously visited entity. For each query pair (h, t), we sample $M = 50$ paths with a maximum length $L_{\max} = 4$. The balancing hyperparameter λ in Equation (3) was selected via grid search on the validation set, with optimal values of 0.7 for FB15k-237, 0.5 for WN18RR, and 0.6 for the maintenance knowledge graph.

The advantage of this strategy is that the GAT attention weights ensure that walks tend toward locally important edges, while the target similarity term guides the walk direction toward target entity t, thereby efficiently sampling high-quality, highly relevant semantic paths.

3.5. Path Encoding and Aggregator

For a sampled path $p = (e_0, r_1, e_1, r_2, \ldots, e_L)$ (where $e_0 = h$, $e_L = t$), it is encoded into a fixed-length vector $\mathbf{p}$. This paper employs a bidirectional GRU as the path encoder:

$$\overrightarrow{h}_i = \text{GRU}(h_{e_i}^{(GAT)}, \overrightarrow{h}_{i-1}) \tag{5}$$

$$\overleftarrow{h}_i = \text{GRU}(h_{e_i}^{(GAT)}, \overleftarrow{h}_{i+1}) \tag{6}$$

$$\mathbf{p} = [\overrightarrow{h}_L; \overleftarrow{h}_0] \tag{7}$$

Here, each node on the path uses its GAT embedding $h^{(GAT)}$ as input, and the final path vector $\mathbf{p}$ is the concatenation of the bidirectional GRU's final hidden states.

For an entity pair (h, t), M paths $p_1, p_2, \ldots, p_M$ are sampled and encoded as $\mathbf{p}_1, \mathbf{p}_2, \ldots, \mathbf{p}_M$. Not all paths are equally important; therefore, attention mechanisms are introduced for weighted aggregation to obtain the global path context vector $c_{h,t}$:

$$u_m = q^T \tanh(W_p \mathbf{p}_m + b), \quad a_m = \frac{\exp(u_m)}{\sum_{m'=1}^{M} \exp(u_{m'})} \tag{8}$$

https://doi.org/10.3390/sym18030439

$$c_{h,t} = \sum_{m=1}^{M} a_m \mathbf{p}_m \tag{9}$$

where W_p, b, and q are learnable parameters. The attention weight a_m reflects the importance of path p_m for the current prediction, enhancing model interpretability.

3.6. Fusion and Prediction Module

To synergistically leverage local neighborhood information and global path information, the GAT embedding $h_h^{(GAT)}$ of head entity h is fused with the path context vector $c_{h,t}$. This paper adopts a gating fusion mechanism to dynamically control information flow:

$$g = \sigma(W_g[h_h^{(GAT)}; c_{h,t}] + b_g) \tag{10}$$

$$h_{\text{final}} = g \odot h_h^{(GAT)} + (1-g) \odot c_{h,t} \tag{11}$$

where g is the gating vector, σ is the sigmoid function, and $\odot$ denotes element-wise multiplication. Finally, the fused head entity representation h_{final}, relation r embedding $\mathbf{r}$, and tail entity t GAT embedding $h_t^{(GAT)}$ are input to the scoring function ϕ. This paper selects the DistMult scoring function:

$$\phi(h,r,t) = \langle h_{\text{final}}, \mathbf{r}, h_t^{(GAT)} \rangle = \sum_i h_{\text{final}}[i] \cdot \mathbf{r}[i] \cdot h_t^{(GAT)}[i] \tag{12}$$

where $\langle \cdot, \cdot, \cdot \rangle$ denotes a trilinear dot product. Model training adopts a negative sampling strategy, using the margin ranking loss function:

$$\mathcal{L} = \sum_{(h,r,t)\in T} \sum_{(h',r,t')\in T'} \max(0, \gamma + \phi(h',r,t') - \phi(h,r,t)) \tag{13}$$

where T is the positive sample set, T' is the corresponding generated negative sample set, and γ is the margin hyperparameter.

We employ DistMult for its efficiency and effectiveness with symmetric relations prevalent in our maintenance knowledge graph. While acknowledging its limitations in modeling asymmetric relations compared to more expressive functions like ComplEx or RotatE, this choice allows us to focus computational resources on the novel path reasoning mechanisms. The framework is modular and can readily accommodate alternative scoring functions in future work.

This chapter provides a detailed introduction to the link prediction model based on GAT attention-guided random walks. The model captures local structure through the GAT Encoder, obtains high-quality semantic paths through the innovative Target-Guided Path Sampling strategy, obtains global context through the Path Encoding and Aggregator, and finally fuses two types of information through a gating mechanism for prediction. This design effectively combines the local and global information of knowledge graphs, providing a powerful tool for knowledge graph completion in equipment maintenance and other fields.

4. Experimental Results and Analysis

4.1. Datasets

This paper selects two widely used public datasets in the field of knowledge graph link prediction: FB15k-237 [12] and WN18RR [13]. Both datasets avoid test leakage problems by removing reversible relations from the original datasets (FB15k and WN18), making the evaluation more challenging and realistic. Table 1 lists detailed statistics for both datasets.

https://doi.org/10.3390/sym18030439

Table 1. Dataset statistics for FB15k-237 and WN18RR benchmark datasets. All columns show counts (no directional preference).

Dataset	Entities	Relations	Training	Validation	Test
FB15k-237	14,541	237	272,115	17,535	20,466
WN18RR	40,943	11	86,835	3034	3134

FB15k-237 is derived from the large-scale general knowledge base Freebase, containing rich real-world facts with diverse relation types and complex structure. WN18RR is derived from the lexical database WordNet, mainly describing semantic relations between words (such as hypernymy, synonym relations), with obvious hierarchical structure characteristics.

In addition to public benchmarks, we evaluate our model on a real-world Equipment Maintenance Knowledge Graph (EMKG) collected from industrial maintenance manuals, historical work orders, and expert interviews of a partnered manufacturing facility. This domain-specific graph captures critical entities and relations for diagnostic and repair procedures. Its schema includes core entity types such as *Fault Symptom*, *Component*, *Tool*, *Maintenance Action*, and *Safety Notice*. Key relation types include `causes`, `requires`, `located_at`, `is_a`, and `has_step`. The dataset is characterized by sparsity, a long-tail distribution of faults, and a predominance of symmetric relations (e.g., `co-occurs_with`). Basic statistics are provided in Table 2.

Table 2. Statistics of the Equipment Maintenance Knowledge Graph (EMKG).

Dataset	Entities	Relation Types	Training Triples	Validation	Test
EMKG	8742	16	45,678	5712	5709

4.2. Evaluation Metrics

Following the general evaluation protocol for link prediction tasks, this paper adopts the following ranking metrics:

Mean Reciprocal Rank (MRR) computes the average of reciprocals of ranks assigned to all correct entities, which is defined as:

$$\mathrm{MRR} = \frac{1}{|Q|}\sum_{i=1}^{|Q|}\frac{1}{\mathrm{rank}_i} \tag{14}$$

where $|Q|$ is the number of test queries, and rank_i is the rank of the correct entity for the i-th query. This metric is particularly sensitive to overall ranking performance.

Hits@N (N = 1, 3, 10) measures the proportion of test triples where the correct entity ranks within the top N positions:

$$\mathrm{Hits@N} = \frac{1}{|Q|}\sum_{i=1}^{|Q|}\mathbb{1}(\mathrm{rank}_i \leq N) \tag{15}$$

where $\mathbb{1}(\cdot)$ is the indicator function. Hits@1 measures precision, while Hits@10 measures recall capability.

All metrics adopt filtered settings, i.e., when calculating rankings, all known true triples in the knowledge graph (all true triples in training, validation, and test sets except the currently predicted triple) are filtered out to avoid negative impacts of known facts on ranking results, making evaluation more accurate.

https://doi.org/10.3390/sym18030439

4.3. Ablation Study

To systematically evaluate the contribution of each core component in the proposed framework, comprehensive ablation experiments were conducted on both FB15k-237 and WN18RR datasets. The ablation study is designed to assess four key architectural choices: the necessity of the entire path reasoning module, the effectiveness of GAT attention-guided sampling versus uniform random walk, the benefit of attention-based path aggregation over simple averaging, and the advantage of gating fusion compared to direct concatenation. For each variant, the corresponding component is removed or replaced while keeping all other settings identical to ensure fair comparison.

The variant w/o Path Module removes the entire global reasoning branch. Specifically, it uses only the GAT encoder to obtain entity embeddings h^{GAT} and directly uses these embeddings with the DistMult scoring function for prediction, without any path sampling, encoding, or aggregation. This reduces the model to a standard GAT-based link predictor.

The results presented in Table 3 demonstrate the effectiveness of each proposed component. Removing the entire path module leads to the most substantial performance degradation, with MRR dropping by 0.032 (9.1%) on FB15k-237 and 0.044 (9.1%) on WN18RR. This significant decline reveals that global semantic path information provides crucial complementary knowledge beyond the local neighborhood structures captured by GAT, particularly for reasoning about complex multi-hop relations. Without path reasoning, the model degenerates to a pure GAT-based approach, confirming that explicit path information is indispensable for capturing long-range dependencies in knowledge graphs.

Table 3. Ablation study results on FB15k-237 and WN18RR datasets. Metrics are reported as MRR↑/Hits@10↑ (higher is better). Bold indicates the complete model with all components.

Model Variant	FB15k-237	WN18RR
Complete Model	0.350/0.535	0.485/0.580
w/o Path Module	0.318/0.492	0.441/0.528
w/o GAT Attention Guidance (uniform random walk)	0.332/0.508	0.462/0.549
w/o Path Attention Aggregation (average pooling)	0.341/0.521	0.473/0.562
w/o Gating Fusion (direct concatenation)	0.345/0.526	0.478/0.570

Building upon this foundation, the attention-guided sampling mechanism proves equally important. When replaced with uniform random walk, the model experiences notable performance drops across both datasets (0.018 MRR on FB15k-237 and 0.023 on WN18RR). This validates the core hypothesis that leveraging GAT attention weights as sampling bias enables the model to efficiently discover high-quality semantic paths that are most relevant to the prediction task. While uniform sampling distributes computational resources uniformly across all possible paths, the guided strategy adaptively concentrates on promising reasoning trajectories, thereby improving both efficiency and effectiveness.

The attention-based path aggregation mechanism further refines the model's reasoning capability. Compared to simple average pooling, the attention mechanism yields moderate but consistent improvements (0.009 MRR on FB15k-237 and 0.012 on WN18RR), indicating that sampled paths contribute unequally to the final prediction. The attention weights successfully identify and emphasize the most informative reasoning paths while downweighting less relevant ones. Similarly, the gating fusion mechanism demonstrates its value through marginal yet consistent gains over direct concatenation, adaptively balancing the contributions of local neighborhood information and global path context based on input characteristics.

The ablation study collectively confirms that all proposed components contribute positively to the model's performance, with the path reasoning module and attention-guided

https://doi.org/10.3390/sym18030439

sampling strategy being the most critical innovations. From a symmetry perspective, the performance degradation observed when removing key components reflects not merely the loss of individual modules but rather the destruction of the learned asymmetric reasoning structure. Specifically, replacing attention-guided sampling with uniform random walk restores path-level symmetry, forcing the model to treat all reasoning chains equally regardless of their structural importance. This symmetry constraint significantly limits the model's ability to focus on task-relevant paths, explaining the substantial performance decline. Similarly, removing attention-based path aggregation eliminates the learned asymmetric weighting of different reasoning chains, preventing the model from distinguishing high-quality semantic paths from noisy ones. The consistent improvements across both datasets demonstrate the robustness and generalizability of the architectural design choices, and validate the effectiveness of breaking path-level symmetry through principled attention mechanisms.

4.4. Comparative Experiments

To comprehensively evaluate the effectiveness of the proposed model, we conducted extensive comparative experiments against a diverse set of representative baseline methods covering different technical paradigms in knowledge graph reasoning. Specifically, we included translation-based embedding models (TransE), convolution-based architectures (ConvE), graph neural network approaches (CompGCN), recent distance-aware GNN frameworks (RE-GNN [54]), a knowledge hypergraph representation learning model (HySAE [55]), and a Heterogeneous Knowledge Graph Attention Network (HKGAT [56]).

These baselines encompass classical embedding techniques, structural message-passing mechanisms, and recent path-aware and subgraph-based reasoning strategies. All models were evaluated on the FB15k-237 and WN18RR datasets under consistent experimental protocols to ensure fair and reliable comparison. Figure 5 shows the performance comparison on (a) FB15k-237 and (b) WN18RR datasets.

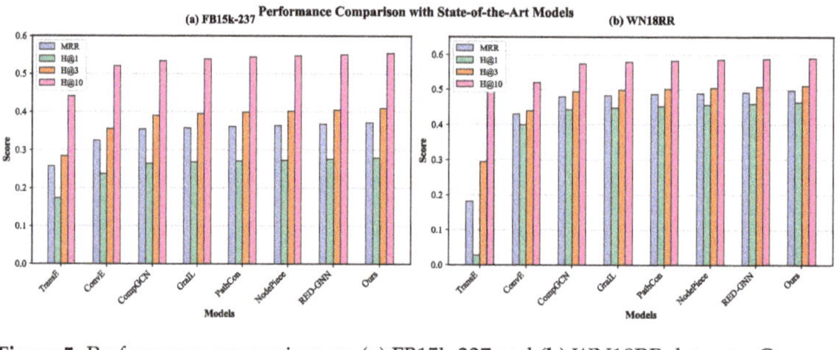

Figure 5. Performance comparison on (**a**) FB15k-237 and (**b**) WN18RR datasets. Our model consistently outperforms baseline methods across all metrics.

Table 4 presents the comparative results across diverse reasoning paradigms. Several important observations can be drawn. The proposed model achieves the best overall performance on both datasets, consistently outperforming classical embedding models and recent subgraph-based and path-aware reasoning frameworks. On FB15k-237, the proposed model attains an MRR of 0.372 and Hits@10 of 0.555, surpassing strong structural reasoning baselines such as RED-GNN and NodePiece. These improvements demonstrate the effectiveness of the attention-guided path sampling and neural path encoding mechanisms in capturing complex relational dependencies beyond local neighborhood aggregation.

https://doi.org/10.3390/sym18030439